Windows NT™ 4
Web Development

Sanjaya Hettihewa

201 West 103rd Street
Indianapolis, Indiana 46290

SAMS.NET Developer's Guide

Copyright © 1996 by Sams.net Publishing

Trademarks

President, Sams Publishing	*Richard K. Swadley*
Publishing Manager	*Mark Taber*
Managing Editor	*Cindy Morrow*
Marketing Manager	*John Pierce*
Assistant Marketing Manager	*Kristina Perry*

Acquisitions Editor
Kim Spilker

Development Editors
Sunthar Visuvalingam
Brian-Kent Proffitt

Software Development Specialist
Cari Skaggs

Production Editor
Keith A. Davenport

Copy Editors
David Bradford
Kristi Hart
Chuck Hutchinson
Anne Owen

Technical Reviewer
Christopher Stone

Editorial Coordinator
Bill Whitmer

Technical Edit Coordinator
Lynette Quinn

Resource Coordinator
Deborah Frisby

Formatter
Frank Sinclair

Editorial Assistants
Carol Ackerman
Andi Richter
Rhonda Tinch-Mize

Cover Designer
Tim Amrhein

Book Designer
Alyssa Yesh

Copy Writer
Peter Fuller

Production Team Supervisor
Brad Chinn

Production
Carol Bowers, Georgiana Briggs,
Mona Brown, Paula Lowell,
Donna Martin, Ian Smith,
Mark Walchle

Indexer
Chris Wilcox

Overview

Contents

II   Business Aspects of Web Publishing

IV Designing Your Web Site

VI   Incorporating Technologies into Your Web Site

VII Maintaining Your Web Site

22 Publicizing Your Web Site   467

VIII   Enhancing the Capabilities of Your Server

Appendixes

Dedication

This book is dedicated to all the Windows NT users who are about to embark on an exciting journey of discovery! It opens the gates of convenience, power, and versatility for your successful deployment of Internet information systems. May the road ahead, at least for us ;-), run on Windows NT!

Acknowledgments

I am indebted to many individuals who helped me complete this project. Although this project consumed me for a few months, the following people helped me complete it and reclaim my life—although temporarily!

I'd first like to thank my acquisitions editor, Kim Spilker, for suggesting this timely project and helping me bring it to fruition. It has been a pleasure working with you and everyone else at Sams.net. Sunthar, Brian, Kristi, Chris, and Keith did a wonderful job editing and developing chapters of this book. Their knowledge in new technologies and foresight helped shape this book into what it is. Copy editors of this book were Anne, Chuck, and David. They did an excellent job editing this book and refining its content. Thanks for all the valuable suggestions and comments! Lynette Quinn is the technical editor coordinator of this book. Many thanks to Cari for putting together the CD-ROM that accompanies this book. I do not personally know everyone at Sams.net who make books like this possible. All the same, I'd like to thank them for helping me complete this project because it would never have been possible without all their help.

I am especially indebted to Sandra for proofreading the last few chapters of this book. I'd probably still be proofreading them if not for you! (You still owe me dinner and a movie, though!) Thanks to Robert for helping me set up and test NT BIND in the wee hours of the morning. Many thanks to Michael for helping me move to my new apartment in the middle of this project and helping me put everything together so I could get back to work.

This book covers numerous Windows NT applications that can be used to publish information on the Internet. The following persons helped me evaluate the applications discussed in this book. I am very much indebted for their help in making this book the most comprehensive source of information for setting up Internet information systems with Windows NT.

iBasic.com	Tom Billings
Internet Shopper	Brian Dorricott
Software.com	Kevin Thau
Metainfo	Jason Morse
egSoftware	Alice F. Boyd
InContext	Craig L. Dudley
FutureTense	BC Krishna
	Gayle Evans
Microsoft	George Bukow
	Benjamin Slivka

Verity	Marguerite Padovani
	Stephany Derry
NetManage	Steve Cirimele
	Ellie Saif
Process Software	Tom Ricci
	Donna Clayfield
	Barbara Gaumond
O'Reilly & Associates	Ellen Elias
	Kimberly Simoni
	Sara Winge

I know there are many others who helped me put this book together. I'd like to thank them for all their help. It has been a pleasure working with them and I look forward to working with them again.

About the Author

Sanjaya Hettihewa is an accomplished Webmaster and a consultant specializing in integrating Windows NT-based information systems on the Internet. He has lived in the Washington, D.C., area for the last six years and is a computer science major attending the University of Maryland. For the last two years, Sanjaya has done extensive research in setting up Internet information systems with Windows NT as well as exploring ways of using Windows NT's unique features to publish information on the Internet. Sanjaya is the co-author of *Designing and Implementing Microsoft Internet Information Server, Internet Information Server Unleashed, FrontPage Unleashed, Internet Explorer Unleashed,* and *Windows NT 3.51 Unleashed,* all by Sams and Sams.net Publishing. Sanjaya can be reached at http://www.NetInnovation.com/ (if you prefer the old-fashioned way, sanjaya@NetInnovation.com).

Tell Us What You Think!

As a reader, you are the most important critic and commentator of our books. We value your opinion and want to know what we're doing right, what we could do better, what areas you'd like to see us publish in, and any other words of wisdom you're willing to pass our way. You can help us make strong books that meet your needs and give you the computer guidance you require.

Do you have access to CompuServe or the World Wide Web? Then check out our CompuServe forum by typing GO SAMS at any prompt. If you prefer the World Wide Web, check out our site at http://www.mcp.com.

> **NOTE**
>
> If you have a technical question about this book, call the technical support line at (800) 571-5840, ext. 3668.

As the team leader of the group that created this book, I welcome your comments. You can fax, e-mail, or write me directly to let me know what you did or didn't like about this book—as well as what we can do to make our books stronger. Here's the information:

FAX: 317/581-4669

E-mail: opsys_mgr@sams.mcp.com

Mail: Dean Miller
       Comments Department
       Sams Publishing
       201 W. 103rd Street
       Indianapolis, IN 46290

Introduction

Welcome to the world of deploying information systems on the Internet with Windows NT! With the growth of the World Wide Web, many organizations are establishing a presence on the Internet. Although until recently a considerable amount of money, time, and effort had to be invested to set up, manage, and administer a good Web site, things have changed. Windows NT is responsible for most of this change. While being a high-performance and robust operating system, Windows NT is user friendly and easy to work with. The purpose of this book is to show you how to exploit the strengths of Windows NT and publish information on the Internet. I hope *Windows NT 4 Web Development* becomes a major resource in your bookshelf.

Why This Book Is Special

The World Wide Web has experienced phenomenal growth during the last few years. This book is different from most books about the Web. Navigating the Web, using various Web browsers, or learning boring details of various HTML tags is not what this book is about. Although use of HTML tags is discussed, it's presented in a concise manner so that you will be able to refer to the information when the need arises. Instead of focusing on details such as how to use HTML, this book will show you how to use new Web publishing tools that exploit the user-friendly environment afforded by Windows NT to make Web publishing easier and more fun.

Although several Web publishing books that discuss how to set up and manage Web sites have been written, most are not written for the Windows NT community. The Windows NT community has lacked a book that comprehensively covers all aspects of setting up and deploying information systems on the Internet using Windows NT. This book is special because it has been written by an author who believes that Windows NT is the best environment to publish information on the Internet. Therefore, as you read along, you will discover various Windows NT tools and shortcuts that will save you time, frustration, and money. You will also benefit from the knowledge the author has gained by administering a Windows NT-based Web server at the University of Maryland for the last two years.

Every author believes his or her book is special. Therefore, I might be biased in my opinion. However, after reading this book and setting up an outstanding Web site with Windows NT, I hope you will agree with me.

Goals of This Book

The primary goal of this book is to provide you with all the information that's necessary to set up an outstanding Internet server with Windows NT. I will walk you through setting up Internet information distribution applications and highlight advantages of using one application over the other. One of the biggest advantages of using Windows NT to host a Web site is how easy it is to publish content on the Web with NT-based tools and applications.

Instead of focusing entirely on details such as the syntax of HTML tags, this book will provide a more abstract point of view when it comes to developing Web sites. Many new tools have been invented to make Web publishing easier. I will evaluate various Windows NT Web publishing tools and provide you with hands-on examples of when such utilities can be used to make Web site development easier. Armed with this knowledge, you will be able to tackle virtually any Web publishing task.

Who Should Read This Book

This book will teach you everything that's needed to set up a Windows NT-based Web site. Although it is written for Web site developers, even if you have little prior knowledge about Windows NT, the Web, or either, you will be able to easily follow this book. The topics covered in this book are all explained in easy-to-understand terms. Screen shots and diagrams are used whenever possible to explain topics. This book should be read by anyone who wishes to utilize Windows NT to host a Web site. Its purpose is to make life easier for those using Windows NT to publish information on the Internet. The Web is made up of a very diverse group of people. Likewise, this book has been written for an equally diverse group of people.

Web Site Developers

As the name suggests, this book is primarily written for Web site developers. The Web has been rapidly expanding for the last few years. As more and more organizations want to establish a presence on the Web, these organizations will need skilled developers who can utilize state-of-the-art Web publishing tools to build Web sites. One of the main goals is to demonstrate how to make use of tools that are available for Windows NT to develop an outstanding Web site in the shortest possible time. Since I cover all aspects of Web publishing, Web site developers will become familiar with virtually all Windows NT tools available to create outstanding Web sites.

Web Site Administrators

The role of Web site administrators is becoming more complicated. In order to maintain an information-rich Web site that is updated frequently and provides users the capability to interact with the server to obtain various information, Web site administrators need to be knowledgeable about various Web publishing tools. Although in the past, most programming was done "in house" when it was needed to develop customized solutions, more and more powerful Web publishing tools are being created for Windows NT. This book will provide an overview of virtually all tools that can be used to make publishing information on the Web easier for developers.

Web Application Programmers

Although originally the Web was used mostly for distributing information, it is increasingly being used for more sophisticated tasks. The Web is providing dynamic content to millions of users when they want it. Due to this, the role of Web application programmers is becoming more important. If you are a Web applications programmer, it is crucial that you stay on top of new Web publishing tools and know how and when to use them. We will cover virtually all Windows NT Web programming interfaces and explain their strengths and weaknesses along with practical applications.

Information Systems Architects

This book is of particular value to information systems architects who have been delegated the task of establishing a Web presence and exploring options available for publishing on the Web. Since this book covers virtually all Windows NT Web publishing tools, information systems architects will be made familiar with the latest tools that are available for publishing on the Web.

Windows NT System Administrators

By the time you read this, a new version of Windows NT will have been released. This release, presently called the Shell Upgrade Release (SUR), is more Internet-aware than any operating system previously released by Microsoft. The SUR release of Windows NT will have not only built-in TCP/IP network support like prior releases of Windows NT, but also various applications designed to serve information on the Internet. Until now, in order to publish information on the Internet with Windows NT, someone had to purchase additional applications such as Web servers and database interface applications. However, with the integration of these services into the core operating system, Windows NT system administrators should be increasingly familiar with Internet Services. Although system administrators might not be directly responsible for publishing information on the Internet, they need to have a working knowledge of tools, utilities, and Web publishing technologies. They also need to be familiar with issues such as security that arise when information is published on the Internet. With the help of this book, a system administrator will become familiar with all aspects of using Windows NT to host a Web site and distribute information on the Internet.

UNIX Web Site Developers

You might wonder why *Windows NT 4 Web Development* should be read by UNIX Web Site Developers. The reason is that no matter how much someone is familiar with the ins and outs of UNIX, virtually everything that has to be implemented on a UNIX-based Web site is a major project. Often, before doing something new, someone has to spend a great deal of time reading "man pages" and figuring out how applications have to be set up, configured, and administered. All this can be expensive and time consuming in a production environment. On the other hand, Windows NT Web development tools are true turnkey solutions. Often, all that's needed to do is to figure out how to run SETUP.EXE and answer a few simple questions during the course of installation. With the aid of this book, a UNIX Web site developer will find out how Windows NT can be utilized to host a Web site that's robust, secure, and much easier to maintain than any UNIX-based Web site.

What You Will Learn from This Book

This book will help you learn all aspects of setting up and managing a Windows NT-based Web site. The book deals with topics ranging from an introduction to the Internet to publishing databases on the Web. To give you a better understanding of how information is presented in this book, listed next are topics covered in various parts of the book.

Part I—Introduction to the World Wide Web

The introductory section providing a quick overview of the Web is for readers who are relatively new to the Web. The purpose of this section is to introduce the reader to the Web as well as explain terms and topics that will be covered in greater detail later. By reading this section, the reader will learn all that's needed to understand even the most advanced topics covered later in this text. However, if you are more familiar with the Web, you might want to skim this section quickly and move on to the next.

Part II—Business Aspects of Web Publishing

The second part, "Business Aspects of Web Publishing," deals with business aspects of the Web. Since information published on the Web can be made available to an audience consisting of a few million users, it is a very powerful medium of information distribution. Since the information that can be distributed is determined only by the bandwidth of the Internet connection, publishing on the Web is free from most of the limitations of traditional information mediums. This section will list ways you can make use of the Web. By demonstrating how others are utilizing the Web and letting you know where in the book you will be shown how to implement similar capabilities, you will have a better perspective of what you will be able to implement.

Part III—Setting Up Your Web Server

The third section, "Setting Up Your Web Server," will demonstrate how to set up your Web server. There are over two dozen Windows NT-based Web servers. To give you an overview of various Web server choices, four of the most popular Windows NT Web servers—including Microsoft Information Server, Netscape Enterprise Server, WebSite, and Purveyor—will be evaluated. This section will also cover Windows NT security issues that you should be aware of when publishing information on the Web. After completing it, you will be able to set up a Web site and configure it to meet your needs. Your Web site will now be ready for the next section of the book, which deals with publishing information on the Internet by designing its contents.

Part IV—Designing Your Web Site

The "Designing Your Web Site" section will cover Web publishing tools that can be used to easily publish information on the Web. One of the greatest advantages in using Windows NT to host a Web site is the large number of tools that are available for Windows NT to publish information on the Web. You will be shown how to exploit the user-friendly environment and tools afforded by Windows NT to create content for your Web site in the shortest possible time. This section will also cover Web page editors and content management utilities that can be used to easily update and manage the contents of your Web site.

Part V—Making Your Web Site Interactive

After designing Web pages and setting them up on your Web server, it is time to add some interactivity to your Web site. Section five, "Making Your Web Site Interactive," demonstrates how to use several tools to make your Web site interactive. Several Web-database interfaces will be evaluated in this section to give you an overview of their relative strengths and weaknesses.

Part VI—Incorporating Technologies into Your Web Site

With the recent increase of commercial uses of the Internet, many new technologies have been invented to satisfy the needs of a diverse user group. It is necessary to keep up with newly emerging Web technologies to exploit what they offer. This section discusses various emerging Web technologies such as Java, JavaScript, and VBScript, demonstrating how they can be used to make your Web site richly interactive.

Part VII—Maintaining Your Web Site

After designing your Web site, setting up various CGI scripts to make the site interactive, and incorporating various new technologies to your Web site, it has to be maintained. The success of a Web site is dependent upon how many repeat visitors it attracts. In this section you will be shown how to maintain your Web site. Web site maintenance issues range from registering your Web site with various Web search engines and Web server cataloging databases to analyzing the log file of your Web server to determine various access statistics.

Part VIII—Enhancing the Capabilities of Your Server

Setting up a Web server alone might not be enough to meet your needs. The final section, "Enhancing the Capabilities of Your Server," demonstrates how to set up additional information services on the Internet. Internet information distribution services discussed in this section include News, Mail, Telnet, FTP, Finger, Mail List, and DNS.

How This Book Is Organized

Information in this book is organized in a sequential manner. The first two parts of the book will explain various new topics quickly and go on to discuss more advanced material. The book is written so that even if you are new to Web publishing, you will be able to understand everything in the book if you read from the first chapter and work your way through. Although material in later chapters builds upon earlier chapters of the book, all chapters are self contained so that if you are familiar with simple Web concepts you will be able to read and understand the chapters you are interested in.

Listed next are topics covered in various chapters of the book.

Chapter 1—What Is the World Wide Web?

The book begins with an introduction to the Web and discusses its architecture, strengths, and weaknesses. By understanding how the Web has evolved and where it is heading, you will be able to set up your Web site with a better perspective of where you are headed. This chapter also discusses terminology that will be used throughout the book.

Chapter 2—Publishing on the World Wide Web with Windows NT

This chapter is devoted to how Windows NT can be utilized to publish information on the Web. When publishing content on the Internet with Windows NT, it's important to be aware of advantages and drawbacks associated with using Windows NT. Then you can exploit the advantages of NT and at the same time find solutions and ways of dealing with the limitations of NT. This chapter first discusses how Windows NT is different from other operating systems, outlining why it's an ideal platform for publishing information on the Internet and why UNIX is not an ideal choice to publish information on the Internet. The last section is devoted to identifying and dealing with the drawbacks of Windows NT.

Chapter 3—Creating Business Web Sites

It's a safe bet that you are reading this book to set up a Web site for you or your organization for business purposes. Even if you are not interested in the business aspects of setting up a Web site, you will benefit from knowing potentially what you can accomplish business-wise. Before developing a Web site, it helps to know how others are using the World Wide Web. Various Web sites presented will give you a few ideas for your Web site.

Chapter 4—Using the Web to Your Advantage

Before setting up a Web site, it's important to understand how to use the Internet to your advantage. You can accomplish this by exploring how you can use the World Wide Web for various business applications. Tips and ideas presented will help you make the best use of your Web site to distribute information on the Internet.

Chapter 5—Determining and Fulfilling Your Requirements

After all the introductory material about the Web and its business aspects, you are now ready to set up your Web site. Before setting up your Web server, you need to select suitable hardware. This chapter will help you analyze your needs and select the best hardware platform to meet them. This chapter will also help you analyze your Internet bandwidth requirements and help you select an Internet connection that is within your budget and yet suits your needs.

Chapter 6—Installing and Using Microsoft Internet Information Server

Microsoft Internet Information Server (IIS) is bundled free with Windows NT Server. Although Microsoft will make a version of IIS available for Windows NT Workstation, it will not be as powerful as the version that ships with Windows NT Server. Internet Information Server is shipped with the Internet Database Connector. In Chapter 6, you will learn how the Internet Database Connector can be used to effortlessly publish any ODBC datasource on the Internet taking advantage of high performance afforded by ISAPI. IIS is a powerful, easy-to-manage server designed to make maximum use of Windows NT's system architecture. You can use it to publish information on the Internet via HTTP, Gopher, and FTP.

Chapter 7—Publishing on the Web with WebSite, Purveyor, and Netscape

There are over two dozen Windows NT Web Servers available. Some of these Web servers are commercial and others are free. The chapter on various Windows NT Web servers will cover three NT Web servers and evaluate their strengths and weaknesses. Choosing the right Web server is an important aspect of setting up your Web site. In the past, Web servers did few other tasks besides serving HTTP requests. This trend, however, is changing. Web servers are increasingly being equipped with powerful new features that can be used to effortlessly publish information on the Internet. Some of these features include database publishing wizards, built-in search engines, and various site management tools. The three Web servers, WebSite, Purveyor, and Netscape Enterprise server were chosen because they are shipped with powerful Web site management tools. After these Web servers are evaluated, their various capabilities will be compared and contrasted outlining their suitability for various tasks.

Chapter 8—Security Considerations

When distributing information on the Internet, you should be concerned about security issues. This chapter will address these concerns that need to be dealt with when setting up a Windows NT Server on the Internet. You can take several steps to protect an NT Server on the Internet against unauthorized access. Although setting up an Internet server that is immune to unauthorized access is virtually impossible, you can take steps to make access harder and, in some cases, prohibitively expensive for someone to gain unauthorized access.

Chapter 9—Advanced HTML Techniques

This chapter provides you with an overview of advanced HTML tags and demonstrates how Netscape and Microsoft enhancements to HTML can be used to make your Web pages more appealing. You can make a Web site more interesting to navigate by using a number of advanced HTML techniques. For example, you can use tables to format objects of a Web page such as text, video clips, and Java applets. You can use frames to make it easier to navigate a Web site and make a Web page's text more attractive to read by applying special attributes such as colors and fonts. Chapter 9 demonstrates how advanced HTML tags can be used to create a visually attractive Web site that is easy to navigate.

Chapter 10—Web Site Development Tools

Several Web site development tools will be discussed in chapter. The chapter first covers several HTML editors that can be used to edit Web pages in raw HTML format as well as in a WYSIWYG environment. Use HTML editors discussed in this chapter to fine-tune HTML code of Web pages. Although raw HTML editors are useful for fine-tuning HTML code, they are not generally recommended for large projects. A new breed of WYSIWYG HTML editors is coming into existence as this book goes to print. Use WYSIWYG HTML editors whenever possible to simplify projects and reduce time wasted worrying about various HTML syntaxes.

InContext WebAnalyzer is a useful Web site management tool. You can use it to manage the contents of a Web site by viewing it from a graphical perspective. As more Web pages are added to a Web site, at some point, keeping track of various Web pages and how they are linked to each other becomes increasingly difficult. This can lead to outdated Web pages and broken links. You can use InContext WebAnalyzer to solve some of these problems by viewing how Web pages at a Web site are linked and locating invalid URLs.

Chapter 11—Adding Multimedia to Your Web Site

When used properly, multimedia can complement the contents of a Web site by making it easier and more interesting to browse for information. Multimedia formats are commonly used on the Internet. When adding multimedia to a Web site, it's important to know strengths and weaknesses of multimedia formats and when to use which formats. Examples and tips provided in this chapter will help you select the best multimedia format and optimize multimedia files at your Web site for transmitting on the Internet. Due to bandwidth limitations, every effort has to be taken to ensure multimedia files are as small as they can be.

Chapter 12—Designing and Managing a Web Site with FrontPage

Although tools discussed in this chapter are very useful for creating Web pages, they do not help much in terms of organizing the contents of your Web site. FrontPage is an application for developing and maintaining Web sites on the Internet. It is also designed to help developers manage their Web sites easily. A major feature of FrontPage is how it allows the creation of fully functional CGI applications without writing a single line of code. The chapter on FrontPage will demonstrate how it can be effectively utilized to simplify Web publishing and create a richly interactive Web site without developing CGI applications. You will also be shown how to use FrontPage wizards and templates to create Web pages.

Chapter 13—Publishing on the Web with Microsoft Office

Microsoft Office is a powerful suite of productivity applications. Internet Assistants available for Microsoft Office can be used to effortlessly publish content on the Internet. These Internet assistants are especially useful for converting large amounts of MS Office files into HTML so they can be published on the global Internet or a local intranet. Internet Assistants available for Microsoft Word, Excel, Access, and PowerPoint will be covered, demonstrating how each of these applications can be used to effectively distribute information on the Internet.

Chapter 14—Designing Web Pages with FutureTense Texture

Texture is a powerful Java-based Web content development application. It can be used to create publications that are highly interactive and exciting to browse. Texture also provides Web content developers better control over publications they create. For example, fonts used in a Texture publication are portable across all platforms that support Java. This is a major advantage since finally, with Texture, Web content developers do not have to be bound with using only one or two standard typefaces. In addition to this, Texture includes a collection of powerful objects that can be used with actions and triggers to create active publications. FutureTense Texture is an ideal solution for creating high impact Web publications that require complete control over the layout, typefaces, and interactive behavior of the publication.

Chapter 15—Making Your Web Site Searchable

Making your Web site searchable is very important so that users browsing it can locate information they need without unnecessarily browsing hierarchies of Web pages. After reading Chapter 15, you can make a Web site searchable in a matter of minutes.

Chapter 16—Introduction to Windows NT CGI Programming

Although a number of off-the-shelf applications can be used to make your Web site interactive, it's always beneficial to know what really happens when CGI scripts are executed on your Web server. This chapter will cover all the fundamentals you need to know about Windows NT CGI programming. After reading this chapter, you will understand how simple CGI scripts work. Armed with this knowledge, you will be able to create customized solutions for various problems you encounter. As an example of how CGI can be utilized to enhance the capabilities of a Web site, you will be shown how to create a CGI script to provide dynamic content based on the browser used to access your Web site. You will also be shown how PERL and C CGI scripts can be set up at your Web site. Security issues you need to be concerned about when setting up CGI scripts will also be discussed in this chapter.

Chapter 17—Advanced Windows NT CGI Applications

PolyForm and iBasic are two useful CGI applications that can be used to create interactive and dynamic Web pages. Although these two applications are not distributed free of charge or included with Windows NT, they can potentially save days or even weeks of CGI application development time. PolyForm is a tool that can be used to create interactive Web forms and iBasic is a server-side scripting language.

Chapter 18—Publishing Databases on the Web

For most organizations and even individuals, databases are a principal way of storing and organizing information in a logical manner. However, out of the box, most Web servers do not offer capabilities for publishing databases on the Web. Although some Web servers support Web database interfaces, some require you to be familiar with a programming language such as Visual Basic. Although Visual Basic is not very hard to learn, there are a number of Web database interactivity applications that are very easy to set up and use. After reading this chapter you will be able to determine which Web-database interactivity applications best meet your needs and publish databases on the Web in just a few minutes.

Chapter 19—Adding Java to Your Web Site

Developed by Sun Microsystems, Java is a programming language that allows developers to design richly interactive multimedia Web pages. The chapter on Java will explain to you the basics of this exciting programming language and how you can set up Java applets at your Web site after downloading them from Java applet distribution sites on the Internet. You will also be shown the fundamentals of the Java programming language and how to use Java to develop applications. After reading this chapter, you will also be able to develop Java applets to solve problems.

Chapter 20—Creating Interactive Web Pages with JavaScript

JavaScript is a new Web publishing technology that has a great deal of potential. Using JavaScript, it is possible to make your Web pages interactive without using CGI. The chapter on JavaScript will demonstrate how to unleash the potential of JavaScript, integrate it to your Web pages and how you can benefit from this integration.

Chapter 21—Unleashing the Power of VBScript

VBScript is an exciting Web interactivity technology developed by Microsoft. The chapter on VBScript will demonstrate how VBScript can be utilized to create interactive Web pages with embedded scripting, automation, and customization capabilities. VBScript can be used to perform a variety of tasks such as validate user input before a form is submitted to a CGI script for processing. The chapter on VBScript will demonstrate how VBScript can be utilized to design richly interactive Web pages. At the end of the chapter, VBScript will be compared to JavaScript, outlining advantages and drawbacks of using one over the other.

Chapter 22—Publicizing Your Web Site

The key to making your Web site popular on the Internet is knowing how to publicize it on the Internet. Although there are millions of users on the Internet, attracting users who will find your Web site useful is not always easy. This chapter will show you how to publicize your

Web site on the Internet and inform users about your Web site. By exploring how to publicize your Web site using a number of ways, you will be able to inform those who are most likely to be interested about the contents of your Web site. After reading this chapter, you will be able to make your Web site well known on the Internet.

Chapter 23—Web Site Design and Maintenance Issues

After setting up your Web site, it needs to be maintained and there are a number of issues you need to be concerned about. The chapter on Web site design and maintenance issues will discuss issues such as legalities you need to be concerned about when distributing information on the Web. Although your Web site might look very attractive when viewed with the latest version of Internet Explorer (or Netscape Navigator) on a large super VGA screen, not all Web surfers are privileged with the same technology. This chapter will provide numerous tips to design the contents of your Web site so that your Web site will look appealing on a wide variety of Web browsers and hardware platforms. Optimizing the contents of your Web site for the Internet will also be discussed in this chapter.

Chapter 24—Utility Applications for Your Server

Maintaining your Web server is a very important part of publishing on the Web. If it is not maintained properly, soon you will start experiencing problems that will distract you from developing your Web site. Issues (such as disk fragmentation and resource management) and tips discussed in this chapter will help you maintain and host your Web site on a healthy server. In addition to maintenance issues, a few Windows NT utility applications will also be discussed in this chapter.

Chapter 25—Setting Up and Configuring the Windows NT FTP Service

After setting up a Web server, the contents at your Web site will be accessible to anyone who has access to a Web browser. However, users might not always have access to a Web browser. In such an instance, if you have set up an FTP server, users will be able to access various files such as documentation and applications by accessing your Web site. The chapter on setting up and configuring the FTP service will demonstrate how to set up the Windows NT FTP service to distribute files on the Internet. You will also be shown how to reduce the load on your Web server by setting up an FTP service and allow users to access files at your Web site using Web browsers.

Chapter 26—Setting Up a Mail Server

The benefits of setting up an SMTP mail server are twofold. First, users will be able to e-mail you with regards to various questions and feedback. Second, you can communicate with these users without utilizing an external mail server setup on another server. By not depending on another mail server for e-mail, you will be able to respond to feedback and communicate with users efficiently using your own mail server.

Chapter 27—Setting Up a Mail-List Server

Benefits of setting up a mail list server are different from the benefits of simply setting up a mail server. Mail list servers are very effective in forming discussion groups. If you are familiar with Internet newsgroups, you can think of an Internet mail list as an Internet newsgroup. However, all discussions that take place in an Internet mail list take place via e-mail. This is because all discussions that occur in a mail list are transmitted to all users who subscribe to that mail list as regular e-mail. Since all discussions are sent to users via e-mail, they tend to pay more attention and read the messages and respond to them more quickly. With newsgroups, users often have to use a special news reading program to read the newsgroups. However, when a mail-list server is used, they can just use their regular e-mail reading application to read and respond to various discussions. This chapter demonstrates how to set up and administer a mail-list server to allow users to participate in discussions.

Chapter 28—Setting Up a Domain Name Server

Some Internet access service providers require that you have your own domain name server (DNS) setup. Domain name servers do the job of translating a domain name alias (`www.NetInnovation.com`) to its corresponding Internet protocol address (206.161.77.220). Even if your Internet access service provider provides you with a DNS, it's always a good idea to set up a local DNS service for backup purposes. This chapter will demonstrate how to set up a DNS service on your server and how to address various issues related to setting up a DNS service under Windows NT.

Chapter 29—Setting Up a Telnet Server

A Telnet server will be very useful to you if you need to access your server from a remote location to perform system administration tasks. After setting up a Telnet service, using any Telnet client you will be able to access your server from anywhere on the Internet. This chapter will demonstrate how to set up a Telnet server under Windows NT. Security issues related to setting up a Telnet server will also be discussed.

Chapter 30—Setting Up an NNTP News Server

Although your Web server can reach a large audience of users, it's not really designed to host a discussion group where users can post comments and questions. Even though Web-discussion applications have been created by a number of companies, they are usually CGI programs that lack the functionality offered by a news reading application. If you would like to host Internet discussion forums on your server, you will need to set up an NNTP (Network News Transport Protocol) server. This chapter demonstrates how to set up an NNTP news server on your NT server so that users can take part in various discussions.

Chapter 31—Setting Up a Web Conferencing System

WebBoard can be used to set up a Web conferencing system and allow users navigating your Web site to interact with each other. Because conference forums set up with WebBoard are accessible via a Web browser, they are easily accessible to users browsing a Web site. A Web site, which is mostly a one-way medium of information distribution, can be turned into a two-way medium of information exchange by setting up a Web conferencing system and making your Web site a rich and diverse source of information.

What's On The CD

The CD-ROM that accompanies this book contains all the source code from the examples of the book. These examples include HTML Web pages, VBScript, Java, JavaScript as well as C and PERL CGI programs. The CD also contains many tools that can be used to publish information on the Web. These utilities consist of a number of freeware and shareware applications and can be used to design Web pages and manipulate graphics at your Web site. By utilizing these tools, you will be able to publish content, write CGI programs as well as manage the contents of your Web site. Since the Web is hampered by bandwidth limitations, you will be able to use graphic manipulation utilities in the CD-ROM to optimize graphics at your Web site for transmitting via the Internet.

What's Needed to Use This Book

It is highly recommended that you have access to a Windows NT workstation or server that is connected to the Internet. Most topics and discussions can be read off-line when you have time. However, examples presented in this book should be done online. This will enable you to understand topics covered in the book more thoroughly and also provide you the opportunity to experiment with examples by making changes to them. The ideal computer to use with this book should have the following configuration or better.

- 486 DX2/66 or better (Pentium processor is recommended)
- 16 MB RAM minimum (over 24 MB RAM highly recommended)
- At least a 28.8 PPP link to the Internet for obtaining new versions of software as well as consult resources on the Internet
- Around 150 megabytes of free disk space for your Web server, Web pages, graphics, Web publishing tools as well as CGI applications and database interfaces

- CD-ROM drive
- Windows NT Server or Workstation version 3.51 or greater (The book is designed for version 4.0)

What's Next?

You are now ready to learn about exciting ways of publishing information on the Web at your own pace by reading the rest of the book. Since the purpose of the first few chapters is to familiarize yourself with various terms and topics, you will be able to go through them fairly quickly. Even if you are familiar with topics covered in the first few chapters, you might want to skim them quickly before moving on to sections that detail various ways of publishing content on the Web. After reading the following chapters, you will be able to set up an outstanding, richly interactive Windows NT-based Web site that is optimized for the Internet. Good luck and have fun!

> **NOTE**
>
> The information in this book is based on beta software. Since this information was made public before the final release of the product, there may be some changes to the product by the time it is finally released. After final product has begun shipping, we encourage you to visit our website, `http://www.mcp.com/sams` for an electronic update starting 09/01/96.
>
> Additionally, if you have access to the Internet, you can always get up-to-the-minute information about Windows NT Server and Windows NT Workstation direct from Microsoft at the following locations:
>
> `http://www.microsoft.com/ntserver`
> `http://www.microsoft.com/ntworkstation`

I

Introduction to the
World Wide Web

1

What Is the World Wide Web?

Welcome to the exciting world of Web site development with Windows NT! As mentioned in the introduction, although this book is written for Web site developers who are already familiar with publishing on the Web, everything covered in this book is presented in a manner that is easy to understand—even if you are new to material discussed in this book. Before new terms and topics are discussed, they are clearly defined so that even if you do not have any prior knowledge of material discussed, you will still be able to follow this book. Although all chapters are self contained, if you are new to Windows NT, or publishing information on the World Wide Web (WWW) with Windows NT, you should read the first four chapters before moving on to other chapters. Chapters 1 through 4 discuss various issues related to developing a Web site using Windows NT. By studying the topics covered in these chapters, you'll be able to more easily understand material covered in other chapters of the book.

Before discussing various Web publishing tools and advanced Web publishing concepts, an introduction and a brief overview of the World Wide Web is in order. This chapter introduces you to the World Wide Web, Web sites, and home pages on the Internet. It is primarily for those who are not already familiar with the World Wide Web. If you are familiar with these topics, you might want to skim this chapter or skip it altogether and move on to the next chapter, which provides an overview of various aspects of choosing Windows NT to develop a Web site.

How It All Began

In order to make the best use of a new technology, it's often important to know how that technology evolved. Although many organizations have increasingly started to make use of the World Wide Web recently, the Internet used to be a very quiet and small network just a few years ago. This section discusses how the World Wide Web evolved into what it is today, and how it is revolutionizing information distribution and retrieval on the Internet.

Until the early 1980s, what is now called *the Internet* was a relatively small network called *ARPAnet (Advanced Research Projects Agency network of the Department of Defense)*. This small network was mainly used as a research tool for about 15 years. After the Internet was created, many universities and government organizations got connected to it to exchange and distribute information. Although at first the Internet was used exclusively for educational purposes, commercial organizations realized the potential of the Internet and connected to it, as well.

The *World Wide Web* was created to address information distribution problems on the Internet. Until the creation of the World Wide Web, almost all information distribution was accomplished through e-mail, FTP, Archie, and Gopher. *E-mail (electronic mail)* became widely used for exchanging information between various groups of people as well as individuals. *FTP (File Transfer Protocol)* was used to transfer files from one computer to another. *Archie* was used to locate various files on the Internet. Due to its very nature, before long information was scattered all over the Internet. Therefore, unless you knew where information you needed was located, you had no way of searching for it. This became a major problem when someone had to navigate the Internet in search of information. Because a well-organized information infrastructure was missing, the Internet could not be used to its full potential.

As a solution to this problem, *Gopher* was invented at the University of Michigan. Gopher is a database of information that is organized by using a hierarchical menu interface. Gopher was designed to narrow a user's search from general information to very specific information by offering the user selections of topics from various layers of menus. To extend the amount of information that can be provided, Gopher sites were often connected to other Gopher sites. Although Gopher proved to be a more efficient way of locating and distributing information, its capabilities were limited. Mainly, information distributed by way of Gopher was virtually limited to plain text, and access to information at various locations was not very well organized. Furthermore, Internet information technologies that were being used around that time were plagued with limitations, such as the following:

- Platform dependence
- Lack of standards
- Incapability of richly formatting content
- Limited virtually to plain text
- Cryptic user interfaces
- Lack of security
- Familiarity with UNIX often required
- Incapability of being extended to accommodate new technologies

Due to these and other limitations, a new platform-independent method had to be invented to distribute information on the Internet. This issue was addressed at the European Particle Physics Laboratory CERN (Conseil Européen pour la Recherche Nucléaire) in Geneva, Switzerland, when *HyperText Markup Language (HTML)* was created. HTML was derived from a document-formatting language called *Standard Generalized Markup Language (SGML)*. HTML was designed to be a document markup language that's easy to learn, use, and transmit over the Internet. HTML is simpler to use and easier to learn than SGML. To transmit HTML documents on the Internet, a *TCP/IP (Transport Control Protocol/Internet Protocol)* based protocol was invented. This protocol became known as *HyperText Transport Protocol (HTTP)*. The World Wide Web was born with the creation of HTTP and HTML. The Web addresses many of the limitations listed earlier by providing content providers with a powerful medium to distribute information. Web servers speak HTTP to transmit HTML files, and Web browsers use HTTP to retrieve HTML files. Web browsers display various objects, both static and interactive (such as text, images, and Java applets), upon retrieving them from Web servers.

With the unification of text, graphics, video, sound, and interactive applications, the World Wide Web has become an exciting medium of information interchange compared to Gopher. Thanks to the World Wide Web, someone looking for information is finally able to browse various information sources and easily travel from one source to another by following various *hyperlinks*. Hyperlinks are objects that refer to *Uniform Resource Locators (URLs)* of Web pages. When a user clicks on a hyperlink, he or she is transferred to the Web page to which the hyperlink is linked. URLs can be thought of as addresses of Web pages. Every Web page has one or more URLs associated with it. With the help of special applications and browsers, the World Wide Web has quickly become a vehicle for text and multimedia distribution on the Internet. The World Wide Web gained much of its popularity after Mosaic (Web browser) was released in 1993 by the *National Center for Supercomputing Applications (NCSA)*.

No matter how rich the content is, if users have no way of searching for this information, it is of little value to anyone. Locating information on the Internet has become easier thanks to the many search engines and Web-site cataloging databases that have been deployed on the Web such as Yahoo (`http://www.yahoo.com/`) and WebCrawler (`http://www.webcrawler.com/`). These databases offer search capabilities that allow users to search for Web sites they are interested in by using a few keywords.

The World Wide Web is perhaps the most influential vehicle of information distribution since the invention of the television. The recent boom in the number of Web sites on the Internet attests to this fact. As more and more people gain access to the World Wide Web through online services or directly by way of a local *Internet Service Provider (ISP)*, many organizations will focus more on using the World Wide Web to keep their customers informed of new products, carry out business transactions, and provide customer service.

Life on the Internet before the World Wide Web

Before the World Wide Web, the Internet was a more educational network than it is now and was primarily used by researchers and students to correspond and share information with each other. Although this was a great way of using the Internet, it was clearly not used to its full potential. Prior to the World Wide Web, because most users accessing the Internet were accessing it via text-based information retrieval applications, life on the Internet was not very pleasant. Although various Internet services such as mail, FTP, and newsgroups existed before the World Wide Web, these services were more or less standalone services and were not very well integrated. Furthermore, in order to have any control over the layout of a document published on the Internet, someone typically had to use a complicated document-formatting language such as Tex or LaTex or along with a special compiler to compile it to a postscript file. These postscript files were usually made available to users through FTP. However, for a user to view these postscript files, a special postscript interpreter or a printer that supports postscript was required. Due to such complexities, most users who could have taken advantage of the Internet were not able to do so.

Why Is the World Wide Web So Popular?

The World Wide Web is so popular because it addresses most limitations of Internet information distribution applications that existed before Web browsers. In the past, virtually everything on the Internet was in plain text format. Due to this, information could not be richly formatted or presented in a way that is easy to browse and search. However, information on the World Wide Web can be formatted to make the information more presentable, easy to view, and easy to understand. For example, when a complex topic is discussed, it is often easier to explain it by using diagrams, charts, video clips, and even interactive applications as opposed to plain text. The World Wide Web offers a medium to present information in a way that combines the strengths of all these visual aids.

Before the World Wide Web, using the Internet generally meant obtaining and using a UNIX shell account, which typically gives the user a UNIX command prompt that can be used to invoke various UNIX text-based applications. Due to the way most UNIX applications work and their often cryptic text-based interfaces, the learning curve was too high for most people to familiarize themselves with UNIX. Although people are generally willing to try out new things, the lack of user-friendly interfaces held back a lot of people from even getting on the Internet. Most people use Microsoft Windows-based or Macintosh-based computers to do most of their work. For these users who are very comfortable with *graphical user interfaces (GUIs)*, learning UNIX text-based applications and their cryptic commands and hot keys became a challenge. Because of this (although the Internet was around for a long time before the World Wide Web), a noticeable commercial growth on the Internet was not visible until the World Wide Web was created with client-end applications for Microsoft Windows and Macintosh platforms. The success of online services such as America Online, CompuServe, and Prodigy is a result of providing users with user interfaces that are powerful but easy to use. For example, most things that can be accomplished with online services can be accomplished on the Internet through Internet bulletin board services and newsgroups for a fraction of the cost of using an online service. However, most users prefer using an online service because it offers the ability to obtain and distribute information with easy-to-use graphical user interfaces. The World Wide Web brings this power not only to users of online services but also to the entire Internet community that has a TCP/IP link to the Internet.

The World Wide Web is platform independent because it is based on a client/server paradigm. Typically, the server platform is transparent to users browsing a Web site. This is another reason for the success of the World Wide Web. Because Internet standards and protocols defined by CERN were not proprietary standards, everyone was free to implement his or her own Web server and Web browser that complies with Internet standards and specifications. Due to this freedom and openness, organizations like NCSA, Netscape, and Microsoft got the opportunity to research and extend existing Internet standards such as HTML to facilitate broader uses of the World Wide Web. Thanks to the effort of such pioneers, the World Wide Web continues to evolve and become a more mainstream medium of information dispersal by giving content providers more options and control over what they publish on the Internet.

Compared to other information distribution vehicles, the World Wide Web is a very attractive medium because the cost of publishing data and making it available to a global audience is relatively low. Furthermore, by registering a Web site with various search engines and Web site cataloging databases, you can potentially get your customers to come to you for information when they need it. This is different from traditional ways of advertising, such as television advertising, in which advertisers take the information directly to their customers.

Clearly, by setting up a Web site, you will be catering to a different kind of audience. Usually someone visiting your Web site is there because he or she needs access to some information. Therefore, when designing your Web site, you should keep in mind that your first priority is to make the information at your Web site as easily accessible as possible.

The Changing Nature of the World Wide Web

Like most technological inventions of this decade, the World Wide Web itself is going through some major changes. What has been witnessed in the last few years is just the beginning of the World Wide Web. Various organizations are just beginning to realize the potential of the World Wide Web and are setting up Web sites on the Internet. Although some of these organizations might not have a clear agenda just yet as to what to accomplish with their corporate Web site, they certainly want to establish a presence on the Internet. Various organizations are using the Web for different tasks.

Although at first the World Wide Web was created so that students and researchers can share information in a timely manner, more and more organizations are beginning to use it for commercial purposes. Because the Web was originally created for noncommercial purposes, it originally lacked secure data transferring protocols. However, this trend is changing thanks to new secure HTTP protocols that encrypt data before it is transferred through the Internet. Thanks to these secure HTTP protocols, even if someone is eavesdropping on what is transferred between a Web server and a Web client, that person will not be able to do any harm with the data because it is encrypted with robust data encryption algorithms such as SSL (Secure Sockets Layer).

Before scripting languages such as VBScript, Web pages used to be static. Thanks to new Web technologies such as Java, JavaScript, and VBScript, content providers will have more control of information they publish on the World Wide Web. These new technologies can be used to create interactive Web pages that respond to various user interactions without utilizing resources of a Web server. As a result of these technologies and secure data transfer protocols, there will be more commercial growth on the World Wide Web. This will induce more organizations, as well as individuals, to get connected to the Internet, and access and distribute information on the World Wide Web. Chances are that once people and organizations discover the wealth of benefits the Internet has to offer, they will start using it more and contribute to the growth and increased use of the World Wide Web. Although some may view the commercialization of the World Wide Web to be detrimental to the well-being of the Internet, increased commercial use will actually benefit the Internet because many new technologies will come into existence to address various limitations of current technologies. These new technologies can also be used for educational purposes just as well as they can be used for commercial purposes. Therefore, although the Web is changing, these changes will make the Internet an even better medium of information retrieval and distribution. For example, Microsoft has announced that their upcoming Windows NT and Windows 95 update will come with Internet Explorer 3.0, which is part of Microsoft's plan to make Internet Explorer the main user interface of both operating systems.

Increased Bandwidth of Internet Connections

In addition to the Web being used for commercial purposes, the content of the Web is also changing. Currently, limited network bandwidth is holding back a lot of development that can take place on the Web. For example, when visiting a Web page that describes something very technical, rather than showing some static images, it will help to show a video clip of various concepts being discussed in action. However, for such content to be distributed, high-speed Internet connections have to be available at reasonable rates across the country. Thanks to the telecommunications reform bill, there will be more competition among *Internet Service Providers (ISPs)*. As a result of this, phone companies will start providing ISDN services at more reasonable rates, which will allow most users to upgrade their relatively slow 14.4 Kbs (kilobits per second) and 28.8 Kbs modem links to 64 or 128 Kbs ISDN links. In addition to this, cable companies will also start offering Internet access service to their customers. Because cable TV wires can carry more information at the same time than ISDN phone lines, when cable companies realize the potential of providing Internet service and start offering it, users will be able to enjoy high-speed Internet connections to their homes. These high-speed Internet connections will make it possible for content providers to provide information composed of text and graphics, as well as video and sound. Such high-speed connections can also be used to distribute video streams on the MBone (Multicast Backbone on the Internet).

Growth of the World Wide Web

Within the past few years, the number of Internet hosts has grown by a scale of a few magnitudes. If you look at Figure 1.1, you will notice that the number of Internet hosts has been almost doubling annually since 1991. Because such a growth was not visible before the birth of the World Wide Web, it is clear that the World Wide Web is responsible for most of this growth.

The recent increase in the number of Internet hosts is a result of an increasing number of commercial organizations establishing a presence on the Web.

FIGURE 1.1.

The Internet has been growing rapidly since 1991.

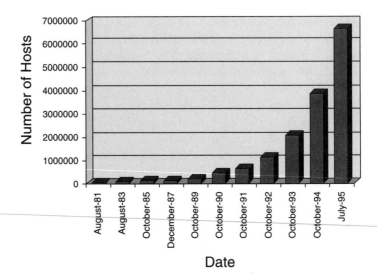

How Others Are Using the World Wide Web

Various organizations are using the World Wide Web for a variety of different purposes, from keeping users informed of new technologies via a Web site to allowing users to interact with each other by setting up forums at a Web site.

Lately, many organizations have begun to utilize the World Wide Web to conduct business on the Internet. Thanks to secure Internet data transfer protocols, it is now possible to conduct business on the Internet without risking an eavesdropper misusing various information provided to the merchant, such as credit card numbers and other personal customer information. To conduct business on the World Wide Web, many vendors have set up secure Web sites where customers can browse an online catalog and immediately make purchases using a credit card. Although such mechanisms are still not widely deployed, very soon they will become more popular than mail-order catalogs where customers call a toll-free number to place orders. The World Wide Web offers the vendor the ability to change prices immediately based upon prevailing market conditions, offer new products as they become available, and take out products from the catalog that are no longer in inventory. These benefits make the World Wide Web a much better medium for transacting business. When a sales catalog is put together for a Web site, several thousand copies of this catalog need not be produced for customer use, saving printing material and money, as well as time. This will allow vendors to pass the savings along to customers and be more competitive.

Organizations that market products and services such as cable TV, long-distance phone service, water, and gas might not be able to serve some Internet users due to geographical limitations. These organizations won't directly benefit from setting up a Web site. However, they have done so for establishing a better public image.

Because information can be immediately made available to millions of users, the World Wide Web is an ideal medium for distributing news. Many news organizations have set up Web sites for distributing news on the Internet. Although some sections of these Web sites are restricted for their customers, usually the latest headlines are made available for anyone to browse.

Some organizations have also begun using the World Wide Web to host discussion groups on the Internet. Some of these discussion groups are hosted by Internet news servers, while others are hosted using sophisticated *CGI (Common Gateway Interface)* programs. By setting up forums to discuss issues related to various products and services being sold by a vendor, use of the product can be encouraged and support costs can be reduced by allowing users to help themselves when they run into problems.

One of the best features about the Internet and the World Wide Web is that many resources are available free of charge for its users. This is partly due the fact that its roots come from an educational and research background where people generally share information with each other for free. This trend has continued despite the increased commercialization of the World Wide Web. Many organizations offer public services to the Internet community as a way of saying thanks for numerous Internet services they make use of. WebCrawler, an Internet search engine maintained by America Online, is an example of such a public service.

In later chapters of the book, you will be shown how to implement various information systems at your Web site to use the Internet to accomplish a variety of tasks. You will then be able to use your Web site to accomplish most of the tasks mentioned previously.

Various Aspects of Publishing on the World Wide Web

The Web is quite different compared to traditional mediums of information distribution such as newspapers, radio, and television. (Yes, it's considered traditional now!) The next few sections explore various advantages and drawbacks of publishing information on the World Wide Web.

Advantages of Publishing on the Web

Recently, many organizations have set up Web sites on the Internet. If you know the name of a company, you can now often get to its Web site by using vname as the the company's Web site address. Also, TV commercials and other product literature increasingly refer to HTTP addresses. This is a harbinger of a new mainstream medium of advertising. The cost savings of publishing on the Web can be very large when it is no longer necessary to print color brochures and mail them to prospective customers. By utilizing the Web, organizations can publish various pieces of product literature on the Web and allow customers to access this information. All this can be done at a fraction of the cost involved in keeping customers informed through traditional methods. Furthermore, information at a Web site can be kept up-to-date as necessary—not something that can be done in a cost-effective manner when printed manuals are involved.

The cost savings and time savings are two of the most significant advantages of using the Web to distribute information. When information is added to a Web site, it is immediately available to millions of users. No other information distribution medium has the capability to distribute information to such a large audience at a relatively minor cost. In addition to being able to provide information in a time-effective manner, by utilizing the Web you can also get customer feedback as soon as a customer transmits the feedback to your Web server. Also, by incorporating multimedia and new technologies such as Java to a Web site, you can make the content of a Web site richly interactive to make the information being presented more appealing to Web surfers.

Drawbacks of Publishing on the Web

Using the World Wide Web to distribute information has some drawbacks. One of the biggest drawbacks is the lack of security standards for transmitting sensitive data on the Internet. Because the World Wide Web was born in an academic environment, security was not initially a major concern. With the increasing commercial use of the Web, however, security has become a major concern. Several companies such as Microsoft and Netscape have come up with various data encryption technologies that can be used to make the Internet a secure place to do business. These security mechanisms, however, are not widely implemented by all Web browsers. Therefore, security concerns arise when sensitive data is transmitted on the Internet. However, this will change when more and more Web browsers (especially proprietary browsers of online services) start supporting various data encryption mechanisms.

Another drawback of publishing on the Web is the lack of content formatting control. Although standard HTML offers many document formatting attributes, its capabilities are somewhat limited. Use of Netscape or Microsoft Enhancements to HTML, however, enables content published on the Web to be better formatted. Unfortunately, not all Web browsers support these HTML "enhancements." This is a major drawback because when special HTML tags are used in a Web page, content might appear almost unintelligible for users who use browsers that do not support HTML tags such as Netscape enhancements to HTML. For example, users of various online services with technologically challenged Web browsers will not be able to enjoy Web sites as much as users who use Netscape Navigator and Microsoft Internet Explorer.

How to Use the Web to Your Advantage

Although there are certain disadvantages when publishing on the Web, its advantages far outweigh the previously mentioned drawbacks. By using the Web judiciously, you will be able to provide content to users in a timely and visually appealing manner. Also, you can use the Web as an efficient medium to communicate with customers and to obtain feedback and other information. In Chapter 16, "Introduction to Windows NT CGI Programming," you learn how to set up a feedback form used to obtain feedback from users browsing your Web site. Furthermore, by using other Internet services such as FTP (File Transfer Protocol), you will be able to distribute software to users visiting your Web site. After reading the rest of this book, you will be able to set up an outstanding Web site and unleash the potential of Web-site development with Windows NT.

Architecture of the World Wide Web

The World Wide Web is made up of Web sites and home pages. Using HTTP, Web servers transmit information requested by Web browsers. The following sections introduce Web sites and home pages.

Web Sites

Web sites can be thought of as TV broadcast stations. However, unlike TV broadcast stations, Web sites broadcast information on a per-demand basis. When a Web browser connects to a Web server and requests information from the Web server, the information is transmitted to the Web browser, and the connection is closed. You can generally have your own Web site up and running in just a few weeks (in all likelihood, much sooner after reading this book!). Refer to Figure 1.2 for a simple diagram of how Web sites and Web clients are connected to the World Wide Web. As you can see in Figure 1.2, the Web is mostly a client/server environment. However, the Web is moving towards a distributed processing environment with the aid of client-side scripting languages such as VBScript and JavaScript.

COMPATIBILITY

Figure 1.2 illustrates how Web servers and clients are linked to the Internet. Because all these Web servers and clients use HTTP to communicate with each other, various hardware platforms and operating systems can act as Web servers and Web clients. Because HTML documents are not platform dependent, they are compatible across a number of hardware platforms.

When a user accesses a page at a Web site, usually more than one HTTP connection is made. Generally, a separate connection is made for each object, such as a graphics file or Java applet, that's embedded in the document being accessed. For example, if you type **netstat** at the command prompt when someone is accessing your Web site, you will notice that usually more than one connection is made by the user accessing your Web site. What you see in Figure 1.3 is the result of a page being accessed by a Web browser. As you can see, several connections are made by the Web browser accessing the page. This is because, typically, a new connection must be made for each object (graphic, sound file, Java applet, and so on) on the page the client is accessing.

FIGURE 1.2.

Users connected to the Internet can access any Web server on the World Wide Web by using a Web browser.

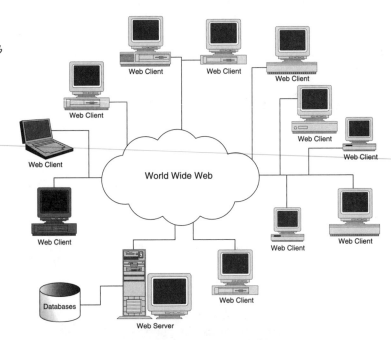

FIGURE 1.3.

Multiple HTTP connections are usually made for a single Web page if it contains embedded graphics or other objects.

```
                        i:\winnt35\system32\cmd.exe
I:\winnt35\system32>netstat

Active Connections

  Proto  Local Address          Foreign Address          State
  TCP    wonderland:80          mccallpm1-10.cyberhighway.net:1585   TIME_WAIT
  TCP    wonderland:80          mccallpm1-10.cyberhighway.net:1586   TIME_WAIT
  TCP    wonderland:80          mccallpm1-10.cyberhighway.net:1587   TIME_WAIT
  TCP    wonderland:80          mccallpm1-10.cyberhighway.net:1588   TIME_WAIT
  TCP    wonderland:80          mccallpm1-10.cyberhighway.net:1589   TIME_WAIT
  TCP    wonderland:80          mccallpm1-10.cyberhighway.net:1590   TIME_WAIT
  TCP    wonderland:80          mccallpm1-10.cyberhighway.net:1591   TIME_WAIT
  TCP    wonderland:80          mccallpm1-10.cyberhighway.net:1592   TIME_WAIT
  TCP    wonderland:80          mccallpm1-10.cyberhighway.net:1593   TIME_WAIT
  TCP    wonderland:80          mccallpm1-10.cyberhighway.net:1594   TIME_WAIT
  TCP    wonderland:80          mccallpm1-10.cyberhighway.net:1595   TIME_WAIT
  TCP    wonderland:80          mccallpm1-10.cyberhighway.net:1596   TIME_WAIT
  TCP    wonderland:80          mccallpm1-10.cyberhighway.net:1597   TIME_WAIT
  TCP    wonderland:80          mccallpm1-10.cyberhighway.net:1598   TIME_WAIT
  TCP    wonderland:80          mccallpm1-10.cyberhighway.net:1599   TIME_WAIT
  TCP    wonderland:80          mccallpm1-10.cyberhighway.net:1601   TIME_WAIT

I:\winnt35\system32>
```

TECHNICAL NOTE

HTTP is a *connectionless* protocol. A connectionless protocol is a protocol that does not need a persistent connection. When an HTTP request is received by a Web server, the data is sent to the client. When the requested data has been transmitted, the connection is closed. Often a request for a page creates more than one connection. This happens if various inline graphics or other objects are on the page. Each connection is good only for retrieving one graphic or other object from the Web server.

Requirements for Setting Up a Web Site

When setting up a Web site, certain key hardware components are required. Hardware requirements for setting up a Web site with Windows NT are discussed in detail in Chapter 5, "Determining and Fulfilling Your Requirements." Various key components of a Web site are illustrated in Figure 1.4. Although some peripherals listed in Figure 1.4 are not required, depending on the nature of your Web site and the information you intend to publish on the Web, having them will make matters much easier for you.

FIGURE 1.4.
The anatomy of a typical Web site.

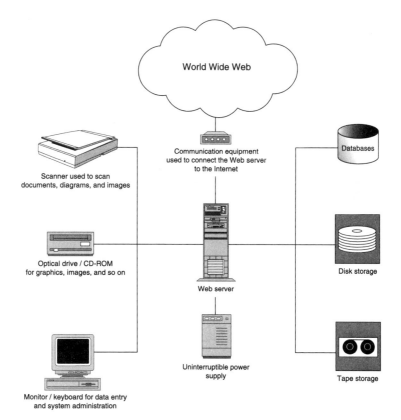

To set up your Web server, a computer capable of running Windows NT and that is connected to the Internet is required. To make matters easy when installing applications and using the contents of the CD-ROM that accompanies this book, a CD-ROM drive is recommended. Furthermore, if you intend to make large amounts of data available for browsing at your Web site, you will also need to set up a Web database interface using CGI. You will be shown how to do this in Chapter 18, "Publishing Databases on the Web."

If you intend to make certain documents and figures that are already in printed form available at your Web site, you can save time by scanning such images and diagrams as opposed to creating them from scratch. Although a tape backup drive and a UPS (Uninterruptible Power Supply) are not required to set up a Web site, these two components can save you a great deal of time as well as money. Because your Web server will be up and running all day, if there is a power failure, Windows NT should be given time to shut down your server successfully. If not, sudden power outages, spikes, and surges can be detrimental to the health of your server. Having a tape backup drive will also be useful in the unlikely event that your hard disk becomes corrupted or someone accidentally deletes some files. A UPS or a tape backup drive can easily pay for itself the first time you use either of them.

How Web Servers Work

The World Wide Web is a collection of servers on the Internet that speak HTTP, which is a "connectionless protocol." Web servers listen for incoming HTTP requests and when an HTTP request is received, the requested data is sent to the client. Refer to Figure 1.5 for an example of this interaction.

FIGURE 1.5.

Web servers serve HTTP requests made by Web browsers by transmitting documents, graphics, and other objects requested.

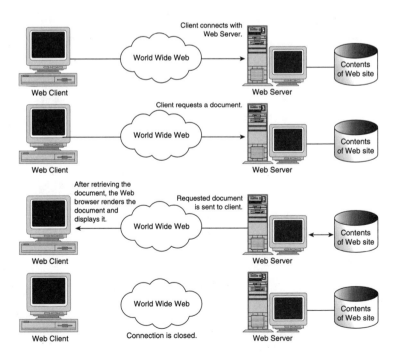

If information requested by a client is simply a Web page consisting of plain text, a few images, sound, or other objects, the Web server simply transmits these objects at the request of the client. More work is involved, however, when dynamic content must be provided by the Web server. CGI is used by Web servers to invoke various applications on the server to provide dynamic content to users browsing a Web site. Refer to Figure 1.6 for a graphical representation of how Web servers invoke CGI scripts to provide dynamic content.

FIGURE 1.6.

Web servers use CGI to process user input and provide dynamic content, possibly from a database, to users visiting a Web site.

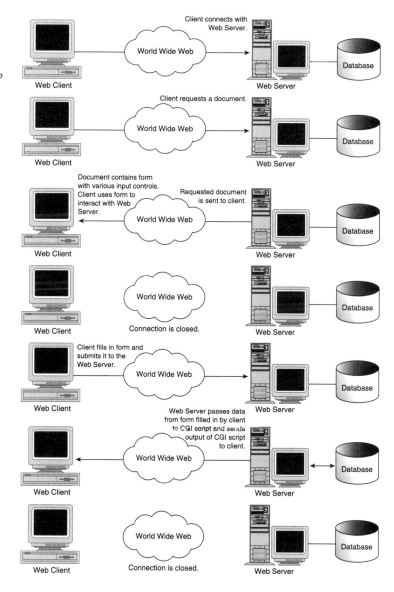

Typically, CGI scripts receive input when a client fills in a form and submits it to the Web server. The Web server then invokes the CGI script after creating certain CGI environment variables. As shown in Figure 1.6, this process begins when a client first requests an HTML document containing a form from the Web server. After the form is sent to the client, the connection is closed. When the user fills in the form and submits it to the server, the server executes the CGI script with the information that was put into the form. The CGI script then processes the data, possibly by accessing a database, and sends a message to the client who invoked the CGI script. This message typically contains the results of processing input provided by the client and provides a link to another page so that the user can continue to browse the Web site.

Information can also be processed at the client side without any interaction with the Web server. Be sure to read Chapter 19, "Adding Java to Your Web Site," Chapter 20, "Creating Interactive Web Pages with JavaScript," and Chapter 21, "Unleashing the Power of VBScript" to learn how various scripting languages can be used to process information at the client side without using resources of the Web server.

TECHNICAL NOTE

Web servers usually listen on port 80 for incoming HTTP requests from Web browsers.

Introduction to Home Pages

Home pages are documents formatted in HTML that might contain inline graphics or other objects. HTML documents are in plain text (usually ASCII) format and can be created with any text editor. In Chapter 10, "Web Site Development Tools," you will be shown how various applications can be used to create HTML files. In Chapter 6, "Installing and Using Microsoft Internet Information Server," and Chapter 7, "Publishing on the Web with WebSite, Purveyor, and Netscape," you will be shown how to set up the Microsoft Internet server or another Web server to host a Web site. Just like the World Wide Web, HTML is evolving. More and more features are being added to HTML to accommodate various needs. HTML has been standardized by the World Wide Web consortium.

URL

For more information about standard HTML and proposed HTML enhancements to standard HTML, visit The World Wide Web Consortium's Web page at

```
http://www.w3.org/hypertext/WWW/MarkUp/
```

Just because a Web browser such as Netscape or Microsoft's Internet Explorer supports a "neat" HTML tag, that doesn't mean that it is a valid HTML. When using HTML enhancements that are beyond standard HTML, you should be aware that when someone looks at your Web site with a browser that supports only standard HTML, your pages might not be rendered properly.

Homepages can contain inline graphics or other objects. Listed here are a few commonly used file formats found in Web pages:

File Type	Extension
AIFF sound	.aiff
AU sound	.au
GIF image	.gif
HTML document	.html or .htm
JPEG image	.jpg or .jpeg
MPEG movie	.mpeg or .mpg
PostScript file	.ps
TIFF image	.tiff or .tif
Plain text	.txt
QuickTime movie	.mov
XBM bitmap image	.xbm

TOOLS

When you embed various objects in file formats not commonly supported by Web browsers, you should always include a link to downloadable software that can be used to view the files you make available.

Various graphics formats like the ones mentioned previously and new technologies such as Java, JavaScript, VBScript, Microsoft Internet Studio, and Virtual Reality Markup Language (VRML) are capable of presenting information to a global audience in a way information has never been presented before.

Web Publishing Tools

To make the task of developing Web sites easier, many Web site development tools are available. Due to the large number of Microsoft Windows users, many Web page development applications are available for Windows NT. These tools can be classified into two categories: Web page development applications and Web database publishing applications. By using Web page development applications, it is possible to develop the static contents of your Web site, and Web database publishing applications allow you to provide dynamic data to users by linking a database on your server to a Web page.

Web Page Development Applications

Many Windows NT Web publishing applications are available for developing Web pages. Although most of these tools are simple HTML editors, a new breed of WYSIWYG Web page creation applications are coming into existence. With these powerful tools, publishing on the Web will become easier and less time-consuming.

Although initial versions of Microsoft Internet Assistant for Microsoft Word were limited in functionality, more recent versions have many added features to make Web publishing tasks easier to handle. For example, the current version of Internet Assistant handles inline images, document backgrounds, various text colors, font attributes, tables, and many other document formatting attributes. Because all these features are accessible through an easy-to-use GUI, someone without any Web publishing experience can publish content on the Web by using Microsoft Internet Assistant. In addition to Microsoft Internet Assistant for Word and FrontPage, other WYSIWYG HTML editors such as Netscape Gold will be available by the time you read this book. In the near future, thanks to these powerful tools, a knowledge of HTML will no longer be necessary to publish on the Web. However, familiarity with HTML will enable you to have more control over what you publish on the World Wide Web.

In addition to Microsoft, other companies, such as Netscape, will be unveiling various Web publishing suites that you can use to publish information on the Web. These Web publishing suites will make setting up and maintaining a Web site easier by enabling you to concentrate on the contents of your Web site instead of worrying about how it should be formatted with HTML.

As powerful Web publishing tools are developed, an HTML knowledge will not even be necessary. Very soon, what word processors such as Microsoft Word did for document publishing will be done to Web publishing by Web publishing suites. Before Word processors came into existence, a person who wanted to create a richly formatted document had to learn a rather complex document markup language and use that and a special compiler to design documents. Thanks to inexpensive microcomputers with feature-rich word processors, this drudgery is no longer necessary.

Web Database Interfaces

Although providing plain text, images, and sound by way of the Web has tremendous potential, the benefits of it are limited. Because one of the main advantages of setting up a Web site is being able to provide information in a timely manner, publishing databases on the Web has many advantages. You can use several Web database applications for Windows NT to publish databases on the World Wide Web. These database publishing applications are easy to install and offer a great deal of functionality. Through the utilization of such interfaces, databases on an NT server can be made available to users browsing a Web site. With the aid of CGI, such database interface applications can be set up to enable users visiting a Web site to update and query databases.

Requirements for Web Publishing

Many Web authoring services will do all your Web authoring for a price. However, if you are setting up your own Web server, you might as well spend some more time familiarizing yourself with Web publishing and do it yourself. To publish on the Web, you can exploit the user-friendly and robust environment of Windows NT. Thanks to many Web publishing applications available for Windows NT, even with no prior Web publishing experience, it's easy to create an outstanding Web site.

To learn Web site development, the single most important thing you need is time. On the Internet, many resources are available that teach you how to publish on the Web. For more information on publishing content on the Web, you might want to visit Yahoo!'s World Wide Web authoring resources page.

URL

Yahoo!'s Web authoring resources page:

`http://www.yahoo.com/Computers_and_Internet/Internet/World_Wide_Web/Authoring/`

The next sections outline a few key requirements for developing a Web site with Windows NT.

Internet Connection

When hosting a Web site, the biggest bottleneck is usually the connection that connects the Web server to the Internet. Therefore, you should obtain the fastest Internet link you can afford for your Web server. Thanks to the new telecommunications reform bill, you will have more freedom when selecting an ISP. Due to the nature of the wire used by cable TV, if your local cable TV company is also providing Internet service, you will be able to obtain a high-bandwidth Internet connection that might even be cheaper than an ISDN connection in some areas. If a cable-based ISP is unavailable in your area, you should consider obtaining an ISDN line for your Web server. A dual channel ISDN line is all digital and can transmit about 4.5 times more data than a 28.8 modem connection in the same amount of time. However, if both options mentioned earlier are unavailable to you, you will have to go along with a 28.8 Plain Old Telephone Service (POTS) Internet connection. This might be painfully slow when you have multiple users accessing your Web site; however, there is a way to provide users accessing your Web site near T1 (high speed/bandwidth Internet connection) speeds while still using only a 28.8 POTS link to the Internet. You learn how this can be accomplished in Chapter 5, "Determining and Fulfilling Your Requirements."

Windows NT Server or Workstation

A Web site can be set up with Windows NT server as well as Windows NT workstation. Although both versions of NT provide a user-friendly, robust, and secure platform to develop a Web site, NT server is optimized for network traffic. Therefore, if you will be hosting a Web site that will be accessed by many users at the same time, it's better to use Windows NT server. Because there are certain restrictions when upgrading from Windows NT workstation to Windows NT server, you should carefully evaluate various benefits and drawbacks before setting up your Web site on a computer that runs Windows NT workstation. Furthermore, Microsoft's Internet Information Server (IIS) is distributed free with Windows NT server and offers a great deal of functionality. Microsoft's Internet Information Server is certainly the most feature-rich, free Web server available for Windows NT! Most likely, a lite version of IIS will be available for Windows NT Workstation 4.0. However, it will not be as powerful as the version of IIS shipped with Windows NT Server 4.0.

COMPATIBILITY

When a Windows NT Workstation installation is upgraded to Windows NT server, it cannot be set up as a Backup domain controller.

Windows NT-Compatible Hardware

Having hardware that's compatible with Windows NT can save time as well as frustration. Windows NT is very sensitive about the hardware it runs on. It's always wise to use hardware that is in the Windows NT hardware compatibility list. This list contains hardware that has been tested with Windows NT. Furthermore, devices in the hardware compatibility list are also guaranteed to have Windows NT drivers. When choosing key system components such as I/O cards, motherboards, SCSI controllers, and mass storage devices, make sure they are compatible with Windows NT. You might save some money at first by going with a product that does not support NT that is from a vendor who denies the existence of NT, but you might end up wasting more money and time when you start having problems.

Time and Patience

You can accomplish a lot with some time and patience. This is especially true when it comes to Web-site development. Although your life as a Windows NT Web-site developer will be much nicer compared to that of a UNIX Web-site developer, some time has to be invested to learn new concepts and technologies. Thanks to the user-friendly environment afforded by Windows NT, you will have many powerful and user-friendly Web-site development tools at your disposal. You will be shown how to use these tools later in the book. Although it might seem time consuming, you should still invest the time in learning how to use the Web page creation, database publishing, and graphic manipulation tools covered in later chapters of the book. By learning how to use these tools and their features, you will be able to develop an outstanding Windows NT Web site.

Patience will pay off splendidly, especially when you start exploring advanced Web-site development tasks such as publishing databases on the Internet and writing CGI and Java programs. Although sometimes it might seem as if nothing works, don't give up! Web-site development is very rewarding when everything finally works the way it should. The more problems you encounter when you do things and the more patience you have, your reward and self-satisfaction at the end of each project will be that much greater!

Summary

This chapter covered various fundamental topics about the World Wide Web that you need in order to understand topics covered in subsequent chapters. You were first introduced to the World Wide Web, its architecture, and its evolution. Next you were shown how Web servers work and how home pages on Web servers can be used to distribute information on the Internet. The section on home pages covered various Web publishing tools and how you can utilize these tools to make Web publishing tasks easier to handle.

What's Next?

The next chapter discusses various aspects of choosing Windows NT to develop a Web site. By understanding various strengths and weaknesses of NT, you'll be able to develop your Web site by taking advantage of the strengths of Windows NT and finding solutions and workarounds for the various limitations of Windows NT.

2

Publishing on the World Wide Web with Windows NT

Prior to Windows NT, virtually all Internet information systems were implemented on UNIX servers. Even now, the majority of Web sites are hosted on UNIX servers. However, most of these servers were set up when Windows NT was still at its infancy in terms of development and deployment in mission-critical applications. The very fact that you're reading this book to deploy information systems on the Internet with NT is a sign of a new operating system standard being set for developing and publishing content on the Internet.

There are many advantages to choosing Windows NT to publish content on the Internet; however, there are also a number of drawbacks in taking this route. UNIX also has its strengths and weaknesses. This chapter compares and contrasts various aspects of choosing one operating system over the other, outlining features and drawbacks of each operating system as it applies to Web site developers.

Because Windows NT is a robust and secure operating system that can manage mission-critical information systems, it is increasingly being used to handle tasks that were delegated only to UNIX servers in the past. Subsequent chapters discuss how you can use Windows NT to develop Web sites and other Internet information distribution systems.

Although comparing and contrasting various aspects of using Windows NT as opposed to UNIX is not directly beneficial to someone developing Web sites with Windows NT, it helps to know strengths and weaknesses of each operating system. Because UNIX has been around for a very long time and is used almost exclusively in educational environments such as universities, many people have grown up with UNIX. Some people have become completely numb to the possibility of the existence of an operating system other than UNIX that can be used to accomplish tasks that were exclusively handled by UNIX servers in the past. In a large corporation, you are bound to meet quite a few of these people. Topics discussed in this chapter will help you, if nothing else, make a valid argument as to why Windows NT is a better operating system for developing and setting up information systems on the Internet. Let us first examine, compared to other operating systems, what's so different about Windows NT.

What's So Different about Windows NT?

Windows NT has been developed from the ground up to be *the* operating system of choice for mission-critical applications. The chief architect of Windows NT is Dave Cutler, designer of the VMS operating system. Along with the NT development team, he combined various aspects of the Mach microkernel (a variant of UNIX developed at Carnegie-Mellon University) and VMS to develop Windows NT. Although Microsoft first started out with MS-DOS running on relatively low-powered processors with limited system resources, system resource requirements for Windows NT are quite different. With the release of Windows NT 4.0, the 80386 platform is no longer supported. Unlike previous versions of MS-DOS, Windows, and even Windows 95, system resource requirements for NT are quite different. Although Microsoft recommends a minimum of 12 MB of RAM for NT Workstation and a minimum of 16 MB for NT server, these requirements are barely sufficient for the operating system, let alone other applications. Requirements for storage space and processing power are equally high for Windows NT. However, NT makes good use of these resources by providing in return a secure, robust, and scaleable environment that helps users be more productive and focus on their work.

Earlier versions of DOS and Windows were plagued with system resource allocation and stability problems, making it hard for users to concentrate on their work. Quite often, rather than coming up with innovative solutions to work-related problems, users came up with innovative ways of working with the operating system. For example, in the olden days, I discovered that if I started applications in a certain order, I could have more of them running at the same time due to the way Graphics Device Interface (GDI) and user resources were allocated. Windows NT's flat memory model frees its users from virtually all system resource allocation problems associated with DOS and Windows 3.*x*. As long as there are enough system resources, NT will happily run multiple applications, preemptively multitasking each of them. NT is clearly not another version of MS-DOS with a new GUI thrown on top of it. In fact, until version 4.0, its user interface looked very much like that of Windows 3.*x*.

Why Not UNIX?

Until recently, someone wanting to establish a presence on the Internet had very few options available apart from UNIX. Due to this reason (at the time of this writing) most Web servers on the Internet are in fact UNIX Web servers. These Web servers are quite capable of hosting a Web site and serving HTTP (HyperText Transport Protocol) requests. However, the development environment offered by UNIX to Web site developers leaves much to be desired. Most often, Web site developers who use UNIX spend a fair amount of time dealing with operating system-imposed inconveniences and cryptic user interfaces of most UNIX applications, which adversely affect their productivity.

Cryptic User Interfaces

Unlike NT, UNIX is not an end-user–oriented operating system known for its user friendliness. In a production environment, this is not very desirable because valuable time will be wasted on learning intricate details of various applications. Besides making users less productive, it also makes it more challenging to train new users.

Steep Learning Curve

Due to cryptic and complicated user interfaces, UNIX applications are typically associated with steep learning curves. This can be very expensive in a production environment where users need to be trained to use various applications.

Because of its complexities, it takes time to learn the ins and outs of UNIX. Although someone with very little experience can be immediately productive with Windows NT, the same is not true for UNIX. As you are undoubtedly aware, employee training can be very expensive. Because most UNIX applications are associated with a steep learning curve, it makes job training unnecessarily time consuming. Because most UNIX applications do not share a common and intuitive user interface, it also makes it hard to replace an employee who is leaving the company—it takes a relatively long time to train a new employee under UNIX. Also, the time and resources invested to train the former employee are lost. On the other hand, when a company uses an operating system such as Windows NT, virtually all investments made on easy-to-use applications are retained because most users require very little or no additional training.

Complicated Installation Procedures

UNIX applications are much more difficult to install and configure than Windows applications. Virtually all Windows applications have *installation wizards* that guide the user through all stages of the installation process, giving the user a chance to configure the application while installing it. Often, without reading any documentation and simply by executing setup.exe, you can install and use a Windows application.

The same is not true for most UNIX applications. Because there are many flavors of UNIX, some UNIX applications are distributed in source code format. This means that before installing the program, the correct source code has to be downloaded and compiled. Due to the subtle inconsistencies between UNIX flavors, it might take hours or even days to fix a compilation problem, especially if the source code is not very well documented. After fixing any compilation problems, due to a lack of installation programs with consistent user interfaces, you may need to read many pages of an instruction manual to learn the peculiar installation and configuration details of a program before installing it.

Because of complicated installation procedures and cryptic user interfaces, virtually everything becomes a major project in UNIX. For example, before using a new application or configuring it, someone typically has to spend a great deal of time reading UNIX man pages and getting to know various configuration issues related to the application being installed or configured. In a production environment, this can be quite expensive due to lost productivity.

Limited Availability of Web Publishing Software

Most Web publishing applications run only on Windows 95 and Windows NT. Using an operating system such as UNIX that lacks sophisticated Web publishing applications is a major drawback when it's used as a Web development platform. Although companies such as Netscape will release UNIX versions of Web publishing applications such as Netscape Gold, most developers will focus only on developing applications for Windows and Macintosh users.

Although several developers have begun developing applications for the Macintosh platform, it's often after they release the Windows version. Therefore, Macintosh users will often be lagging behind in having access to state-of-the art Web publishing tools. For example, the

Macintosh version of Netscape that supports Java was released several months after the Windows version.

At the time of this writing, only a small number of Internet content creation tools were available for UNIX. This trend will change in the future when UNIX Web site developers start demanding better applications. However, by that time, Windows applications would have gone through several stages of development and will offer more advanced features.

Lack of Development Tools

In UNIX, virtually all programs are developed using a simple text editor and a command line compiler. This makes it harder for a less-experienced programmer to develop applications.

On the other hand, with Windows NT, even a novice can create an application with Visual Basic to manipulate a database in a matter of minutes. Leveraging this kind of power to even novice users makes NT a very powerful but easy-to-use Web publishing platform.

A new breed of Web content development applications is coming into existence. Similar to integrated programming environments found in Microsoft Visual C++ and Borland C++, these development applications offer an integrated environment to develop content for the World Wide Web. Microsoft FrontPage, Future Tense Texture, and Microsoft Internet Studio are all examples of integrated Web publishing applications. You can utilize these applications to create richly interactive Web pages and publish large amounts of information in a timely manner. Most of these applications will not be available for UNIX for some time. Lack of availability of such applications limits what can be accomplished by choosing UNIX to develop content for the Internet.

Security: Freely Available Source Code

The source code of some flavors of UNIX is freely available. This is good from a programmer's point of view because various aspects of the operating system can be customized to meet various needs, but this might cause security problems. For example, a potential hacker can carefully go over the code in search of various vulnerabilities and exploit these vulnerabilities for malevolent acts. On the other hand, very few people have access to the source code of Windows NT, making it hard for potential hackers to go over the code in search of vulnerabilities of various security algorithms.

Some might argue that the availability of source code is good because vulnerabilities of security algorithms can be found by others and made public; however, there is a flip side. What if someone finds a vulnerability and doesn't make it public—worse yet, publicizes it in an *underground* Internet forum to a group of other hackers? If information about a vulnerability of a security algorithm falls into the wrong hands, this can seriously compromise the security of many servers that use the same code.

Is Linux Really Free?

One argument commonly made by many UNIX advocates is that Microsoft's Windows NT is a very expensive solution. They are also very quick to point out the fact that Linux, a version of UNIX for Intel microprocessors, is essentially free. However, most of these advocates do not want to discuss various aspects of using Linux, such as high administration costs and lack of powerful applications to simplify various tasks and complete them sooner. Although initially it might be a very inexpensive solution, UNIX requires a lot more care and nurturing than Windows NT. Although NT also requires attention every now and then, system administration tasks associated with NT are very easy to learn and perform. On the other hand, UNIX system administration takes longer to learn, and it costs a fair amount of money to have a UNIX guru around.

In a production environment, human resource costs are several times more than software and hardware costs put together. This is because unlike software and hardware, human resource expenses are not one-time investments. A user-friendly operating system makes users more productive by providing them with an environment that is easy to work with. UNIX, with all its cryptic user interfaces, falls short in providing users with such an environment to work in.

Furthermore, due to the large installed base of Windows users, many software development companies are aggressively creating productivity applications for making it simpler to perform routine tasks and make users more productive. However, such an effort is not very visible in the UNIX world. Most UNIX applications are prohibitively expensive for most organizations because these applications are written for a substantially smaller installed user base. Although UNIX systems are regarded as open systems, some aspects of these systems are very closed. Because there are a lot of different flavors of UNIX, an application that runs on one version may not necessarily run on another. This makes UNIX application development more expensive than Windows application development, and these costs are passed down to customers.

As mentioned earlier, Linux is really not a free solution after you start doing any work with it. On the other hand, although NT will initially cost more than Linux, in the long run, it will prove to be more expensive due to high maintenance costs and lost productivity. Investing in Windows NT will yield increased productivity and cut back the time it takes to accomplish various tasks, such as publishing content on the Internet.

Why Choose Windows NT?

Windows NT addresses most drawbacks of UNIX outlined earlier. Although NT is not by any means the perfect operating system or the solution to all your problems, it does have a lot to offer. After setting up a Web server, publishing content on the Web is very easy thanks to many Web publishing applications available for NT. Because you are reading this book, you must already have some very good reasons for choosing Windows NT to publish information on the Web. In the next few sections, various pros and cons of choosing Windows NT will be discussed in detail. By understanding these pros and cons, you will be able to exploit various capabilities of NT to your advantage.

Benefits of Using Windows NT

Windows NT offers many benefits over other operating systems. By making use of these benefits, you will be able to be more productive and publish content on the Internet by exploiting various capabilities of Windows NT. The following are just some of features of Windows NT that you can take advantage of when setting up information systems on the Internet.

Compatibility with Windows 3.x and DOS Applications

Backward compatibility with most Windows 3.x and DOS applications is a major strength of Windows NT. Thanks to this backward compatibility, those who have invested in 16-bit productivity applications and utilities can continue to use them with Windows NT. There are literally tens and thousands of Windows 3.x and DOS applications that have been developed for a variety of tasks. By choosing a platform that is capable of running these applications, Web site developers will be able to save time by using these utilities and continue to benefit from previously made software investments.

User Friendly Environment/Ease of Use

Ease of use is an important factor to consider when choosing a development platform. Ease of use of the operating system and various applications being used directly affects the productivity of users. When an operating system is not user friendly or an application has a user interface that is too cryptic, a great deal of time can be wasted by figuring out how to perform various tasks as opposed to actually performing them and moving on to something else. Windows NT provides users with a familiar environment that is easy to work with. This increases user productivity and results in more time being spent on finding innovative solutions to various problems as opposed to finding various innovative ways of dealing with an operating system that is not user friendly.

I personally know people who use Windows Notepad along with an FTP program to make changes to documents of their corporate Web server simply because they don't want to deal with the cryptic environment of UNIX. Due to the changing nature of this high-tech world, people sometimes change jobs, and new employees need to be hired to deal with the increasing workload. In order to replace an employee who is leaving, someone else has to be trained; similarly, new employees being hired also require some degree of training. Both of these situations can be very costly in a development environment that's not very easy to use. For these reasons, it's important that the operating system used to publish content on the Internet offers an environment that's both user friendly and easy to use. Using such an operating system makes users more productive by freeing them from the time-consuming drudgery associated with most UNIX-based applications. Because Windows NT provides a user-friendly environment it is an ideal Web site development platform.

Low Administration Costs

After setting up a Web site, it needs to be fine-tuned every now and then to keep things running at maximum efficiency. Operating systems that have cryptic user interfaces are hard to manage and give way to high administration costs. Prior to Windows NT, a UNIX guru was often required to set up Internet information systems. Although some system administration experience is still necessary, this is no longer a requirement thanks to Windows NT. Because NT is extremely easy to administer through various GUI administration tools, even someone who is relatively new to Windows NT can quickly learn how to use them. Also, unlike various versions of UNIX that need to be recompiled to make certain modifications, the maximum that can result as a major system configuration change in NT is having to reboot the server. Using an operating system that is easy to administer saves time and cuts back on administration costs.

True Turnkey Solutions

Windows NT is a true turnkey solution. Often, all that's required to install and configure an application is to run setup.exe and answer a few questions during the course of the installation process. In a production environment, such ease of use and simplicity can potentially save hours or even days of lost productivity wasted on figuring out various intricate installation and configuration details of an application. For example, this book covers how to set up dozens of Internet information distribution applications using Windows NT. In order to follow this book, all that's required is that you be familiar with basic NT system administration tasks. If Windows NT applications are not true turnkey solutions, a book such as this, which comprehensively covers dozens of Internet information distribution applications, would not have been possible.

Cost Savings

Windows NT is a very cost-effective operating system. With as little as around $2,000, it's possible to set up a fully functional Internet server with NT in a matter of days (or even hours with the right resources at hand). One of Microsoft's visions has always been making use of inexpensive hardware to accomplish various tasks that were traditionally carried out with more expensive hardware. Windows NT follows this tradition by providing its users with a cost-effective and scaleable operating system.

A major reason for the success of the PC industry is low prices. Unlike most other technologies, as PC technology evolves and new, better, and faster components are created, prices usually go down. This is not always true for various proprietary hardware platforms that cost several times more. Windows NT users can use inexpensive PC technology to publish content on the Internet. Because NT is scaleable, when more processing power is needed, NT users can move on to either a faster, multiprocessor PC server or a high-performance RISC- (Reduced Instruction Set Computer) based server. Few operating systems offer this much flexibility while still protecting investments made for various software applications.

Backed by Microsoft and Netscape

Although it took them some time to realize the potential of the Internet, Microsoft has made a firm commitment to developing Internet software for Windows NT. At the moment, there is a fierce battle between Microsoft and Netscape to develop Internet content publishing applications. Microsoft is the worldwide leader in developing software for personal computers, and Netscape specializes in creating innovative cutting-edge Internet applications. Both these companies have a lot to offer the Internet, and their competition will make each other create even better applications. Because both Netscape and Microsoft develop software for Windows NT, NT users will be able to benefit from this competition. Because no other operating system is in a position to benefit from this competition as much as Windows NT users, those who use another operating system will be at a disadvantage.and will not have the kind of selection that Windows NT users have.

Why NT Is an Ideal Web Server Platform

At the time of this writing, most Web servers deployed on the Internet were UNIX-based servers, but this trend is likely to change as more and more people discover advantages of using NT to set up Web servers and other Internet information publishing applications. There are over a dozen Web servers available for Windows NT. Because such a large number of Web servers have been developed for NT, more choices are available when setting up a Web site with Windows NT.

Integrated with Productivity Applications

Many Windows applications are integrated with other applications using technologies such as *Object Linking and Embedding (OLE)* and *ActiveX*. Note that OLE and ActiveX mean the same thing for all practical purposes. For example, a Microsoft Excel spreadsheet can be easily embedded in a Microsoft Word document. Such integration makes users more productive by giving them the opportunity to think of several applications as one application and to use various strengths of each application. Although most Windows applications are integrated, they don't always provide a means of exporting content in a format such as HTML. However, this trend is likely to change by the time you read this book. Future versions of Microsoft Office and other applications will be more Internet aware. For example, in the near future, you will be able to publish an entire Microsoft Excel spreadsheet on the Internet simply by exporting it as an HTML file. Furthermore, you will be able to export content in such a way that if the data that was used to create the Excel spreadsheet changes, the changes will be automatically updated to the HTML file that was exported. Such level of integration and automation can save development time and help Web site developers focus less on routine tasks and more on innovative ways of publishing content on the Internet.

Consequences of Choosing Windows NT

The consequences of using Windows to develop and publish content on the Internet are two-fold. First, you will lose the benefits of using UNIX, and second, you will have to deal with some drawbacks of Windows NT. However, as you learn shortly, there are a number of ways to deal with the various limitations and drawbacks of Windows NT. By understanding these drawbacks and their possible remedies, you will be able to make the most use of what Windows NT has to offer.

Why Forgo the Benefits of Using UNIX?

Listed next are various benefits of UNIX that will be lost by choosing Windows NT. However, all these benefits are not completely lost. For example, you can use many third-party applications to deal with various limitations of Windows NT.

Time Tested

UNIX has been around for about two decades. Over this long time period, many organizations have come to depend on the performance and robustness of UNIX. Unlike UNIX, Windows NT does not have a long track record because it has not been around as long. Although this is likely to change in the future, at the moment, Windows NT does not have the time-tested reputation of UNIX.

Availability of Source Code

The source code for some UNIX applications is distributed along with the application which enables end users to make various changes to the application and customize it to meet their needs. However, the same is not true for most Windows applications. This is a disadvantage for those who wish to customize applications by modifying its source code. However, most NT applications are highly customizable using a GUI and registry keys. Therefore, this will not be a major disadvantage for most people.

Highly Customizable

Most UNIX applications are highly customizable to meet various specialized needs of end users. However, many Windows applications are increasingly using the Windows NT registry to store various configuration information. Often, applications can be highly customized by making modifications to documented registry keys.

Drawbacks of Using Windows NT

Just like UNIX, there are a number of drawbacks associated with using Windows NT. By being aware of these drawbacks, you will be able to find solutions to those that affect you.

Relatively New Technology

Windows NT has been around for only a few years. Compared to UNIX, which has been around for approximately two decades, this is a very short period of time. However, within this time, Microsoft has made a tremendous amount of progress with NT. This progress continues as more powerful and feature-rich versions of Windows NT are released. After the release of Windows NT 4.0, Microsoft intends to release a new version of NT nearly every year, adding a host of new features to the operating system. Thanks to these features and increased deployment of Windows NT in mission-critical applications, in the near future, Windows NT will become known as an operating system that can be trusted with managing information systems of a large enterprise. However, until this happens, Windows NT will be treated as new technology, and this will hold back some of its potential.

False Sentiments/Misconceptions about NT

Some still believe that Windows NT is just another version of DOS with a new user interface. As discussed earlier, Windows NT is a very different operating system built from the ground up for a different purpose. However, some people fail to or don't want to believe this. If you work for a large company, you're bound to meet a few of these people. Although such attitudes don't directly affect what can be accomplished with NT, they often get in the way of using it to solve tasks more efficiently and quickly. These false sentiments and misconceptions sometimes turn into a drawback of using Windows NT.

Lack of Standards

Over the last few years, many developers have created various Web servers for Windows NT. As a result, in order to augment limitations of existing standards, various developers have come up with their own standards. *NSAPI (Netscape Application Programming Interface)* and *ISAPI (Internet Server Application Programming Interface)* are examples of such standards. Although these standards have been created to address limitations of existing standards and to optimize how information is distributed by Web servers, they can also cause some chaos and compatibility problems.

Command Line Has Limited Capabilities

Compared to various flavors of UNIX, whose command line comprises many utilities and a rich scripting language, Windows NT's command prompt leaves a lot to be desired. However, a number of third-party command line extension tools can be used to make NT's command prompt more powerful. For example, by using the Hamilton C shell for Windows NT, various command line tools usually found only on UNIX systems can be used from NT's command prompt. In addition to this, the Hamilton C shell also provides a rich scripting environment in which you can create C shell scripts to accomplish various tasks that are too complicated for NT batch files. In addition to this, a number of GNU UNIX utilities have also been ported to Windows NT. The GNU tools can be downloaded free of charge from the Internet.

> **URL**
>
> You can download from the Internet various UNIX-like tools for Windows NT to enhance the capabilities of NT's command prompt:
>
> ```
> ftp://ftp.cc.utexas.edu/microlib/nt/
> ftp://ftp.cygnus.com/pub/sac/
> ```

Software Might Cost More Initially

Windows NT might initially cost more compared to operating systems such as Linux. In order to publish information on the Internet with NT, you typically need to purchase a copy of Windows NT along with a few productivity applications. This might be a problem for someone working with a limited budget. However, when calculating expenses, development costs also need to be taken into consideration. In the long run, Windows NT is a more cost effective solution. Because a number of shareware and freeware applications are available for NT, initial costs can be kept down by using these applications until more powerful applications are needed (and can be afforded).

Although Windows NT has its own share of drawbacks and limitations, most of these can be addressed with third-party applications and utilities. A number of freeware, shareware, and commercial applications have been created to address various limitations of Windows NT. By using these applications, most drawbacks associated with using Windows NT can be solved.

How NT Will Affect the Future of the Internet

Windows NT has the potential to alter the way information is published on the Internet. Thanks to NT, many organizations and individuals are now able to establish a presence and publish content on the Internet without having to invest a large amount of time or money. Prior to NT, complexities and expenses associated with setting up Internet information systems held back many individuals and organizations from getting connected to the Internet and using it to conduct business. However, with the aid of NT, these organizations and individuals can now be a part of the most resourceful global computer network in the world and contribute something meaningful to the Internet.

Summary

When publishing content on the Internet with Windows NT, it's important to be aware of various advantages and drawbacks associated with using Windows NT. Then you can exploit the advantages of NT and at the same time find solutions and ways of dealing with the various limitations of NT. This chapter first discussed how Windows NT is different from other operating systems, outlining why it's an ideal platform for publishing information on the Internet.

Prior to Windows NT, virtually all Internet information systems were set up using UNIX servers. You then learned why UNIX is not an ideal choice to publish information on the Internet, with the various drawbacks and limitations of UNIX being outlined. Then various advantages of using Windows NT were discussed and how you can benefit from them by saving time and money. The last section was devoted to identifying and dealing with the drawbacks of Windows NT. Now that you're aware of the strengths and weaknesses of Windows NT, you're ready to begin publishing content on the Internet.

What's Next?

The next section discusses the various business aspects of using Windows NT to create Web sites and other Internet information services. By understanding the different ways of using the Internet to conduct business on the Internet, you will be able to effectively make use of the information services described in later chapters.

II

Business Aspects of
Web Publishing

3

Creating Business Web Sites

Although, the Internet was initially used for nonprofit educational and research activities, it is increasingly being used for business applications. When building a Web site, it helps to know how other organizations are using the Internet to effectively distribute information. The purpose of this chapter is not to give you an overview of browsing the Internet for information or a tour of a few interesting Web sites. Instead, the chapter provides you with an overview of how you can use your Web site to effectively distribute information on the Internet. Subsequent sections are devoted to various categories of Web sites. A few Web sites of each category are discussed in each section. This discussion includes various characteristics of the Web site being discussed. Depending on how information is presented at each Web site, you may want to incorporate ideas and tips presented in later sections to enhance your Web site and make it easier to navigate.

Web Search Engines

Web search engines play a major role in keeping the Web connected by indexing Web sites and allowing users to search for various keywords. After setting up your Web site, you should register it with as many search engines as you can.

Yahoo!

Yahoo! is a comprehensive database of Web sites that is indexed by hand. When URLs are submitted for review, they are looked over by someone and are manually placed in a certain category. This makes life a little easier for Web surfers because they can select a category they're interested in and visit various Web sites that have been indexed under that category. As you can see in Figure 3.1, a user can locate Web sites with Yahoo! either by typing in a keyword or selecting from a hierarchical list of categories. Tables are used at Yahoo!'s Web site to organize various categories and format them side by side. Yahoo! is a very widely used Web search engine. When new URLs are added to your Web site, you should register them with Yahoo!. In Chapter 22, "Publicizing Your Web Site," you're shown how to register your Web site with Yahoo! and other Web site cataloging databases.

WebCrawler

WebCrawler is different from Yahoo!. Unlike Yahoo!, WebCrawler is not individually indexed and grouped into various categories. Although you can use Yahoo! to effectively search for various Web sites based on a certain category, WebCrawler is more suitable for searching Web sites by using a *keyword*. As shown in Figure 3.2, WebCrawler's search page uses pull-down menus to customize various aspects of a search. Because it's not manually indexed, WebCrawler can index more URLs than Yahoo! and is used a great deal by Web surfers to find Web sites. Chapter 22 shows you how to register URLs with WebCrawler.

FIGURE 3.1.
Yahoo! Web site.

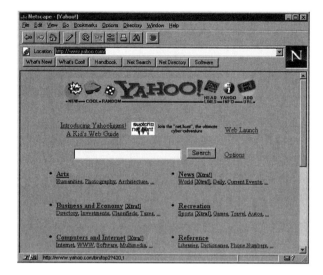

FIGURE 3.2.
WebCrawler Web site.

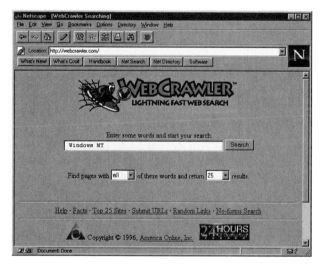

Infoseek

Infoseek is another Web cataloging database that many Web surfers use to locate Web sites. As you can see in Figure 3.3, Infoseek uses *frames* to organize its Web site and makes it easier for users to navigate the site for information. In Chapter 10, "Web Site Development Tools," you are shown how to use frames to make a Web site easier to navigate.

FIGURE 3.3.
Infoseek Web site.

Corporate Web Sites

The next few sections highlight various characteristics of a few corporate Web sites and discuss how you can incorporate similar ideas to your Web site. In later chapters, you are shown how to implement various features of the Web sites, such as search engines and animated GIF files.

Microsoft

Microsoft's Web site extensively uses small icons and tables to organize its contents. As you can see in Figure 3.4, the icons used in Microsoft's page makes it more pleasant to navigate it for information. Also, pay attention to the button bar at the top of the screen. It's a good idea to add a similar button bar to your Web pages so that no matter what page a user is in, he or she can always send you feedback and comments by clicking on a button. Having a "What's New" page that lists new additions to a Web site is also very helpful to Web surfers. In addition to this, you should also set up a CGI search engine at your Web site so that users can use it to search your Web site for information. You are shown how to set up a search engine in Chapter 15, "Making Your Web Site Searchable."

Netscape

You might want to add to the main Web page of your Web site a graphic similar to the one in Netscape's Web page, as shown in Figure 3.5. Although a picture of a sailboat is not directly relevant to products sold by Netscape, it conveys a deeper meaning. To a certain extent, the picture of the sailboat is pleasing to the eye and gives the impression that Netscape is about navigating a sea of information. If you find an image that's relevant to what your Web site is about, you could add it to the main Web page of your Web site. When adding such images, be careful about vertical space. No matter how beautiful or meaningful your image is, if it takes three fourths of the browser's vertical space and takes a few dozen seconds to load over a modem line, it will actually make a negative impression. When adding such images, keep them small. As you can see in Figure 3.5, the size of the image in Netscape's Web page is not too big. Just below the image, as Netscape has done, you can then include a table of contents or latest developments related to your organization.

FIGURE 3.4.

Microsoft Corporation Web site.

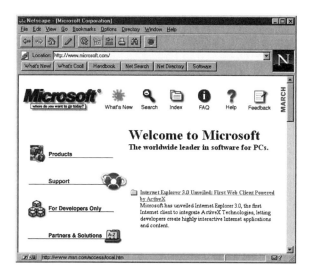

FIGURE 3.5.

Netscape Web site.

Intel

Intel uses state-of-the-art Web technologies to make their Web site easier and more exciting to navigate. The graphic shown in Figure 3.6 is actually an animated GIF file. Although you can't see it by looking at the figure, the animated GIF file is created so that sparks of lights go from the eyes of the woman's face toward blocks of text around her eyes. By incorporating such special effects to a Web site, you can make it more exciting to navigate. You're shown how to create animated GIF files in Chapter 11, "Adding Multimedia to Your Web Site."

FIGURE 3.6.
Intel Web site.

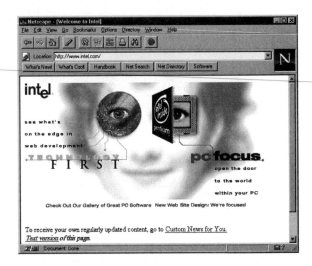

Public Service Web Sites

Not all Web sites on the Internet are solely used for business purposes. Some Web sites have been set up by various individuals and organizations as public services for the Internet community. Such Web sites make the Internet a very unique information distribution medium. For just the price of accessing the Internet via a local Internet service provider, a user can often find virtually all the information he or she needs free of charge. After setting up a Web site, it's possible to attract more users and make it well known on the Internet by using it to provide a useful public service.

On-line Dictionary of Computing

The Free On-line Dictionary of Computing Web site, shown in Figure 3.7, has been set up for users to look up various terms related to computing. Such a service can be set up by creating a database of words and definitions and linking it to a Web page via CGI. By reading Chapter 18, "Publishing Databases on the Web," you can find out how to link a database to a Web page.

FIGURE 3.7.

*Free Online Dictionary of
Computing Web site.*

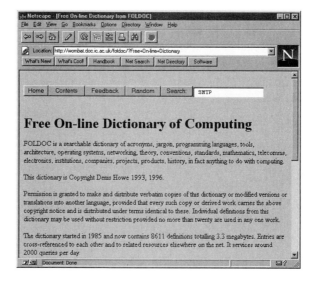

The Electric Postcard

You can use the Electric Postcard Web site to send postcards to people. This Web site is an example of a distinct service being offered by a Web site free of charge for Internet users. Such a service can potentially attract many Internet users and make a Web site well known all over the Internet. Although setting up such a Web site is not directly beneficial business-wise, it can turn into an extra source of revenue by accommodating advertisements. In Chapter 17, "Advanced Windows NT CGI Applications," you're shown how to set up a CGI script to display a few icons that are advertisements, one after the other.

FIGURE 3.8.

Electric Postcard Web site.

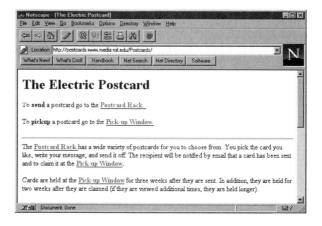

Doctor HTML

You can use the Doctor HTML Web site to validate the quality of HTML used at your Web site. Recently, quite a few HTML tags have been created by companies such as Netscape and Microsoft to augment limitations of HTML 2.0. The CGI program that is linked to the Doctor HTML Web page analyzes the quality of HTML used at your Web sites and lets you know if technologically challenged Web browsers will have problems with your page. As you can see in Figure 3.9, sophisticated CGI scripts can be created and linked to a Web page. Chapter 16, "Introduction to Windows NT CGI Programming," and Chapter 17 demonstrate how CGI scripts can be developed and linked to a Web page.

FIGURE 3.9.

Doctor HTML Web site.

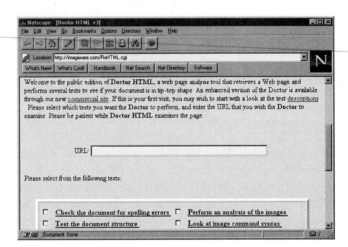

Web Periodicals

Most computer magazines are now available on the Internet for browsing free of charge. The following sections list a few interesting periodicals on the Internet.

ZD Net Home Page

The ZD Net Web page is a great example of a Web site that uses graphics effectively to make a Web site easier and more exciting to navigate. As you can see in Figure 3.10, no screen space is wasted. Most of the screen space is used to highlight a product or service offered by ZD Net, with the remainder used for advertisements. When adding graphics to a Web site, you should be careful about graphics that are too large and take too long to download. However, you can create a high-impact and easy-to-navigate Web site by using small but descriptive graphics similar to the ones used in Figure 3.10. ZD Net's page also uses a Java marquee to inform Web browsers of latest news. You can use such a Java script to compliment the layout of a Web site. In Chapter 19, "Adding Java to Your Web Site," you're shown how to add similar Java applets to a Web page.

FIGURE 3.10.

ZD Net home page.

PC Magazine on the Web

PC Magazine on the Web home page, shown in Figure 3.11, is another example of a Web page that uses tables to format text and graphics to make maximum use of screen space. Although it's not as richly formatted as ZD Net's page, PC Magazine's page is still attractive and easy to navigate because it has made good use of screen space. As you can see, by using tables, it's possible to format the contents of a Web page so that most of it will fit on one page. This makes a Web site easier to browse because users don't have to scroll up and down the Web page in search of information.

Computer Shopper

Computer Shopper's page is different from ZD Net's page and PC Magazine's page. The major difference is the fact that Computer Shopper uses a graphic to format its contents rather than a table. As you can see in Figure 3.12, this has given the author of the Computer Shopper page more control over the layout of text and graphics. However, this extra control comes with a price. Graphic files such as the one in Computer Shopper's page might take a long time to load over slow modem lines. If you intend to use such a graphic at your Web site instead of a table, plain text, and a few small graphics, be sure it's not larger than about 30 KB in size.

FIGURE 3.11.
PC Magazine on the Web.

FIGURE 3.12.
*Computer Shopper
Web site.*

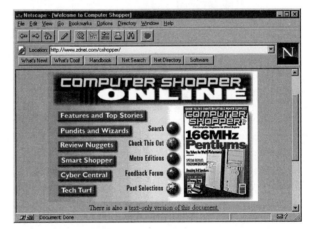

Metropolitan Information Services

The World Wide Web is a great medium for distributing metropolitan information to local residents. With traditional information distribution mediums, cost has always been a major factor when distributing local information to a relatively small group of people in a certain area. On the other hand, by using a Web site, information can be made available to local residents in a format that is interactive and rich in multimedia at a significantly lower price.

Traffic Cameras

The traffic camera shown in Figure 3.13 is a great example of a metropolitan information service that takes advantage of multimedia capabilities of the World Wide Web.

FIGURE 3.13.

Traffic camera.

Weather Service

The INTELLiCast Washington DC area weather page is another example of a useful metropolitan information service. Rather than wait until someone announces the weather on radio or TV, it's easier to take a look at the INTELLiCast Washington DC area weather page when browsing the Web. Although such information services are not currently as widely used as they should be, when more people discover the virtues of the Web and get connected to it, Web sites like the one shown in Figure 3.14 will be more widely used and will provide a valuable service to the community.

Apartment Guide

The apartment connection home page, shown in Figure 3.15, locates apartments for users after they fill in an online form and submit it. The information supplied by the user is then searched against a database of apartments for various search criteria such as location, type, and cost of apartment. After reading Chapter 16, "Introduction to Windows NT CGI Applications," Chapter 17, "Advanced Windows NT CGI Applications," and Chapter 18, "Publishing Databases on the Web," you will be able to set up a similar service.

FIGURE 3.14.
INTELLiCast Washington DC area weather page.

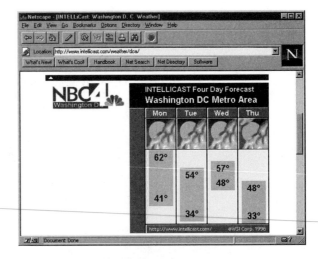

FIGURE 3.15.
The Apartment Connection Web site.

Discussion Forums

You can create discussion forums on the Web by using applications such as WebBoard and Network News Transport Protocol (NNTP) news servers. Listed next are examples of how you can use CGI applications and NNTP servers to host Internet discussion forums.

WebBoard

WebBoard is a *WINCGI (Windows Common Gateway Interface)* application that can be used effectively to host discussion forums on the Internet. As shown in Figure 3.16, by using WebBoard, users who visit a Web site can discuss various issues by posting messages. WebBoard takes the interactive nature of a Web site to a whole new level by allowing users to communicate with each other. You're shown how to set up WebBoard at your Web site in Chapter 31, "Setting Up a Web Conferencing System."

FIGURE 3.16.
Online discussion forum
hosted by using WebBoard.

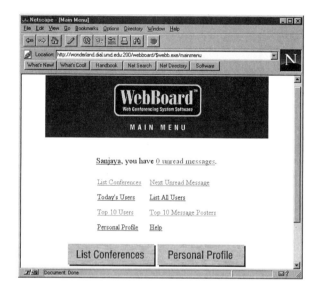

Netscape Newsgroups

Netscape uses newsgroups to provide customer service and technical support to its users (see Figure 3.17). News servers are well suited for hosting online discussion forums on the Internet. In Chapter 30, "Setting Up an NNTP News Server," you learn how to set up a news server and use it to host public discussion forums.

FIGURE 3.17.
Netscape newsgroups.

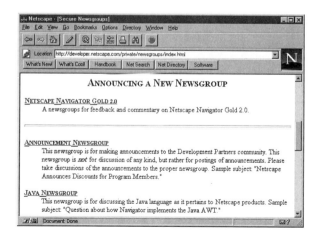

Product Catalogs

Due to low costs associated with publishing content on the Internet, the Web is an ideal medium to distribute a product catalog to a large audience. Listed next are a few organizations that have realized the potential of using the Web to publish product catalogs.

Macmillan Information SuperLibrary

The Macmillan Web site shown in Figure 3.18 is used to distribute information about books published by Macmillan. An attractive imagemap similar to the one in Macmillan's Web site makes it easier and more interesting for users to navigate a Web site for information. Various tips for creating and optimizing graphics for the Internet are presented in Chapter 11, "Adding Multimedia to Your Web Site."

FIGURE 3.18.

Macmillan Information SuperLibrary Web site.

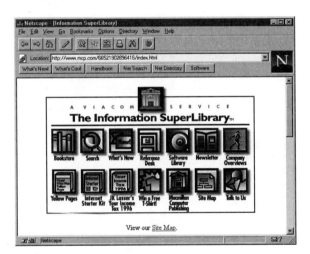

Internet Shopping Network

Some organizations depend entirely on the Internet for selling merchandise. The Internet Shopping Network (ISN) is an example of such an organization. As you can see in Figure 3.19, Web browser space is very efficiently used in ISN's Web page to make it easier to navigate it without extensively using scroll bars. When creating graphics for your Web site, like ISN, you should make an effort to make the maximum use of Web browser space.

FIGURE 3.19.
Internet Shopping Network Web site.

Resource Centers

A number of Internet resource centers have been created to distribute information about various products and services. A few such Web sites are listed in the next few sections.

The BackOffice Resource Center

Another good example of using tables to format the contents of a Web site can be found in Figure 3.20. The BackOffice Resource Center uses tables to format icons and text. Because icons found in Figure 3.20 are relatively small, they load fast and don't get in the way of someone browsing the Web site through a slow modem link.

FIGURE 3.20.
BackOffice Resource Center Web site.

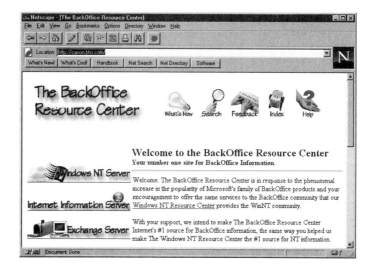

Netscape Development Partners' Net Site

The Web site shown in Figure 3.21 is used by Netscape to inform its development community about various new technologies and announcements. Netscape Development Partner's Web site is a secure Web site that is open only to members of the Netscape development partners program. Access to this Web site is restricted through a user ID and a password. Refer to Chapter 6, "Installing and Using Microsoft Internet Information Server," and Chapter 7, "Publishing on the Web with WebSite, Purveyor, and Netscape," to learn how to restrict access to a Web site based on a username and password. You can use such an authentication mechanism to allow only specific users access to certain information at a Web site.

FIGURE 3.21.

Netscape Development Partners' Web Site.

News Services

The World Wide Web is perhaps the best medium to distribute information to a global audience. Usually, there is a time lag associated with publishing news and distributing it to a large audience. This time delay is virtually eliminated when the World Wide Web is used.

Weather Reports

CNN's regional weather Web site is updated with the latest weather every 12 hours. As shown in Figure 3.22, you can use the Web to distribute continuously changing information.

FIGURE 3.22.

CNN's regional weather Web site.

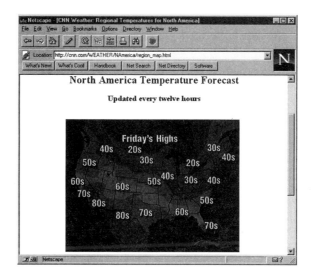

CNN's Web Site

You can use an imagemap similar to the one in Figure 3.23 to present a menu and make it easier to navigate a Web site. Chapter 10, "Web Site Development Tools," illustrates how you can add imagemaps to a Web site. CNN uses its Web site to distribute up-to-the-minute information to Internet users. Because information can be made available for browsing as soon as it's put together, the Internet is an ideal medium to publish news. Although the same is true for cable news broadcasts to television sets, it's not as interactive as the Web. Another disadvantage of news broadcast to television sets is the fact that everything is linear. For example, if a person turns on the television at five minutes past the hour in search of headline news, he or she will have to wait another 25 minutes to find out that day's news headlines. On the other hand, someone browsing the CNN Web site can easily find the latest headline news and browse interesting articles in any order.

FIGURE 3.23.
CNN's Web site.

Product Advertising

The World Wide Web is an ideal medium for advertising products. When information is published on the Web, it's available to a large audience of users. Because the costs associated with publishing information on the Internet are relatively low, the World Wide Web is a very cost-effective medium to publish product information and advertise a product. A few Web sites that advertise various products are listed next.

Paint Shop Pro

The Paint Shop Pro Web page shown in Figure 3.24 is used to distribute information and demonstration copies of Paint Shop Pro. By using a horizontal background image, the page shown in Figure 3.24 has been made to look more attractive. Chapter 10 demonstrates how to create background effects similar to the one used in the Paint Shop Pro Web page.

WebTrends

Frames can make a Web site easier to navigate when used properly. As you can see in Figure 3.25, the WebTrends page is divided into two sections. The top half shows information, and the bottom half shows various topics that are available for browsing. The bottom half is very useful to someone browsing the WebTrends Web site. Rather than backtrack all the way to the main home page to visit a different page, users can simply use the index provided in the bottom half to visit various Web pages effortlessly. In Chapter 10 you learn how to effectively use frames to make a Web site easier to navigate.

FIGURE 3.24.

Paint Shop Pro product information and software distribution Web site.

FIGURE 3.25.

WebTrends Web page.

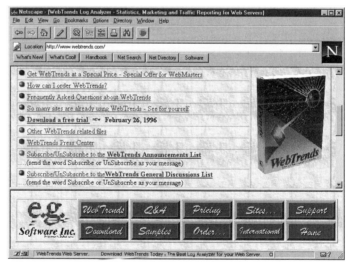

Software Distribution

The World Wide Web is a great medium for distributing software. Although there are security concerns associated with using the Internet to distribute software, when distributing information and demonstration copies of applications, such security concerns do not always apply. Listed next are a few examples of how you can use the Internet to distribute software.

Internet Shopper

Internet Shopper uses the World Wide Web to distribute copies of NTMail to its customers (see Figure 3.26). After downloading the software, if users like NTMail, they can register the software and keep on using it by typing in a special registration key. Because NTMail is freely available for download from virtually anywhere in the world, it has become a widely used SMTP/POP/Mail-List server for Windows NT. Refer to Chapter 27, "Setting Up a Mail-List Server," for more information about the NTMail SMTP/POP/Mail-List server. By making software widely available to a large group of people, as in the case of Netscape Navigator, it can become very popular and widely used.

FIGURE 3.26.

Internet Shopper's NTMail distribution Web site.

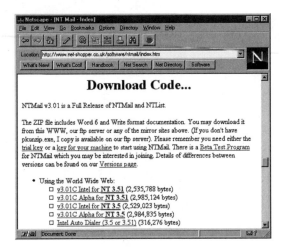

Microsoft Internet Explorer

As you can see in Figure 3.27, the Microsoft Internet Explorer download page is not really optimized for space. A relatively large graphic takes up a significant portion of a Web browser's vertical space but provides very little information in return. When adding graphics to your Web site, try to avoid this. Always make an effort to make graphics compact and informative. Although the graphic used in Figure 3.27 is attractive, it might appear to be rather displeasing to someone browsing it with a 640×480 monitor.

FIGURE 3.27.

Microsoft Internet Explorer software distribution Web site.

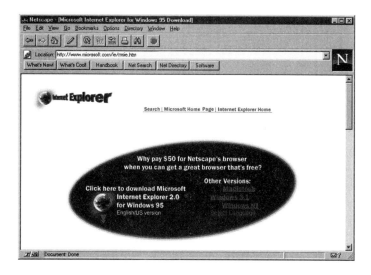

FIGURE 3.28.

Before users can download MS Internet Information server, they need to fill in a form and submit it.

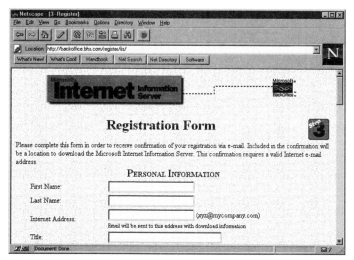

Microsoft Internet Information Server

When distributing software on the Internet, rather than just creating an HTML link to the distribution file, it's often helpful to know who is downloading the software. You can find this out by setting up a form similar to the one shown in Figure 3.28. After users fill in the form and submit it, they can be provided with a URL that they can use to download the software. Having information such as the e-mail addresses of those who download the software is very useful. For example, e-mail addresses supplied can be added to an announcement-only mail list to keep users informed of new releases of software. Setting up a form similar to the one shown in Figure 3.28 is discussed in Chapter 16, "Introduction to Windows NT CGI Programming." If you wish to add e-mail addresses to an Internet mail list, Chapter 27, "Setting Up a Mail-List Server," demonstrates how to set up a mail-list server by using software included in the CD-ROM that accompanies this book.

Summary

Before developing a Web site, it helps to know how others are using the World Wide Web. Various Web sites presented to you in this chapter may have given you a few ideas for your Web site. Various special effects used by the Web sites shown in previous sections, such as animated GIF files, are not too complicated to implement. In later chapters, you're shown how to implement similar special effects and characteristics found in the Web sites described in this chapter.

What's Next?

Various organizations and individuals are increasingly getting connected to the Internet. The next chapter, "Using the Web to Your Advantage," discusses various aspects of using the World Wide Web to distribute information. By learning various unique capabilities of the World Wide Web and how you can exploit them, you will be able to make the best use of resources you invest to establish a presence on the Internet.

4

Using the Web to Your Advantage

Many organizations and individuals are increasingly establishing a presence on the Internet to distribute information and conduct business. Over 150,000 World Wide Web servers were active in 1995. With the deployment of more Web sites on the Internet and intranets, this number is estimated to be as high as two million by 1998. Although many Web sites are being deployed on the Internet each day, some Web sites fail to use the Web to its fullest potential. Before establishing a presence on the Internet, it's worthwhile to explore how you can use a Web site to your advantage by exploiting various characteristics of the World Wide Web.

Understanding the audience of a Web site is crucial to its success. Unlike traditional information distribution mediums, the audience of a Web site is quite different in terms of personal factors such as nationality, education, language, and geographical location, as well as technical factors such as software, Internet bandwidth, and capabilities of hardware and software the audience uses. When designing a Web site, you should take all these factors into consideration. The success of a Web site depends on understanding its audience and providing content to meet various information needs of users browsing the Web site. When developing contents of a Web site, you should also take into consideration technical expertise of users and software used to browse a Web site. No matter how interesting a Web site might look when viewed with the latest version of Netscape or Internet Explorer, if most users use a different Web browser, they won't be able to appreciate various Netscape and Internet Explorer enhancements of a Web site.

The World Wide Web offers a number of advantages not found in traditional mediums of information distribution. These features enable content developers to use the Web for a variety of tasks. Understanding various advantages of using the World Wide Web enable you to make the best use of your Web site.

In order to use the World Wide Web to your advantage, you should explore various ways you can use the Web for business purposes. Setting up a Web site and adding a few HTML files to it is just the tip of the iceberg. The World Wide Web offers a medium to publish information that is both richly interactive and extensible via new and innovative applications. For example, in Chapter 31, "Setting Up a Web Conferencing System," you learn how to set up online discussion forums on the World Wide Web by using a CGI application called WebBoard. You will be able to use the World Wide Web to its maximum potential by using similar applications presented throughout the remainder of this book.

Understanding Your Audience

The Internet consists of a global audience of users. These users have different resources and technical capabilities. When designing a Web site, you should first determine its audience. Due to its global nature, it's not always easy to determine the audience of a Web site. However, the following list of factors will help you understand your audience better.

Bandwidth of Internet Link

When designing Web content, by far the most important thing you should be concerned about is the bandwidth available to users when they access your Web site. No matter how well a Web site is put together, if it takes a few minutes for a page to load over a relatively slow modem link, that Web page is of little use to you or your users.

Operating System Used

Depending on the kind of content published at a Web site, the operating system used by site users should also be taken into account. For example, when making files stored in common Windows formats such as .WRI (Windows Write) that are available to Internet users, you should think of Macintosh and UNIX users. Due to lack of helper applications, these users might be unable to view the contents of files stored in special file formats such as Windows Write.

Although there are estimated to be around 150 million Windows users, most of these users are still using a version of Windows 3.*x*. Therefore, when adding new technologies such as Java to a Web site, you should be aware that some users are unable to view Java applets. At the time of this writing, no Java-capable browsers were available for Windows 3.*x*. In addition to that, Windows 3.*x* versions of Internet Explorer are usually not as feature rich as Windows NT and Windows 95 versions of Internet Explorer.

Browser Software Used

The browser software used by Web site visitors is an important factor that you should take into account when developing content for a Web site. A Web site that looks attractive when viewed with the latest version of Netscape or Internet Explorer can look less than appealing when viewed with a technologically challenged Web browser. Therefore, it's important to keep an eye on various Web browsers used to access your Web site. You can do this by examining the Web server's access log file as shown in Chapter 24, "Utility Applications for Your Server." You need to make sure that content at your Web site is still legible when viewed with a less advanced Web browser.

Technical Sophistication of Users

You should also be aware of the technical sophistication of your audience when developing content for your Web site. For example, if most users browsing your Web site barely know how to type in a URL to their Web browser, you should not expect them to know how to download a helper application and install it into their Web browser so they will be able see various text at your Web site rotate in different colors.

Information Needs

Information needs of users greatly differ from one user to the other. For example, the information needs of a user browsing Coca Cola's Web site (`http://www.cocacola.com/`) differ greatly from those of someone browsing CNN's Web site (`http://www.cnn.com/`). A person browsing CNN's Web site is interested in accurate, up-to-date news. On the other hand, a person browsing Coca Cola's Web site is probably browsing it for entertainment purposes.

Advantages of Using the World Wide Web

There are many advantages of using the World Wide Web to distribute information. The following sections list some of these advantages.

Global Audience

Content published on the World Wide Web is immediately available to a global audience of users. This makes the World Wide Web a very cost-effective medium to publish information to a large audience at a very low cost.

Immediate Distribution of Information

When information is added to a Web site, it's immediately available for browsing by millions of Internet users. The World Wide Web is an ideal medium of information distribution because it takes away the time lag associated with publishing content and actually making it available to users.

Relatively Inexpensive

It is relatively inexpensive to publish information on the Internet. At a fraction of the cost to publish information by traditional methods, various organizations and individuals can now distribute information to millions of users. It costs only a few thousand dollars to establish an Internet presence and publish content on the Internet.

Easy Integration with Internal Information Systems

Internet information systems deployed on the Internet with Windows NT can be easily integrated with internal information systems managed with office productivity applications such as Microsoft Office. Because Windows is the native operating system for most productivity applications, internal information repositories can easily be made available for browsing through a Windows NT Web server. There are estimated to be over 10 million office and productivity application users. Virtually all major application and office software vendors have made plans to make their applications more Internet aware. For example, using Internet Assistant for Microsoft Word, it's possible to publish MS Word documents on the World Wide Web in HTML. These documents can then be viewed by Internet users through Web browsers.

Powerful Content Publishing Tools

A new breed of Internet-aware applications will start emerging in software stores by the time you read this. These applications will enable users to develop content for the World Wide Web in an environment they are familiar with and publish it to the World Wide Web by simply saving the content as an HTML file. In addition to software developers making existing applications Internet aware, various new, powerful, and easy-to-use Internet content publishing applications are also being developed. These applications will make the task of publishing content on the Internet even easier. Most of these applications are developed for Windows users. Because you will be using Windows NT, you will be able to take advantage of these applications when developing content for your Web site.

Multimedia

The capability to incorporate multimedia into Web pages is a major advantage of using the World Wide Web to publish information. For example, many Web sites use sounds and video clips to make the content easier and more interesting to browse.

Formatting Capabilities

Content published on the World Wide Web can be richly formatted by using various HTML tags and graphic formats. The capability to do this is a major reason for the success of the World Wide Web. In addition to using HTML tags and various multimedia formats in Web pages, various interactive controls can also be added to a Web page. This capability allows Web site content developers to create "active" Web sites. For example, before a user sends some information to a Web server for processing, a VBScript or JavaScript subroutine can be used to verify information typed in by the user. Various formatting capabilities, along with technologies such as Java and VBScript, make the World Wide Web a richly interactive medium that you can use to distribute information to millions of users.

New Technologies

Various new technologies have been created to provide Internet content developers more control over the content they publish on the Internet. These technologies include new programming languages such as VBScript, Java, and JavaScript, as well as various additions to standard HTML 2.0 such as tables and frames. Web site content developers can make use of these new technologies to develop informative Web sites that are easy to navigate.

Internet Software Developers

According to Microsoft, there are approximately three million Visual Basic developers. These developers will be able to immediately make use of various Microsoft technologies such as ActiveX and VBScript and create applications for the Internet. Most of these developers will be able to leverage their skills to the Internet by exploiting capabilities of VBScript and other Internet application development languages such as Java. Many software developers are increasingly embracing the Internet and developing applications for it. Various applications developed by these developers will make the Internet an even more powerful medium of information distribution.

Using the World Wide Web for Business Applications

You can use the World Wide Web for a number of business applications. Although many organizations have set up Web sites on the Internet, they fail to use the Internet to its maximum potential. The following sections list a few business applications for which you can use the World Wide Web.

Product Advertising

You can use the World Wide Web to advertise various products. Before purchasing a product, customers will be able to look up various product specification sheets and find out additional information. You can use the multimedia capabilities of the World Wide Web to make available not only various product specification sheets but also audio files, images, and even video clips of products in action.

Distribute Product Catalogs

The World Wide Web is a very effective medium for distributing product catalogs. In the old days, putting together a product catalog used to be very costly in terms of time and money needed to publish and distribute it. The World Wide Web changes all this by allowing content developers to put together a sales catalog and make it available to millions of users immediately. Furthermore, unlike printed product catalogs that are usually updated around once a month, product catalogs on the World Wide Web can be updated as needed to respond to various changing market conditions.

Online Surveys

Traditional methods of performing surveys are often relatively slow and expensive compared to online surveys conducted on the Internet. For example, in order to find out various needs of customers or what they would like to see in a future product, it's often necessary to compile a list of addresses and mail a questionnaire to many customers. The success of such an attempt is not always guaranteed and can be very costly in terms of mailing the questionnaires and entering responses to a database and analyzing it. On the other hand, you can use the World Wide Web to automate the whole process. For example, you can set up a CGI script to conduct online surveys. Results of such a survey can be automatically updated to a database. This database can then be used to keep a pulse on various opinions and needs of customers. Publishing databases on the World Wide Web is covered in Chapter 18, "Publishing Databases on the Web."

Announcements

With the World Wide Web, you can distribute various announcements to millions of users in a timely manner. Because there is virtually no time lag from the time it takes to publish information to making the information available to users, the Web is an ideal medium to publicize announcements. As more people discover the virtues of the Web and get connected to the Internet, the Web will become the medium of choice for many organizations and individuals to publicize various announcements.

Provide Technical Support

You can also use a Web site to provide technical support to users. Because Web pages can be updated immediately with new information, various technical support literature can be immediately modified in light of new findings and developments. This can be accomplished without having to distribute changes to all users affected by any changes using traditional mediums of information distribution, which are often quite costly compared to the World Wide Web.

Create Online Discussion Forums

By using applications such as WebBoard, it's possible to set up online discussion forums on the Web. You will learn how to set up WebBoard at your Web site in Chapter 31, "Setting Up a Web Conferencing System."

Obtain Customer Feedback

The interactive nature of the World Wide Web is ideal for obtaining customer feedback. You can easily set up a CGI script to obtain customer feedback about a product or service. Because customer feedback submitted by customers can be read immediately, it's possible to respond to various customer concerns in a timely manner, increasing customer satisfaction and quality of customer service.

Summary

Before setting up a Web site, it's important to understand how to use the Internet to your advantage. You can accomplish this by exploring how you can use the World Wide Web for various business applications. The tips and ideas presented in earlier sections will help you make the best use of your Web site to effectively distribute information on the Internet.

What's Next?

The next chapter will help you determine and fulfill various requirements related to setting up a Web site on the Internet. The chapter begins with an introduction to various Internet connection types outlining their capabilities and drawbacks. Depending on your needs, budget, and various Internet links available in your area, you will be able to select an Internet link that best suits your needs after learning about the different Internet connection types. Due to budget limitations, if you can't afford a high-speed Internet link, you will be shown how to utilize a secondary Web server to get the maximum use out of a POTS (Plain Old Telephone Service) link. You're introduced to the various Internet connection types, their suitability, and other issues related to choosing the right Internet connection to meet your needs. Hardware requirements for setting up an Internet server with Windows NT will also be covered. After discussing various hardware options, the chapter concludes with an overview of the software needed to set up a Windows NT-based site.

III

Setting Up Your
Web Server

5

Determining and Fulfilling Your Requirements

Before installing Web server software and developing your Web site, you need to determine and fulfill various requirements, such as an Internet connection and a server to host your Web site. The bandwidth of the Internet connection and the hardware you select is crucial to what you can accomplish with your Web site. Quite often, the biggest bottleneck of a Web site is its Internet connection. This chapter gives you an overview of the various hardware, Internet connection options, and Web servers that you can use to host a Web site with Windows NT. You will be knowledgeable of various hardware platforms that are capable of running Windows NT and also learn about the advantages and drawbacks of selecting one hardware platform over another.

Various types of Internet connections available are also discussed, highlighting their capabilities and price/performance issues. If all you can afford at the moment is a low-speed modem connection, you are shown how to use your modem connection and still provide users near T1 or T3 access to your data. There are currently over two dozen Web servers available for Windows NT. Although this proves the acceptance of Windows NT as an ideal platform to host a Web site, it can make choosing the best Web server very confusing. Five Web servers, including Microsoft Internet Information Server, are discussed in the next two chapters to give you an overview of the strengths and deficiencies of various Web servers. Rather than discuss specific features and capabilities of Web servers, this chapter provides a brief overview of Web servers available to set up a Web site with Windows NT. In addition to hardware, Internet connection types, and Web servers, issues related to choosing Windows NT Server as opposed to Windows NT Workstation are also discussed.

Figure 5.1 contains a list of requirements that need to be fulfilled before developing a Web site with Windows NT. All requirements in Figure 5.1 up to the fourth requirement, "Select Web Server Software," are thoroughly discussed later in this chapter. Installing and configuring the Web server you select is discussed in Chapter 6, "Installing and Using Microsoft Internet Information Server," and Chapter 7, "Publishing on the Web with WebSite, Purveyor, and Netscape."

FIGURE 5.1.

Requirements for setting up a Web site on the Internet with Windows NT.

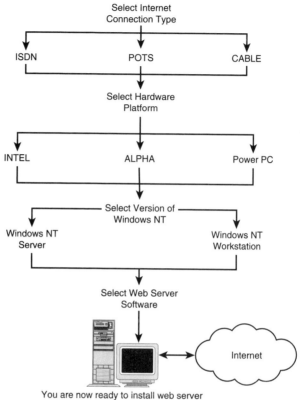

You are now ready to install web server software and begin developing your web site.

Choosing the Right Internet Connection

As mentioned earlier, the biggest bottleneck of your Web site is most likely its Internet connection link. When multiple users begin accessing your Web site at the same time, things can get painfully slow if you don't have enough Internet bandwidth to transmit data requested by your users. This section provides you with an overview of various Internet connection types and how to choose the best connection type based on your needs and other factors, such as availability and affordability.

As shown in Figure 5.1, the first thing you should do is obtain an Internet link for your Web site. If you are planning on hosting a Web site for your company, it's best to obtain your own Internet domain name. Because Internet Service Providers (ISP) can take as long as a few weeks to set up an Internet access account and register your domain name, it is best that you contact an ISP in your area and request an Internet connection before proceeding any further. Internet access prices vary from one ISP to another. If there are a number of ISPs in your area, you can save at least a few hundred dollars by shopping around. If all you can afford right now is a 28.8

kbps (kilobits per second) POTS (Plain Old Telephone Service) link to the Internet, you will be shown a tip that enables you to provide content to users browsing your Web site at near T1 speeds using your 28.8 kbps link to the Internet in the "Using Another Server" section.

> **TIP**
>
> When selecting an Internet domain name, select a name that is easy to remember. This makes it easy for users to remember your Web site and lets others know about it. Also, be careful when you abbreviate long words. Although you can abbreviate "Internet" with something like "intrnt," "Internet" is much easier to remember than "Intrnt."

Bandwidths of Various Connection Lines

Most likely, your Web server's biggest bottleneck will be the limited bandwidth of your Internet connection. If possible, you should use at least an ISDN (Integrated Services Digital Network) link to the Internet. As you can see from the chart in Figure 5.2, even a basic, single B channel ISDN line is several times faster than a 28.8 POTS connection.

FIGURE 5.2.

ISDN Internet links have a higher bandwidth than POTS Internet links.

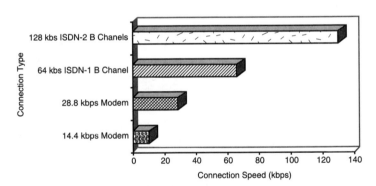

Another reason for using an ISDN link is that it does not need to be up all day for your Internet link; you will be using the line only when data is transferred, so you can disconnect when the line is not in use. Because ISDN lines are typically charged based on usage, this can save you money. This is practical with ISDN lines because of their fast call setup and disconnect times, typically about one second. On the other hand, as you can see in Figure 5.3, a POTS link usually takes about 30 seconds to establish a call.

FIGURE 5.3.

ISDN connect/disconnect speeds are faster than POTS connect/disconnect speeds.

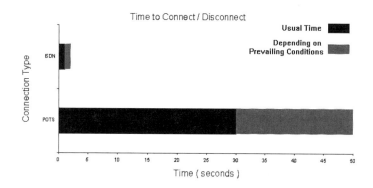

Using Another Server

If you are unable to afford an ISDN or a T1 link at the moment, you can use another server to store all your graphics and other nontext objects and use your POTS link exclusively for transmitting HTML text files.

If you will be starting out with a 28.8 kbps (kilobits per second) POTS link to the Internet, you should not get carried away with too many graphics. However, if you do have a few graphics and you start getting more and more hits, your Web surfers might become frustrated with the slow data transfer rates of your Web server. To avoid this, there is a very low-cost solution. You can simply find a Web space provider with a fast link to the Internet (that is, T1 or T3) who rents out space on a Web server. This service is inexpensive, usually less than $20 a month. Afterward, you can simply move all your graphics files to this Web server. In your page, you can call the graphics files on the other Web server rather than the graphics on your own server. This can make a significant difference because you will be using the slow POTS link only for transmitting HTML files to users who access your Web server. Because large objects such as graphics files can be stored on another server, users will go to the other server for all inline graphics and other large objects. This frees up your relatively limited Internet bandwidth for transmitting plain-text HTML files and processing user input.

> **TIP**
>
> When Internet bandwidth available to you is limited, use a secondary server to distribute relatively large objects such as graphic files.

For example, suppose that you have a local inline image called `WindowsNT.gif` that's embedded in a Web page with the following HTML tag:

```
<img src="/graphics/icons/WindowsNT.gif">
```

You can free up your bandwidth for this graphic by moving `WindowsNT.gif` to another server (for example, www.server.com) and changing the preceding tag to the following:

```
<img src="http://www.server.com/graphics/icons/WindowsNT.gif">
```

You can conserve your bandwidth by following this tip because HTTP is a connectionless protocol. Therefore, after a connection is made for a Web page or other object (image, video clip, Java application, and so on), the page or other object is transmitted, and the connection to the Web server is closed. Subsequently, for various inline images and objects of a page, a Web browser can be instructed to go to a different Web server.

Because it's possible to use another server to store your graphics, you might wonder why you shouldn't just store everything on the other server and skip all the chapters until the next section where Web site design issues are discussed. Although it is possible to use a secondary server to store most of your Web site's content, you will be unable to offer your users any kind of interactivity when using another server. Many Web space providers do not allow access to the CGI directory of their Web server because doing so can lead to some very serious security breaches. The CGI directory is where all interactive Web applications are stored. More information on this and other security issues is provided in Chapter 8, "Security Considerations." By setting up your own Web server, however, it is possible to provide users accessing your Web site dynamic information as well as to publish databases on the Internet.

Suitability of Various Internet Connections

Due to its low bandwidth, a POTS link is suitable for only limited Web traffic. By using another server to store your graphics files, you will be able to get the maximum use from your POTS link by using it exclusively for transmitting HTML text files. However, as you get more accesses and the size of your pages increase, a POTS link will no longer be adequate. This is when you need to consider an alternative, such as ISDN.

Although ISDN has been around for a while, it's still not as widely used as it should be. ISDN technology has a lot of potential. If you look at it from your telephone company's point of view, you'll see that providing ISDN is much simpler. Virtually all your phone conversations are transmitted digitally within your phone company's circuits; only the line from your phone company to your site is analog. The phone company actually has to convert digital signals to analog before sending this signal to your site. By using ISDN, you make the job simpler for the phone company because the phone company doesn't need to worry about converting digital signals to analog. Unfortunately, current prices do not reflect this advantage. At the time of this writing, maintaining a 24-hour link to the Internet using a single-channel ISDN link (64 kbps) can cost as much as $650 per month for the ISDN line, plus ISP (Internet Service Provider) charges. Ironically, a second phone line for a 28.8 kbps link to the Internet is only about $17, plus ISP charges. This means that for about twice the bandwidth of a 28.8 kbps link to the Internet, one might have to pay over 38 times! You might want to give your local phone company a call and consider what they want to charge you and what you get in return before going with ISDN.

NOTE

The previous cost of $650 a month was calculated for a 24-hour single channel ISDN line. Because you can bring down the line when it's not in use, the cost will be lower. However, it can still cost several times more than a regular phone line.

Apart from ISDN and POTS, a third option might be available to you for Internet access. In all likelihood, you can get a much better deal if your local cable company provides Internet access services in your area. Due to the nature of the coaxial cable that delivers cable TV, by choosing a cable-based Internet connection you will typically get a bandwidth of over 4 megabits per second. Such a connection can be up to 350 times faster than a 28.8 kbps dial-up modem connection! For more information about a cable-based Internet access provider, you might want to visit the following URL.

URL

For information about a cable-based Internet access provider:
`http://www.tci.east-lansing.mi.us/metshome.htm`

Choosing the Right Connection

Choosing the right Internet connection is an equation that depends on several variables, such as your bandwidth requirements, expected Web traffic, availability and cost of ISDN in your area, and, of course, your budget for the Internet link.

Recently, cable companies have been exploring the possibility of providing Internet service. If ISDN prices seem to be too high or unreasonable for you, you might want to check with your local cable company to see if they offer Internet service or if they plan to do so. The bandwidth your cable company can provide you is much greater than what ISDN offers. If cable companies realize the potential of providing Internet services at a reasonable cost, the Internet will become a much nicer place to live!

This section has covered various kinds of Internet connections that are available to connect your Web site to the Internet. The next section addresses hardware compatibility issues as well as advantages and drawbacks of selecting an Intel-based, Alpha-based, or Power PC-based hardware platform to host your Web site.

Choosing the Right Hardware for the Job

The hardware you need for your Web site depends on the kinds of services you will be setting up on your Web server. When you are hosting a Web site, by far the most important factors as far as performance is concerned are input/output performance and the amount of memory available apart from the bandwidth of your Internet connection.

This priority changes somewhat dramatically when you start getting into 40 to 60 simultaneous users running various Common Gateway Interface (CGI) applications. If these CGI programs query and update a database on your server, raw input/output performance and RAM are not going to be enough. In such an event, although adding more memory will increase performance, you will need a powerful server to host your Web server. When choosing your hardware, you need to think about the magnitude of traffic you expect your Web server to generate.

TIP

Regardless of the hardware platform you go with, be sure that your Web server is on an NTFS (NT File System) partition. This will enhance the performance of your Web server as well as provide better security. NTFS, unlike FAT, is also a recoverable file system. In the event of a power failure, when the system comes back online, NTFS is typically able to reconstruct disk volumes and return them to a consistent state within a few seconds.

PERFORMANCE

To increase performance, if possible, you should set up your Web server on another hard disk (not just another partition on the same hard disk, but a different physical hard disk). For example, if your Web server is set up on the same hard disk as other applications, whenever these applications are used at the same time with the Web server, your Web server will be competing for the attention of the hard drive head along with other applications. On the other hand, if a separate hard disk is used, your Web server will have its own hard drive head for accessing data. For best results, a high-performance SCSI-2 Wide/Ultra Wide hard drive with an RPM (Revolutions Per Minute) rate of 7200 should be used.

Platforms Suitable to Run NT

Although Windows NT runs on several hardware platforms, Intel is the most widely used. Lately, however, Power PC-based and Digital Alpha-based servers have been gaining popularity due to their high performance. Various tradeoffs are involved when choosing one platform over another. Depending on your current and anticipated needs, you need to choose the right server platform. Advantages and drawbacks of selecting one platform over another are discussed next.

Using an Intel-Based Web Platform

Hosting your Web server on an Intel-based Web server might be the most practical solution for you. Intel-based servers are generally less expensive than Alpha-based or Power PC-based servers. If you do not need an extremely high-performance server, an Intel-based server will do fine. Often, your biggest bottleneck will be the bandwidth of the line connecting you to the Internet. Therefore, unless you are thinking about burdening your Web server with other tasks that require a fair amount of processing time, you will be fine by going with an Intel-based server. Being able to utilize many applications written for Intel-based computers to develop your Web site is another advantage in choosing an Intel-based Web server. According to Robert Denny, developer of the popular Windows NT Web Server WebSite, an Intel-based Web server running Windows NT is perfectly capable of saturating a T1 line.

PERFORMANCE

If you'll be going with an Intel-based Web server, it might be a good idea to purchase a server that supports Symmetric Multi Processing (SMP). By investing in a server that supports SMP under Windows NT, if you outgrow your server you can simply add another processor. However, before purchasing an SMP server, be sure to discuss Windows NT compatibility issues with your vendor. Windows NT might require a special HAL (Hardware Abstraction Layer) from the vendor to take advantage of the second processor.

Using a Power PC-based or DEC Alpha-Based Web Platform

Power PC and Alpha servers are clearly high-performance servers that can be utilized for other tasks in addition to hosting a Web site. If you're employing your Web server for internal use (it's an easy way of distributing information), you want a fast system. If you're using it as a proxy server, you also want a fast system. Proxy servers cache network information requests to save bandwidth and provide faster access to information. A Web server on a Power PC-based or Alpha-based server will do fine in the latter case.

On the downside, Power PC-based and Alpha-based servers generally require more RAM to run the same application programs that run on an Intel-based computer. Lack of software or delayed release of software is another downside. Although this situation might change in the future, at the moment, most software vendors are focusing most of their resources on Intel-based platforms.

Due to costs associated with developing software on non-Intel platforms, most applications are available only for Intel-based computers. This can be a problem if you intend to develop as well as host your Web server on a non-Intel platform. Make sure that you are comfortable with available software for the Windows NT platform you choose.

Hardware Requirements for Each Platform

The following sections discuss the minimum hardware requirements for a basic Windows NT-based Web server. Depending on whether you'll provide additional services, such as hosting a database or providing mail services, you'll need more RAM and/or processing power.

The following are minimum hardware requirements for an Intel-based Web server:

486 DX2/66 or better
16 MB of RAM (24 MB or more highly recommended)
Around 100 MB of free disk space on an NTFS partition
At least a 28.8 PPP (Point-to-Point Protocol) link to the Internet
UPS that supports Windows NT
CD-ROM drive

PERFORMANCE

With 16 MB of RAM, you can basically get by for a Web site. If, however, you are planning to run a few other applications or set up a database on your Web server, a RAM upgrade to 24 or 32 MB will make a tremendous difference. Depending on what else the Web server is used for, more RAM will be needed.

You can also boost the performance of your Web server by using more than one hard disk and/or by using a dual-channel/wide SCSI card. By having Windows NT reside on one hard disk, your data files on another, and your application programs on another, you can increase the performance of your server. Also, when setting up page file space, you can increase the performance of your server by splitting your page files over two or more physical hard disks.

The following are minimum hardware requirements for an Alpha-based or Power PC-based Web server:

Any Alpha-based or Power PC-based server
32 MB of RAM
At least a 64/128 kbps ISDN link to the Internet
Around 100 MB of free disk space on an NTFS partition
CD-ROM drive
UPS that supports Windows NT

Price/Performance Issues

Although Power PC-based and Alpha-based Web servers are inherently more powerful than existing Intel-based servers, they tend to be more expensive. Unfortunately, most software vendors don't seem to port their NT software to non-Intel platforms; therefore, the number of application programs available for non-Intel platforms is limited. This might be an issue for you if you are going to use the same machine to develop your Web site because tools for non-Intel platforms are limited. With the recent Microsoft-Digital alliance, however, and the development of an Intel 486 emulator for the Alpha, things might change in the near future. If you are going to link your Web site to a large database or if you are planning to use one server for other tasks, such as Microsoft Exchange Server, a DHCP server, or an RAS server, in addition to hosting a Web server, then using a Power PC or an Alpha server makes sense. If not, your best bet would be to go along with an Intel-based server. Also, with the introduction of new Pentium Pro-based servers that are optimized for 32-bit operating systems such as Windows NT, you will be able to enjoy a higher level of performance from Intel-based servers.

COMPATIBILITY

Currently, an Intel emulator for Alpha computers running Windows NT exists. This emulator, however, will run only those Windows applications that do not require Windows to be run in 386-enhanced mode. In other words, the new 32-bit applications will not work with this emulator. In the near future, however, you might expect to see an Intel emulator that will run 32-bit Windows applications on an Alpha. With the aid of such an emulator, Alpha users will be able to benefit from the large number of Windows applications written for the Intel platform.

Importance of an Uninterruptible Power Supply (UPS)

The importance of having an *Uninterruptible Power Supply (UPS)* can't be stressed enough when you're dealing with an operating system like Windows NT that will be serving up documents on the Web 24 hours a day. A sudden power failure in the middle of a disk read/write operation can be detrimental to the health of your server. What's really bad about such an incident is that a file might get corrupted, and you might never know about it until you need the file. Although NTFS provides many safeguards to prevent such incidents from happening, you should never take a chance with your data. It's always wise to invest in a UPS that will shut down your server safely in the event of an extended power outage. Depending on your hardware, you need to choose a UPS that's at least capable of providing power until Windows NT has enough time to shut down various services and applications running on your server.

TIP

When selecting a UPS for your server, be sure it *supports* Windows NT. Although you can use the UPS application that comes with Windows NT, many UPS vendors bundle software with added functionality that gives you more control and features, such as the capability to perform scheduled server shutdowns and restarts.

Windows NT Server or Workstation

This section is mainly for those who are exploring the possibility of using NT Workstation to host a Web site. If you are already using NT Server or plan to use NT Server to host your Web site, please skip to the next section, "Choosing Your Web Server." There are a number of differences between Windows NT Server and Workstation; however, when hosting and developing a Web site, most of these differences apply only if you will be using the same computer for other purposes (such as file and print services) in addition to hosting a Web server. Although as far as software is concerned, virtually all software that runs on Windows NT Server runs on Windows NT Workstation and vice versa; the exception to this rule is certain Microsoft software and a handful of third-party tools that require NT Server.

Microsoft Internet Information Server (MS IIS) will be bundled with Windows NT Server version 4.0 and will not be compatible with Windows NT Workstation. Although a somewhat trimmed down version of MS IIS will work with NT Workstation, the current release (version 1.0) does not. Therefore, if you'd like to use MS IIS, you will have to use Windows NT Server. Although you'll save some money by using NT Workstation, because MS IIS is free, the price difference between the combined price of NT Workstation and a commercial Web server will be almost the same as NT Server and MS IIS.

As mentioned earlier, the price difference is really not a very big issue. When managing a Web site, time is very valuable. Tools that save development time will eventually save you money. Therefore, ease of use and features such as database and search engine support are very important when selecting a Web server. Unlike Web servers such as WebSite Purveyor and Netscape (covered in Chapter 7, "Publishing on the Web with WebSite, Purveyor, and Netscape"), MS IIS is new. Although MS IIS is well integrated with Windows NT and comes with integrated Gopher, Web, and FTP capabilities, it lacks some features such as database wizards and search engines found in other Web servers. Therefore, even if you decide to use Windows NT Server, you should read Chapter 7 for an overview of various Windows NT Web servers and features they offer. After reading the next two chapters, you might decide that even if MS IIS is free, it lacks features available in other Web servers. In which case, you can run both MS IIS and another Web server at the same time to take advantage of features of both servers. You can do this by configuring one Web server to run on the default HTTP port (port 80) and the other to run on a different port. More information about this will be provided in the following two chapters.

Availability of MS IIS is not the only advantage of selecting NT Server. Unlike NT Workstation, NT Server is optimized for network applications—an advantage when hosting a Web server. For example, because NT Server can be configured to use more memory for network applications, most of your system resources can be invested to ensure network applications are provided with adequate system resources. If you use the same computer for a variety of other tasks such as providing file and print services, you can expect better performance when using Windows NT Server.

Windows NT Server also includes support for Microsoft BackOffice components. By choosing Windows NT Server, all your BackOffice applications will be integrated with Windows NT Server and MS IIS. As mentioned earlier, there are a number of advantages in choosing Windows NT Server to host a Web site. However, to take advantage of these capabilities, you need to use MS IIS, various BackOffice components, or utilize the same server for other applications, such as file and print services.

After reading the next two chapters, if you are interested in a Web server other than MS IIS, you will be able to get by with NT Workstation. However, by selecting NT Workstation, Microsoft applications such as MS IIS, various BackOffice components, and Microsoft Internet Studio might not be available to you. Microsoft Internet Studio, a Web publishing application that can be used to distribute richly formatted, interactive Web pages on the Internet, requires MS IIS.

When developing a Web site, it's easier to make the decision at an early stage and begin with either NT Workstation or NT Server. For example, if you installed NT Workstation on a computer and decided later to install NT Server and make it a Primary or Backup Domain Controller (PDC/BDC), you need to install NT Server as a new installation because an NT Workstation installation cannot be upgraded to an NT Server BDC or PDC. Speaking from experience, re-installing NT, other applications, and copying .DLL and .INI files from one directory to another so that applications continue to work as they should is not a very pleasant experience. It can take as much as a few days before things are more or less back to the way they used to be. Therefore, in the long run, it will save you both time and money to decide whether to use NT Workstation or NT Server when you first start out.

Choosing Your Web Server

About two dozen Web servers are available for hosting Windows NT-based Web sites. Various Web servers support various features. Because capabilities of Web servers change frequently, this chapter does not discuss features of specific Web servers. Instead, an overview of useful Web server features and their benefits are discussed. By browsing URLs of Web servers, you will be able to obtain the most up-to-date information about their capabilities and features. More detailed information about Web servers is provided in Chapter 7. The four Web servers covered are Netscape, WebSite, Purveyor, and the FREE EMWAC Web server. These four Web servers were selected because they are four of the most widely used Windows NT Web servers, and they offer a lot in terms of enhanced features and tools. However, it does not mean you should ignore other Web servers. A special requirement of yours might be better met by a different server. In addition to the four Web servers mentioned earlier, MS IIS will be covered in Chapter 6.

Useful Web Server Features

When selecting Web server software, you should keep a few things in mind. One of the most important considerations is how easy the Web server is to set up and administer. For example, the Netscape server uses forms to administer all aspects of the server. Therefore, by entering a user ID and a password, the Web site administrator can administer all aspects of the server from a remote location. Such a feature might be very useful to you if you don't always have ready access to your Web server.

Another feature you should look for is the degree of security each server provides. The level of security you need depends on what you will be using your server for. If your Web site will be providing only unclassified information to users browsing your Web site, security will not be a major concern for you. When providing sensitive information over the Web, however, you should ensure that such information is transmitted only via a secure medium in which the Web server encrypts the data before it is transmitted. However, the server you choose should at least support restricting access to part of your server with user names and passwords. Some Web servers allow the creation of user groups and assign various permissions to users on a per-group basis. If you deal with a large number of users, this feature will be useful to you. Some Web servers can use the Windows NT user database to authenticate users who want to access various areas of your Web site. Such a feature will be handy if you need to allow access to parts of your Web site to users of your NT server. Having the capability to restrict access based on the client's IP (Internet Protocol) address might be useful to you, also. By utilizing this feature, you can deny access to visitors browsing your Web site from various domains and countries.

> ### SECURITY
>
> You should never determine the identity of a user accessing your Web site based on the IP address of the Web client. You can trick your Web server by misrepresenting the IP address from which the client is accessing your Web server. Before transmitting sensitive data, you should authenticate the user with a user ID and password using a secure medium.

If you are using your Web server to distribute security-sensitive data, you should make sure that your Web server encrypts the data before transmitting it over the Web. This is especially important if you will be transmitting or receiving valuable data such as customer credit card numbers.

Your Web server should also give you control over *directory browsing*. Directory browsing is the capability of a Web server to list the contents of a directory when a URL is given without a filename but with a directory, as shown in Figure 5.4.

FIGURE 5.4.

When directory browsing is enabled, users will be able to leaf through the entire directory structure of your Web site.

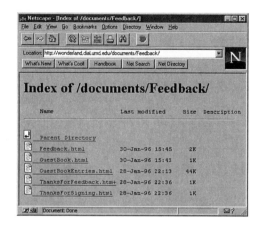

If you want to make sure that Web surfers can get to certain pages only if they know the complete URL name of a file, you should disable directory browsing. Otherwise, someone visiting your Web site will be able to traverse your directory structure and obtain various files you did not intend anyone to have access to.

Support for CGI scripts is a definite must for a Web server. CGI scripts enable you to interact with visitors browsing your Web site by providing dynamic content and immediately responding to user input. You should make sure that your Web server provides CGI scripts with access to CGI environment variables and supports *server-side includes*. Server side includes are special commands that can be embedded in HTML files. These commands are processed by the Web server before the HTML is transmitted to a Web browser. Some Web servers also enable you to interface with Visual Basic programs. This feature will be very useful to you if you are familiar with Visual Basic programming, because you can utilize the power and ease of Visual Basic to interact with users browsing your Web site.

PERFORMANCE

By using server-side includes, you can make information in your static HTML pages change based on various conditions. However, server-side includes should be used sparingly because they tax your Web server by making it take longer to process HTTP requests.

In addition to the previously mentioned features, a few other features are standard for most Web servers; however, you should ensure that your Web server supports these features. After setting up your Web site, you will realize that your Web server's "log file" keeps increasing in size every day. This log file logs all your Web server accesses; it is the key to determining who accessed what from your Web server and when they accessed it. Many different log file analyzing programs are available. To use most of these programs, you should make sure that your Web server generates logs in CERN/NCSA common log format.

Having a mechanism to automatically archive log files is another plus. This feature renames the current log file, creates a new log file, and starts logging Web server accesses to the new log file. Depending on the number of hits your Web site receives, you should typically recycle your log file about once a week. By recycling your log file on a regular basis, such as once a week, you will be able to compare Web server access statistics. However, if you do this at an irregular interval, such as once in every five or six days, analyzing your log file and comparing Web server accesses statistics will become a rather challenging task. Old log files should be archived for future reference. In Chapter 24, "Utility Applications for Your Server," you will be shown how to use a log file analyzing application to find out various access statistics for your Web site.

Last, but not least, is the price of the Web server. Currently, about two dozen Web servers are available that will run on Windows NT. Some of these Web servers are free and in most cases will meet your needs. If, however, you are very concerned about security and performance, you might want to go for a commercial Web server that will better suit your needs.

To summarize the preceding discussion, the following lists the features you should look for when choosing a Web server:

- The Web server generates logs in CERN/NCSA common log format.
- The server includes performance measurement logs and tools.
- The server can be configured to prohibit access by domain name and IP address.
- Access can be controlled by requiring a password based on user IDs and user groups.
- Access to data hierarchies can be configured based on the IP address of the client accessing the Web site.
- The server supports server-side includes.
- The server supports directory browsing.
- CGI scripts have access to all CGI environment variables.
- The server has a built-in search engine.
- The server has built-in database connectivity.
- Easy setup and administration are available via a GUI.
- The server can be administered while it is running.
- The server can be administered remotely.
- The server can serve different directory roots based on the IP address of the client.
- The server offers automatic archival of log files.

NOTE

In case you run into a problem, support provided for free Web servers is limited. It might take as much as a few days to hear from someone if you encounter a problem. If expeditious support is a must for you, consider using a commercial Web server.

Web Servers Available for Windows NT

Table 5.1 lists Web servers for Windows NT. Because capabilities of different Web servers change, features of specific Web servers are not covered in this chapter. Instead, by visiting Web sites listed here, you will be able to find the most up-to-date information.

Table 5.1. Web servers and related information.

Web Server	URL to Visit for More Information
Alibaba	`http://alibaba.austria.eu.net/`
Commerce Builder	`http://www.aristosoft.com/ifact/inet.htm`
Communications Builder	`http://www.aristosoft.com/ifact/inet.htm`
Folio Infobase	`http://www.folio.com/`
FolkWeb	`http://www.ilar.com/folkweb.htm`
FrontPage	`http://www.microsoft.com/frontpage/`
HTTPS	`http://emwac.ed.ac.uk/html/internet_toolchest/` `https/contents.htm`
Internet Office Web Server	`http://server.spry.com/`
NaviServer	`http://www.gnnhost.com/index.htm`
NetPublisher	`http://netpub.notis.com/`
Netscape Commerce	`http://www.netscape.com/comprod/` `netscape_commerce.html`
Netscape Communications	`http://www.netscape.com/comprod/` `netscape_commun.html`
PowerWeb	`http://www.cyberpi.com/`
Purveyor	`http://www.process.com/prod/purveyor.htp`
Quarterdeck WebServer	`http://arachnid.qdeck.com/qdeck/demosoft/` `WebServr/`
SAIC	`http://wwwserver.itl.saic.com/`

continues

Table 5.1. continued

Web Server	URL to Visit for More Information
SuperWeb Server	http://www.frontiertech.com/products/superweb.htm
Web Commander	http://www.flicks.com./
WebBase	http://www.webbase.com/
WebNotes	http://webnotes.ostech.com/
WebQuest	http://www.questar.com/webquest.htm
WebSite	http://website.ora.com/

TIP

You should join *Internet mail lists* that have been set up to discuss various issues related to the Web server you are using. You can learn more about hosting a Web site and publishing information on the Internet. Also, if you have a question, you can ask for help and get answers. Various Windows NT mail lists are discussed in Appendix A, "Windows NT Resources on the Internet."

If you are looking for a free Web server to get you started, you should consider the *SAIC server* and the *EMWAC Web server*. These servers support many basic features that will enable you to get started very quickly. Both servers are administered via graphical user interfaces and are very easy to install and administer. For more information on installing and configuring them, refer to their documentation found at the previously listed Web sites. Installation and administration issues related to the EMWAC server are discussed in Chapter 7.

Summary

This chapter covered issues related to determining and fulfilling various requirements before setting up a Web site. You were introduced to various Internet connection types, including their capabilities and drawbacks. Depending on your needs, budget, and various Internet links available in your area, you can now select the Internet link that best suits your needs. If you cannot afford a high-speed Internet link, you can utilize a secondary Web server to get the maximum use out of a POTS link.

You were introduced to hardware platforms suitable for hosting a Windows NT Web site.

Although Alpha-based and Power PC-based computers are very high-performance server plat-forms, software for them is limited. For this reason, it might be more productive for you to choose an Intel-based server to develop your Web site.

You now have an overview of the software needed to set up a Windows NT-based site. You know the various advantages of selecting Windows NT server over Windows NT Workstation and cases in which you can make do with NT Workstation. From the various Web server ap-plications that are available, you know what features you should look for while selecting the right one to host your Windows NT- based Web site. You also know where to go on the Web for more information about the various Windows NT Web Server applications.

What's Next?

The next two chapters discuss issues related to setting up and configuring five Windows NT Web servers. After finding out more about these Web servers and evaluating your needs, you will be able to select the Web server that best meets your needs. The next chapter, "Installing and Using Microsoft Internet Information Server," discusses installation, configuration, and administration issues related to MS IIS.

6

Installing and Using Microsoft Internet Information Server

Microsoft Internet Information Server (IIS) is a Web, FTP, and Gopher server developed by Microsoft to exploit various capabilities of Windows NT and to publish content on the Internet. Compared to other Windows NT Web servers, IIS offers many unique features. IIS's security model is based on NTFS security permissions. This is a major advantage, because the security of a Web site hosted with IIS can be easily managed using File Manager. Although at the time of this writing IIS is available only for Windows NT server, most likely a special version of IIS will be available for Windows NT Workstation by the time you read this. The following sections discuss how IIS can be installed and used to publish information on the Internet.

Installing Internet Information Server

Installing IIS is easy. A copy of IIS will be included in the Windows NT 4.0 distribution CD-ROM. The latest version of IIS can be downloaded from Microsoft's IIS Web page. It's always best to check the IIS Web site for a more recent version of IIS before installing the version included in the Windows NT 4.0 distribution CD-ROM. After downloading IIS, copy it to a temporary directory and decompress the archive by executing the executable program with the -d argument. This will extract contents of the IIS distribution archive into various subdirectories. You can skip this step if the file SETUP.EXE is found in the CD-ROM's IIS directory.

URL

You can obtain the most up-to-date information about MS Internet Information Server from the official Internet Information Server Web page by visiting the following URL:

`http://www.microsoft.com/InfoServ/`

CAUTION

Before continuing to install IIS, it's a good idea to make sure that no other Web servers are running on port 80 of your NT server. If you already have a Web server installed and would like to continue using it, change its port to a different port number so that the installation program will not have any problems binding IIS to port 80 (default port for HTTP). The same applies to FTP. If you wish to use the FTP server included with IIS, stop the Windows NT FTP service by using the command `net stop "FTP Server"`.

When SETUP.EXE is executed, the installation program presents you with a dialog box similar to the one shown in Figure 6.1. In this dialog box, you can select various IIS components to be installed. It is highly recommended that you make sure the Internet Server Manager checkbox is checked. If it is not checked, you will have to use the Windows NT Registry to make changes to IIS. If you have already installed ODBC drivers on your system, you may deselect the ODBC Drivers and Administrator checkbox. The same applies to Microsoft Internet Explorer.

FIGURE 6.1.

You can selectively install various components of IIS.

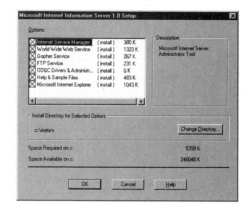

If you wish to change the default directory in which IIS is installed, click Change Directory and specify another directory by using a dialog box similar to the one shown in Figure 6.2. For security purposes, it is highly recommended that you install all IIS components in an NTFS partition.

FIGURE 6.2.

Install IIS on an NTFS partition.

Next, you need to specify root directories for all three Internet publishing services. This is accomplished by using a dialog box similar to the one shown in Figure 6.3. These three directories do not have to be sister subdirectories. However, you might find it easier to manage the directory structure if they are sister subdirectories. Be sure to specify directories in an NTFS partition because IIS uses NTFS security.

If you have already installed the NT FTP service that's part of the NT TCP/IP utilities package, the IIS installation program asks if you'd like to disable it, as shown in Figure 6.4. Because the FTP server that ships with IIS is more powerful and easier to administer than the FTP service that's part of the NT TCP/IP services package, it's recommended that you allow the installation program to disable the previously installed FTP service. Note, however, that after the previously installed FTP server is disabled, you cannot restart it using the Services application in the Control Panel. The FTP Server included with IIS can be configured using the Internet Server Manager. Unlike the standard FTP server that's part of the TCP/IP services package, IIS FTP Server statistics can be logged to an ODBC data source. Performance Monitor can also be used to monitor IIS FTP Server statistics in real time. In addition to that, several useful configuration settings that have to be modified using the registry in the FTP Server that's part of the NT TCP/IP services package can be modified using an easy-to-use dialog box when using the FTP Server that's part of IIS.

FIGURE 6.3.

Specify directories in an NTFS partition to be used as root directories by the FTP, Gopher, and Web publishing service.

FIGURE 6.4.

The IIS installation program gives you the option to disable the FTP service that's part of the NT TCP/IP services package if it's already installed.

The next dialog box prompts you to install the SQL Server driver, as shown in Figure 6.5. After this driver is installed, Microsoft SQL Server databases can be published on the Web using the Internet Database Connector. When the dialog box in Figure 6.5 appears, click OK to continue installing IIS. Note that MS SQL Server is required for a few sample ISAPI applications shipped with IIS.

After the SQL Server driver is installed, the message box in Figure 6.6 appears, telling you that IIS is successfully installed on your system. All Internet publishing services selected earlier are now ready for use.

At the end of the installation process, four new icons are added to the NT start menu. These icons appear in Figure 6.7. In the "Configuring the Microsoft Internet Information Server" section, you are shown how to use the Internet Service Manager to configure various aspects of IIS.

FIGURE 6.5.

SQL Server driver install dialog box.

FIGURE 6.6.

A message box appears confirming that Internet Information Server is fully installed.

FIGURE 6.7.

Four new icons are added to the NT Start menu by the IIS installation program.

It's possible to immediately begin publishing content on the Web by using the Web Publishing Service of IIS. If you connect to your computer at this point by using a Web browser, you'll see a Web page similar to the one in Figure 6.8. Use this Web page to get familiar with how IIS works and to try out the CGI and database applications that ship with IIS. Be sure to check out the guest book application. It demonstrates how IIS's Internet Database Connector can be used to update and view a Microsoft SQL database. Although these applications are not production-quality applications, they will give you some idea of how IIS can be used to interact with users browsing a Web site. At some point, you'll need to change the default Web page shown in Figure 6.8 and replace it with one of your own Web pages.

If you look at User Manager, you'll notice that the IIS installation program has created a new user account. Before publishing information on the Internet with IIS, it's crucial that you understand the importance of this account and how it's used by the IIS Web Publishing Service. As you can see in Figure 6.9, the full name of the account created for the IIS is Internet Guest Account. The name of this account depends on the name of your server. For example, if the name of your server is INTERNET, the name of the account created for the IIS is IUSR_INTERNET. This account will be referred to as the *Internet Guest Account* in future sections.

FIGURE 6.8.

Internet Information Server default Web page.

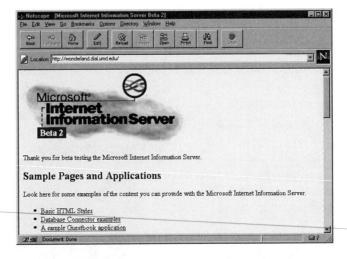

FIGURE 6.9.

The installation program creates a new NT user account to be used by the Internet Information Server.

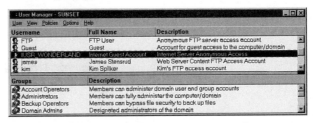

Internet Information Server File Permissions

It's important that you understand how IIS implements security and user authentication before publishing information with it. It's easy to control who has access to what files at your Web site because IIS uses NTFS security. The Internet Guest Account should have read permission for all public files freely available to users browsing a Web site without a username and a password. A part of a Web site's directory structure can be *restricted* by revoking file and directory access from the Internet Guest Account and by giving it to users who are allowed to access files in a certain directory structure. Note that these users should also be assigned the Windows NT user right "Log on Locally." More information about this is presented in the following section. When file access permission is revoked from the Internet Guest Account and is assigned to a few Windows NT users, a username and a password that has enough permission to access the data has to be supplied before IIS allows a browser to view the data. IIS supports three kinds of username/password authentication methods:

■ **Basic clear text authentication.** Although basic authentication is encoded, it's very easy for a hacker to decode it and obtain a user's username and password. If this is the only authentication mechanism you use, be sure not to make any sensitive data available to the Internet using basic clear text authentication! Generally, you should treat content published on the Internet with basic clear text authentication as content that might possibly be accessed by any unauthorized person with a *stolen* username and a password. All Web browsers support basic clear text authentication.

■ **SSL user authentication.** *SSL (Secure Sockets Layer)* authentication is typically used along with basic authentication to ensure that usernames and passwords are encrypted before transmission.

■ **Windows NT Challenge/Response authentication.** This is a very secure way to authenticate users. However, this works only with Internet Explorer. When Windows NT Challenge/Response authentication is selected, before a username and a password are sent to the server, they're encrypted. That way, someone, possibly with malicious intent, eavesdropping on a connection will not be able to use the same username and password to gain access to the Web site.

Configuring the Microsoft Internet Information Server

The next few sections discuss how you can configure IIS to suit your needs. IIS is configured by using the Internet Service Manager icon shown in Figure 6.7. When Internet Service Manager is invoked, it looks similar to Figure 6.10.

FIGURE 6.10.

The Internet Service Manager application is used to configure various aspects of IIS.

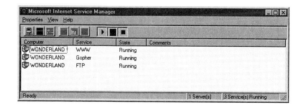

It's easy to locate the NT Server or Internet service you wish to administer by using the View option of the Internet Service Manager menu. Various server views appear in Figure 6.11 and Figure 6.12.

FIGURE 6.11.

Internet Service Manager with servers grouped by server name.

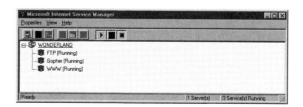

FIGURE 6.12.

*Internet Service Manager
with servers grouped by
various Internet Services
(FTP, Gopher, WWW).*

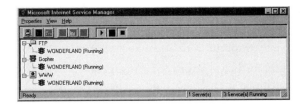

Configuring WWW Publishing Service

You can select the WWW publishing service to configure from the IIS manager menu shown in Figure 6.10, 6.11, or 6.12. After selecting the WWW publishing service you wish to configure, either double-click on it or use the right mouse button to select `Service Properties`. You then can configure various aspects of the WWW Publishing Service.

WWW Publishing Service Properties

As shown in Figure 6.13, the Service tab of the WWW Publishing Service can be used to configure key aspects of the WWW publishing service. It's recommended that you don't change the default settings for Connection Timeout and Maximum Connections. However, after monitoring the number of connections at any given time by using Performance Monitor, you might want to increase this value if you have sufficient network bandwidth to accommodate additional connections. In the "Monitoring Performance of Internet Information Server" section, you're shown how to use Performance Monitor to monitor the performance of IIS. Performance Monitor is a utility shipped with Windows NT that can be used to monitor various statistics of Windows NT resources and applications.

FIGURE 6.13.

*The Service tab of the
WWW Publishing Service.*

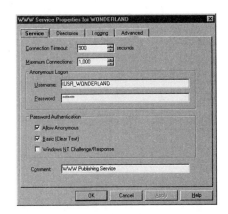

As mentioned earlier, IIS uses Windows NT user accounts and NTFS security to enforce file access permissions. The username and password specified for Anonymous Logon is used to determine if an anonymous user requesting an object from IIS is permitted to have that object.

It's recommended that IIS be allowed to use the Internet Guest Account shown in Figure 6.13. By using File Manager, you can control which objects anonymous users have access to by assigning file permissions to the Internet Guest Account.

If your Web site is a public Web site, make sure that the Allow Anonymous checkbox in Figure 6.13 is checked. If you want to protect parts of your Web site with a username and a password, make sure that the Basic (Clear Text) checkbox is checked. As Figure 6.14 shows, you are then warned about the consequences of using clear text passwords. As a rule of thumb, never use clear text passwords to safeguard sensitive data from unauthorized users unless an encryption algorithm such as SSL is used.

FIGURE 6.14.

You should not use clear text passwords to restrict access to sensitive data.

The Windows NT Challenge/Response authentication method is much safer than clear text user authentication because user authorization information is encrypted before it's transmitted over the Internet. However, at the time of this writing, only Internet Explorer was capable of handling Windows NT Challenge/Response authentication. Unless you're certain most users visiting your Web site use Internet Explorer, it's recommended that you stay away from Windows NT Challenge/Response authentication for now.

You can specify a comment for the WWW Publishing Service by typing it in the space provided for Comment. This comment will show up in Internet Service Manager under "Comments."

Configuring WWW Publishing Service Directories

You can use the Directories tab shown in Figure 6.15 to configure how IIS handles directories. As you can see in Figure 6.15, several directory mappings have already been set up by the IIS installation program.

It's very easy to add directory mappings to the Web Publishing Service. For example, you can use the Add button to add a CGI (Common Gateway Interface) directory mapping to the WWW Publishing Service. Applications in this directory can then be executed by users using a Web browser. After pressing the Add button, the Directory Properties dialog box appears, as shown in Figure 6.16. In this dialog box, you can select a directory and an *alias* for it. The alias specified in Figure 6.16 for the CGI directory is cgi-bin. You can use this alias to execute applications in the H:\Publish\WWW\CGI-BIN directory by using a URL such as `http://server.name.com/cgi-bin/application.exe`. Because the cgi-bin directory contains applications, the Execute checkbox is selected in Figure 6.16; this enables the WWW Publishing service to execute applications requested by users and return the output. If the virtual directory points to a network resource using a Universal Naming Convention (UNC) share name, a username and a password that has access to the share can be specified in the space provided for Account Information. Note that this option is visible only if a UNC share name is typed in.

FIGURE 6.15.

The directories tab of the WWW Service properties dialog box can be used to configure various directory settings.

FIGURE 6.16.

Directory Properties dialog box.

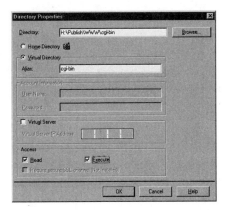

IIS supports virtual servers. You can use the Virtual Server checkbox if a server has more than one IP address. The virtual server feature is handy for setting up Web servers for several companies on one server. For example, you can use the virtual server feature to host Web servers for www.Microsoft.com and www.IBM.com on the same computer (assuming you own both domain names, of course!). Note that properties have to be set separately for each virtual server.

Finally, you can select the Require Secure SSL Channel checkbox if SSL is installed on your server. SSL encrypts data before it's transmitted to users browsing a Web site.

The Enable Default Document checkbox, shown in Figure 6.15, is used to specify the name of the file that is sent by default if a URL is given without a filename. For example, when a user accesses a Web site with the URL http://www.company.com/, the filename specified under Enable Default Document is sent to the user. If the file is not found or if a filename is not specified under Enable Default Document, the user is presented with a list of files and directories, as shown in Figure 6.17, if directory browsing is allowed. Otherwise, the user is presented with a message similar to the one shown in Figure 6.18.

FIGURE 6.17.
A list of files and directories appears if a URL without a filename is used and directory browsing is allowed.

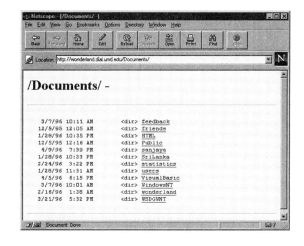

FIGURE 6.18.
An Access Forbidden message appears if a URL without a filename is used and directory browsing is not allowed.

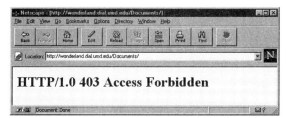

The Directory Browsing Allowed checkbox, shown in Figure 6.15, is used to specify if IIS should return a list of files and directories if a URL is given with a filename. For example, `http://wonderland.dial.umd.edu/document` refers to a subdirectory. If directory browsing is allowed, the user sees a list of directories, as shown in Figure 6.17. On the other hand, if directory browsing is not allowed, the user will see a message similar to the one shown in Figure 6.18.

Logging Web Publishing Service Accesses

Web server accesses can either be logged to an SQL/ODBC database or a plain text file. WWW Publishing Service access logging is configured by using the Logging tab shown Figure 6.19. Unless you have special software to analyze data logged to an SQL/ODBC database, it's recommended that you allow IIS to log Web server accesses to a plain text file. Refer to Chapter 24, "Utility Applications for Your Server," for more information about analyzing Web server access log files.

FIGURE 6.19.

WWW Publishing Service access logging dialog box.

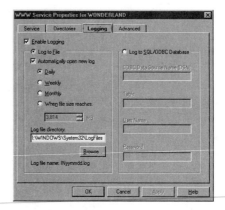

Web Publishing Service Access Control

The Advanced tab of the WWW Service Properties dialog box shown in Figure 6.20 is used to grant and deny access to various computers on the Internet. You might want to use this dialog box to deny access to one or more Internet computers.

FIGURE 6.20.

WWW Publishing Service advanced properties dialog box.

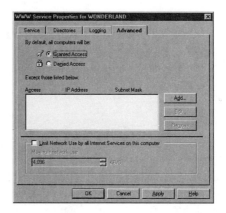

For example, it's possible to deny access to a computer by the name of www.hacker.com by selecting the "Denied Access" radio button and by clicking the Add button. You can use the dialog box shown in Figure 6.21 to specify which IP addresses should be denied access. If you don't know the IP address of a computer but only its domain name (www.hacker.com), simply click the ellipsis button shown in Figure 6.21, and you can enter the domain name as shown in Figure 6.22.

FIGURE 6.21.
Deny Access On dialog box.

FIGURE 6.22.
You can use the DNS Lookup dialog box to look up an Internet computer by its domain name.

The Limit Network Use checkbox, shown in Figure 6.20, is handy for limiting network bandwidth that will be used by all Internet services (managed by IIS) running on the computer being administered. As shown in the "Monitoring Performance of Internet Information Server" section, use Performance Monitor to determine network bandwidth used by IIS before changing the default value. If it's necessary to use this option to severely limit network bandwidth, it's a good indication that you need to upgrade your Internet link. If this isn't possible, at least move all large graphics files to another server.

Configuring FTP Publishing Service

You can use the FTP Publishing Service to distribute files on the Internet. Before using it in a production environment, it's recommended that the FTP Publishing Service be configured to suit your needs. Just select the FTP Publishing Service you wish to configure from the Internet Service Manager and double-click it. The FTP Publishing Service is configured by using a tabbed dialog box similar to the one shown in Figure 6.23.

> **TECHNICAL NOTE**
>
> The default TCP/IP port of the FTP Service is 21.

The dialog box shown in Figure 6.23 is identical in many ways to the dialog box in Figure 6.13. To avoid redundancy, this section covers only those dialog box options that are different. The Allow only anonymous connections checkbox and the Current Sessions button are the only options that are different between Figure 6.23 and Figure 6.13.

FIGURE 6.23.

FTP Publishing Service configuration dialog box.

Anonymous Connections

You can check the Allow only anonymous connections checkbox to ensure that Windows NT users do not compromise the security of your NT server by using their usernames and passwords to log on to the FTP Publishing Service. Usernames and passwords used to authenticate users to access the FTP server are transmitted in clear text format. This means that anyone who has a *protocol analyzer* and access to your network or the part of the Internet that the authentication data is transferred across can intercept usernames and passwords used by authorized users and gain unauthorized access to your system. If you deselect this option, be aware that every time a user logs on with a username and password, the same username and password can be used by an unauthorized person. As a security precaution, advise your users not to store sensitive files on the FTP server. If they should store sensitive files, ask them to please encrypt the files by using a powerful encryption algorithm such as Pretty Good Privacy (PGP).

Administering FTP Sessions

You can use the Current Sessions button to find out which users are logged on to the FTP server at any given time by using the dialog box in Figure 6.24. You can use the same dialog box to disconnect users from the FTP server. Regular users have a face next to their username; anonymous users have a question mark next to the e-mail address used to access the FTP server. For example, the anonymous user shown in Figure 6.24 has used the e-mail address BillGates@Microsoft.com to access the FTP server.

FIGURE 6.24.

FTP User Sessions dialog box.

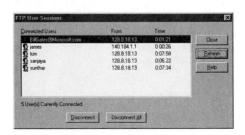

FTP Publishing Service Messages

You can use the Messages tab shown in Figure 6.25 to specify various messages displayed to users connecting to the FTP server. As shown in Figure 6.25, you can specify a Welcome message and an Exit message, as well as a Maximum connections message by using this dialog box.

FIGURE 6.25.

FTP Publishing Service messages dialog box.

FTP Publishing Service Directories

Directories of the FTP Publishing service can be configured by using the Directories tab shown in Figure 6.26. This dialog box is very similar in functionality to the dialog box in Figure 6.16. The only difference is the Directory Listing Style option. This option is used to specify if the FTP Publishing Service should return an MS-DOS– or UNIX–style directory listing. It's recommended that the UNIX radio button be selected because some Web browsers expect the directory listing format of FTP servers to be in the UNIX (ls -l) directory listing format.

FIGURE 6.26.

FTP Publishing Service directories dialog box.

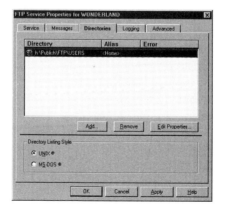

Home Directories of FTP Server Users

It's very easy to specify home directories for FTP users. The only requirement is to have the directory structure set up so that all users share the same parent directory and their home directories correspond to their usernames. For example, if H:\Publish\FTP\Users is the parent directory, home directories of the two users Sunthar and Kim should be H:\Publish\FTP\Users\Sunthar and H:\Publish\FTP\Users\Kim, respectively. The parent directory of user home directories can be specified as shown in Figure 6.27. Note that the directory H:\Publish\FTP\Users is configured as the Home Directory of the FTP Publishing Service. Again, be sure users don't store any sensitive files on your system that are accessible via FTP.

FIGURE 6.27.

FTP Publishing Service home directory configuration dialog box.

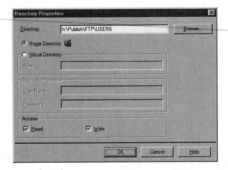

The Logging and Advanced tabs of the FTP Publishing service are identical in functionality to that of the WWW Publishing Service discussed earlier. Please refer to the earlier discussion for more information about using these two configuration tabs.

Configuring the Gopher Publishing Service

IIS also includes a Gopher server. Although the Gopher protocol is becoming less and less popular by the day due to inherent limitations of the Gopher protocol, almost anyone who has access to the Internet has access to a Gopher client. This is especially true for users who still access the Internet through UNIX shell accounts. The Gopher server is administered by using the Gopher Publishing Service properties dialog box, shown in Figure 6.28.

TECHNICAL NOTE

The default TCP/IP port of the Gopher Service is 70.

FIGURE 6.28.
Gopher Publishing Service properties dialog box.

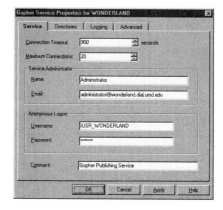

The dialog box in Figure 6.28 is very similar to the dialog box in Figure 6.13, which was discussed in detail earlier. The only difference is the space provided for Service Administrator information. The name and e-mail address of the Gopher server administrator can be specified as shown in Figure 6.28.

The Gopher Service directories dialog box shown in Figure 6.29 is very similar to the dialog box in Figure 6.16, which was discussed in detail earlier. Note that the home directory of the Gopher service is H:\Publish\Gopher. This information is used in the following section where you're shown how to publish information on the Internet with the Gopher server.

FIGURE 6.29.
Gopher Publishing Service directories dialog box.

Publishing Information with the Gopher Server

It's very easy to publish information on the Internet with the Gopher server. To a certain extent, it's similar to publishing an entire directory structure of information on the Internet. However, as you learn shortly, there is one extra required step to publish information by using the Gopher service than merely copying files to the Gopher directory structure.

As mentioned earlier, the home directory of the Gopher Publishing Service used in this exercise is H:\Publish\Gopher. The directory structure of H:\Publish\Gopher is shown in Figure 6.30. Note that there is a file by the name of Welcome.txt in the home directory of the Gopher server. The contents of this file are shown in Figure 6.31. Shortly, you find out how easy it is to publish this file and directory structure on the Internet with the Gopher server.

FIGURE 6.30.

Directory structure of the Gopher server's home directory.

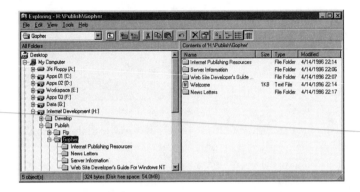

FIGURE 6.31.

Contents of file Welcome.txt.

At this point, if a user connects to the Gopher Publishing Service, he or she sees a directory listing similar to the one shown in Figure 6.32. Note how the file Welcome.txt in Figure 6.32 is marked as a binary file. This is because, by default, all files published with the Gopher Publishing Service are assumed to be binary files. At this time, you might want to create a text file in your Gopher server directory and notice that if you click it, it is downloaded as a binary file.

You can solve this problem by creating a tag file for the text file Welcome.txt. You create a tag file by using the following syntax:

```
gdsset -c -g<number> -f <"file description> -a <"administrator's name"> -e <e-mail
➥address> <filename>
```

FIGURE 6.32.

Directory listing of the home directory of the Gopher Publishing Service.

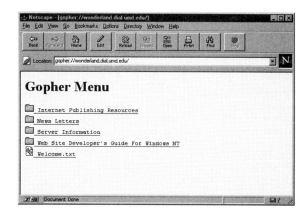

Explanations of various command-line argument substitutions are listed here:

-c:—Edits or creates a new file.

-g<number>:—Specifies the type of file according to the file type table shown next. Simply replace <number> with the single digit File Type Code from the file type table.

-a <"administrator's name">:—Name of administrator.

-e <e-mail address>:—Administrator's e-mail address.

<filename>:—Name of file.

The following is the file type code table for publishing various kinds of files with the Gopher Publishing Service.

File Type Code	File Type Description
0	Text file
1	Gopher directory
2	CSO phone book server
3	Error
4	Binary Hexadecimal Macintosh file
5	MS-DOS binary archive
6	UNIX UUencoded file
7	Index search server
8	Telnet session
9	Binary file

Listed next is the actual command used to publish the file Welcome.txt on the Internet with the Gopher Publishing Service. This command should be typed at the Windows NT command prompt. Note the various command-line arguments that are used and the output of the gdsset application.

```
H:\publish\Gopher>gdsset -c -g0 -f "Welcome Message" -a "Sanjaya" -e
↪sanjaya@erols.com Welcome.txt
 Old Tag contents for H:\publish\Gopher\Welcome.txt
 Tag information for H:\publish\Gopher\Welcome.txt
        Object Type = 9
      Friendly Name = Welcome.txt
         Admin Name = Default Admin Name
        Admin Email = Default Admin Email
 Gopher Object Type = 0
 Gopher FriendlyName = Welcome Message
 Tag information for H:\publish\Gopher\Welcome.txt
        Object Type = 0
      Friendly Name = Welcome Message
         Admin Name = Sanjaya
        Admin Email = sanjaya@erols.com
H:\publish\Gopher>
```

At this point, if a user connects to the Gopher server, he or she sees a directory listing similar to the one shown in Figure 6.33. Compare the directory listing in Figure 6.32 with the listing in Figure 6.33. Note how the description of the file is now changed to Welcome Message from Welcome.txt. Also, note the icon of the text file is changed to a text file icon from a binary file icon. If a user clicks on the text file rather than a prompt to download the file, the user now sees the actual contents of the text file, as shown in Figure 6.34.

FIGURE 6.33.

Directory listing of the home directory of the Gopher Publishing Service after a tag file is created for Welcome.txt.

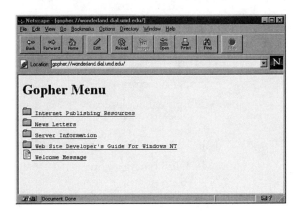

FIGURE 6.34.

Contents of text file Welcome.txt viewed via the Gopher Publishing Service.

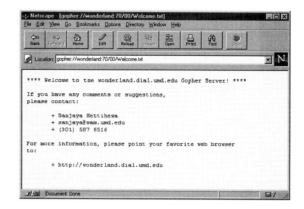

Monitoring Performance of Internet Information Server

Various IIS statistics can be monitored using Performance Monitor. Performance Monitor is invoked by executing the Performance Monitor icon in the Administrative Tools Windows NT Start Menu folder. In order to monitor various IIS statistics, after invoking Performance Monitor, select Edit | Add To Chart from the menu bar. The dialog box shown in Figure 6.35 appears. Use this dialog box to choose various IIS statistics to monitor by selecting an IIS object and counter as shown in Figure 6.35. Each object has various counters associated with it. After selecting a counter to monitor, click the Add button.

FIGURE 6.35.

A number of IIS statistics are available to be monitored with Performance Monitor.

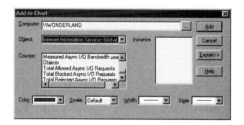

Counters selected using the Add to Chart dialog box can be monitored using Performance Monitor as shown in Figure 6.36. Performance Monitor is especially useful for finding bottle necks. For example, the `Bytes Total/sec` counter of the `HTTP Service` object can be monitored to determine if Internet bandwidth available is sufficient to serve HTTP requests.

FIGURE 6.36.

Selected IIS statistics can be monitored with Performance Monitor.

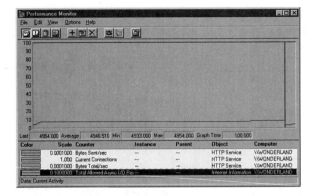

Summary

Microsoft Internet Server is bundled free with Windows NT server. Although Microsoft intends to make a version of IIS available for Windows NT Workstation, it will not be as powerful as the version that ships with Windows NT server. There are many commercial Web servers available for Windows NT. Most of these Web servers come bundled with additional software, such as database setup connectivity wizards and search engines. On the other hand, although IIS is a very powerful server, it doesn't include any database setup wizards or search engines. Such features have to be added separately by using custom CGI (or ISAPI) or third-party applications.

IIS is a powerful, easy-to-manage server designed to make maximum use of Windows NT's system architecture. You can use it to publish information on the Internet via HTTP, Gopher, and FTP.

What's Next?

At the time of this writing, over a dozen Web servers are available for Windows NT. Although this proves the success of Windows NT as an ideal operating system for setting up Web sites, it can certainly make things rather confusing when selecting a Web server. The next chapter discusses a number of Web servers available for Windows NT, highlighting advantages and drawbacks of choosing one Web server over the other.

7

Publishing on the Web with WebSite, Purveyor, and Netscape

As this book goes to press, more than two dozen Web servers run on Windows NT. Although covering all Web servers is beyond the scope of this book, this chapter covers three important Web servers: WebSite, Purveyor, and Netscape. (The Microsoft Internet Information Server is covered in the preceding chapter.) These Web servers were selected because they are three of the most widely used Windows NT Web servers and offer a lot in terms of features, performance, and ease of use.

Internet Information Server (IIS) is freely available to Windows NT users. As you will learn shortly, however, IIS lacks several features found in other Windows NT Web servers. Although IIS is a powerful server, it doesn't include the comprehensive Web site management tools offered by WebSite and Purveyor. IIS requires a few add-ons to do some of the tasks that can be accomplished easily with some of the Web servers discussed in this chapter. Therefore, the fact that you run Windows NT Server does not necessarily mean IIS is your best Web server solution. If you are using Windows NT Server, however, you still might want to install IIS because it is provided free, is integrated with Windows NT, and offers many advanced features. It's important to note that you are not limited to running only one Web server on an NT machine. For example, the test system used to write this book has five Web servers installed on the same machine. Each Web server uses a different TCP/IP port. By installing two or more Web servers in different ports, you enjoy the best of two worlds by being able to mix and match features of the various Web servers. Although this might seem to be rather complicated, it is not. More than one Web server can be used to serve HTTP documents at a Web site by installing them in two different ports. Although this does not make much of a difference when serving HTML documents, this capability is extremely useful when creating various advanced CGI, WinCGI, or ISAPI applications.

According to a Microsoft presentation at the 1996 Professional Developer's Conference in San Francisco, Microsoft will be releasing a less powerful version of IIS for Windows NT Workstation. Although information about this less powerful version of IIS was limited when this book went to print, it is likely that more information about such a server will be available at Microsoft's Web site by the time you read this. At the time of this writing, IIS is available only for Windows NT Server. If you wish to set up your Web site with Windows NT Workstation, such a limitation might concern you. The personal Web server included with NT Workstation is most likely only going to have a Web server—unlike IIS which also includes a Gopher and FTP server. However, the Workstation version of IIS will support ISAPI, just like IIS. All three Web servers discussed here, however, support both Windows NT Workstation and Windows NT Server fully. For a discussion on using Windows NT Workstation or Server to publish information on the Internet, refer to Chapter 5, "Determining and Fulfilling Your Requirements."

Various aspects of installing, configuring, and using the aforementioned Web servers are discussed in the following sections. Note that the following sections are not meant to cover all aspects of these three Web servers comprehensively. For additional information about the various servers discussed in the following sections, visit their respective Web sites.

Installing and Using WebSite Web Server

WebSite is a widely used Windows NT Web server that is not only rich in features, but also easy to use. WebSite can be installed and configured in just a few minutes to publish information on the Web. Because it is compatible with WinCGI (Windows Common Gateway Interface) and CGI (Common Gateway Interface), there are many *server-side* solutions available for WebSite. These server-side applications can be used to further enhance the capabilities of WebSite.

Note that there are two versions of WebSite: WebSite Standard and WebSite Professional. This section is based on WebSite Professional. In addition to features of WebSite Standard, WebSite Professional supports the two major Web cryptographic security systems: Secure Hypertext Transfer Protocol (SHTTP) and Secure Sockets Layer (SSL).

URL

Information about the WebSite Web server can be obtained from O'Reilly's Web site:

`http://Website.ora.com/`

Before discussing the features of WebSite, the next section covers various issues related to installing and configuring WebSite in order to publish information on the Internet. Afterward, advanced features of WebSite are discussed, with an emphasis on how these features can be used to manage a Web site effectively.

Installing WebSite

It only takes a few minutes to install WebSite. To begin installing WebSite, simply run the `setup.exe` file. The setup program asks you for a directory to install WebSite, as shown in Figure 7.1. Use this dialog box to type in a directory and press the Next button to continue.

FIGURE 7.1.

Selecting the destination directory for WebSite.

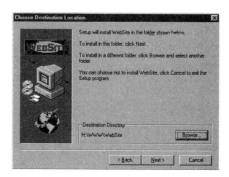

After clicking the Next button, you see a dialog box similar to the one shown in Figure 7.2. Using this dialog box, you can select the various WebSite components you want to install. The released version of WebSite Professional will likely have a few extra components, including an option to install Cold Fusion, which is an application that can be used to effortlessly publish databases on the Web. Unless you have already installed Cold Fusion Professional on your system, install the version of Cold Fusion shipped with WebSite. When installing WebSite, make sure that Server, Essential Tools, and Samples are selected for installation. Very little can be accomplished with WebSite without these components! If you have Internet Explorer, Netscape Navigator, or another preferred browser installed on your computer, you can deselect the checkbox next to Spyglass Enhanced Mosaic Browser. As you will see in Chapter 10, "Web Site Development Tools," HotDog is a powerful HTML editor. It is, however, a *raw* HTML editor. If you are only comfortable with WYSIWYG HTML editors, you may deselect the checkbox to install HotDog. If not, select to install it and give it a try. After selecting WebSite components to install, click the Next button.

FIGURE 7.2.

Various WebSite components can be selectively installed.

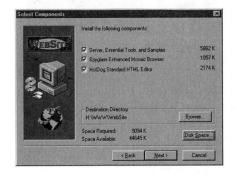

The next dialog box, shown in Figure 7.3, can be used to specify details about an existing Web you might have already set up on your server. This directory will become WebSite's "document root directory" after it is installed. As you can see in Figure 7.3, the document root directory does not have to be a child of the WebSite installation directory. It is recommended that you keep the two separate. Doing so will enable you to easily switch from one Web server to another. If directory browsing is enabled on the Web server, the contents of the directory "directory" are sent to the user when he or she enters a URL such as http://server.com/directory. Before this listing is sent out, the Web server checks the directory for an "index file." The index file is sent by default, if it is present, when a URL is given with a directory name and no filename. The same is true when someone looks up a Web site with the URL http://server.com/ . If the server's index file is present on the Web server's root directory, it will be sent to the user. If not, the contents of the root directory will be displayed. The "Index doc" data entry field is used to specify the name of WebSite's index file. Usually, index.html is used as the index file of a Web server, and it is recommended that you leave the default value as it is. After typing in the two values, press the Next button to continue.

FIGURE 7.3.

Existing Web information dialog box.

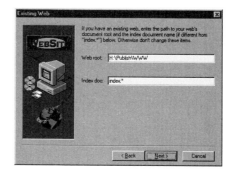

The next dialog box is used to specify if WebSite should be automatically started when you login to your NT Server. If you select it to be automatically started, WebSite will be added to your Startup folder. Note that this does not mean WebSite will not run as a Windows NT service. Shortly, you will be shown how to setup WebSite to run as a Windows NT service. If you would like to set up WebSite to function as a Windows NT service, select Manual Start and click the Next button. Otherwise, select WebSite to be added to the Startup folder.

FIGURE 7.4.

Server Run Mode dialog box.

The installation program will then ask you for your Internet server's IP address. Type your Internet address and click the Next button. You will then be asked for the Web site administrator's e-mail address. This is usually `Webmaster@your.company.com`. Click the Next button after entering the e-mail address of the Web site administrator. WebSite will then install itself by copying all its files, updating the registry, and adding a new folder to your Start menu. The folder added to the Start menu is shown in Figure 7.5. Note that this section is based on a beta version of WebSite Professional. The released version of WebSite Professional, which will be available by the time you read this, is likely to have several additional icons.

FIGURE 7.5.
WebSite Start menu folder.

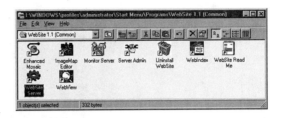

That's all there is to installing WebSite. WebSite can now be used to publish information on the Internet by adding files to the document root directory specified earlier during installation. Locate the WebSite Server icon in the folder shown in Figure 7.5, and double-click it to start WebSite. At this time, you can verify your WebSite installation by looking up `http://localhost/wsdocs/readme.html` with a Web browser. If WebSite was successfully installed on your system, you will see a Web page similar to the one shown in Figure 7.6. Use this Web page to test your WebSite installation and learn how to use some of its features. Select the Server Self-Test option to verify WebSite is successfully installed on your system. If you have Microsoft Access and Visual Basic Professional 4.0 installed on your system, be sure also to select the Access/VB CGI Sample option to discover how WebSite can be used to interface with Visual Basic applications.

FIGURE 7.6.
Verifying WebSite installation.

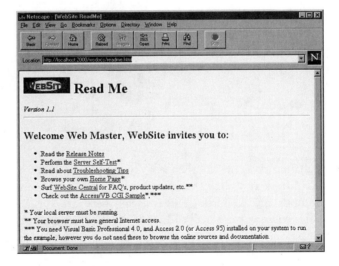

Configuring WebSite

Most aspects of WebSite can be customized using the WebSite Server application shown in Figure 7.7. The WebSite Server application can be launched by double-clicking the Web Server icon shown in Figure 7.5. The purpose of this section is to offer a brief overview of how WebSite can be configured to meet various needs. It does not cover all aspects of configuring WebSite. Instead, it demonstrates the customizability of the Web server by discussing several key configuration settings.

FIGURE 7.7.
WebSite Server application.

General Settings

The WebSite Server Properties dialog box, shown in Figure 7.8, is used to configure various aspects of WebSite. Select Control | Properties from the main menu of the WebSite application shown in Figure 7.7 to invoke the WebSite Server Properties dialog box. The WebSite Server Properties dialog box can be used to configure several key aspects of WebSite. As you can see in Figure 7.8, the default port of WebSite can be changed by specifying a port number in the Normal Port data entry field. This feature is particularly useful when running more than one Web server on the same computer. When changing the default port number (80), it is recommended that you select a port number over 1024 because port numbers below that might already be used by other Internet services. By default, WebSite is configured to run as an application. The Run Mode drop-down list can be used to configure WebSite to run as a Windows NT Service or an application. If it is configured to run as an application, the Web server will only run if a user is logged on to the NT Server. This is not desirable for a Web server. It is recommended that you use the Run Mode drop-down list and configure WebSite to run as a Windows NT Service.

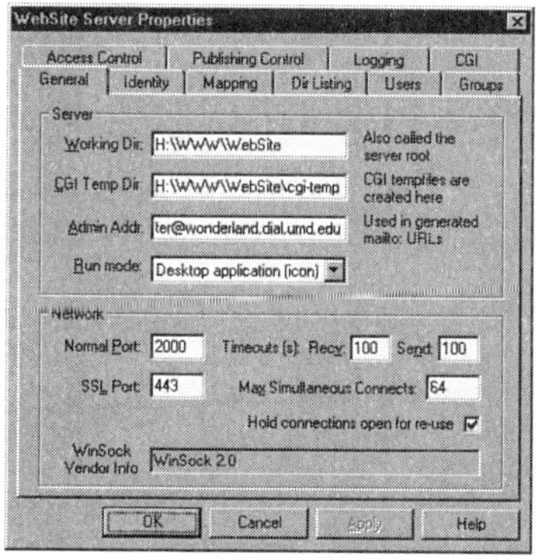

FIGURE 7.8.
The General tab of the WebSite Server Properties dialog box.

Identity Settings

The Identity tab, shown in Figure 7.9, is used to specify various Web server identity settings. By default, the Web server's Internet address will be displayed in the space provided for Server Name. The identity tab is useful to host virtual Web sites with WebSite. By clicking the Multiple Identities checkbox, it is possible to configure WebSite to act as the Web server for two or more Internet addresses (such as www.abc.com and www.123.com).

If you are using WebSite Professional, the dialog box in Figure 7.9 can also be used to generate *digital certificates* by clicking the Certs... button. After installing a digital certificate, WebSite can be used to conduct secure transactions over the Internet. Consult WebSite documentation for more information about installing digital certificates and using WebSite to conduct secure transactions over the Internet. Visit the following Web site for information about digital certificates and public key encryption.

URL

For information about digital certificates and public key encryption, try this URL.

www.verisign.com/docs/pk_intro.html

FIGURE 7.9.

The Identity tab of the WebSite Server Properties dialog box.

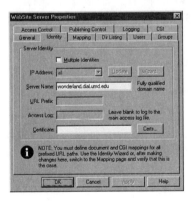

Directory Mappings

The Mapping tab of the WebSite Server Properties dialog box can be used to create several different kinds of directory mapping *aliases*. By default, only information in subdirectories of WebSite's document root directory can be published on the Internet. The dialog box shown in Figure 7.10 can be used to create directory mapping to other subdirectories. After a directory mapping is created for another directory, information in that directory can be published on the World Wide Web with WebSite.

FIGURE 7.10.

The Mapping tab of the WebSite Server Properties dialog box can be used to create directory mappings.

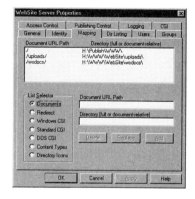

Directory Listing Settings

When a user types in a URL without a filename at the end, if the *default document* specified in Figure 7.3 is not found, a directory listing will be sent to the user. The format of this directory listing can be customized using the Dir Listing tab of the WebSite Server Properties dialog box (see Figure 7.11). This feature can be disabled by removing the checkmark from the Enable Directory Listings checkbox.

FIGURE 7.11.

The Dir Listing tab of the WebSite Server Properties dialog box is used to configure various directory listing settings.

Managing Users

WebSite supports restricting access to various parts of a Web site using a username and a password. The WebSite user database can be managed using the Users tab of the WebSite Server Properties dialog box. As shown in Figure 7.12, the user database of WebSite is similar to that of Windows NT. Just like the Windows NT user database, WebSite users can be part of various user groups.

FIGURE 7.12.

*The Users tab of the
WebSite Server Properties
dialog box is used to
manage WebSite users.*

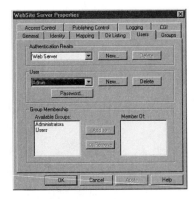

Managing Groups

WebSite user groups can be managed using the dialog box shown in Figure 7.13. The Groups tab of the WebSite Server Properties dialog box can be used to create and select Authentication Realms. Afterwards, WebSite user groups can be assigned to the Authentication Realm that was selected or created.

> **NOTE**
>
> A Realm is a set of usernames and group names associated with a directory or virtual path. Realms can be used to limit access to parts of a Web site.

FIGURE 7.13.

*The Groups tab of the
WebSite Server Properties
dialog box is used to
manage various WebSite
user groups.*

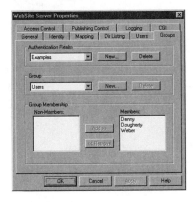

Configuring CGI

The CGI tab of the WebSite Server Properties dialog box can be used to configure how CGI scripts are executed by WebSite. The CGI settings configuration tab is shown in Figure 7.14. When entering this dialog box for the first time, WebSite warns you that any changes to made to various data entry fields can cause undesired results. Click OK to acknowledge this dialog box. If you place a checkmark on the checkbox in this dialog box, this dialog box will not be shown again. Consult WebSite documentation for customizing various CGI settings in this dialog box.

FIGURE 7.14.

The CGI tab of the WebSite Server Properties dialog box is used to configure various CGI settings.

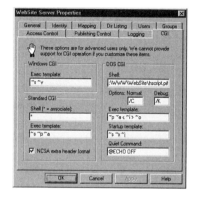

Access Logging

Access logging is an important aspect of a Web server. A Web server's access log file is the key to determining who accessed what from the Web server. As you can see in Figure 7.15, log files generated by WebSite can be extensively customized to allow Web server accesses. The Logging tab of the WebSite Server Properties dialog box can also be used to specify the format of the access log file and whether WebSite should perform DNS reverse lookups. If your Web server log analyzing program supports DNS reverse lookups, it is recommended that you turn off this feature because it will speed the time it takes WebSite to serve an HTTP request. Refer to Chapter 24, "Utility Applications for Your Server," for more information about analyzing access log files generated by Web servers. Chapter 24 demonstrates how a Web server log analyzing application can be used to perform reverse DNS lookups on IP addresses and generate graphical Web server access statistics.

FIGURE 7.15.

The Logging tab of the WebSite Server Properties dialog box is used to configure how WebSite logs HTTP requests.

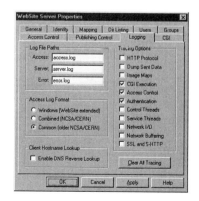

Publishing Settings

The Publishing Control tab, shown in Figure 7.16, is used to restrict access to various URLs. A URL path can be typed in by clicking the New button and users and user groups can be assigned to it using the Add button. When the Add button is pressed, users and user groups can be selected using a dialog similar to the one shown in Figure 7.17. In addition, if you are running WebSite Professional and have installed a digital certificate, the Require SSL connection checkbox can be used to make sure information is encrypted before it is transmitted.

FIGURE 7.16.

The Publishing Control tab of WebSite Server Properties dialog box can be used to restrict access to various parts of a Web site.

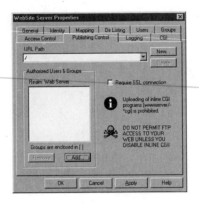

Users and groups can be selected using the Available Users & Groups dialog box shown in Figure 7.17. Note that unlike usernames, user group names are enclosed in square brackets.

FIGURE 7.17.

The Available Users & Groups dialog box.

Access Control

The Access Control tab shown in Figure 7.18 is handy for controlling various WebSite access settings. The Access Control dialog box can be used restrict access to part of a Web site, enable secure transactions, and to disable directory listings. Use the Require SSL Connection checkbox to configure WebSite to encrypt data using SSL before transmitting it by way of the Internet. Before a user can access a protected object, the user should provide a valid username and password, and should also connect from a host that is allowed to access objects served with WebSite. The logical OR users and class checkbox can be used to configure WebSite to enable a user to access a protected object if either criterion is met.

FIGURE 7.18.
WebSite security settings can be managed using the Access Control tab of the WebSite Server Properties dialog box.

WebSite Tools

A number of very powerful tools are included with WebSite. These tools make it easier to publish information on the Internet using WebSite.

MapThis! for Creating Image Maps

An image map creation tool is bundled with WebSite. It can be used to create image maps by drawing various shapes on an image as shown in Figure 7.19. After the image map is created, it can be saved in several different image map formats.

URL

MapThis! can also be downloaded from the following FTP site:

```
ftp://ftp.digital.com/pub/micro/msdos/win3/util/mpths110.zip
```

FIGURE 7.19.
Map This!, an image map creation tool bundled with WebSite, can be used to easily create image maps.

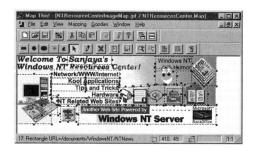

Cold Fusion for Publishing Databases

WebSite ships with a database publishing application called Cold Fusion. Cold Fusion can be used to effortlessly publish databases on the Web. Refer to Chapter 18, "Publishing Databases on the Web," for more information about using Cold Fusion to publish databases on the World Wide Web.

WebIndex for Making a Web Site Searchable

WebIndex is an application that can be used to easily make a Web site searchable in a matter of minutes. Refer to Chapter 15, "Making Your Web Site Searchable," for more information about WebIndex and how it can be used to make a Web site searchable.

WebView for Managing a Web Site

WebView is a Web site management tool that can be used to manage the contents of a Web site graphically as shown in Figure 7.20. WebView can be used to locate files to edit, graphically view how various files in a Web site are connected to each other, and invoke other WebSite tools. WebView is also handy for locating *broken links* at a Web site. WebView graphically displays the nature of various objects at a Web site. For example, broken URLs are marked with a cross, and links to external URLs are marked with a globe.

FIGURE 7.20.

WebView, a Web site management tool, can be used to easily manage the contents of a Web site.

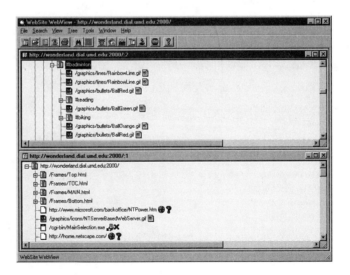

QuickStats for Web Server Statistics

Although QuickStats is not very detailed, it can be used to obtain a brief summary of Web server statistics (as shown in Figure 7.21). QuickStats can be invoked by selecting Tools | QuickStats from WebView's main menu.

FIGURE 7.21.

QuickStats can be used to obtain a brief summary of Web server statistics.

Why Choose WebSite?

There are a number of reasons for selecting WebSite over other Web servers. Some features of WebSite that are not implemented well on other Web servers are listed next. If these features are important to you, you might want to consider obtaining a copy of WebSite and setting it up at your Web site either as a *primary* (installed on port 80) or *secondary* (installed on a port greater than 1024) Web server. For example, if you are comfortable with WebSite's database features, you might want to use it for publishing databases on the Internet.

A major advantage of using WebSite is the fact that it includes several powerful Web development tools. For example, a Web site published on the Web with WebSite can be made searchable in less than five minutes using WebIndex. In addition to that, a Web site hosted with WebSite can be easily made interactive using WinCGI (the CGI development environment of WebSite) and various development tools such as Visual Basic. WebSite is also well documented and includes a comprehensive instruction manual that details all its features.

Installing and Using Purveyor Web Server

Process Software's Purveyor is another powerful and feature-rich Web server. It can be installed and used to publish information on the Internet in a matter of minutes. This section discusses various issues related to installing and using Purveyor to publish information on the Internet. Be sure to visit Process Software's Web site for the most up-to-date information about Purveyor.

URL

Visit Process Software's Web site for the most up-to-date information about Purveyor Web server:

`http://www.process.com/`

Installing Purveyor

Purveyor can be installed in a few minutes by running the file setup.exe. When setup.exe is run, the installation program asks you for your name, company name, and the Purveyor serial number. If you have not yet purchased Purveyor, you can obtain an evaluation serial number from Purveyor's Web site and use it to evaluate Purveyor. Purveyor is tightly integrated with Windows NT. The Purveyor installation program installs several File Manager and Performance Monitor extensions. Therefore, be sure to close File Manager and Performance Monitor before beginning to install Purveyor. The File Manager extensions can be used to control various aspects of Purveyor and Performance monitor extensions can be used to monitor the performance of Purveyor. There are two versions of Purveyor, the regular version and the Encrypt version. The Encrypt version has all the features of the standard version and can, in addition, be used to conduct secure transactions over the Internet.

The Purveyor installation program first presents a dialog box similar to the one shown in Figure 7.22. This dialog box can be used to specify the directory Purveyor should be installed in. After specifying a directory, click the Continue button.

FIGURE 7.22.
Selecting the destination directory of Purveyor.

The Purveyor installation program will then install Purveyor, register itself as a Windows NT Service, and display a dialog box as shown in Figure 7.23. When this dialog box displayed, although Purveyor is installed, it has not yet been started to serve HTTP requests. Click the Start button to start Purveyor. If you already have a Web server running on port 80, it is not recommended that you start Purveyor while the other Web server is running. Either stop the other Web server before Purveyor is started, or change Purveyor's default TCP/IP port as described shortly. In the latter case, click the Exit button.

FIGURE 7.23.
Purveyor NT Setup dialog box.

After Purveyor is installed, a folder similar to the one shown in Figure 7.24 will be added to the Windows NT Start menu. Icons in this folder can be used to configure various aspects of Purveyor. The Link Browser and Log Viewer applications can be used to manage a Web site published with Purveyor. You will be shown how to use these applications shortly.

FIGURE 7.24.

Purveyor applications.

As shown in Figure 7.25, the installation program adds a Purveyor icon to the Control Panel. This icon can be used to configure various aspects of Purveyor. The next section discusses how Purveyor can be configured to suit various needs by executing the Purveyor icon. Note that the Purveyor configuration application can be invoked using the Control Panel or the Windows NT Start menu.

FIGURE 7.25.

Purveyor can be configured using the Control Panel.

Customizing Purveyor

The purpose of this section is to offer a brief overview of how Purveyor can be configured to meet various needs. It does not cover all aspects of configuring Purveyor. Instead, it demonstrates the customizability of the Web server by discussing several key configuration settings. As shown in Figure 7.26, the Purveyor configuration application is broken down into several tabbed dialog boxes. The next few sections briefly discusses some of these dialog boxes.

Main Settings

The Main Settings tab can be used to configure several key configuration settings. By default, Purveyor's TCP/IP port is set to 80. The default port number can be changed using the TCP/IP Port data entry field as shown in Figure 7.26. This feature is particularly useful for running more than one Web server on the same computer. The Server Control buttons can be used to stop, start, pause, and resume the Web server. Access to certain parts of a Web site can be restricted by clicking the Access Control button, which in turn invokes the Windows NT File Manager. Purveyor adds several icons to the File Manager tool bar. These icons can be used to restrict access to part of a Web site published with Purveyor.

FIGURE 7.26.

The Main Settings tab of the Purveyor Configuration dialog box.

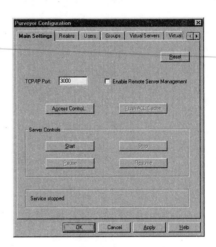

Creating Realms

A Realm is a set of usernames and group names associated with a directory or virtual path. Realms can be used to limit access to parts of a Web site. The Realms tab of the Purveyor Configuration dialog box can be used to create and delete Realms. Purveyor's user authentication system is extensible by creating DLLs to record user and group database information. An external DLL can be specified by clicking the Use External Authentication DLL checkbox shown in Figure 7.27 and providing the full pathname of the DLL. Refer to Purveyor documentation for more information about creating External Authentication DLLs.

Managing Users

The Users tab of the Purveyor Configuration dialog box can be used to manage users. As shown in Figure 7.28, the Users tab can be used to insert, edit, and delete users. Users created with this tab can be assigned to various groups using the tab shown in Figure 7.29. Access to various parts of a Web site can then be restricted by users and user groups.

FIGURE 7.27.

The Realms tab of the Purveyor Configuration dialog box.

FIGURE 7.28.

The Users tab of the Purveyor Configuration dialog box.

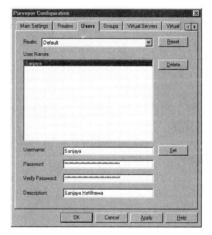

Managing Groups

Purveyor user groups can be managed using the Groups tab of the Purveyor Configuration dialog box. As shown in Figure 7.29, this dialog box can be used to create, edit, and delete user groups. Groups created with this dialog box fall under various Realms created in the dialog box shown in Figure 7.27. After a group is created, users can be added to the group by selecting them and clicking the Add button. After Realms, users, and user groups are created, the Purveyor | Edit Access control can be selected from the File Manager main menu to restrict access to parts of a Web site with a username and a password. Note that a Purveyor menu option is added to File Manager's tool bar by the Purveyor installation program.

FIGURE 7.29.

The Groups tab of the Purveyor Configuration dialog box.

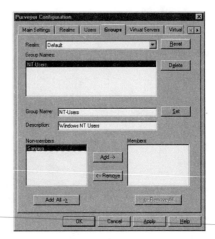

Managing Virtual Servers

The Virtual Servers tab can be used to configure Purveyor to host Web sites for several Internet domain names. As shown in Figure 7.30, this tab can be used to specify a host name and assign it a document root directory, and to specify a default filename. Directory browsing and CGI settings of virtual servers can also be configured using the Virtual Servers tab. Refer to Purveyor documentation for more information about managing virtual servers.

FIGURE 7.30.

The Virtual Servers tab of the Purveyor Configuration dialog box.

Creating Virtual Paths

Virtual Paths are aliases to various directories. Virtual paths can be used to create directory mapping to directories that are not part of the Web server's document root, as shown in Figure 7.31. In this case, a virtual path is created to a user's FTP directory. Virtual paths can also be used to shorten long URL names.

FIGURE 7.31.
Creating virtual paths.

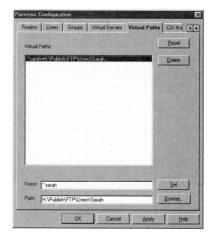

Creating CGI Extension Mappings

The CGI Mapping tab, shown in Figure 7.32, is useful for associating file extensions with various programs. This feature is handy for using CGI scripts that need to be interpreted by another program. For example, the CGI mapping example in Figure 7.32 demonstrates how the .pl extension is mapped to the PERL interpreter. After this is done, PERL scripts can be executed by simply using the PERL script name without giving out the location of PERL.EXE. If you use PERL scripts at your Web site, it is recommended that you create CGI extension mappings for them. CGI extension mappings can be used to avoid security breaches related to users abusing PERL for malicious intent. Users with malicious intent can hack PERL and execute various commands by passing complex arguments into PERL.EXE.

FIGURE 7.32.
Creating CGI extension mappings.

Access Logging

The tab in Figure 7.33 can be used to log Web server accesses. Access logging is an important part of any Web server, and Purveyor supports several powerful access logging features. Purveyor can be configured to log only specific Web server accesses. For example, it is possible to exclude Web server accesses from certain IP addresses. It is also possible to use the Create New Log File pull-down list to configure Purveyor to create a new access log file every hour, day, week, month, or year. It is recommended that the Web server access log file be configured so that a new log file is created each week.

FIGURE 7.33.

Logging Web server accesses.

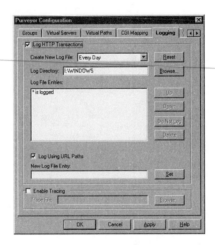

Logging Templates

The Logging Templates feature can be used to further customize Web server access log files. The tab shown in Figure 7.34 can be used to specify the log file format of the access log file and also various parameters that should be included in it.

Proxy Support

The tab in Figure 7.35 can be used to configure Purveyor to function as a Proxy server. This is a powerful and unique feature of Purveyor. A Proxy server is typically set up at a firewall between a local Intranet and the global Internet. Purveyor provides Proxy services for HTTP, FTP, and Gopher. As shown in Figure 7.35, Purveyor can be configured so that only certain IP addresses can use HTTP, FTP, and Gopher services provided by the Purveyor Proxy server.

NOTE

Purveyor can be configured to function as an HTTP, FTP, and Gopher Proxy server.

FIGURE 7.34.
Access logging templates.

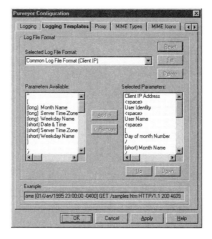

FIGURE 7.35.
Configuring a Proxy server.

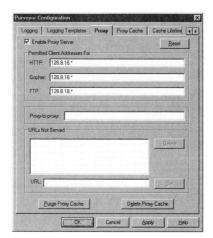

MIME Types

The MIME Types tab, shown in Figure 7.36, is handy for creating and editing various MIME types. MIME types are used by clients connecting to a Web server to determine the type of various objects transmitted by the Web server.

Purveyor Tools

Purveyor includes a number of useful tools that can be used to manage a Web site. Some of these tools are discussed next.

FIGURE 7.36.
Specifying MIME types.

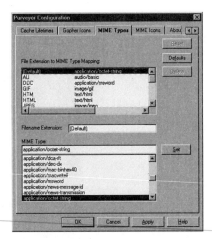

Verity Topic Search Engine

Purveyor is shipped with the Verity Topic search engine. Although it is powerful, the Verity Topic search engine is not as easy to use as the search engine supplied with WebSite because it isn't GUI oriented. However, the Verity Topic search engine is more powerful than the one supplied with WebSite and is highly customizable—although it might take you a while to learn how to use it. Refer to Chapter 15, "Making Your Web Site Searchable," for more information about how the Verity Topic search engine can be used to make a Web site searchable.

Link Browser

Link Browser is a handy application for finding and repairing broken links at a Web site. As shown in Figure 7.37, Link Browser displays graphically how Web pages at a Web site are connected to each other.

Log Viewer

Log Viewer can be used to analyze Web server access log files generated by Purveyor. As shown in Figure 7.38, Log Viewer is ideal for viewing the contents of a log file. The Report and Query menus of Log Viewer can be used to analyze Web server access log files and obtain various statistics about the log files being viewed.

Database Wizard

The Database Wizard can be used to easily publish databases on the Web using Purveyor. Any ODBC-compliant database can be published on the Web with Database Wizard. Refer to Chapter 18, "Publishing Databases on the Web," for more information about how Database Wizard can be used to publish databases on the Web.

FIGURE 7.37.

Link Browser.

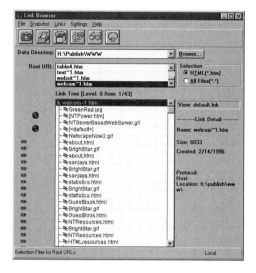

FIGURE 7.38.

Log Viewer.

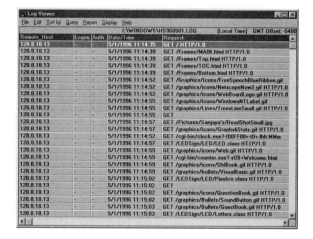

Why Choose Purveyor?

Purveyor is a powerful Web server that can be used to publish information on the Web easily. Its ease of use complements its powerful features. Purveyor also includes a Proxy server. Therefore, in addition to serving HTTP requests, Purveyor can also be used to provide HTTP, FTP, and Gopher Proxy services to users on your LAN.

Purveyor supports ISAPI, which is a powerful CGI programming interface developed jointly by Microsoft and Purveyor. ISAPI does not have some of the drawbacks of CGI because ISAPI applications, unlike CGI applications, are loaded to memory only once.

Purveyor is shipped with several powerful Web publishing tools such as the Database Wizard, Verity Topic search engine, Log Viewer, and Link Browser. These tools compliment Purveyor's advanced features and make it an ideal Web server solution.

Installing and Using Netscape Web Server

The Netscape server is one of the oldest servers available for Windows NT. As this book goes to print, a new line of Netscape servers is being developed by Netscape. This section is based on Netscape Enterprise Server that should be released by the time you read this. Among other features, the Netscape Enterprise Server includes SSL 3.0, client-side certificates, MKS Revision control, WYSIWYG Web page editing through Netscape Gold, Verity search engine, and advanced access control. If you are familiar with Java or JavaScript, the Netscape Enterprise Server supports Java and JavaScript applications.

The Netscape Enterprise Server is part of a suite of new Netscape servers that provide search, mail, news, proxy, and advanced scripting services. If you do not need the advanced capabilities of the Netscape Enterprise Server, such as SNMP management, Revision Control, integrated Verity full text search engine, and database connectivity, you might want to consider the less expensive FastTrack Server. Visit *Netscape Server Central* for the most up-to-date information about various Netscape servers.

URL

Try the URL for Netscape Server Central:

```
http://home.netscape.com/comprod/server_central/index.html
```

Installing Netscape

The Netscape Enterprise Server can be downloaded from Netscape's Web site. After downloading it, copy it to a temporary directory and execute the distribution file. You will then see a dialog box similar to the one shown in Figure 7.39. This dialog box is used to specify the target directory of the Netscape Enterprise Server.

After clicking the Next button, the Server Setup application displays your Internet address. If the address displayed is correct, click the Next button. If not, correct it and press the Next button. You will then be presented with a dialog box that can be used to select an administration username and a password. This username and password will be used later to configure the Netscape server. After typing in a username and a password, as shown in Figure 7.40, click the Next button.

FIGURE 7.39.

The target directory selection dialog box.

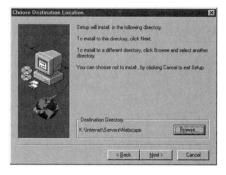

FIGURE 7.40.

The administration username and password selection dialog box.

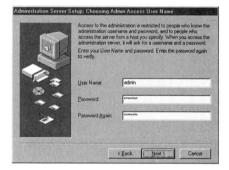

The Netscape Enterprise Server is administered using Netscape Navigator. As you'll see shortly, this is done by connecting to a certain port on your computer. The dialog box in Figure 7.41 can be used to select this port. By default, the installation program randomly picks a port that is not being used. If you wish, you may pick a port number over 1024 that's easier to remember, as shown in Figure 7.41.

FIGURE 7.41.

Choosing an administration port.

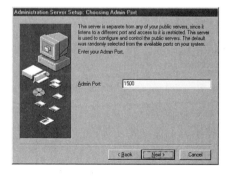

The Netscape server administration program runs as a certain Windows NT user that can be specified using the next dialog box. If you would like to use the default local system user account, simply click the Next button. Otherwise, select a different user and click the Next button. The next two dialog boxes can be used to select the Web server's document root directory and its port. The document root directory does not have to be a child of the Netscape server directory. By default, Netscape server listens on port 80 for incoming HTTP requests. If you would like to use the Netscape server as a secondary server, enter a different port, as shown in Figure 7.42.

FIGURE 7.42.

Changing the default port of Netscape server.

Configuring Netscape

Netscape Enterprise Server is configured using Netscape Navigator. This is a useful feature, especially if you need to administer the Netscape server remotely over the Internet. After installing the Netscape server, connect to it using the port specified in Figure 7.41. For example, if the server's Internet address is `your.server.com` and the administration port specified in Figure 7.41 is `1500`, the server can be administered using the URL `http://your.server.com:1500/`. When first connecting to the administration server, you will be asked for a username and a password as shown in Figure 7.43. Note the how the dialog box displays the server address and the port number of the administration server.

> **NOTE**
>
> The Netscape Enterprise Server can be remotely configured using Netscape Navigator. This feature is particularly useful if you do not always have ready access to the NT machine running Netscape Enterprise Server.

FIGURE 7.43.

Validating the administration username and password.

After the administrator username and password are validated, a Web page similar to the one shown in Figure 7.44 will be displayed. This Web page can be used to administer the *administration server* as well as the *public Web server.* The Administration Server is used to administer various aspects of the administration server as well as the public server. The public server is used to distribute information on the Internet. The Install a new Netscape Enterprise Server button can be used to install a new server. The Remove a server from this machine button can be used to remove an exsiting server installation. The Configure Administration button is used to configure various aspects of the administration server. The Netscape Administration Server can be configured so that only users connecting from trusted domains can connect to the administration server and make changes to the Netscape Server configuration.

> **NOTE**
>
> The Netscape Administration Server can be configured to allow only users from trusted domains to administer the Netscape Server.

FIGURE 7.44.

Netscape Administration Server Web page.

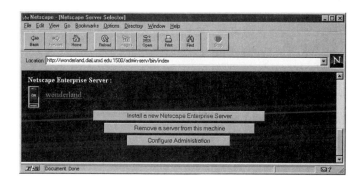

Installing a New Server

As described earlier, a new Netscape server can be installed on a different port by clicking on the Install a new Netscape Enterprise Server button. When this button is pressed, a Web page similar to the one shown in Figure 7.45 will be displayed. This Web page can be used to specify various settings of the new server, including its identifier name and port number.

Configuring Administration Server

Default settings of the administration server can be changed by clicking on the Configure Administration button in the Web page shown in Figure 7.44. Once this button is pressed, the Web page shown in Figure 7.46 can be used to configure various aspects of the administration server. This Web page is particularly useful for controlling which computers can connect to the administration server. In addition, SSL can be enabled to make sure an unauthorized person does not take control of the Netscape server using an intercepted username and password.

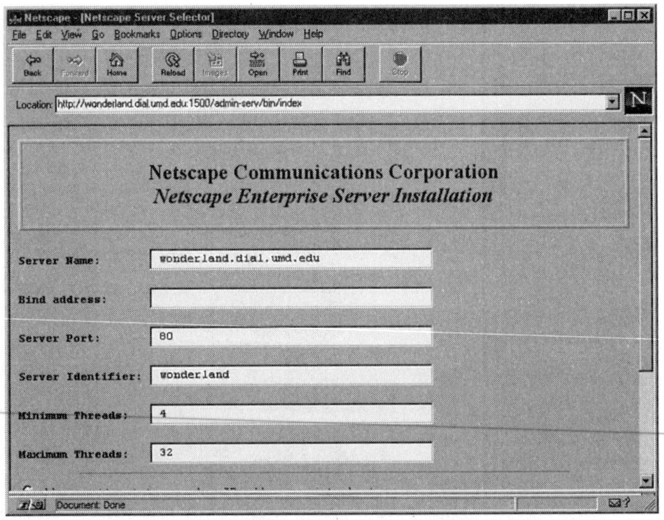

FIGURE 7.45.

New server installation Web page.

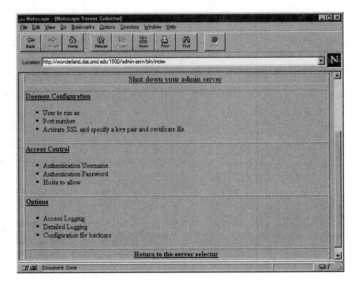

FIGURE 7.46.

Administration server configuration page.

Configuring Enterprise Server

The Enterprise Server configuration Web page, shown in Figure 7.47, can be used to administer all aspects of a Netscape Enterprise Server. This Web page can be invoked by selecting a server from the list of servers shown previously in Figure 7.44. The Server Manager will then display the server configuration page for the selected server. This Web page can be used to start and stop the selected Netscape server. As you can see in Figure 7.47, the Enterprise Server configuration Web page is highly customizable. It uses frames to display various server settings and makes it easier to select various configuration options. The next few sections discuss a few useful Netscape server configuration Web pages to demonstrate how the Netscape server can be customized to suit various needs. Consult Netscape server documentation for additional server configuration information.

FIGURE 7.47.

Enterprise Server configuration Web page.

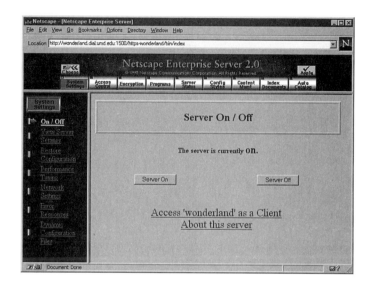

Configuring Server Settings

The Web page shown in Figure 7.48 can be used to customize several key settings of the Netscape Enterprise Server. This Web page can be used to view various server settings and make modifications to them. A setting displayed on this Web page can be modified by clicking it with the mouse.

FIGURE 7.48.

Configuring server settings.

Performance Tuning Enterprise Server

The System Setting option of the main menu can be used to fine tune the Netscape server for performance. The Web page shown in Figure 7.49 can be used to increase performance by caching DNS entries. The DNS caching feature used by the Netscape server enhances performance by remembering DNS lookups and not performing a DNS lookup for a certain client several times unnecessarily. The values shown in Figure 7.49 can be used to increase the performance of a high-traffic Web site hosted with the Netscape server.

FIGURE 7.49.

Performance tuning Web page.

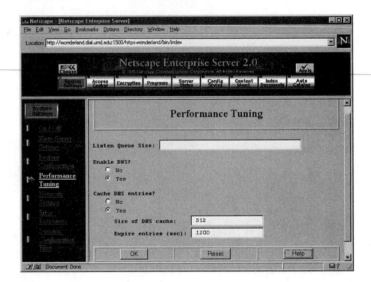

Customizing Error Responses

Usually, if an error occurs when processing an HTTP request, the Web server displays a rather crude and unfriendly error message. The Web page in Figure 7.50 can be used to create customized Web pages for various error conditions. Rather than assigning HTML files for various error conditions, it is also possible to execute a CGI script and display its output. This is a very powerful feature. For example, a CGI program can not only display an error message, but keep track of the number of unauthorized accesses made by a user. The CGI script can then either send an e-mail message or page the Webmaster—with all the details—if a user is attempting to breach the security of the Web server.

Creating Users

The Access Control menu option can be used to restrict access to parts of a Web site with a username and a password. After users are created, access to certain areas of a Web site can be restricted with a username and password by using a Web page similar to the one in Figure 7.51.

FIGURE 7.50.
Customizing error responses.

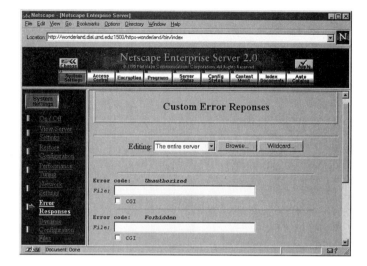

FIGURE 7.51.
Creating users.

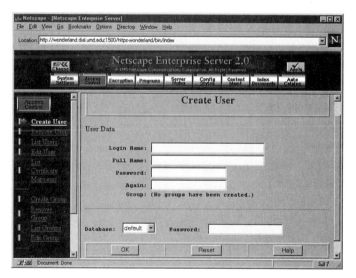

Enabling Encryption

The encryption menu option can be used to configure Netscape to encrypt information before it is sent over the Internet. By installing a digital certificate and enabling Encryption, the Netscape server can be used to carry out secure transactions over the Internet using the Web page shown in Figure 7.52.

URL

This is the URL for the Verisign Web site:

`http://www.verisign.com`

FIGURE 7.52.
Encryption settings Web page.

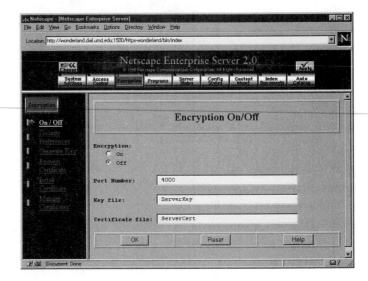

Generating Server Statistics

The Netscape server includes several utilities that can be used to manipulate and analyze Web server access log files. The Web page in Figure 7.53 demonstrates how the Netscape server administration program can be used to view the access log file of the Web server.

Why Choose Netscape?

The Netscape Server has been gone through several years of development and has been optimized for performance. This makes Netscape an ideal Web server solution for a high-traffic Web site. In addition to its high performance, as demonstrated earlier, the Netscape server is also highly customizable. The fact that Netscape Navigator can be used to administer all aspects of the Web server from anywhere on the Internet complements its customizability.

Netscape is ideal for developing custom Web applications because it supports Java, JavaScript, and LiveScript. These scripting languages can be used to create customized Web pages and leverage capabilities of Java and JavaScript to server-side Web applications.

Netscape also includes several tools that can be used to easily enhance the capabilities of a Web site. For example, the built-in search engine can be used to make a Web site searchable in a matter of minutes. Refer to Chapter 15, "Making Your Web Site Searchable," for more information about how the Verity Topic search engine, which is included with Netscape Enterprise Server, can be used to make a Web site searchable.

The Netscape Server is a feature rich, powerful, and highly customizable Web server that is ideal for hosting high-traffic Web sites.

FIGURE 7.53.
Server statistics Web page.

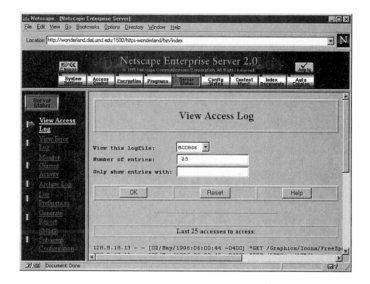

Choosing the Right Web Server

Regardless of what various Web server vendors claim, there is no single *right* Web server that is ideal for all purposes. Each Web server has its own strengths and weaknesses, just as each reader who reads this chapter has different needs and expectations. A few things you might want to consider when selecting a Web server follow:

- Performance
- Security
- Ease of use and administration
- Customizability
- Database publishing tools
- Support for server-side scripting languages
- Availability of a search engine
- Web site management tools
- Remote administration
- Support for ISAPI and WinCGI
- Cost

Both WebSite and Purveyor are easy to use and are shipped with several Windows-based Web site development tools. Select either of these Web servers if you are looking for an easy-to-use Web server that uses familiar Windows dialog boxes to administer and customize various aspects of the server.

On the other hand, the Netscape server offers remote Web server administration through the Netscape Navigator. This is a useful feature because the Netscape server can be administered from anywhere on the Internet using either a Windows-, Macintosh-, or UNIX-based workstation. Generally, if you will be managing a large Web site, the Netscape server is a better solution because it is part of a larger suite of Netscape Internet servers. The Netscape server has been in development for a relatively long period of time and has been optimized for performance. At the time of this writing, the Netscape server does not support ISAPI. This is a drawback if you wish to develop ISAPI applications to customize your Web site. As mentioned earlier, however, because it is possible to install Web servers on different ports, it is possible to mix and match features of various Web servers.

The previous sections provided a brief overview of three feature-rich and widely used Web servers that are available for Windows NT. The best way to select the right Web server for you is to download a trial version of a server and try it out. All Web servers discussed in this chapter offer extended trial periods. You can then put the Web server into use and decide if you are comfortable with its features and capabilities.

Summary

Choosing the right Web server is an important aspect of setting up your Web site. In the past, Web servers did few other tasks besides serving HTTP requests. This trend, however, is changing. Web servers are increasingly being equipped with powerful new features that can be used to effortlessly publish information on the Internet. Some of these features include database publishing wizards, built-in search engines, and various site management tools.

What's Next

Security is an important aspect of any Internet server. Windows NT is a modern operating system that is built with security in mind. Most of these security countermeasures, however, are of little use if they are not used. The next chapter discusses various issues that relate to securing an Internet-connected server against unauthorized access.

8

Security Considerations

Security is an important aspect of any Internet server. When you're publishing information on the Internet, you should be aware of various security threats and take precautions to guard against them. In this chapter, you examine various ways of making your Internet server more secure. Note that this chapter does not cover security issues related to all Internet information distribution applications discussed in this book. Security issues specific to various applications are covered in their respective chapters. Chapter 15, "Making Your Web Site Searchable," for example, includes a section on preventing unauthorized changes to the search engine. The purpose of this chapter is to provide an overview of various steps that you can take to make an NT server on the Internet more secure. Note the expression "more secure." Security risks are always associated with connecting a server to the Internet. The possible threat to security does not mean that you should not set up a server on the Internet. You simply should take whatever precautions necessary to make it harder and more expensive for someone to try to break into your system.

The first few sections of this chapter are devoted to discussing various security countermeasures that you can implement to secure an NT server on the Internet. The last major section is devoted to various Internet security resources on the Internet. You should visit Web sites listed here to obtain the most up-to-date information about Internet security.

Disabling the Windows NT Guest Account

If you have not done so already, disable the Windows NT guest account. Anyone can use this account to gain access to your system. If you have an FTP server set up at your site, this account can be especially dangerous because a user with malicious intent can potentially destroy information on your system using this account.

Using NTFS Security and Disk Partitions

Devoting an entire disk partition for Internet publishing is recommended if you can afford to do so. This partition should contain not only the FTP and Web server document root directories but also binary files of various Internet services. This setup makes it easier for you to control access to various directory structures and manage security. If you follow this advice, you can use NTFS security to restrict access to all other disk partitions. Using NTFS partitions exclusively is highly recommended. As shown in Figure 8.1, access to files and directories in an NTFS partition can be restricted to only certain users and user groups. Figure 8.1 demonstrates how you can revoke access to a certain directory from the Internet guest account (the account used by Internet Information Server) and assign it to the Administrators group, a certain user, and the System user.

FIGURE 8.1.

You can restrict access to files and directories in NTFS partitions by using the File Manager.

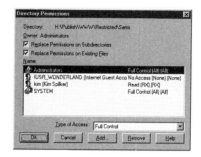

Controlling Directory Browsing

Directory browsing is a feature available in most Web servers. A URL typically contains a directory and a filename. If a user types in a URL without a filename at the end of it, a listing of files in the directory is sent to the user, if the "default document" (usually, `index.html`) is not present in that directory. Look at Figure 8.2 for an example of how a user can use the directory browsing feature to obtain a list of files and directories in a directory.

FIGURE 8.2.

Listing of files and directories when directory browsing is turned on.

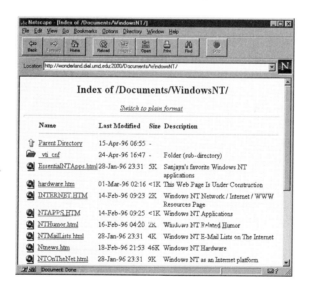

Depending on the structure and nature of information at your Web site, this capability has advantages as well as disadvantages. If your Web site is an *open* Web site and you want to share as much information as possible, enable directory browsing. If your Web site contains information that should be accessed in a particular order, however, disable directory browsing. You can, for example, distribute software using a Web server. All the applications distributed through the Web server can be in a certain directory. For record keeping and statistical analysis purposes, you might want to make sure that users fill in a form and submit it before they are given permission to download various applications. If directory browsing is enabled, a technically inclined user might figure out how to skip registering by typing in the name of the directory in which the applications are located and downloading all the applications in that directory.

Note that a middle ground also exists. You can disable directory browsing only on certain directories. For these directories, simply create a "default document" (usually, index.html) Web page and copy it to directories in which you want to disable directory browsing. Your Web server might allow you to disable directory browsing on certain directories using a special menu or configuration file. Refer to your Web server documentation for more information.

Controlling Access to CGI Directories

Controlling access to the CGI directory of your Web server is very important. Only trusted users should have access to this directory. Any user who has access to the CGI directory of a Web server can easily execute programs on your Web server using a Web browser. For this reason, never allow any user to have access to the CGI directory via FTP. FTP uses clear text usernames and passwords. Therefore, someone who has access to part of your local network or the part of the Internet over which the authentication data is transmitted can monitor FTP transactions with a simple protocol analyzer. A protocol analyzer can be used to obtain usernames and passwords of users authorized to access your system. An unauthorized user, possibly with malicious intent, can then access your system via FTP, pretending to be an authorized user, and execute any application on your system by copying it to the CGI directory.

Enabling Auditing

Use resource auditing capabilities of Windows NT to monitor critical resources of your Internet server. From the User Manager's main menu, select Policies | Audit. The Audit Policy dialog box that appears can be used to turn on auditing (see Figure 8.3).

FIGURE 8.3.
You can audit various system resources by using User Manager.

After you enable auditing with User Manager, select a directory and then choose Security | Auditing from the File Manager main menu. The Directory Auditing dialog box in Figure 8.4 then appears. Use the options in this dialog box to audit critical areas of your Internet server.

FIGURE 8.4.

The Directory Auditing dialog box.

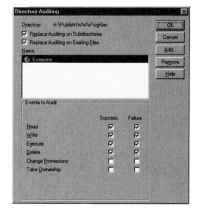

You can use the Event Detail dialog box in Figure 8.5 to monitor possible breaches of security. The event in this figure was logged as a result of an unsuccessful login attempt.

FIGURE 8.5.

Unsuccessful login attempt recorded.

CAUTION

Be careful when auditing various system resources. Do not get carried away and audit too many activities because they clutter your Event Log and slow down your system. Limiting auditing to access failures is generally a good ideal. Otherwise, the Event Log becomes cluttered with too many events, making it virtually impossible for you to locate critical information.

Allowing FTP Access to Your Web Site

You can use FTP to allow users to upload contents to your Web site. When you allow users to FTP to your server, take the time to make sure that your users are aware that anything they upload to the Web server via FTP can be viewed by someone eavesdropping on the network connection. If users upload sensitive material to your server via FTP, make them use a powerful data encryption mechanism such as Pretty Good Privacy (PGP). Visit the following Web site for information about PGP.

URL

Yahoo!'s PGP information Web page:

```
http://www.yahoo.com/Computers_and_Internet/Security_and_Encryption/
PGP___Pretty_Good_Privacy/
```

Monitoring Event Viewer

You should also take the time to monitor Event Viewer entries periodically to detect any suspicious activities. The Event Log contains valuable information that should be monitored. Devoting some time, at least once every few days, to go over the Event Log looking for any suspicious activities is a good idea. Refer to Figure 8.6 for a typical Event Viewer listing.

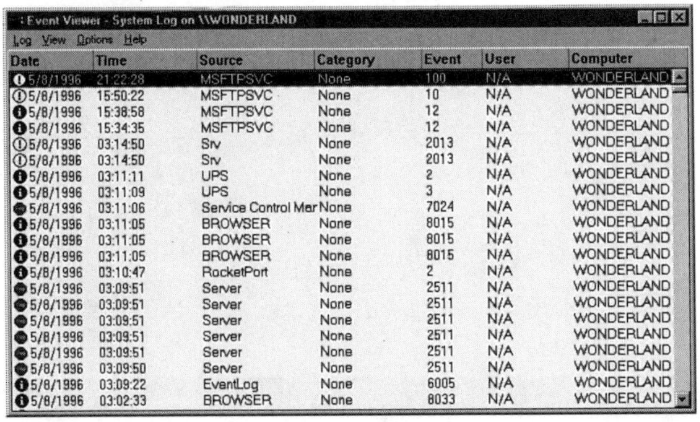

FIGURE 8.6.

An Event Viewer listing.

You can obtain additional information about various events displayed in the Event Viewer by selecting an event and double-clicking it. The dialog box in Figure 8.7 is invoked by double-clicking the event selected in Figure 8.6.

FIGURE 8.7.

Detailed information about an event displayed in the Event Viewer.

Monitoring Access Log Files

If you detect suspicious activity, monitoring access log files is a good idea. Log files can easily be several megabytes is size. Manually going over access log files, therefore, is not a very good idea. If you detect repeated suspicious activity, however, you can use the access log file to obtain additional information. If several messages appear in the Event Log, similar to the one shown in Figure 8.7, for example, you can use the access log file to obtain additional information such as the IP address of the user who tried to access the system. Figure 8.8 demonstrates how the access log file can be used to obtain detailed information about the event in Figure 8.7. In this example, the time and date of the event in Figure 8.7 are used as an index to locate the corresponding access log file entry. Refer to your Web or FTP documentation and configuration settings for the location of the access log file.

FIGURE 8.8.

You can use access log files to obtain detailed information about various suspicious activities.

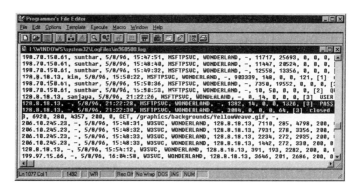

Hiding PERL.EXE

Perl is a powerful language that you can use for a variety of purposes. It is particularly suitable for creating CGI applications to process user input. However, do not place PERL.EXE in your CGI directory. A user with malicious intent can potentially use PERL.EXE to execute commands on your NT Server. Rather than place PERL.EXE in your CGI directory, create a CGI extension mapping and place PERL.EXE in a directory that's not accessible via your Web server. Refer to your Web server documentation for information about creating CGI extension mappings.

Publishing Sensitive Information

Sensitive information should never be distributed with a Web server unless the data is encrypted before it is transmitted via the Internet. Note that although you can restrict access to parts of a Web site by IP address, users can spoof IP addresses. Therefore, you should never use IP addresses to restrict access to sensitive information. The same goes for basic user authentication. Unless Windows NT challenge/response user authentication is used, someone monitoring connections to your Web server can easily intercept usernames and passwords of authorized users, and then can use them to gain unauthorized access to your system.

Enabling Encryption on the Web Server

If you use your Web server to conduct sensitive transactions over the Internet, enable encryption on your Web server to make it virtually impossible for someone to monitor your Web server traffic. Although a user who has a great deal of processing power can still monitor HTTP transactions to and from your server, doing so is prohibitively expensive. The purpose of enabling encryption is to make monitoring Web server traffic that is encrypted with a mechanism such as SSL too expensive.

Using Windows NT Challenge/Response User Authentication

If you are hosting your Web site with MS Internet Information Server, you can use Windows NT challenge/response user authentication to make sure that usernames and passwords are encrypted before they are transmitted over the Internet. Although doing so improves security, you have a trade-off. At the time of this writing, only Internet Explorer supports Windows NT challenge/response user authentication. Use this method of user authentication to improve security if you are certain all your users use Internet Explorer. Note that Windows NT challenge/response user authentication does not encrypt information transmitted via the Internet; it encrypts only usernames and passwords.

Simulating Unauthorized Break-Ins

You also would be wise to test the security of your NT system by trying to gain unauthorized access to it. You can do so with the aid of various administrative tools. Visit the following Web site for information about a utility that can be used to find weak passwords on NT systems. You can use such a utility to make sure that poor passwords chosen by your users do not compromise the security of your system by detecting them before a potential breach of security occurs.

URL

ScanNT (Password cracker for Windows NT):

```
http://www.omna.com/yes/AndyBaron/pk.htm
```

Using Internet Security Resources on the Internet

Many Internet security resources are available on the Internet. You should visit the Web sites listed in the following sections to learn more about Internet security and various ways of protecting an Internet server against unauthorized access. Monitor these Web sites for the most up-to-date information related to Internet security.

The World Wide Web Security FAQ

The World Wide Web Security FAQ contains many Internet security resources. Visit it to find information about various common security holes and how to protect your system from unauthorized accesses.

URL

World Wide Web Security FAQ:

```
http://www-genome.wi.mit.edu/WWW/faqs/www-security-faq.html
```

Information Security Web Site

Visit the Information Security Web site for news articles related to information about data security and Internet Web security.

URL

Information Security Web site:

```
http://www.newspage.com/NEWSPAGE/cgi-bin/walk.cgi/NEWSPAGE/info/d2/d10/
```

Almost Everything You Ever Wanted to Know...

Visit the "Almost Everything" Web site to learn about various Internet security topics. Although some topics discussed apply only to UNIX systems, reading about them will give you a thorough understanding of some of the issues related to Internet security.

URL

"Almost everything you ever wanted to know about security (but were afraid to ask!)" Web page:

`http://www.cis.ohio-state.edu/hypertext/faq/usenet/security-faq/faq.html`

Yahoo!'s Internet Security and Encryption Web Page

Yahoo!'s Internet Security and Encryption Web page lists numerous Internet security Web pages. Visit it often for the most up-to-date information related to Internet security and encryption.

URL

Yahoo!'s Internet Security and Encryption Web page:

`http://www.yahoo.com/Computers_and_Internet/Security_and_Encryption/`

NT Web Server Security Issues

The following Web site lists many useful suggestions for securing an NT Web server on the Internet. Visit it to learn about various security precautions that you can take to prevent unauthorized access to an NT Web server.

URL

NT Web Server security issues:

`http://www.telemark.net/~randallg/ntsecure.htm`

NT FTP Server Security Issues

If you need help setting up the Windows NT FTP server and securing it to prevent unauthorized access to your system, visit the following Web page. It contains information about Windows NT FTP server security issues.

URL

NT FTP Server security issues:

`http://mushin.wes.army.mil/ntpermit.htm`

Summary

You can take several steps to protect an NT server on the Internet against unauthorized access. Although setting up an Internet server that is immune to unauthorized access is virtually impossible, you can take steps to make access harder and, in some cases, prohibitively expensive for someone to gain unauthorized access.

What's Next?

To make a Web site more interesting to navigate, you can utilize a number of advanced HTML techniques. You can use tables, for example, to format various objects of a Web page such as text, video clips, Java applets, and so on. You also can use frames to make navigating a Web site easier. The next chapter demonstrates how you can use various advanced HTML techniques to create attractive Web pages.

IV

Designing Your Web Site

9

Advanced HTML Techniques

As mentioned in the introduction, the purpose of this book is not to provide a comprehensive overview of various HTML tags. However, a few relatively new and useful HTML tags are discussed in the following sections. You can use these HTML tags to make a Web site easier and more interesting to navigate. An increasingly large amount of applications are being developed to create content for the World Wide Web in a WYSIWYG environment that utilizes various advanced HTML tags. However, knowing how these tags work comes in handy when it's necessary to fine-tune the HTML code. The advanced HTML tips and techniques presented shortly will help you make your Web site easier and more interesting to browse by formatting its contents in an attractive manner. Refer to *Teach Yourself Web Publishing with HTML 3, Premier Edition,* by Laura Lemay, Sams.net Publishing (1-57521-014-2), for additional information about various HTML 3.0 tags.

Tables

Tables are very helpful for formatting the contents of a Web page. You can place various objects such as graphics, video clips, text, and Java applets in a certain part of a Web page by using tables. Many Web sites use tables to organize the contents of a Web page and make maximum use of Web browser space. In the next few sections, you learn how easy it is to use tables to format the contents of a Web site and to control where objects appear in a Web page.

The syntax of the HTML tag used to create tables is very simple. Listed next are descriptions of various HTML tags you can use to create and customize tables. At the time of this writing, the HTML 3.0 standard was not yet implemented on all Web browsers. However, Netscape Navigator and Internet Explorer are two of the most widely used Web browsers on the Internet, and they both support most proposed HTML 3.0 tags. The following sections list HTML tags you can use to create tables. These tags are compatible with both Internet Explorer and Netscape Navigator, with the exception of a few HTML tags.

> **NOTE**
>
> If you'd like to experiment with them, you can find the HTML examples listed next on the CD-ROM (\Chapter-09) that accompanies this book.

Table Data Containers

The following HTML tags act as containers for table data. Text and other objects placed within these data containers appear inside the table. After table containers are discussed, the next section shows you how to change their attributes.

The `<TABLE>` `</TABLE>` Tag

```
<TABLE>
… contents of the table…
  <TABLE>
    … contents of embedded table…
  </TABLE>
</TABLE>
```

The `<TABLE>` `</TABLE>` tag is used to define a table. All contents of a table should appear inside the two HTML tags `<TABLE>` and `</TABLE>`. Note that it's possible to have one table embedded inside another table. Contents of objects contained in a table are left aligned by default.

The `<TR>` `</TR>` Tag

```
<TR>
  … contents of a table row
</TR>
```

You can create table rows with the two HTML tags `<TR>` and `</TR>`. Contents of objects contained in a row are left aligned by default.

The `<TD>` `</TD>` Tag

```
<TD> table data </TD>
<TD> table data </TD>
```

Table data is enclosed within the two HTML tags `<TD>` and `</TD>`. Objects inside the table data tag are left aligned by default.

The `<TH>` `</TH>` Tag

```
<TH>table header data</TH>
<TH>table header data</TH>
```

This tag is used to define table headers. Text defined in between the two HTML tags `<TH>` and `</TH>` are identical to text defined between the two HTML tags `<TD>` and `</TD>`. The only difference is the fact that text defined within table header tags appears in bold and is centered by default.

The `<CAPTION>` `</CAPTION>` Tag

```
<CAPTION>table caption</CAPTION>
```

The caption of a table can be defined with the two HTML tags `<CAPTION>` and `</CAPTION>`. By default, table captions appear horizontally centered, on top of a table. Table captions can be formatted as follows. Note that `<ALIGN>` and `<VALIGN>` can be used together.

<CAPTION ALIGN=LEFT>—Displays caption left aligned.

<CAPTION ALIGN=CENTER>—Displays caption centered between the left and right borders of a table.

<CAPTION ALIGN=RIGHT>—Displays caption right aligned.

<CAPTION VALIGN=TOP>—Displays caption above the table.

<CAPTION VALIGN=BOTTOM>—Displays caption below the table.

Note that Netscape Navigator handles caption alignment differently. Use <CAPTION ALIGN=TOP> to display a caption on top of a table, and use <CAPTION ALIGN=BOTTOM> to display a caption below a table in Netscape Navigator. Netscape does support VALIGN inside table cells, just not inside captions.

Using Table Data Containers

The following example shows how the HTML tags discussed earlier can be used to create a table with data. The HTML code of the table shown in Figure 9.1 is listed next.

```
<HTML>
<HEAD><TITLE>HTML Table Demonstration</TITLE>
</HEAD>
<BODY BGCOLOR="#FFFFFF" TEXT="#000000"
LINK="#0000FF" VLINK="#FF7500" ALINK="#FF4B9A">

<TABLE BORDER=1>
<CAPTION ALIGN=TOP>Caption of table</CAPTION>
<TR>
  <TH>Table</TH><TH>header</TH><TH>data</TH>
</TR>
<TR>
  <TD>Regular </TD><TD>table </TD><TD>data </TD>
</TR>
<TR>
  <TD>Hello </TD><TD>World! </TD>
</TR>
<TR>
  <TD>Tables </TD><TD>are </TD><TD>fun! </TD>
</TR>
</TABLE>

</BODY>
</HTML>
```

Formatting Attributes of Table Data Containers

You can modify the attributes of various table data containers by using the following HTML tags. A description of the tags that you can use to modify table attributes, as well as examples of how you can use them, are listed next.

FIGURE 9.1.
Simple table created with various table data containers.

Colors

Most HTML tags that take an RGB (Red, Green, Blue) color value also take predefined color names that are easy to remember. The following colors are supported by Internet Explorer:

Red	Aqua	Green	Silver
Maroon	Navy	Purple	Grey
Black	Yellow	Blue	Teal
Lime	White	Fuchsia	Olive

A few RGB color values that come in handy when assigning colors to HTML objects are listed next. You might want to bookmark this page so you can refer to the following table when assigning RGB colors to objects of Web pages such as table cells, frames, and so on. You can also use the following Web site to obtain RGB codes of various colors.

URL

You can obtain RGB codes of various colors from the following Web site:

`http://www.infi.net/wwwimages/colorindex.html`

Table 9.1. RGB colors and values.

Name of Color	*RGB Color Code*
Aquamarine	#70DB93
Baker's Chocolate	#5C3317
Black	#000000
Blue	#0000FF
Blue Violet	#9F5F9F
Brass	#B5A642
Bright Gold	#D9D919

continues

Table 9.1. continued

Name of Color	RGB Color Code
Brown	#A62A2A
Bronze	#8C7853
Bronze II	#A67D3D
Cadet Blue	#5F9F9F
Cool Copper	#D98719
Copper	#B87333
Coral	#FF7F00
Cyan	#00FFFF
Corn Flower Blue	#42426F
Dark Brown	#5C4033
Dark Green	#2F4F2F
Dark Green Copper	#4A766E
Dark Olive Green	#4F4F2F
Dark Orchid	#9932CD
Dark Purple	#871F78
Dark Slate Blue	#6B238E
Dark Slate Grey	#2F4F4F
Dark Tan	#97694F
Dark Turquoise	#7093DB
Dark Wood	#855E42
Dim Grey	#545454
Dusty Rose	#856363
Feldspar	#D19275
Firebrick	#8E2323
Forest Green	#238E23
Gold	#CD7F32
Goldenrod	#DBDB70
Grey	#C0C0C0
Green	#00FF00
Green Copper	#527F76
Green Yellow	#93DB70
Hunter Green	#215E21
Indian Red	#4E2F2F

Name of Color	*RGB Color Code*
Khaki	#9F9F5F
Light Blue	#C0D9D9
Light Grey	#A8A8A8
Light Steel Blue	#8F8FBD
Light Wood	#E9C2A6
Lime Green	#32CD32
Magenta	#FF00FF
Mandarin Orange	#E47833
Maroon	#8E236B
Medium Aquamarine	#32CD99
Medium Blue	#3232CD
Medium Forest Green	#6B8E23
Medium Goldenrod	#EAEAAE
Medium Orchid	#9370DB
Medium Sea Green	#426F42
Medium Slate Blue	#7F00FF
Medium Spring Green	#7FFF00
Medium Turquoise	#70DBDB
Medium Violet Red	#DB7093
Medium Wood	#A68064
Midnight Blue	#2F2F4F
Navy Blue	#23238E
Neon Blue	#4D4DFF
Neon Pink	#FF6EC7
New Midnight Blue	#00009C
New Tan	#EBC79E
Old Gold	#CFB53B
Orange	#FF7F00
Orange Red	#FF2400
Orchid	#DB70DB
Pale Green	#8FBC8F
Pink	#BC8F8F

continues

Table 9.1. continued

Name of Color	RGB Color Code
Plum	#EAADEA
Quartz	#D9D9F3
Red	#FF0000
Rich Blue	#5959AB
Salmon	#6F4242
Scarlet	#8C1717
Sea Green	#238E68
Semi-Sweet Chocolate	#6B4226
Sienna	#8E6B23
Silver	#E6E8FA
Sky Blue	#3299CC
Slate Blue	#007FFF
Spicy Pink	#FF1CAE
Spring Green	#00FF7F
Steel Blue	#236B8E
Summer Sky	#38B0DE
Tan	#DB9370
Thistle	#D8BFD8
Turquoise	#ADEAEA
Very Dark Brown	#5C4033
Very Light Grey	#CDCDCD
Violet	#4F2F4F
Violet Red	#CC3299
Wheat	#D8D8BF
White	#FFFFFF
Yellow	#FFFF00
Yellow Green	#99CC32

Borders

By using the <BORDER> tag, it's possible to control the appearance of a table border. Refer to Figure 9.2 for an example of what the following HTML code looks like.

```
<HTML>
<HEAD><TITLE>HTML Table Demonstration</TITLE>
</HEAD>
<BODY BGCOLOR="#FFFFFF" TEXT="#000000" LINK="#0000FF" VLINK="#FF7500"
ALINK="#FF4B9A">

<TABLE BORDER=0>
<CAPTION ALIGN=TOP>Table with BORDER=0</CAPTION>
<TR><TD>This </TD><TD>is </TD><TD>a </TD></TR>
<TR><TD>demonstration of </TD><TD>table </TD><TD>borders</TD></TR>
</TABLE>

<TABLE BORDER=1>
<CAPTION ALIGN=TOP>Table with BORDER=1</CAPTION>
<TR><TD>This </TD><TD>is </TD><TD>a </TD></TR>
<TR><TD>demonstration of </TD><TD>table </TD><TD>borders</TD></TR>
</TABLE>

<TABLE BORDER=2>
<CAPTION ALIGN=TOP>Table with BORDER=2</CAPTION>
<TR><TD>This </TD><TD>is </TD><TD>a </TD></TR>
<TR><TD>demonstration of </TD><TD>table </TD><TD>borders</TD></TR>
</TABLE>

<TABLE BORDER=3>
<CAPTION ALIGN=TOP>Table with BORDER=3</CAPTION>
<TR><TD>This </TD><TD>is </TD><TD>a </TD></TR>
<TR><TD>demonstration of </TD><TD>table </TD><TD>borders</TD></TR>
</TABLE>

</BODY>
</HTML>
```

FIGURE 9.2.

The border of a table can be controlled with the <BORDER> *tag.*

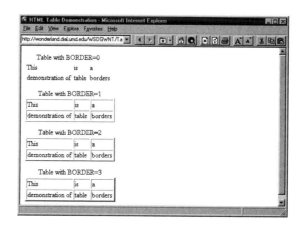

Border Colors

You can assign colors to various borders of tables by using the following HTML tags inside tags used to define various parts of a table, such as <TABLE> and <TD>. Border colors were not supported by Netscape Navigator at the time of this writing.

- `BORDERCOLOR=<RGB color name>`—Used to specify the normal color of border. For example, `<TABLE BORDER=3 BORDERCOLOR=#0000FF>`.

- `BORDERCOLORLIGHT=<RGB color name>`—Used to specify the light color border of a 3D table. For example, `<TABLE BORDER=3 BORDERCOLORLIGHT=#0000FF>`.

- `BORDERCOLORDARK=<RGB color name>`—Used to specify the dark color border of a 3D table. For example, `<TABLE BORDER=3 BORDERCOLORDARK=#0000FF>`.

Background Colors

Internet Explorer supports various background colors in tables as well as table cells. The syntax of the background color tag is `<BGCOLOR=<colorname>>`. The color name can be either an RGB color code or a color name such as Black, White, Yellow, and so on. The following example demonstrates how background colors can be assigned to tables and table cells:

```
<HTML>
<HEAD><TITLE>Table Background Color Demonstration</TITLE>
</HEAD>
<BODY BGCOLOR="#BFBFBF" TEXT="#000000" LINK="#0000FF" VLINK="#FF7500"
➥ALINK="#FF4B9A">

<TABLE BORDER=8 BGCOLOR=LIME >
<CAPTION ALIGN=TOP>This entire table is Lime</CAPTION>
<TR><TD>Table </TD><TD>with </TD><TD>lime background </TD></TR>
</TABLE>

<TABLE BORDER=8 BGCOLOR=Lime >
<CAPTION ALIGN=TOP>This entire table is Lime with multi colored cells</CAPTION>
<TR>
<TD BGCOLOR=Yellow> BGCOLOR = Yellow </TD>
<TD BGCOLOR=Aqua> BGCOLOR = Aqua </TD>
</TR>
<TR>
<TD BGCOLOR=White> BGCOLOR = White </TD>
<TD BGCOLOR=Silver> BGCOLOR = Silver </TD>
</TR>
</TABLE>

</BODY>
</HTML>
```

FIGURE 9.3.

Background colors can be assigned to an entire table or individual cells of a table.

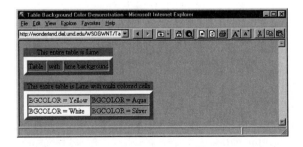

Background Images

In addition to background colors, you can assign background images to a table or individual cells of a table. The syntax of the background image tag is very similar to that of the background color tag. The only difference is the fact that a URL of a background image is specified in the background image tag. The syntax of the background image tag is BACKGROUND="URL of background image". An example of using background images in a table and cells of a table is listed next. If you wish to experiment with this example, you can find it in the CD-ROM (Chapter-09\Tables\Table4.htm).

```
<HTML>
<HEAD><TITLE>Table Background Image Demonstration</TITLE>
</HEAD>
<BODY BGCOLOR="#DFDFDF" TEXT="#000000" LINK="#0000FF" VLINK="#FF7500"
➥ALINK="#FF4B9A">

<TABLE BORDER=8 BACKGROUND="GreenAndWhitePaper.gif" >
<CAPTION ALIGN=TOP>
<H2>A background image is used in this table</H2>
</CAPTION>

<TR>
<TD BACKGROUND="YellowStucco.gif" >
<H3>This cell has its own background image. A background image was added to
this cell with the BACKGROUND="YellowStucco.gif" HTML tag</H3></TD>
<TD BACKGROUND="BluePaper.gif" >
<H3>This cell has its own background image. A background image was added to
this cell with the BACKGROUND="BluePaper.gif" HTML tag</H3></TD>
</TR>
</TABLE>

</BODY>
</HTML>
```

FIGURE 9.4.

A background image can be tiled in a table or cell of a table.

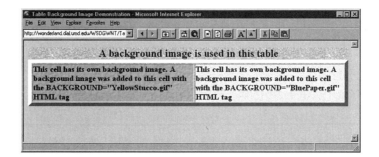

Aligning Contents of a Table

The data containers <TABLE>, <TR>, <TH>, and <TD> can be aligned with <ALIGN> and <VALIGN>. The <VALIGN> tag is used to align the contents of a container to its top or bottom. The default is center or middle aligned. The <ALIGN> tag is used to align the contents of a container to its left or right border. By default, the contents are center or middle aligned. A few examples of these two tags are listed next:

- `<TABLE ALIGN=RIGHT>`—Table with contents right aligned.
- `<TD ALIGN=LEFT>`—Contents of the table cell is left aligned.
- `<TABLE VALIGN=TOP>`—Contents of the table is aligned to its top.
- `<TD VALIGN=TOP>`—Contents of the table cell is aligned to its top.

URL

Tables are implemented in Microsoft Internet Explorer according to the HTML specification at the following URL:

`http://www.microsoft.com/ie/author/htmlspec/tables.htm`

URL

Visit the following Web site for more information about how tables are implemented in Netscape Navigator:

`http://home.netscape.com/assist/net_sites/tables.html`

Merging Table Rows and Columns

Rows and columns of a table can be merged together by using the two HTML tags `<COLSPAN>` and `<ROWSPAN>`. These two tags can be used very easily to extend a row or column of a table. The following example demonstrates how rows and columns of a table can be joined together. Note that `<COLSPAN>` and `<ROWSPAN>` can be used only to extend areas of a table cell defined by the two HTML tags `<TH>` and `<TD>`.

```
<HTML>
<HEAD>
<TITLE>Table Column/Row merge demonstration</TITLE>
</HEAD>
<BODY BGCOLOR="#DFDFDF" Table Data="#000000" LINK="#0000FF"
VLINK="#FF7500" ALINK="#FF4B9A">

<TABLE BORDER=8>
<CAPTION ALIGN=TOP>
<H2>ROWSPAN / COLSPAN Demonstration</H2>
</CAPTION>

<TR>
  <TD ROWSPAN=2>Description</TD>
  <TD COLSPAN=2>Amount of Transaction</TD>
  <TD>Balance</TD>
</TR>
```

```
<TR>
  <TD>Withdrawal</TD><TD>Deposit</TD>
  <TD ALIGN=RIGHT>$ 150</TD>
</TR>
<TR>
  <TD>Won Publishers Clearinghouse Lottery </TD> <TD></TD>
  <TD>$ 1,000,000</TD><TD ALIGN=RIGHT>$ 1,000,150</TD>
</TR>
<TR>
  <TD>Paid off Washington DC parking tickets </TD> <TD ALIGN=RIGHT>$500,000</TD>
  <TD></TD><TD ALIGN=RIGHT>$ 500,150</TD>
</TR>
<TR>
  <TD>Bought MS Bob (For Windows NT) </TD> <TD ALIGN=RIGHT>$100</TD>
  <TD></TD><TD ALIGN=RIGHT>$ 500,050</TD>
</TR>
<TR>
  <TD>Closing balance</TD>
  <TD COLSPAN=3 ALIGN=RIGHT>$ 500,050</TD>
</TR>
</TABLE>

</BODY></HTML>
```

FIGURE 9.5.

Rows and columns of a table can be made to span additional rows and columns by using <COLSPAN> *and* <ROWSPAN>.

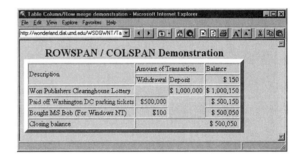

Frames

When used properly, frames can make a Web site easier to navigate, as shown in Figure 9.6. Frames allow Web content developers to have more control over the layout of a Web page. For example, frames can be used to display an index of a Web site in one frame while users use another frame to browse various Web pages.

As you can see in this figure, the contents of a Web site can be broken down into various sections by using frames. In the example in Figure 9.6, A Java applet is used to display various messages at the top of the page. Because the Java applet is in a frame, when users navigate the Web site, they will still be able to view various messages that scroll on the Java applet's LED display. A help icon is also placed beside the Java applet in case a user needs help navigating a Web site that has frames. Note that the help icon is actually an animated GIF file with the four frames Click, Here, For, and Help. The Java applet was displaying the For frame when the screen capture was taken, just in case you were wondering what the For icon was for! If you're interested in creating animated GIF files for your Web site, refer to the section on animated GIF files in Chapter 11, "Adding Multimedia to Your Web Site."

FIGURE 9.6.

You can use frames to organize the contents of a Web site more efficiently and make it easier to navigate.

The two middle frames display most of the data. The frame to the left side can be used as an index of Web pages, and the one to the right is used to display various pages selected by the user. The bottom frame can be used to perform common functions such as return to the main Web page, provide feedback, and so on. The following section demonstrates how easy it is to add frames to a Web site.

Before discussing various HTML tags used to create frames, a simple example is presented next to introduce you to frames. Then the HTML tags you can use to create frames are discussed. You then learn how to create a more complicated frame set.

URL

You can obtain more information about how frames are implemented in MS Internet Explorer from the following Web site:

```
http://www.microsoft.com/ie/author/html30/frames.htm
```

URL

You can obtain more information about how frames are implemented in Netscape Navigator from the following Web site:

```
http://home.netscape.com/assist/net_sites/frames.html
```

Adding Frames to a Web Site

The syntax of frames resembles the syntax of tables in many ways. Refer to Figure 9.7 for a simple example of a set of frames. The frames in Figure 9.7 were generated with the HTML code listed after the following two paragraphs.

As you can see in the following code listing, the <BODY> tag of the Web page is replaced by the <FRAMESET> tag. The <FRAMESET> tag is used to specify frames in a frame set. HTML tags that you can use to create frame sets are discussed in detail in the "Syntax of Frames" section.

Use the two tags <NOFRAMES> and </NOFRAMES> to display a message to users using technologically challenged Web browsers. HTML code between these two tags are ignored by frames compatible Web browsers. You might want to include the same URLs contained in various frames here to make it easier for technologically challenged users to navigate your Web site.

```
<HTML>
<HEAD>
<TITLE>Simple Frame Demonstration</TITLE>
</HEAD>

<FRAMESET COLS="120,50%,*">

<NOFRAMES>
Please use a Web browser such as Internet Explorer 3.0 or
Netscape Navigator to view this page in frames!
</NOFRAMES>

    <FRAME SRC="contents.htm">
    <FRAME SRC="contents.htm">
    <FRAME SRC="contents.htm">

</FRAMESET>
</HTML>
```

FIGURE 9.7.

Simple frames demon-stration.

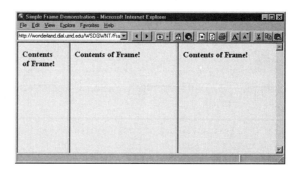

The examples presented in this section refer to a file by the name of contents.htm. The contents of the file contents.htm used in the examples of this section are listed next. When creating a frame set, a filename has to be specified for each frame. Please note that you may substitute contents.htm with another file you may have created when experimenting with various examples in this section. You can find all examples in this section on the CD-ROM (Chapter-09\Tables) that comes with this book.

```
<HTML>
<HEAD><TITLE>Contents of Frame</TITLE>
</HEAD>
<BODY BGCOLOR="#FAEFB6" TEXT="#000000"
LINK="#0000FF" VLINK="#AA21A5" ALINK="#FF0080">

<H3><B>Contents of Frame!</B></H3>

</BODY>
</HTML>
```

Syntax of Frames

The `<FRAME>` tag is used to define a frame in a frame set. You can use the following HTML tags inside the `<FRAME>` tag:

- `<SRC=<Filename of frame>>`—Used to specify the URL of the document associated with a frame. The contents of the file referred to by the URL are displayed in the frame by the Web browser.

- `<NORESIZE>`—By default, users can resize frames by using the mouse. However, when the `<NORESIZE>` tag is used, users are no longer able to resize the frame.

- `<NAME=<Name of Frame>>`—Can be used to assign a name to a frame.

- `<SCROLLING=<"Yes" or "No">>`—By default, if the contents of a frame don't fit inside the frame, a scroll bar is displayed automatically. This can be manually controlled by using the `<SCROLLING>` tag. For example, `<SCROLLING="Yes">` can be used to make a frame always display a scroll bar.

- `<MARGINWIDTH=<Size in Pixels>>`—Can be used to specify left and right margins of a frame.

- `<MARGINHEIGHT=<Size in Pixels>>`—Can be used to specify upper and lower margins of a frame.

- `<FRAMEBORDER=<"Yes" or "No">>`—At the time of this writing, this tag was supported only by Internet Explorer. This tag can be used to either display or hide the border of a frame.

The `<FRAMESET>` tag is used to define various attributes of frames. HTML tags that can be used within the `<FRAMESET>` tag are listed here:

- `<ROWS=<"format of rows in a frame set">>`—Used to specify the number of frames in a frame set along with how much space should be given to each frame. Each frame in the frame set is separated by commas. A pixel value, a percentage, or a relative value can be given to any frame in a frame set. For example, if a frame set has two frames and one should have 75 percent of the browser space, and the other should have 25 percent of the browser space, `<ROWS="75%,25%">` would be used. In the same manner, if one frame should have 125 pixels and the other should have the remainder of browser space, `<ROWS="125,*">` would be used to create the two frames. Note that the % sign can be used to specify a relative size, a number is used to specify an absolute size, and an asterisk is used to specify the remainder of available browser space.

- `<COLS=<"format of columns in a frame set">>`—Used to specify the number of frames in a frame set along with how much space should be given to each frame. Refer to the previous discussion about the `<FRAME>` tag for more information about how individual frames can be formatted.
- `<FRAMEBORDER=<"Yes" or "No">>`—At the time of this writing, this tag was supported only by Internet Explorer. This tag can be used to display or hide the border of a frame.
- `<FRAMESPACING=<Size in pixels>>`—Can be used to create spaces between frames. At the time of this writing, this tag was supported only by Internet Explorer.

Because it can be used to display the contents of a URL a user clicks on one frame in another frame. The `<TARGET>` tag is especially useful. The `<TARGET>` tag can be used inside certain HTML tags as demonstrated next:

- `<A TARGET=<TargetName> HREF="…">`—When a user clicks on a URL defined with the `<HREF>` tag, its contents will be displayed in the frame identified by `<TargetName>`.
- `<BASE TARGET=<TargetName>>`—The frame identified by `<TargetName>` will be used as the default frame for URLs defined within a page.
- `<FORM TARGET=<TargetName>>`—Specifies the frame where output of a form submission should be redirected to.

In addition to the name of a frame, the following values can be substituted with `<TargetName>`.

- `"Name of a window or frame"`—As mentioned earlier, a frame can be given a name. For example, if a frame named `"MainContents"` was created, contents of various URLs can be displayed in that frame by including a `TARGET="MainContents"` in URLs (for example `<A TARGET="MainContents" HREF="filename.html>Click here</A>`).
- `"_TOP"`—Loads a URL into the full body of a window.
- `"_PARENT"`—Loads a URL into the immediate parent of the container the hyperlink was in.
- `"_BLANK"`—Loads a URL into a new blank window.
- `"_SELF"`—The URL is loaded to the same window or frame the hyperlink was in.

A More Complicated Demonstration of Frames

A slightly more complicated example of frames appears in Figure 9.8. The source code of the frame set in Figure 9.8 is listed here:

```
<HTML>
<HEAD>
<TITLE>Simple Frame Demonstration</TITLE>
</HEAD>

<FRAMESET ROWS="40,*,40>

<NOFRAMES>
Please use a Web browser such as Internet Explorer 3.0 or
Netscape Navigator to view this page in frames!
</NOFRAMES>

  <FRAME SRC="contents.htm">

  <FRAMESET COLS="120,*">

    <FRAME SRC="contents.htm">

    <FRAMESET ROWS=",50">
      <FRAME SRC="contents.htm">
      <FRAME SRC="contents.htm">
    </FRAMESET>

  </FRAMESET>

  <FRAME SRC="contents.htm">

</FRAMESET>

</HTML>
```

FIGURE 9.8.

*A more complicated
demonstration of frames.*

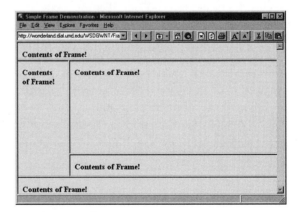

Text Special Effects

Several HTML tags introduced by Microsoft and Netscape give content developers more control over various typefaces they can use in documents published on the Web. Some of the more useful HTML tags that can be used to control various attributes of typefaces in Web pages are listed next. Although, at the time of this writing, Internet Explorer was the only Web browser that could display TrueType fonts, this might have changed by the time you've read this. All examples in the following sections can be found on the CD-ROM (Chapter-09\Fonts).

Font Sizes

By using `<FONT SIZE=<Size Of Font>>`, it's possible to change the size of a font. As shown in the following example, `<Size Of Font>` can be used to increment and decrement a number from the base font size with + and -. Refer to Figure 9.9 for an example of how you can use the preceding HTML tag to control font sizes. The HTML code used to generate the Web page shown in Figure 9.9 is also listed next for your reference:

```
<html>
<head>
    <title>Font Size Demonstration</title>
</head>

<body text="#000000" bgcolor="#FFFFFF" link="#0000EE"
vlink="#551A8B" alink="#FF0000">

<font SIZE=-2>Font Size - 2</font><BR>

<font SIZE=-1>Font Size - 1</font><BR>

Regular Font Size <BR>

<font SIZE=+1>Font Size + 1</font><BR>

<font SIZE=+2>Font Size + 2</font><BR>

<font SIZE=+3>Font Size + 3</font><BR>

<font SIZE=+4>Font Size + 4</font><BR>

</body>
</html>
```

FIGURE 9.9.

You can control font sizes by using the `<FONT SIZE=#>` *HTML tag.*

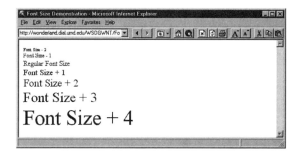

Text Colors

You can specify text colors by using the `<font COLOR="#<RGB Color value>">` HTML tag. An example of how this is accomplished appears in Figure 9.10. You might want to look at the file

Chapter-09\Fonts\Fonts2.htm on the CD-ROM that comes with this book and experiment with it; you probably can't tell the difference between colors too much from the grayscale figure shown next. The HTML source code of Figure 9.10 is also provided for your reference:

```
<html>
<head>
   <title>Font Color Demonstration</title>
</head>

<body text="#000000" bgcolor="#FFFFFF" link="#0000EE"
vlink="#551A8B" alink="#FF0000">

<H3><font COLOR="#008000">Font COLOR="#008000"</font><BR>

<font COLOR="#808000">Font COLOR="#808000"</font><BR>

<font COLOR="#FF0000">Font COLOR="#FF0000"</font><BR>

<font COLOR="#0000FF">Font COLOR="#0000FF"</font><BR>

<font COLOR="#FF00FF">Font COLOR="#FF00FF"</font><BR>

<font COLOR="#800080">Font COLOR="#800080"</font><BR>

<font COLOR="#000040">Font COLOR="#000040"</font><BR></H3>

</body>
</html>
```

FIGURE 9.10.

Colors can be assigned to text by using the <FONT COLOR=#RGB_CODE> *HTML tag.*

Using TrueType Fonts

At the time of this writing, MS Internet Explorer is the only Web browser that supports TrueType fonts. However, by the time you read this, several other Web browsers would have started supporting TrueType fonts, as well. Prior to Web browsers that support TrueType fonts, Web content developers had no way of controlling the appearance of a certain typeface. Web browsers that support TrueType fonts lift this restriction by giving Web content developers full control over the appearance of text in a Web page. Text of a Web page can be assigned a certain font by using the <FONT FACE> extension to HTML. This extension can be used to specify a primary font and several secondary fonts. If the primary font is not available on the user's system, a secondary font specified in the <FONT FACE> tag will be used. If you're confused, the following syntax definition and example of the <FONT FACE> tag should make this clearer:

Syntax: `<FONT FACE="<Font-1>,<Font-2>,<Font-3>">`

In the preceding syntax definition, if `<Font-1>` is unavailable, `<Font-2>` will be used, and if `<Font-2>` is unavailable as well, `<Font-3>` will be used.

An example of the `<FONT FACE>` tag appears in Figure 9.11.

FIGURE 9.11.

You can use the `<FONT FACE>` *HTML tag to assign TrueType fonts to text in a Web page.*

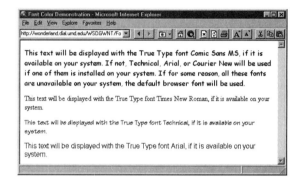

URL

Visit the Microsoft Typography Web page at the following URL for more information about TrueType fonts on the Web:

`http://www.microsoft.com/truetype/content.htm`

HTML 2.0 Specification

Although there is no official HTML at the time of this writing, an official standard exists for HTML 2.0. Because HTML 2.0 tags are understood by virtually all Web browsers, it is beneficial to be familiar with various standard HTML 2.0 tags. Browse the following Web page to learn more about various HTML tags defined in the HTML 2.0 specification and how these tags can be used to format the contents of a Web page.

URL

Official HTML 2.0 specification:

`http://www.w3.org/pub/WWW/MarkUp/html-spec/html-spec_toc.html`

Summary

You can make a Web site more interesting to navigate by utilizing a number of advanced HTML techniques. For example, you can use tables to format objects of a Web page such as text, video clips, and Java applets. You can use frames to make it easier to navigate a Web site. You can make a Web page's text more attractive to read by applying special attributes such as colors and fonts.

What's Next?

This chapter discussed a number of advanced HTML tags in detail. However, the HTML tags discussed in this chapter had to be manually added to a Web page. This can be frustrating as well as time consuming when working on a large project. The next chapter discusses a number of applications that you can use to create content for the Internet. Because most of these applications take care of HTML details, they help content developers concentrate more on the content they are publishing rather than on the intrinsic details of HTML.

10

Web Site Development Tools

At the time of this writing, dozens of Web site development tools are available for Windows NT. The purpose of this chapter is to provide an overview of some of these tools and demonstrate how you can use them to develop a Web site. In the first few sections, you learn about Web page creation tools that you can use to create and edit Web pages. The last section is devoted to InContext WebAnalyzer, an application that you can use to analyze the contents of a Web site. Although you cannot use this application to create Web pages, it is helpful for managing the contents of a Web site.

As you create Web pages, you might at some point need to edit Web pages in *raw* HTML format to fine-tune the HTML code. Having several feature-rich HTML editors handy to edit Web pages is always useful. In the next few sections, you examine several feature-rich HTML editors that you can use to create and edit raw HTML files. Except for Netscape Gold and InContext Spider, virtually all Web page creation applications discussed next are raw HTML editors.

In addition to this chapter, be sure to read Chapter 12, "Designing and Managing a Web Site with FrontPage," and Chapter 13, "Publishing on the Web with Microsoft Office," to learn how various Microsoft Internet information publishing applications can be used to develop content for the Web.

HTML Assistant Pro

A useful HTML editor, HTML Assistant Pro uses floating toolbars and icons to make it easier to mark Web pages with various HTML tags, as shown in Figure 10.1. Visit the following Web site for additional information about HTML Assistant Pro. You can download a freeware copy of HTML Assistant Pro from the same Web site.

URL

HTML Assistant Pro home page:

`http://www.brooknorth.com`

Refer to Figure 10.1 for an example of how a Web page can be edited using HTML Assistant Pro. In addition to various toolbars that can be used to insert HTML tags, HTML Assistant Pro also includes several useful Web page development utilities. You can use Background Assistant to select background and text colors. You also can use the dialog box shown in Figure 10.2 to assign a background image to a Web page.

FIGURE 10.1.

Editing a Web page with HTML Assistant Pro.

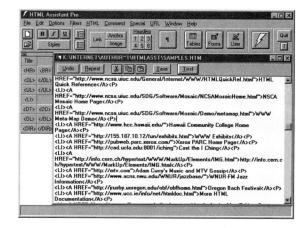

FIGURE 10.2.

You can use HTML Assistant Pro Background Assistant to assign attributes visually to various Web page elements.

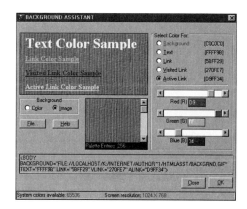

HotDog Pro

You can use HotDog Pro, a powerful HTML editor, to edit multiple Web pages (see Figure 10.3). It is ideal for working with several HTML files at the same time. In addition to its resourceful toolbars, HotDog Pro also includes a number of useful features such as a Web browser and a spell checker. Visit the HotDog Web site for additional information about this editor and to download an evaluation copy of it.

URL

HotDog home page:

`http://www.sausage.com/hotdog32.htm`

FIGURE 10.3.
HotDog Pro is ideal for working with several HTML files at the same time.

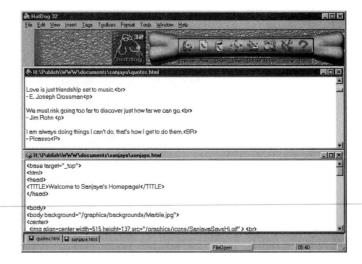

HoTMetaL Pro

Although HoTMetaL Pro is similar to most HTML editors, it has one major difference. Virtually all HTML editors enable users to type in virtually any HTML tag. With HoTMetaL Pro, however, you can use only certain HTML tags in Web pages. This capability is a major advantage if you are interested in making sure that all your Web pages conform to the HTML 2.0 standard. One major drawback is that it imposes restrictions on HTML tags that you can use in Web pages being edited. HoTMetaL Pro therefore is not as flexible as other HTML editors. This inflexibility somewhat defeats the purpose of using an HTML editor in the first place: the purpose being to gain more control over the HTML code of a Web page.

As shown in Figure 10.4, HoTMetaL Pro marks HTML tags with special markers. This useful feature can be used to separate HTML code visually from the contents of a document. Use HoTMetaL Pro if you are concerned about your HTML. Be aware that if you use HoTMetaL Pro, however, you can use only HTML tags that have been programmed into it. Visit the following Web site for the most up-to-date information about HoTMetaL Pro.

URL

HoTMetaL Pro information Web page:

`http://www.sq.com/products/hotmetal/hmp-org.htm`

FIGURE 10.4.
HoTMetaL Pro highlights HTML tags with special markers.

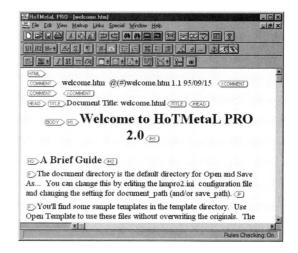

Netscape Gold

Netscape Gold is a powerful Web page development tool. Unlike Web page development tools discussed previously, Netscape Gold is a WYSIWYG HTML editor. Because Netscape Gold supports *Netscapisms* (or "Netscape enhancements to HTML"), you can use it to create attractive Web pages easily. Visit Netscape's Web site for the most up-to-date information about Netscape Gold.

URL

The Netscape Communications Corporation Web site:

`http://home.netscape.com/`

You can use Netscape Gold to create Web pages using the Netscape Page Wizard, as shown in Figure 10.5. You can use the Page Wizard to type interactively in various elements of a Web page and select Web page attributes such as background and text colors. After you customize the page, you can use Netscape Gold to download the Web page, edit it, and publish it on the Web.

Another useful feature of Netscape Gold is its capability to edit any Web page browsed with Netscape navigator. If you select the Edit button, you can download and edit a Web page being browsed. Note that you cannot browse the Web, find interesting Web pages, download them to your computer using Netscape Gold, and then publish them at your Web site. Doing so may cause legal repercussions due to violations of copyright law. This feature is mostly useful for editing templates and your own Web pages. Visit the following Web site for information about copyright law.

FIGURE 10.5.

You can use the Netscape Page to create Web pages with Netscape Gold.

URL

Information about copyrights:

`http://www.patents.com/copyrigh.sht`

As shown in the Properties dialog box in Figure 10.6, Netscape Gold also includes powerful editing capabilities that you can use to format the contents of a Web page. Although Netscape Gold is a powerful Web page development tool, it lacks useful features found in other Web page development tools, such as a WYSIWYG table creation tool and a spell checker. For this reason, Netscape Gold is not recommended for large Web site development projects.

FIGURE 10.6.

You can use the Properties dialog box to format various objects of a Web page.

Web pages created with Netscape Gold can be published on the Web using FTP, as shown in Figure 10.7. After you specify the address of an FTP server, a username, and a password in the Editor Preferences dialog box, you can transfer a Web page being edited with Netscape Gold to a remote server with just the click of a button.

FIGURE 10.7.

Web pages created with Netscape Gold can be published on the Web using FTP.

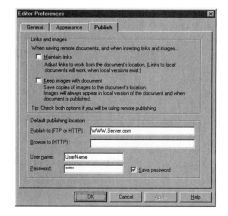

InContext Spider

As shown in Figure 10.8, InContext Spider has a different screen layout than the layouts of other HTML editors. Although it is a WYSIWYG HTML editor, it does not hide HTML from the user. The left pane contains various HTML tags used in the Web document. The object (text, graphic, and so on) formatted with an HTML tag in the left column is displayed in the right column. This useful feature ensures that Web pages created with InContext Spider are syntactically correct. Visit the InContext Spider information Web page for additional information about InContext Spider.

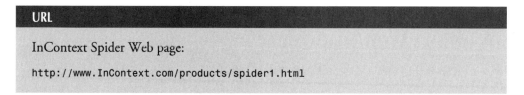

URL

InContext Spider Web page:

`http://www.InContext.com/products/spider1.html`

Spider Mosaic, the Web browser included with InContext Spider, can be used to preview pages created with Spider, as shown in Figure 10.9.

FIGURE 10.8.

A Web page edited with InContext Spider.

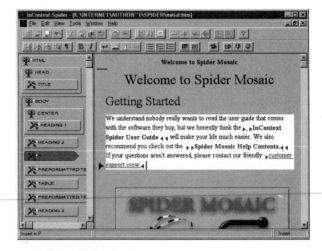

FIGURE 10.9.

Previewing a Web page edited with InContext Spider.

InContext WebAnalyzer

InContext WebAnalyzer is different from various Web site development tools discussed earlier. It is not an application that you can use to create Web pages. Instead, it is a useful tool for managing and analyzing the contents of a Web site. As your Web site increases in size, with additional hyperlinks, documents, and graphics, being able to look at your Web site from a graphical perspective will save you a great deal of time. It is often helpful to find out how various documents in a Web site are connected and check the Web site for broken links. As you learn in this section, WebAnalyzer is a useful tool for performing all these tasks. In this section, you learn how you can use various features of WebAnalyzer to manage a Web site. Download and experiment with a copy to discover features that are not discussed in this section. Visit the following Web site for additional information about InContext WebAnalyzer.

URL

InContext WebAnalyzer information Web page:

`http://www.InContext.com/products/analyze.html`

As mentioned previously, you can use InContext WebAnalyzer to comprehensively analyze a Web site graphically. Refer to Figure 10.10 for an example of a Web site being analyzed with InContext WebAnalyzer. As you can see, WebAnalyzer is broken down into three panes. The bottom pane displays critical information about various URLs at a Web site. Note that you can sort information displayed in the bottom frame by clicking on the corresponding column label. The right pane displays how various objects at a Web site are connected. When you select a page in this pane, all URLs of that Web page are displayed in the left pane, as shown in Figure 10.10.

In addition to InContext WebAnalyzer, Microsoft FrontPage, covered in Chapter 12, "Designing and Managing a Web Site with FrontPage," also can be used to manage the contents of a Web site.

FIGURE 10.10.

A Web site being analyzed with InContext WebAnalyzer.

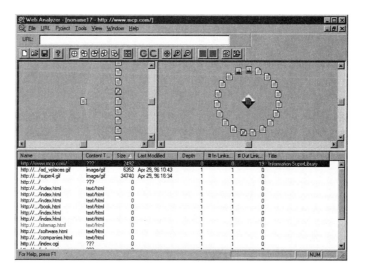

To generate a comprehensive report of a Web site being analyzed with WebAnalyzer, choose Project|Make Report from the main menu. After you create a report, you can view it by using a Web browser, as shown in Figure 10.11.

FIGURE 10.11.

You can generate a comprehensive report for a Web site by using InContext WebAnalyzer.

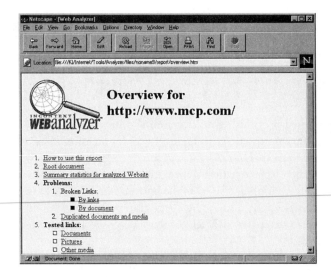

You can select various options of the Web page in Figure 10.11 to obtain detailed statistics, as shown in Figure 10.12. Figure 10.12 contains the Web page displayed when "Summary statistics for analyzed Website" is selected from the Web page in Figure 10.11. You can use the summary displayed to obtain information about various objects used at a Web site.

FIGURE 10.12.

Vital statistics of a Web site.

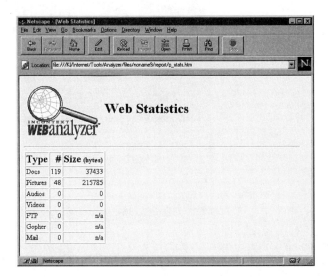

As more Web pages are added to a Web site, broken links inevitably pop up when pages are deleted or renamed. Although broken links might not be a problem for a Web site with only a few Web pages, tracking down broken links manually becomes increasingly difficult. Broken links found at some corporate Web sites attest to this fact. You've probably come across a few broken links at various corporate Web sites. You can use the Web page shown in Figure 10.13 to easily track down broken URLs of a Web site.

FIGURE 10.13.
*You can use InContext
WebAnalyzer to find
broken links of a Web site.*

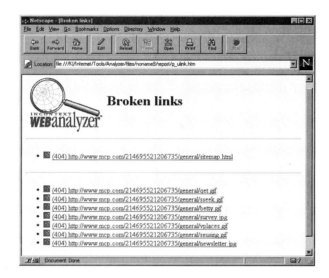

You can obtain additional information about a broken URL displayed in Figure 10.13 by selecting it. When you select a broken URL, you can obtain additional information by using a Web page similar to the one shown in Figure 10.14. Note that the Web page in Figure 10.14 not only displays the broken URL, but also the links to the broken URL.

FIGURE 10.14.
*Detailed information
about a broken link.*

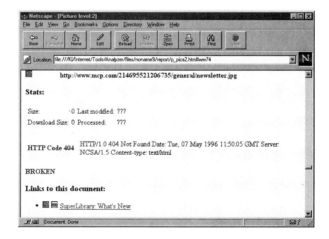

Summary

You can use the HTML editors discussed in this chapter to fine-tune HTML code of Web pages. Although these HTML editors are not ideal for large Web projects, they are well suited for projects that require complete control over the HTML code. You also can use various HTML editors discussed here to create and edit Web pages easily.

Although HTML editors are useful for fine-tuning HTML code, they are not generally recommended for large projects. A new breed of HTML editors is coming into existence as this book goes to print. Use WYSIWYG HTML editors whenever possible to simplify projects and reduce time wasted worrying about various HTML syntaxes. However, the flexibility offered by WYSIWYG HTML editors is not always sufficient for some projects. Use raw HTML editors discussed here in such instances so that you have more control.

InContext WebAnalyzer is a useful Web site management tool. You can use it to manage the contents of a Web site by viewing it from a graphical perspective. As more Web pages are added to a Web site, at some point, keeping track of various Web pages and how they are linked to each other becomes increasingly difficult. This can lead to outdated Web pages and broken links, if a Web page is renamed or deleted. You can use InContext WebAnalyzer to solve some of these problems by viewing how Web pages at a Web site are linked and locating invalid URLs.

What's Next?

When used properly, multimedia complements the contents of a Web site by making it easier and more interesting to navigate for information. A number of multimedia formats are commonly used on the Internet. When you add multimedia to a Web site, you need to know strengths and weaknesses of various multimedia formats and know when to use what format. The next chapter discusses various multimedia formats and outlines benefits of choosing one format over the other. After you read the next chapter, you will know which format is appropriate and also how to use several graphics manipulation tools to create transparent, animated, and interlaced GIF files. Because bandwidth is a precious and limited resource on the Internet, the next chapter also provides several tips that you can use to optimize graphics for the Internet.

11

Adding Multimedia to Your Web Site

Multimedia is increasingly becoming an important part of content published on the Internet. When it's used properly, multimedia makes it easier and more interesting to navigate a Web site. Although most graphics can easily be created and added to a Web page, to optimize graphics for the Internet, there are a few more things that need to be accomplished. Also different types of graphics formats are suitable for various tasks. Knowing when to use which format can make your Web site easier to navigate by offering your Web surfers graphics that are optimized for the Internet. Before discussing the different graphics formats and their suitability for different tasks, it's time to examine why you should go to all the trouble to add multimedia to a Web site and to optimize graphics for the Internet.

Going Beyond Plain Text

Although information is a Web site's most valuable asset, when it's used properly, multimedia can enhance the information viewing experience. Multimedia complements the contents of a Web site by making it more attractive and easier to navigate. Although some prefer not to incorporate multimedia to a Web site for fear of distracting users, by not using multimedia these people fail to use the World Wide Web to its fullest potential. Although too much of any good thing is usually not very good, adding a few images and other multimedia objects to a Web site makes it easier and more enjoyable to browse.

Multimedia often acts almost like eye candy. For example, when discussing the final results of a technical experiment, the reader is probably tired of reading a few pages of information. When presenting the final results to the reader, relying on a plain text chart might not make a very big impact. However, if the plain text data is converted to a few graphical charts that are exported as GIF files, the impact will be far greater.

In addition to providing a more effective way of distributing information, multimedia also helps Web surfers locate information they need faster. For instance, when a user is presented with a menu consisting of a few items, in order to find an interesting topic the user often has to read all the items in the menu. On the other hand, if graphic icons are added to the menu, rather than reading lines of text, the user will be able to quickly single out interesting topics by scanning the graphics. This not only saves time but also makes the whole information retrieval experience more interesting.

Commonly Used Multimedia Formats

Table 11.1 lists the multimedia formats commonly used on the Internet and a brief description of each format.

Table 11.1. Commonly used multimedia formats.

Extension	Common/Complete Name	Description
AVI	Audio Video Interleaved	A motion video format commonly used under Windows.
BMP	Windows Bitmap	A graphics format native to Windows. BMP files are often quite large and are not suitable for low bandwidth Internet use.
GIF	GIF	*GIF* stands for *Graphics Interchange Format.* The GIF format was originally developed by CompuServe. It is now one of the most popular graphics formats on the Internet.
JPG	JPEG	A graphics format optimized for compressing "natural images." JPEG should not be used when sharp borders or text are part of the image.
MOV	QuickTime	A motion video format commonly used in Apple Macintosh computers. QuickTime was developed by Apple. A Windows version of the QuickTime viewer is available for Windows.
MPG	MPEG	A motion video format that exploits various characteristics of the JPEG format and similarities between various frames to compress video files.
TIF	Tagged Image File Format	A graphics format used to retain very detailed information about a graphic. TIF files are usually very large in size and are not suitable for general Internet use. Unless you have art majors looking at classic artwork with subtle changes in

continues

Table 11.1. continued

Extension	Common Name	Description
		color and brightness, you should not use this format for Internet graphics.
WAV	Microsoft Waveform	An audio file format commonly used under Windows. By reducing the frequency and sampling rate of WAV files, file sizes can be reduced by sacrificing sound quality, and vice versa.
AU	u-law file format	An audio format commonly used on the Internet. Most Java applets use this audio format.
XBM	X Window Bitmap	A commonly used graphics format in the X Window environment.

When adding multimedia to a Web site, it's very important to use platform-independent multimedia. Sometimes it's frustrating for users to find multimedia files at a Web site but have no way of viewing them. You should provide URLs to download viewers for various multimedia files at your Web site, especially if the Web site will be visited by many not-so-computer-literate users.

Multimedia and Bandwidth

Multimedia is significantly more bandwidth-intensive than plain text. Therefore, it's important not only to stay within the bandwidth of your Internet link, but also to be considerate toward users who might be connected to the Internet via a POTS Internet link.

You should be particularly careful about bandwidth restrictions when adding multimedia to your Web site. Although you might have a relatively fast connection to the Internet, not everyone has that luxury. If your target audience includes large corporations, don't think that all your users will automatically have high-speed Internet links to their desktops. A company may have just gotten connected to the Internet, and its employees may be using only a 56 KB leased frame relay connection to the Internet. Such an Internet link can be painfully slow when several users use it to browse the Web.

It's undesirable to have large, bulky graphics that might take as much as a few minutes to load over a slow modem link to the Internet. Such graphics waste Internet bandwidth and might actually discourage a user from visiting your Web site. When adding graphics and multimedia to a Web site, take the time to experiment with various graphics formats and optimize them for the Internet. You're shown ways of judiciously using different graphics formats and optimizing them for the Internet shortly.

Graphics File Creation Tools

A large number of graphics file creation tools are available for Windows NT. The following sections list some of my favorite graphics creation applications. Although some applications are shareware, some are commercial applications. If you intend to create high-impact graphics, I recommend that you look into purchasing a powerful graphics file creation tool. Various graphics applications listed next have many useful features. Not all of these features are comprehensively covered in this chapter. Instead, you're provided with a brief overview of the application and are referred to a URL for more information.

LView Pro

LView Pro is an all-purpose graphics manipulation tool. It supports a wide variety of graphics formats and is ideal for converting graphics from one format to another. In addition to this, LView has provisions for applying special effects to graphics. Refer to Figure 11.1 for an example of what an image loaded in LView Pro looks like. As shown in Figure 11.1, you can apply special effects to an image by using its Retouch menu.

FIGURE 11.1.

LView Pro is an all-purpose graphics file manipulation utility.

URL

You can download the latest version of LView Pro from

`http://world.std.com/~mmedia/lviewp.html`

Paint Shop Pro

Paint Shop Pro is another useful general purpose Windows graphics creation utility. Although it's not a particularly powerful tool for applying advanced graphics special effects, Paint Shop Pro is sufficient for most tasks. A major advantage of using Paint Shop Pro over other utilities is its capability to handle more than one image at a time. As shown in Figure 11.2, Paint Shop Pro supports an *MDI (Multiple Document Interface)* user interface. For this reason, it's possible to work with more than one image at a time. This is sometimes a major advantage when working with graphics at a Web site. The tool bar to the left side of Figure 11.2 is also very handy when applying special effects to images.

FIGURE 11.2.

Paint Shop Pro is a powerful image-viewing, editing, and converting application.

URL

You can download the latest version of Paint Shop Pro from

`http://www.jasc.com/psp.html`

CorelXARA

Once you begin publishing content on the Internet, you'll need a powerful image-viewing and editing tool capable of performing advanced graphics manipulation tasks such as graduated transparency layers and anti-aliasing, and various text manipulation tasks such as fitting text to a path. The shareware tools mentioned earlier are not capable of handling such advanced graphics manipulation tasks. If you intend to create high-impact graphics for your Web site, CorelXARA is a very powerful application that will meet virtually all your needs. Refer to Figure 11.3 for an example of a graphic loaded to CorelXARA.

FIGURE 11.3.

You can apply many powerful special effects to a graphic by using CorelXARA.

Another useful CorelXARA feature is its clipart and fill catalog shown in Figure 11.4. You can use this tool to catalog all your graphics files. When designing a graphic, you can then select various graphics from this catalog, simply drag them from the catalog window, place them on the workspace, and resize them to meet your needs.

FIGURE 11.4.

The clipart and fill catalog is a very useful CorelXARA tool.

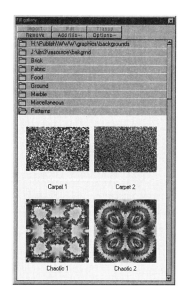

MetalWorks

MetalWorks is a very handy application for creating and optimizing graphics for the Internet. Although MetalWorks is not as feature rich as other applications discussed earlier, it has many powerful features for creating graphics for Web sites. Listed next are a few tasks for which you can use MetalWorks.

URL

You can obtain additional information about MetalWorks from

`http://www.sq.com/products/mtlworks/mtl-home.htm`

Making Icons into Buttons

It's easy to add borders to images by using MetalWorks. In order to add a border to an image, first load it into MetalWorks, as shown in Figure 11.5.

FIGURE 11.5.

Graphic loaded to MetalWorks before a border is applied. By loading an image to MetalWorks, you can apply various special effects to it.

After loading the file, choose Effects | Border to add a border to it. You are then presented with the Border dialog box, shown in Figure 11.6. This dialog box is used to specify various settings for the image's border. First, select the pixel width of the border by using the Width scroll bar. It's recommended that you select a setting of around 6 pixels. A large button frame can be distracting and needlessly increases the file size, making it take longer to transmit via the Internet. Then, by using the scroll-down list, select the color of the frame and whether you want the frame to be raised, inverted, or basic.

Before clicking on OK, you can view the setting you selected by using the View button. If you don't like the selection you made, make another selection and click on the View button. After you're satisfied with the settings of the border, click OK. MetalWorks then creates a border around your graphic, as shown in Figure 11.7.

FIGURE 11.6.

You can adjust border settings by using the Border dialog box.

FIGURE 11.7.

Graphic after a border is applied to it.

NOTE

Adding borders to photographic images saved in the JPEG format is not recommended. JPEG compression works best when the image being compressed does not have any sharp borders or lines. Although adding a border to a JPEG image might look nice, it takes away any image compression you gain by using the JPEG format. As a rule of thumb, add borders only to images stored in the GIF format.

Embossing Graphics

You can also use MetalWorks to emboss graphics. Embossing gives graphics a special look by making them appear as if they're carved on a stonelike object. After loading a graphic to MetalWorks, as shown in Figure 11.7, you can emboss it by selecting Effects | Emboss from the main menu. You then see the Emboss dialog box, as shown in Figure 11.8.

FIGURE 11.8.

You can select the light angle used to emboss a graphic by using the Light Angle scroll bar.

Specify the light angle in degrees used to emboss the graphic by using the scroll bar provided in this dialog box. After you're happy with a value, click on View to preview your selection. If you're content with your choice, click on OK to apply the setting you selected, and the image will be embossed, as shown in Figure 11.9.

FIGURE 11.9.

The graphic shown in Figure 11.7, embossed by MetalWorks.

In addition to embossing and adding borders, you can also use MetalWorks to make the backgrounds of GIF files transparent.

MetalWorks also makes it easy to optimize graphics for the Internet. By using MetalWorks to reduce the number of colors, you can reduce file sizes, making it easier to transmit them via the Internet. All these features, along with the capability to create imagemaps, makes MetalWorks a very handy utility that you can use to enhance and optimize graphics for the Web.

All about GIF Files

Out of all the graphics formats used on the Internet, *GIF (Graphics Interchange Format)* is perhaps the most widely used graphics format. It's so famous for several reasons. Unlike JPEG files, GIF files are not optimized for storing images resembling natural photographs. GIF is an all-purpose graphics format that can be used to store various graphics and images. The GIF format should be used to store graphics files that do not resemble natural photographs.

A major advantage of using the GIF format is its capability to allow a certain color to be transparent. For example, when adding a GIF file graphic into a Web page, if you make its background transparent, you can give the impression that it's *floating* in the background. You are shown how to do this in the Transparent GIF Files section.

GIF files also support *interlacing*. Interlacing is the capability to save a GIF file so that it becomes visible in bands. The banding effect makes the GIF file appear out of focus at first, and as more information about the graphic is retrieved, the image appears more focused. After you're shown how to make the background of GIF files transparent, you're shown how to *interlace* GIF files in the Interlacing GIF Files section. Various advantages and drawbacks of interlacing files are also discussed shortly.

Unfortunately, GIF files have a few limitations. Although these limitations are not applicable for some tasks, they make GIF files unsuitable for others. GIF files are limited to only 256 colors. This may cause color shifting and other undesired side effects.

Transparent GIF Files

You can give your Web site a professional touch by making the backgrounds of GIF files transparent. When someone looks at a transparent GIF file with a browser, the graphic's background becomes the background color of the browser. This gives the impression that the graphic is *floating* in the background, which adds a sophisticated touch to the graphic.

CAUTION

Making the background color of a photograph transparent can adversely affect the rest of the photograph. Photographs saved in the GIF format are not suitable for making a certain background color invisible unless the background color doesn't appear anywhere else in the photograph. Photographs are usually very rich in colors, and a GIF file can have only 256 colors. Because only 256 colors are used, it's a good bet that the background color is used somewhere else in the photograph. Consequently, if you make that color "invisible," it's going to make the photograph look bad because parts of it will also be invisible. If this happened in a photograph of a person, it could make him or her look like an alien! However, if a GIF file's background color is distinctly different from other colors in the graphic, you will have better luck making its background transparent.

Creating Transparent GIF Files

By using Paint Shop Pro, it's very easy to make the background of a GIF file transparent. Before doing this, you need to determine the *index color* of the background by loading the graphic to Paint Shop Pro, as shown in Figure 11.10.

FIGURE 11.10.

Graphic loaded to Paint Shop Pro before its background is made transparent. Note that the eyedropper tool is selected to find the index value of the background color.

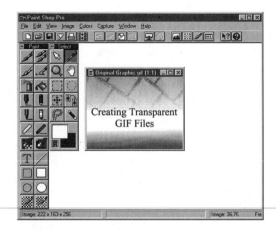

After loading the graphic, select the eyedropper tool. The mouse pointer turns into an eye-dropper when it's moved over the graphic. At the same time, if you look at the bottom status bar next to the image's resolution and color depth, a number of digits and characters are shown. These digits and characters are in the following format:

(`X-coordinate`, `Y-coordinate`) (**I**:`IndexColor`, **R**:`RedValue`, **G**:`GreenValue`, **B**:`BlueValue`)

> **NOTE**
>
> The index color is shown only if the image loaded to Paint Shop Pro is a GIF file. If it's not, save it as a GIF file before proceeding further.

The only number you need to pay attention to is the *IndexColor* value. When you move the mouse over the part of the image you want to be made transparent, make a note of its index color value. You'll need this information shortly. For the purpose of this example, the index color of the white background is 255. This graphic is included on the CD-ROM. If you wish, you can examine it yourself. After making a note of the index value, choose File | Save As to bring up the Save As dialog box shown in Figure 11.11. From the List Files of Type pull-down list, select GIF CompuServe. Next, select GIF 89A - Non Interlaced as the File Sub-Format. Then select a valid directory and type in a filename.

After typing in a filename and selecting a valid directory, click the Options button. This brings up the GIF Transparency Options dialog box shown in Figure 11.12. You can use this dialog box to specify the index color of the image's background color that should be made transparent. Because 255 is the index color of the background, click Set the Transparency Value to type **255** and click OK. Use a new filename when saving the graphic by using the Save As dialog box in Figure 11.11. This way, if something should go wrong in the conversion process, you won't lose the original file. Then, click OK in the Save As dialog box to save the graphic with its background color set to transparent.

FIGURE 11.11.

Saving a graphic as a GIF file.

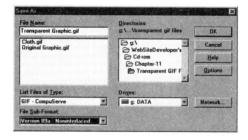

FIGURE 11.12.

The background color of the graphic is made transparent by specifying its index value.

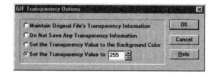

The graphic before its background was made transparent appears in Figure 11.13. As you can see, its white background stands out.

FIGURE 11.13.

Original graphic loaded to Netscape before its white background was made transparent.

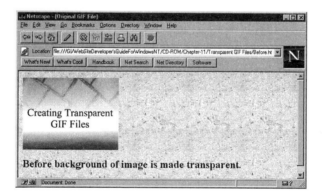

As you can see in Figure 11.14, when the white background of the graphic is made transparent, it no longer stands out against the background. If you'd like to see these two figures in color, refer to \Chapter-11\Transparent GIF Files\Before.html and \Chapter-11\Transparent GIF Files\After.html on the CD-ROM that comes with this book.

FIGURE 11.14.

Graphic loaded to Netscape after its white background is made transparent.

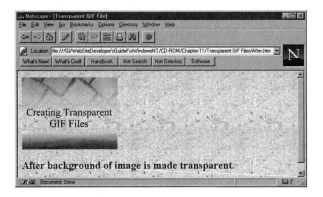

Interlacing GIF Files

If you have photographs at your Web site stored in the GIF format, it's a good idea to interlace them. What is *interlacing*? You may have noticed how some graphics on Web sites appear in bands. First, the graphic will look out of focus, and then get clearer and more focused as more data about the graphic is sent to the Web browser. Adding this effect to a GIF file is called *interlacing*.

Interlacing photographs at your Web site allows someone who's not interested in the entire picture to go to another page rather than wait for the whole picture to load. You can use the interlace feature only on graphics stored in the GIF format. Although a similar feature is available for JPEG files (Progressive JPEG), it's not widely supported or backward-compatible.

PERFORMANCE

Interlaced GIF files are more CPU-intensive than noninterlaced GIF files, so be careful when using interlaced GIF files. Even though interlacing makes your graphics look neat, interlaced GIF files are larger than noninterlaced GIF files and generally take longer to display, especially if the client's computer has a relatively slow processor or a poor video card. Therefore, don't get carried away with interlacing and interlace all the GIF files at your Web site! Interlacing is a useful tool, but you should use it for the right job. Generally, interlacing should be used when displaying photographs because you can guess what the final photograph will look like from an early rendering of an interlaced GIF file. The same is not true for GIF files that contain text.

How to Interlace a GIF File

You can interlace a GIF file very easily by using Paint Shop Pro. In order to interlace a GIF file, first load it to Paint Shop Pro as shown in Figure 11.15. You can use any file format compatible with Paint Shop Pro to create an Interlaced GIF file.

FIGURE 11.15.

Original graphic loaded to Paint Shop Pro.

After loading the file, choose File | Save As. When the Save As dialog box appears, as shown in Figure 11.16, select a directory and type in a filename. Next, select GIF - CompuServe as the List Files of Type and Version 89a - Interlaced as the File Sub-Format.

> **NOTE**
>
> If the file does not contain any transparency information, you may save the file as Version 87a - Interlaced.

FIGURE 11.16.

Saving a graphic as an interlaced GIF file.

Animated GIF Files

You can use animation to give GIF files a certain flair. Netscape Navigator supports animated GIF files since Netscape 2.0 beta 05. An animated GIF file can be thought of as a collection of GIF files separated by each other with a time delay. Although at the time of this writing only a handful of Web browsers supported animated GIF files, this is most likely to change by the time you read this book. Also, Microsoft Internet Explorer 3.0 supports animated GIF files.

Before Netscape and Microsoft made an agreement with America Online (AOL), around five million people were accessing the World Wide Web by using a technologically challenged Web browser that was not even sure how to parse a table. By the time you read this, this situation will have changed; Internet Explorer will suddenly become the default Web browser for around five million users. Because in the long run Internet Explorer and Netscape are going to be two of the most widely used Web browsers, you can add some flair to your Web site by using animated GIF files.

URL

You can download many free animated GIF files from

`http://www.teleport.com/~cooler/MMMM/index.html`

GIF Animations and Technologically Challenged Browsers

First, some good news. Animated GIF files are backward-compatible with Web browsers that support only regular GIF files. However, only the first frame of the animated GIF file will be visible to someone looking at it using a Web browser that does not support animated GIF files. When creating animated GIF files, you should keep this in mind. For example, you might want to create an animated GIF file with four frames. These four frames can each have a word that makes up a complete sentence. For example, "Click here for help" will have the following four frames:

Click
Here
For
Help

Although it makes sense to start this animating with "Click" because it's the first word of the sentence, this is not a very good idea. What if someone browses your Web site with a browser that does not support animated GIF files? They will then just see an icon that says "Click." But click *what* and *why*? Because Web browsers that do not support animated GIF files show only the first frame, seeing an icon that says "Click" can be somewhat confusing to some users. To remedy this problem, it's more desirable to start the animation in the following order:

Help
Click
Here
For

After making the suggested change in the animation sequence, a user browsing a Web site with a technologically challenged Web browser will see an icon that reads "Help" rather than "Click"

(Help is a lot less ambiguous than Click). At the same time, after a few iterations of the animation sequence, those who use an advanced Web browser will figure out what the animation is about. As you can see, with a little effort, you can create animated GIF files so that they are *completely* backward-compatible with earlier Web browsers.

GIF Animations and CPU Utilization

When using a new multimedia format, you should be aware of some of its side effects. The current implementation of animated GIF files (at least on the Netscape browser) is not very efficient. Although this does not make a big difference for a relatively small animated GIF file, the same is not true for large animated GIF files. In Figure 11.17, you see an animated GIF file that's found in one of Netscape's Web pages. Although you can't notice this from the figure, the wheels shown in the image are animated, and they actually turn. This is a rather elaborate GIF file and looks very impressive.

FIGURE 11.17.

An animated GIF file found in one of Netscape's Web pages.

However, the animated GIF file shown in Figure 11.17 is rather CPU-intensive. The animation consumes approximately 70 percent of the CPU resources on a 90 MHz Pentium computer. As you can see in the CPU utilization chart generated by QuickSlice in Figure 11.18, the System Process barely has around 25 percent of CPU resources free when the animation is running.

You should take into account CPU utilization issues related to animated GIF files when creating and adding them to your Web site. Make an effort to keep animated GIF files as small as possible. As a rule of thumb, try to keep them smaller than 100×100 pixels. Also, avoid having more than one animated GIF file in one page unless they are small animations (smaller than 50×50 pixels). What's shown by QuickSlice is merely a snapshot of CPU utilization.

This is not a very accurate representation of CPU utilization over a certain time period. What's shown in Figures 11.19 and 11.20 are Performance Monitor CPU utilization charts before and after loading Netscape's Web page. As you can see in Figure 11.20, after Netscape's page is loaded, CPU utilization is up by an average of about 70 percent.

FIGURE 11.18.

CPU utilization of various applications when the page in Figure 11.17 is loaded.

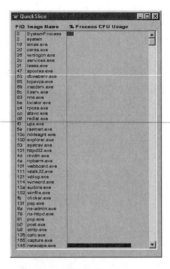

FIGURE 11.19.

Performance Monitor monitoring CPU utilization before Netscape's page is loaded. Note that average CPU utilization is 7.48 percent.

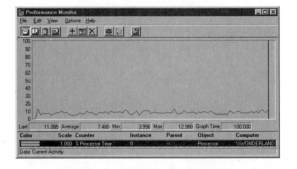

FIGURE 11.20.

Performance Monitor monitoring CPU utilization after Netscape's page is loaded. Note that average CPU utilization is now 77.825 percent.

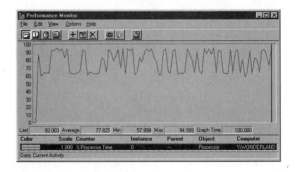

Creating a GIF Animation

You can create animated GIF files easily by using GIF Construction Set for Windows. For the purpose of this example, you are shown how to create an animated bullet icon. Unlike regular bullet icons, the animated bullet icon consists of ten colors, and every three seconds the bullet changes its color. You are shown how to create this animation later in this section. Listed next are the steps you need to take in order to create a GIF animation:

1. Create individual GIF files for the animation.

2. Load individual GIF files into GIF Construction Set for Windows.

3. Set necessary transparency and delay settings for animation.

URL

GIF Construction Set for Windows is a utility that you can use to create animated GIF files. This utility is *bookware*; you can register the program by purchasing a certain book and by answering a question. You can download GIF Construction Set for Windows from

`http://www.mindworkshop.com/alchemy/gifcon.html`

Before creating the animation with GIF Construction Set for Windows, you have to create ten multicolored bullets. These bullets are simply multicolored circles. You can use a number of graphics utility programs to create the ten files needed for the animation. The ten graphics used in this example were created with CorelXARA, as shown in Figure 11.21. If you wish to follow along, these graphics are on the CD-ROM that accompanies this book (\Chapter-11\GIF Animations\RoundBullets).

FIGURE 11.21.

You can create graphics needed for a GIF animation by using a graphics manipulation utility such as CorelXARA.

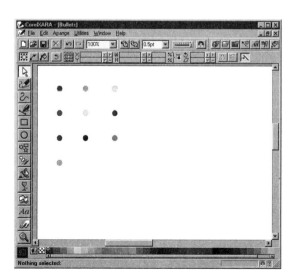

After creating the graphics, as shown in Figure 11.22, they need to be *exported* as GIF files. Use descriptive names when exporting several graphics that will become part of an animation. This will make it easier for you to determine which file is which when creating the animation.

FIGURE 11.22.

Before creating a GIF animation, a graphic has to be created for each frame. Use descriptive names when saving graphics that are part of an animation.

When saving various graphics that are going to be part of an animation, you should pay attention to the dimensions of the graphics because you'll need this information later. By default, the GIF animation program allocates an area of 640 × 480 for the GIF animation. You should typically change this value to the largest graphic that's part of the animation. Usually, when a graphic is exported, you are shown information about the graphics, such as dimensions, in a dialog box similar to the one shown in Figure 11.23.

FIGURE 11.23.

You should keep track of the dimensions of graphics that are going to be part of a GIF animation.

After saving the graphics needed for the animation, invoke GIF Construction Set for Windows to create the animation. When GIF Construction Set for Windows is first invoked, it looks like Figure 11.24. On the left side, you see a listing of directories. Use this directory listing to select the location of your animated GIF file. Then choose File | New to begin creating an animated GIF file.

FIGURE 11.24.

When GIF Construction Set for Windows is first invoked, use the directory listing to select a directory for the GIF animation.

At this point, you will see a header at the top with a dimension of 640 × 480. This value should be changed to the dimensions of the largest graphic that's part of the animation. In order to change the dimension of the header, select it and press the Edit button. You're then presented with an Edit Header dialog box, as shown in Figure 11.25.

FIGURE 11.25.

The Edit Header dialog box is used to specify the dimensions of the animation.

Use the Edit Header dialog box to specify the width and height of the animation. Screen width corresponds with the width of the largest graphic of the animation, and screen depth corresponds with the height of the largest graphic. After setting these values, click OK to continue. The animation can now be created by adding various objects such as controls, images, loops, comments, and plain text. In order for the animation to iterate for a while, a loop control has to be added. To do this, click the Insert button, and you'll see a button bar identical to the one in Figure 11.26. In order to add a loop, click the Loop button in the dialog box shown in Figure 11.26.

FIGURE 11.26.
You can add different objects to an animation.

With the Insert Object dialog box, you can add a number of objects to an animation. The following lists each object you can insert and a description of each:

Control: Define time delays for various animation sequences.

Image: Used to specify images that are part of an animation.

Loop: Used to specify the number of times the animation should iterate. Note that you can add only one *loop block* to an animation. The loop block contains information about the number of iterations of the animation.

Comment: Add comments to an animation. Use this to add a copyright notice to the animation.

Plain Text: Used to insert text blocks to animation.

After clicking the Loop button, the Edit Loop Block dialog box appears, as shown in Figure 11.27. Use this dialog box to type in the number of times the animation should iterate. After typing in a number, click OK to continue.

FIGURE 11.27.
The Edit Loop Block dialog box.

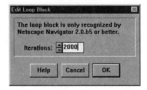

After inserting the loop block, various images that are part of the animation have to be inserted. This can be done in pairs. Each image being inserted has two objects: a control object and an image object. The control object holds the time delay for the animation sequence, while the image object holds the image that will be displayed after the time delay specified in the control object. Now you can insert a control object and an image object.

By clicking the Insert button in Figure 11.24, first insert a control object and then insert an image object. When adding an image object, you need to specify the image that will be added by using a dialog box similar to the one shown in Figure 11.28. After selecting a file using this dialog box, press OK to continue.

FIGURE 11.28.

Use the Open file dialog box to select images for an animation.

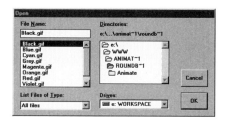

You then need to select a palette for the new image using the dialog box in Figure 11.29. Listed next are descriptions of various choices you can make at this point.

Use a local palette for this image: Use this format to make sure no color shifts or dithering effects are introduced into the image. Dithering is the process of blending two or more colors to produce a different color. However, this is not a very suitable format for computers with video cards that support only 256 colors. When this setting is used with such a video card, and another image is displayed on top of the previous image, it may cause undesired side effects.

Use a local gray palette for this image: Unless the image is already grayscale, this format is not recommended because it converts the image into grayscale.

Remap this image to the global palette: This causes all local colors of the image to be remapped by the closest matching colors of the global palette. Because it adversely affects color-sensitive images, this setting is *not* recommended for photographs.

Dither this image to the global palette: This setting is more suitable for photographic images.

Use this image as the global palette: If no other image blocks exist, you can use this option to import the global palette of the image being added.

Use it as is: This option is not recommended unless you like taking chances with the quality of your animated GIF files. When this option is used, if colors required by the image are not available in the global palate, it can make your graphics look very bad due to color substitutions and approximations.

> **TIP**
>
> When adding images to an animated GIF file, use the 15-bit quantize (which limits the possible values to a discrete set of values) to produce better results. However, this option is more CPU-intensive, and you may have to wait longer.

FIGURE 11.29.

*After selecting an image
for the animation, a color
palette has to be selected
for it.*

After adding the image, select the control that was added earlier and click the Edit button. You are then presented with the Edit Control Block dialog box, as shown in Figure 11.30.

FIGURE 11.30.

*The Edit Control Block
dialog box.*

You can use this dialog box to specify a transparent color, animation sequence delay, and what the image will be replaced with after it is displayed. All ten graphics files used in this example have a white background. The final animation will look much nicer if the white background is made transparent so only the circular bullet is visible. This can be done by clicking the Transparent color checkbox and by clicking the wide box next to it. As shown in Figure 11.31, you will then see a list of colors. From this list, select the color you want to be made transparent.

NOTE

At this point, if you don't see any other colors but black, this is because you probably selected the black bullet. Simply add another control and an image, and the color box will look similar to Figure 11.31.

FIGURE 11.31.

Transparent color selection dialog box.

Then enter a number for the delay period using the Edit Control Block dialog box. Note that this value is specified in 1/100 seconds. In order to have a three-second delay, enter 300 in the space provided for Delay in Figure 11.30. Then select how you would like this image to be replaced after the delay period. The Edit Control Block dialog box will now look similar to the one shown in Figure 11.30. Click OK to continue and repeat it for all other images. The GIF Construction Set for Windows window should now look similar to Figure 11.32.

FIGURE 11.32.

The GIF Construction Set for Windows dialog box after all images and controls of the animation are added.

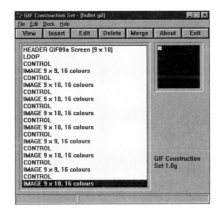

At this point, you might want to add a comment to the animation or insert a copyright notice to it. You do this by clicking Insert and Comment. After a comment block is added, double-click it to edit it. You can then add a comment to the animation you just created, as shown in Figure 11.33.

The animated GIF file is now created and can be used as a regular GIF file. When it's viewed with either a viewer or Web browser that does not support animated GIF files, only the first frame will be visible. However, when it's viewed with a graphics viewer or Web browser that supports animated GIF files, all ten frames of the animation will be visible, one after the other in three-second intervals. As shown in Figure 11.34, the animated bullet created in this example can be added to a Web page as a regular inline GIF image. The Web page shown in Figure 11.34 can be found on this book's CD-ROM under the directory \Chapter-11\GIF-Animations\RoundBullets\Animate.

FIGURE 11.33.

You can use the Edit Comment dialog box to add a comment to a GIF animation.

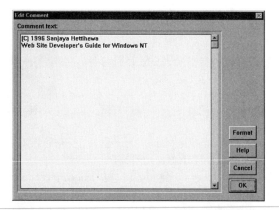

FIGURE 11.34.

You can use animated GIF files as inline images of a Web page as if they were regular GIF files.

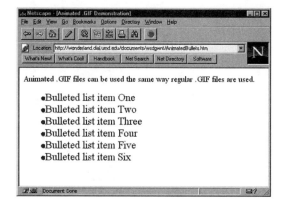

All about JPEG Files

JPEG (pronounced *jay-peg*) stands for *Joint Photographic Experts Group*, the original name of the committee that wrote the standard. Next to GIF, JPEG is the second most widely used still-image format on the Internet. Unlike GIF, JPEG is not an all-purpose graphics format. JPEG exploits a certain limitation of the way we see things to compress photographic images. Humans are more sensitive to brightness than color. You will learn more about the JPEG format shortly.

URL

Visit the following URL for more information about the JPEG format:

`http://www.cis.ohio-state.edu/hypertext/faq/usenet/jpeg-faq/part1/faq.html`

When to Use the JPEG Format

JPEG works well on photographs, naturalistic artwork, and similar material. When displaying photographs at your Web site, you should convert your pictures to JPEG format, which is a standardized image compression mechanism. JPEG can be used to compress color or grayscale images, and it works best when the image being converted to JPEG has "natural colors" (like those found in photographs of humans, trees, sunsets, forests, lakes, and beaches).

Advantages of JPEG

Photographs saved in the JPEG format are often much smaller than those saved in the GIF format. Because you will typically gain a 4:1 compression ratio with JPEG, as opposed to GIF, your images will be much smaller as long as they resemble photographs with natural colors. Having small images is a great advantage when pictures have to be transmitted over the Internet. Web surfers with slow Internet links will particularly appreciate the small file sizes.

By using JPEG, your graphics can be in 24-bit color instead of the 8-bit color used in the GIF format, which supports only 256 colors. On the other hand, JPEG supports up to 16.7 million colors.

Limitations of JPEG

You should never convert a cartoon or line art image to JPEG format. The resulting image will often be much bigger than the original! The same is true for images containing letters because JPEG has a hard time compressing graphics files that have sharp edges. JPEG is a poor choice for any graphic containing letters, cartoons, sharp edges, or line drawings.

Progressive JPEG Files

Progressive JPEG files are very similar to interlaced GIF files; however, they are not backward-compatible. Unless you're certain that a very large percentage of your Web surfers use a browser that can handle progressive JPEG files, it's recommended that you use this format sparsely.

There are a number of benefits of using progressive JPEG files. Progressive JPEG files load faster than regular JPEG files. A demonstration of this can be found at the Netscape Web site, as shown in Figure 11.35.

> **URL**
>
> You can find a Progressive JPEG demonstration at Netscape's Web site at the following URL:
>
> `http://www.netscape.com/eng/mozilla/2.0/relnotes/demo/pjpegdemo.html`

FIGURE 11.35.

Progressive JPEG files load faster than regular JPEG files (elapsed time 11 seconds over a 28.8 Kbps Internet link).

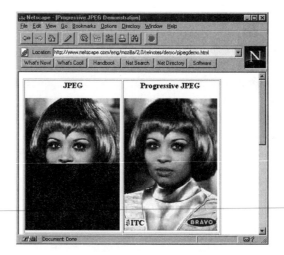

Because some browsers don't support progressive JPEG files, when you add them to your Web site, be sure to create a link to a regular JPEG file in case a technologically challenged user visits your Web site. At the time of this writing, the following four Web browsers are the only ones I am aware of that support progressive JPEG:

- Netscape 2.0
- Enhanced Mosaic 2.1
- Microsoft Internet Explorer
- OmniWeb 2.0
- Microsoft Internet Explorer

URL

Visit the following URL for more information about the progressive JPEG image compression format:

```
http://www.cis.ohio-state.edu/hypertext/faq/usenet/jpeg-faq/part1/faq-doc-
➥11.html
```

Creating Progressive JPEG Files

Progressive GIF files can be created easily by using a graphics utility called LView Pro. Refer to the earlier section on Graphics File Creation Tools for the URL of LView Pro. In order to create a Progressive JPEG file, first load the image into LView Pro. Then choose File | Properties. This shows you the LView Pro Properties dialog box. Locate the JPEG (Normal) tab in this dialog box and click it. You are presented with a tabbed dialog box similar to the one in Figure 11.36. To save all JPEG images as Progressive JPEG images, simply locate the Compression settings section and click the Progressive compression checkbox. From now on, all JPEG files that you save will be saved as Progressive JPEG files.

FIGURE 11.36.

LView Pro can be configured to save images as Progressive JPEG files.

JPEG Images and Frames

Although frames might look nice, you should not add frames to JPEG files. Whatever file size reduction you gain by converting an image to JPEG will be lost when a frame is added to it. For example, Figure 11.37 contains a JPEG image without a frame. (This image is approximately 18 KB, as you see later in Figure 11.39.)

FIGURE 11.37.

Original JPEG graphics file without a frame.

Adding a frame to the graphic can make the image in Figure 11.37 almost twice as large. The image shown in Figure 11.38 is a copy of the image shown in Figure 11.37; the only difference is a frame has been added to it. As you can see in the right side of Figure 11.39, adding a frame to the JPEG file in Figure 11.37 made it almost twice as large by adding an extra 17 KB to the file. For this reason, you should be very careful when adding frames to JPEG files because they get in the way of JPEG compression.

FIGURE 11.38.

JPEG graphics file with a frame.

FIGURE 11.39.

The JPEG file with a frame is almost twice as large as the JPEG file without a frame.

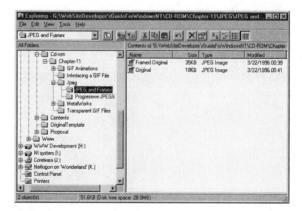

Optimizing Graphics for the Internet

You might wonder why you should go to all this trouble to optimize your graphics by reducing graphics file sizes by just a few kilobytes. Although the reduction of each file might not be that much, the kilobytes add up when you have more than one graphic on a page and more than one person accessing your Web site at the same time. Most Web surfers are connected to the Internet by relatively slow POTS lines to the Internet.

Reducing the Number of Colors

As mentioned, graphics saved in GIF format can have up to 256 colors. However, unless you have a photograph saved in GIF format, you probably aren't using all 256 colors. Chances are you can use only a fraction of them and still have your graphic look remarkably similar to the original file. By reducing the number of colors used in a graphic, you can actually reduce the file size by as much as 40 percent, depending on the graphic. To reduce the number of colors, experiment with various amounts of colors until your graphic looks almost identical to the original graphic.

Using Thumbnails

It's not desirable to add large graphics to your Web pages without warning. This can be very frustrating for a user accessing your Web site via a relatively slow modem link to the Internet. Rather than adding a large graphic or image file to a Web page, it's more desirable to create a small *thumbnail* representation of the graphic. You can then let users know that if they click the thumbnail, the user will see the graphic or image in full size. It will also be helpful to let the user know the file size.

Tips for Reducing File Sizes

Reducing file sizes of graphics is key to making a Web site easier to navigate, especially for those accessing it through relatively slow POTS links to the Internet. Listed in the next sections are a few tips that will aid you in the process of reducing graphics file sizes.

Blur Images before Making Them Smaller

Most graphic utilities have an option to blur images. When reducing the size of a graphic, especially a graphic containing text and other fine detail, it's recommended that you make the image blur before reducing its size.

The reason for this is very simple. When a graphic is reduced in size, small details such as lines and text tend to appear jagged because they are relatively small. On the other hand, when an image is blurred, such details become spread out. When an image is then reduced in size, jagged lines are not visible because fine lines get spread out when the image is blurred.

Add Text after Converting to 256-Color Format

Due to its intrinsic nature, text is very sensitive to graphics file size reductions and changes in color. For this reason, you should always add text to graphics when you're done adding other special effects.

Graphics File Size Issues

Make sure the images on your Web site are as small as possible. If you have large graphics files at your Web site, users with slow modem links might get frustrated and leave your Web site. After all the work you've put into setting up your Web site, you don't want that to happen. If you need to have large graphics files, you should let the user decide if he or she wants to see them. This can be done by showing a thumbnail representation of the graphics file and allowing the user to click the image if he or she is interested in seeing the image magnified. Keeping your graphics small will also make them load faster. In particular, try to limit the graphic's height. Vertical space is "golden" on a Web page, quite apart from loading speed. When users look at your Web pages, they generally expect to see some information. It might look rather unappealing if most of your user's screen is taken up by a large graphics file that takes several seconds to load.

Summary

When used properly, multimedia can compliment the contents of a Web site by making it easier and more interesting to browse for information. Various multimedia formats are commonly used on the Internet. When adding multimedia to a Web site, it's important to know strengths and weaknesses of various multimedia formats and know when to use which formats. Examples and tips provided in this chapter will help you select the best multimedia format and optimize various multimedia files at your Web site for transmitting via the Internet.

What's Next?

FrontPage is an application that is well integrated on other Microsoft Office applications. With FrontPage, it's easy to manage the contents of an entire Web site by using its various GUI Web administration tools. FrontPage also includes a number of special server applications that can be used to set up CGI programs to gather data from users browsing a Web site. The next chapter introduces you to Microsoft FrontPage and demonstrates how it can be used to make Web site development and administration easier.

12

Designing and Managing a Web Site with FrontPage

FrontPage is a powerful Web site development tool. Not only can it be used to edit Web pages, but it also can be used to manage your Web site. The next few sections demonstrate how FrontPage can be used to develop and manage the contents of a Web site. More information about FrontPage can be obtained from Microsoft's Web site.

URL

The Microsoft FrontPage Web site can be found at
`http://www.microsoft.com/frontpage/default.htm`

Installing FrontPage

Installing FrontPage is as easy as downloading it from Microsoft's Web site and running the file `setup.exe`. When the FrontPage installation program is executed, it will display a dialog box similar to the one shown in Figure 12.1. Use this dialog box to specify the directory in which FrontPage should be installed. Three optional FrontPage components also can be selected to be installed using the same dialog box. It is recommended that you make sure the "Client Software" component is checked. The Client Software component consists of the FrontPage Explorer and Editor. Select the "Personal Web Server" check box if you would like the FrontPage server to be installed on your system. If your Web server is compatible with FrontPage Server Extensions, you do not have to install the FrontPage Web Server. Visit the FrontPage Web site for the most up-to-date list of Web servers supported by FrontPage. At the time of this writing, FrontPage Server Extensions are compatible with the Netscape Commerce Server, Netscape Communications Server, and WebSite. However, by the time you read this, FrontPage will support several other Web servers including Internet Information Server by Microsoft.

NOTE

If you select to install the "Personal Web Server" component, be sure no other Web server is running on port 80 of your system. If another Web server is using port 80, the FrontPage Web server might have problems binding to port 80 of your server. If you would like to install the FrontPage server for testing purposes and have already installed a server such as Internet Information Server, there is a way to get the FrontPage server to use a different port. In the later case, stop the other server for the duration of the installation process. After FrontPage is installed, and its port is changed, you can continue to use the previous server as you did earlier.

FIGURE 12.1.
*FrontPage component
selection dialog box.*

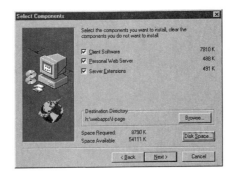

If you wish to install FrontPage extensions for your Web server, place a check mark by the Server Extensions checkbox. Afterwards, click the next button to continue.

Use the Select Program Folder dialog box shown in Figure 12.2 to select the folder in which FrontPage should be installed. When FrontPage is installed, the string of text you specify in Figure 12.2 will become a branch of the Windows NT start menu. The scroll down list can be used to install FrontPage into an exiting start menu folder.

FIGURE 12.2.
*Select Program Folder
dialog box.*

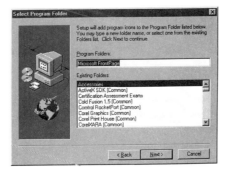

When all the files are copied, the installation program will display a dialog box identical to the one shown in Figure 12.3. FrontPage is now installed on your system. Before the installation programs terminates, it might check the IP address of your system and display a confirmation dialog box. As soon as FrontPage is installed on your system, the FrontPage Explorer can be started by checking the checkbox in Figure 12.3.

FrontPage consists of several separate programs. Depending on components you selected in Figure 12.1, the FrontPage installation program will install various FrontPage applications and insert them into a start menu folder as shown in Figure 12.4.

FIGURE 12.3.
Setup Complete dialog box.

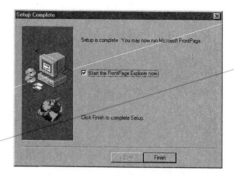

FIGURE 12.4.
FrontPage application icons.

FrontPage Server

If your Web server is not compatible with Windows NT, you can use the FrontPage server to experiment with FrontPage and create a Web site. After creating Web pages, they can be transferred to the production Web server. The FrontPage server looks similar to Figure 12.5. It can be launched from the Windows NT Start menu. You may need to edit several configuration files to configure the FrontPage server if you wish to run it on a different port other than port 80.

FIGURE 12.5.
FrontPage server.

Changing the Default Port of the FrontPage Server

By default, the FrontPage server is installed on port 80. If you have another Web server running on port 80, this can cause problems because both servers cannot share the same port. As described shortly, this problem can be solved by changing the default port of the FrontPage server by editing several configuration files. Note that the following instructions are based on FrontPage 1.1. If you are using a later version of FrontPage, refer to its documentation for the most up-to-date information about changing the default port of the FrontPage Web server. If you've already installed "server extensions" for the FrontPage server, invoke the FrontPage Server Administrator application and select "Uninstall" to remove server extensions from the FrontPage server. Once the port number of the FrontPage server is changed, you can reinstall server extensions for the FrontPage server. The port used by the FrontPage server can be changed by editing the file H:\FrontPageWebs\Server\conf\httpd.cnf, assuming you installed the FrontPage server in the H:\FrontPageWebs directory. As shown in Figure 12.6, to change the port of the FrontPage server, locate the line containing the server port information and type in the new port number.

FIGURE 12.6.

The default port of the FrontPage server can be modified by editing the httpd.cnf *file.*

> **CAUTION**
>
> When changing the default port of a Web server, selecting a port below 1024 can potentially cause problems in the future.

You can now install server extensions for the FrontPage server and start it in a different port. If you had another Web server running on port 80, that Web server can be restarted and used as usual.

FrontPage Server Administrator

The FrontPage server administrator is used to manage server extensions installed on various Web servers managed with FrontPage. It also can be used to make sure Web server extensions are installed properly as well as enable and disable authoring on a server. The next few sections discuss how FrontPage Server Administrator can be used to manage and administer server extensions. When it is first invoked, the FrontPage Server Administrator dialog box will list Web servers that can be authored with FrontPage as shown in Figure 12.7. By default, if you selected to install the FrontPage server, only contents of the FrontPage server can be managed using FrontPage Explorer. As you will learn shortly, it is easy to manage and author the contents of a Web site using FrontPage Explorer. However, FrontPage server extensions have to be installed on a server before it can be managed using FrontPage Explorer. Therefore, it is recommended that you install FrontPage server extensions for your Web server as shown in the next section. Make sure FrontPage supports your Web server before attempting to install FrontPage server extensions on your Web server. If your Web server is not supported by FrontPage, you can still use the FrontPage server to design and manage the contents of your Web site. In the latter case, skip the following section and proceed to the Managing Server Extensions section.

FIGURE 12.7.
*FrontPage Server
Administrator dialog box.*

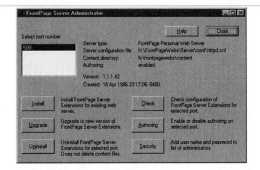

Installing Server Extensions

It is easy to install server extensions for additional Web servers as long as they are supported by FrontPage. Click the Install button in the dialog box shown in Figure 12.7 to install server extensions for an existing Web server. You then will be presented with a dialog box similar to the one shown in Figure 12.8. Use this dialog box to select the type of your Web server and press OK to continue. Note that for the purpose of this demonstration, FrontPage server extensions will be installed on a WebSite Web server that is configured to run on port 200. (Again, when changing the port number of a secondary Web server running on your server, do not follow my example and use a port number below 1024. Always use port numbers above 1024 to avoid potential conflicts.)

FIGURE 12.8.
*Configure Server Type
dialog box.*

FrontPage then will gather information about your Web server and display a confirmation dialog box similar to the one shown in Figure 12.9. Simply press the OK button to continue and FrontPage will install server extensions for the Web server selected earlier. If you are installing FrontPage server extensions on a WebSite Web server, and have it configured for multiple domain names, enter multiple domain name information when asked for it. Otherwise, leave the dialog box asking for multiple domain name information blank and press the OK button to continue.

FIGURE 12.9.
Confirmation dialog box.

After server extensions are installed for a new Web server, its port will be added to the FrontPage Server Administrator dialog box as shown in Figure 12.10. Server extensions and authoring settings of each server then can be configured by selecting the server port you wish to administer and following directions in the next section.

FIGURE 12.10.
FrontPage Server Administrator dialog box after installing server extensions for an additional Web server.

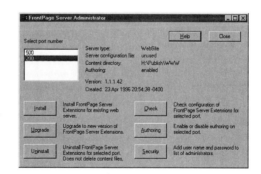

Managing Server Extensions

The Upgrade button of the dialog box shown in Figure 12.10 can be used to upgrade server extensions of a Web server to the server extensions of the current version of FrontPage. This feature is particularly useful after upgrading to a newer version of FrontPage. When the Install button is pressed, a dialog box identical to the one shown in Figure 12.11 will ask for confirmation to upgrade the server extensions of the Web server selected.

FIGURE 12.11.

Server Extensions upgrade dialog box.

The Uninstall button can be used to uninstall server extensions from a Web server. When the Uninstall button is pressed a dialog box similar to the one shown in Figure 12.12 will ask for confirmation before proceeding to uninstall server extensions from the Web server selected. As mentioned in Figure 12.12, this action will not delete the contents of a Web site. Only FrontPage server extensions will be removed.

FIGURE 12.12.

Server extensions uninstall dialog box.

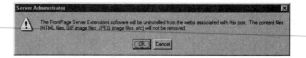

The Check button can be used to verify whether server extensions for a Web server have been installed properly. When the check button is pressed, if a dialog identical to the one shown in Figure 12.13 is not displayed, it means the server extensions have not been installed properly; in which case, you might want to try and reinstall FrontPage server extensions using the Install button.

FIGURE 12.13.

The Check button of the FrontPage Server Administrator can be used to check the status of server extensions installed on a Web server.

The Authoring button can be used to control if a Web server's content can be authored using FrontPage. When the Authoring button is pressed a dialog box similar to the one shown in Figure 12.14 will confirm that you wish to change authoring settings on the Web server selected.

FIGURE 12.14.

Enable/Disable Authoring dialog box.

The Security button is used to administer various security settings of FrontPage server extensions. It can be used to assign a password to a Web of documents managed by FrontPage as well as limit which computers can manage a Web site using FrontPage server extensions.

When the security button is pressed, a dialog box similar to the one shown in Figure 12.15 will be displayed. This dialog box can be used to specify a username and a password that can be used to author a Web site managed with FrontPage.

FIGURE 12.15.

A username and password can be used to make sure unauthorized persons do not make changes to your Web site using FrontPage.

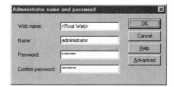

The Advanced button in the dialog box shown in Figure 12.15 can be used to specify which computers can use FrontPage to manage the contents of a Web site. If your Web site will only be managed by computers in your own domain, it is recommended that you change the default setting to match your domain name's IP address. Note that this dialog box accepts numeric Internet IP addresses. Your IP address can be found by executing the "FrontPage TCP_IP Test" icon. This icon can be found in the FrontPage Start Menu folder shown in Figure 12.4. When it is executed, it will display your IP address as shown in Figure 12.16.

FIGURE 12.16.

The FrontPage TCP/IP Test application can be used to find the IP address of your computer.

If you would like to make sure no other computers can make modifications to your Web site using FrontPage, you might want to enter your IP address in the dialog box shown in Figure 12.17. Even if you do not specify an IP address in Figure 12.17, FrontPage still requests a username and a password before users are allowed to make changes to your Web site. When specifying an IP address, it has to be a numeric IP address that has four digits (1-256) separated by periods. A wildcard character (*) can be used instead of a digit. For example, 128.*.*.* allows all computers whose IP addresses begin with 128 to administer a FrontPage *Web*.

FIGURE 12.17.

Internet address restriction dialog box.

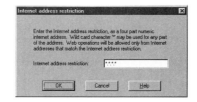

FrontPage Explorer

FrontPage Explorer is a powerful utility that can be used to view your Web site from a different perspective. Although it is possible to view the contents of a Web site using File Manager or Windows NT Explorer, these applications were not meant to be used to view the contents of a Web site. For example, when you look at your document root directory using a utility such as Windows NT Explorer, you will most likely see several directories and files. However, you will not be able to find out information such as what these files are, what is in these files, or if they have any URLs that point to your Web site or other Web sites. Most importantly, there is no way to find out if hyperlinks at your Web site actually work at all without checking them individually.

FrontPage Explorer solves all these problems by enabling Web site developers to look at Web sites they create in a new perspective. This section will demonstrate how FrontPage explorer can be used to effortlessly manage the contents of a Web site. When it is first invoked, FrontPage explorer looks similar to the window in Figure 12.18. Select File | Open Web from the dialog box shown in Figure 12.18 to invoke the Open Web dialog box shown in Figure 12.19. After selecting a Web using the Open Web dialog box, you can manage it using FrontPage Explorer.

FIGURE 12.18.
FrontPage Explorer.

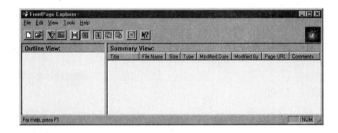

After invoking the Open Web dialog box, type in the address of your server as shown in Figure 12.19. If the server you wish to manage is installed in a different port than port 80, specify its port name by preceding the port number with a colon. Afterwards, click the List Webs button in Figure 12.19 and you will see various Webs installed on the Web server you selected. Select <Root Web> as shown in the Open Web dialog box and press OK to continue. You then will have to type in a username and password to administer the Web you selected in Figure 12.19.

FIGURE 12.19.
Open Web dialog box.

FrontPage Explorer then will extract information about the Web selected in Figure 12.19 and display the information graphically as shown in Figure 12.20. After you install FrontPage, it defaults to the Summary View. Select View | Link View from the menu bar to see the Link

View. As you can see in Figure 12.20, the Outline View pane lists various home pages and the Link View pane graphically displays various URLs that are part of the Web page selected in Outline View. If you wish to edit a Web page shown in Link View, simply double-click it. You then will be able to edit it using FrontPage editor. Note the plus and minus buttons that appear to the upper-left corner of some Web pages. Also note how the Web tree of the page selected in Figure 12.20 is expanded and how there is a minus sign to the upper-left corner of this page. If a Web page has a plus sign to its upper-left corner, it means that document has URLs that link to other Web pages. If you click the plus sign, the plus sign will change into a minus sign and you will see all the URLs in that page as shown in Figure 12.20.

FIGURE 12.20.

FrontPage explorer can be used graphically to view the contents of a Web site.

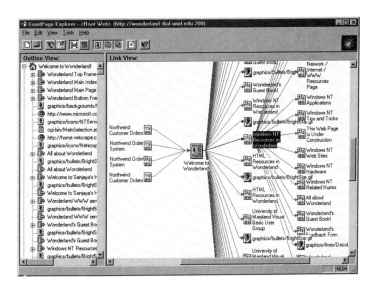

Although the graphical view shown in Figure 12.20 is useful for viewing how Web pages in a Web site are connected to each other, it does not give much information about various files at a Web site. More detailed information about a Web site can be obtained by selecting View | Summary View from the main menu. As you can see in Figure 12.21, Summary View is ideal for obtaining detailed information about a Web site. Note that various columns in Summary View can be sorted by clicking the description label at the top of each column. This feature is powerful. For example, certain Web pages at your Web site might use graphics files that are too large to be transferred over a POTS link in a reasonable period of time. Such graphics files can be easily singled out by clicking the Size column and sorting files based on their file size.

As you can see in Figure 12.21, FrontPage Explorer is a powerful tool that can be used to graphically manage the contents of a Web site. FrontPage Explorer can be used to exploit capabilities of FrontPage because it is integrated with various components of FrontPage, such as the To Do List and the program that verifies URLs of Web pages. Be sure to spend some time with FrontPage Explorer to become more familiar with it and realize its potential.

FIGURE 12.21.

*Summary View can be used
to obtain detailed
information about various
files at a Web site.*

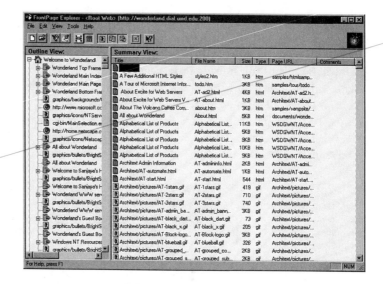

FrontPage To Do List

The FrontPage To Do List can be used to keep track of various tasks that have to be done as shown in Figure 12.22. Because it is integrated with other components of FrontPage, such as the program that checks for broken links, the FrontPage To Do List is ideal for keeping track of various tasks that have to be done to maintain a Web site. The FrontPage To Do List can be invoked by selecting Tools | Show To Do List from the main menu.

FIGURE 12.22.

FrontPage To Do List.

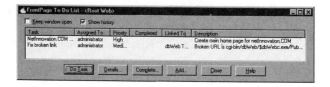

New tasks can be added to the To Do List by clicking the Add button. When the Add button is pressed, a dialog box similar to the one shown in Figure 12.23 will be displayed to gather information about the task being added to the To Do List. As shown in Figure 12.23, this dialog box can be used type in the name and description of a task along with its level of priority.

FIGURE 12.23.

Adding a task to FrontPage To Do List.

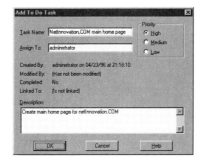

Verifying Links

After setting up a Web site, it is inevitable that at some point the Web pages are going to have broken URLs for objects that no longer exist. It is important that you check your Web site periodically for broken links. An application that can be used to verify links at a Web site is included with FrontPage. This utility can be invoked by selecting Tools | Verify Links from the main menu. As you can see in Figure 12.24, the Verify Links utility can be used to locate invalid URLs of a Web site as well as Web pages that contain them.

FIGURE 12.24.

FrontPage can be used to verify URLs of a Web page.

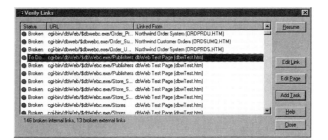

If you want, you can add a broken link to the To Do List so you can take care of it another time. Refer to Figure 12.22 for an example of a broken link added to the To Do List. Invalid URLs can be added to the To Do List by clicking the Add Task button in Figure 12.24. It is also possible to immediately correct broken links by clicking the Edit Link button and correcting the URL as shown in Figure 12.25. Also, the Edit Page button can be used to edit the Web page containing the broken URL.

FIGURE 12.25.
FrontPage can be used to
verify URLs of a Web page.

FrontPage Editor

The FrontPage Editor is a powerful WYSIWYG HTML editor that can be used to create Web pages with Tables, Frames, and other HTML 2.0 enhancements. The purpose of this section is not to comprehensively cover all aspects of the FrontPage Editor. However, a few key features of it will be discussed shortly to provide you an overview of some of its capabilities.

Designing Web Pages Using the FrontPage Editor

The FrontPage Editor is a powerful HTML editor that can be used to create and edit Web pages. Although it is possible to invoke the FrontPage Editor as a stand-alone application or through the FrontPage Explorer, it is recommended you first open an exiting Web and then open the FrontPage Explorer. This will enable you to use features of FrontPage Explorer to create and edit Web pages. It is recommended that you spend some time and become familiar with FrontPage Explorer because it can be used to view Web pages at a Web site in a more natural manner, and you can edit Web pages by simply double-clicking them. The next few sections will help you get started with FrontPage. Before proceeding to the next section, bring up FrontPage Explorer, select a Web, and then select Tools | Show FrontPage Editor from the main menu. Doing this will enable you to save Web documents edited with FrontPage into an exiting Web.

Document Attributes

Various document formatting attributes of a Web page can be defined using the FrontPage editor. For example, when creating a new document, you might want to assign colors to various elements of the Web page. This can be done by selecting Edit | Properties from the main menu. You then will be presented with a dialog box similar to the one shown in Figure 12.26. This dialog box can be used to assign a title to a Web page to customize its appearance.

Text in a Web page can be formatted by first selecting the text using the mouse and selecting Format | Characters from the main menu. By using a dialog box identical to the one shown in Figure 12.27, you then will be able to format the text you selected. The Choose button can be used to change the color of the text selected. This feature is handy for emphasizing a paragraph or heading. After selecting various text formatting options, press the OK button to apply them to the text selected.

FIGURE 12.26.

Page Properties dialog box.

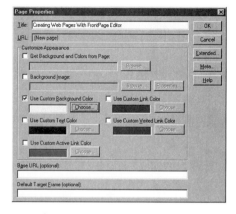

FIGURE 12.27.

Text formatting dialog box.

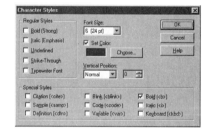

Frames

Frames can make a Web site easier and more interesting to navigate when they are used properly. It's easy to create a multiframe Web page with FrontPage. In order to create a Web page with frames, select File | New from the main menu. You then will be presented with the dialog box shown in Figure 12.28. Use the scroll down list in this dialog box to select the Frames Wizard as shown in Figure 12.28 and press OK to continue.

FIGURE 12.28.

Frames Wizard can be used to create a Web page with frames.

The next dialog box, shown in Figure 12.29, can be used to create a multiframe Web page using a custom grid or frames template. Generally, you should select to create a multiframe Web page using a custom grid if you are familiar with Frames and have an unusual frame set in mind. If not, select to create a Web page using a frames template. After selecting "Pick a template," click the next button.

FIGURE 12.29.

Frame creation technique dialog box.

You then will see a dialog box similar to the one shown in Figure 12.30. This dialog box can be used to select the layout of various frames on your Web page. Select a layout you like and press the OK button to continue. When selecting the layout of frames, be considerate toward users who might browse your Web site with 640 × 480 resolution monitors. After creating a frame set, take a look at it after resizing your Web browser window to 640 × 480 pixels to make sure everything is legible.

FIGURE 12.30.

Frame layout selection dialog box.

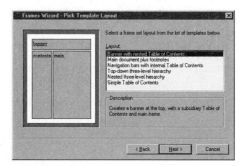

When creating Web pages with frames, be aware that some Web browsers do not support frames. Although the percentage of users using technologically challenged Web browsers is going down, you should make sure a user browsing your Web site with an older browser can still view the contents of your Web site. A Web page that will be shown to users whose browsers do not support frames can be specified using the dialog box shown in Figure 12.31.

FIGURE 12.31.

Alternate content page URL for Web browsers that do not support frames.

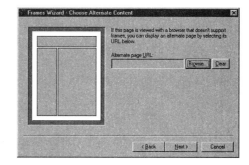

FrontPage will finally ask you for the title of your multiframe Web page and its filename as shown in Figure 12.32. Fill in the information requested and click the Finish button to continue. FrontPage then will create your multiframe Web page.

FIGURE 12.32.

Page information dialog box.

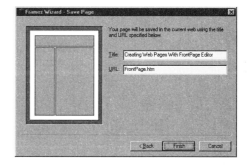

If you go back to FrontPage Explorer, you will see the multiframe Web page that was just created as shown in Figure 12.33. Note how the Web page that was just created is broken down into three separate Web pages. Each of these Web pages holds the contents of a frame. A frame can be edited by selecting and double-clicking the corresponding file in the Link View pane of FrontPage Explorer.

FIGURE 12.33.

Multiframe document just created when viewed with FrontPage Explorer. Various frames can be edited by double-clicking them.

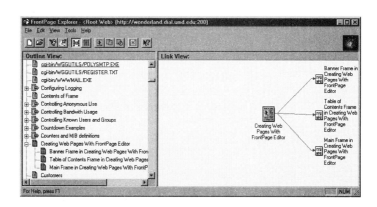

Tables

The table menu option can be used to add tables to a Web page. The following example illustrates how a table can be inserted to a Web page. Select Table | Insert Table to insert a table into a Web page. You then will see a dialog box similar to the one shown in Figure 12.34. This dialog box can be used to specify the number of columns and rows of a table as well as several other attributes.

FIGURE 12.34.
Insert Table dialog box.

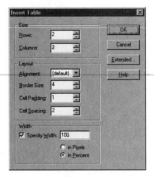

After a table is created, text and images can be inserted to various cells the same way text and images are inserted into regular Web pages. Images can be inserted by selecting Insert | Image from the main menu. By default, a two-column table has equal width. As shown in Figure 12.35, this is not ideal for some cases. The image in Figure 12.35 is cut off because the left column takes up too much space. This can be fixed by placing the mouse pointer on the left column and clicking the right mouse button. You then will see the pop up menu shown in Figure 12.35.

FIGURE 12.35.
The right mouse button can be used to format cells in a table.

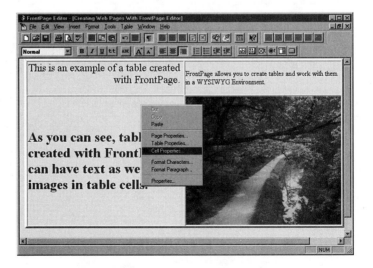

Select Cell Properties as shown in Figure 12.36 to change the width of the left column. You then will see a dialog box that can be used to define the width of a column as shown in Figure 12.36. In order to reduce the width of the left column, a lower percentage value can be specified for the width of the column. A cell width value of 30 percent is used in this example to reduce the size of the left column.

FIGURE 12.36.

Cell Properties dialog box.

Refer to Figure 12.37 for the result of the modification made in Figure 12.36. Note how the entire image now can be displayed on the window when the width of the left column is reduced. Tables are useful for formatting the contents of a Web site. As demonstrated in this example, the right mouse button can be used to format cells of a table and have more control over the contents of a table cell.

FIGURE 12.37.

Table after its left column size is reduced.

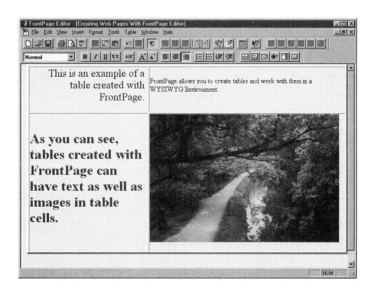

FrontPage Scripts

FrontPage scripts can be used to effortlessly add CGI programs to a Web site. For example, if you would like to set up a guest book at your Web site, one can be set up with FrontPage in just a few minutes. Setting up a guest book is as simple as Selecting File | New from the main menu and selecting the Guest Book option as shown in Figure 12.38.

FIGURE 12.38.

Selecting Guest Book template.

The Guest Book template then will be loaded into the FrontPage Editor as shown in Figure 12.39. You then can edit the Guest Book page as you want by changing the font and maybe adding a few images. Afterwards, select File | Save from the main menu to save the guest book Web page.

FIGURE 12.39.

Editing Guest Book Web page.

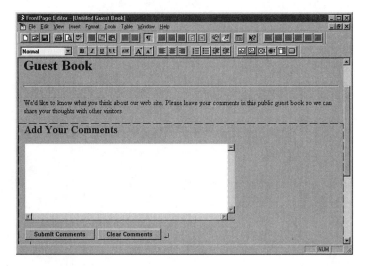

The file save dialog box, shown in Figure 12.40, can be used to save the guest book Web page and give it a title. After typing in a title for the Web page and a filename for the guest book, click the OK button to save the file.

FIGURE 12.40.

Saving Guest Book Web page.

Users now can connect to your Web server and sign your guest book using the filename specified in Figure 12.40. Refer to Figure 12.41 for an example of how a user can connect to your Web server and sign the guest book.

FIGURE 12.41.

The guest book setup using the FrontPage Editor is immediately functional.

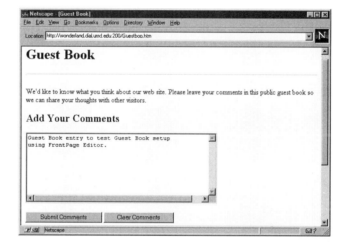

After a user types in a guest book entry and presses the Submit Comments button, the information is sent to a FrontPage CGI (Common Gateway Interface) program for processing. After the information is processed, FrontPage will display a message as shown in Figure 12.42. This message also has a link to go back to the previous page.

When a user either clicks the link to go back to the previous page or manually goes back and reloads the guest book Web page, the entry that was just added will be displayed as shown in Figure 12.43. As you can see from this example, CGI applications that are built into FrontPage are powerful. For example, a guest book can be set up using FrontPage—without writing a single line of CGI code—in about five minutes. Experiment with other FrontPage CGI scripts and incorporate them into your Web site to make it more interactive.

FIGURE 12.42.
*Guest book entry
confirmation message.*

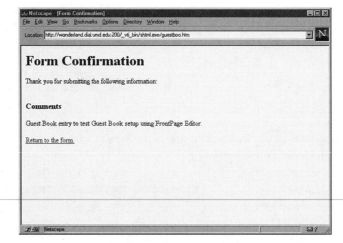

FIGURE 12.43.
*Guest book entry
confirmation message.*

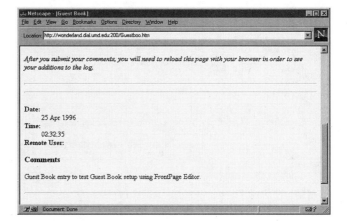

Creating Web Pages Using Templates

Web pages also can be created using predefined document templates. In order to create a document using a predefined template, select File | New from the main menu and select a template that best resembles the page you wish to create. Experiment with various FrontPage templates and become more familiar with using them. You then will be able to save time by using templates to create routine Web pages.

Summary

FrontPage is a powerful, yet easy-to-use Web page development application that can be used to manage the contents of a Web site. Because FrontPage is part of Microsoft Office, it is likely that it will be integrated with various Microsoft Office applications in the future. Because FrontPage can be used to create interactive Web pages without writing CGI programs or worrying about details of HTML, it is an ideal application to be used to easily create content for a Web site.

What's Next?

Microsoft Office is a powerful suite of productivity applications. Various Internet assistants for Microsoft Office can be used to effortlessly publish content for the Web using Microsoft Applications. These Internet assistants are especially useful for converting large amounts of MS Office files into HTML so they can be published on the global Internet or a local intranet. The next chapter demonstrates how Microsoft Word, Excel, Access, and PowerPoint can be used to create content for the World Wide Web.

13

Publishing on the Web with Microsoft Office

Various Microsoft Office applications can be used to publish information on the Internet. This capability is particularly useful for effortlessly publishing existing MS Office documents on the Web. There are many advantages to using MS Office Internet Assistants to create content for your Web site. One of the most significant benefits is the capability to enable those who create content to publish it on the Internet without waiting for someone else to convert it into HTML. For example, the person who puts together a sales report is probably not a Web developer. Having someone else convert the sales report into an HTML file is not only a waste of resources but can also be time consuming. On the other hand, using Internet Assistant for MS Word or Excel, the person who created the sales report can easily publish the information on the Internet or an intranet without waiting for someone else to go through the sales report and add a few funny HTML tags here and there.

Visit the Microsoft Office Web site for more information about using various Internet Assistants to publish content on the Internet.

> **URL**
>
> The Microsoft Office Web site is located at
>
> `http://www.microsoft.com/msoffice/`

Microsoft Office and the Internet

The next few sections will demonstrate how MS Word, Excel, PowerPoint, and Access documents can be published on the Web using various Internet Assistants. Internet Assistants are special add-on programs that can be downloaded from Microsoft's Web site. These applications are designed to seamlessly integrate with various office applications and extend their functionality by allowing office documents to be saved as HTML documents. Note that most Internet Assistants covered in later sections require Microsoft Office for Windows 95.

> **URL**
>
> Microsoft's Internet tools for Microsoft Office Web page can be found at
>
> `http://www.microsoft.com/MSOffice/MSOfc/it_ofc.htm`

Publishing on the Web with Microsoft Word

Microsoft Word is a feature-rich word processing application. Internet Assistant (IA) for MS Word can be used to effortlessly publish Word files on the Internet. As you will be shown shortly, it can also be used as a WYSIWYG HTML editor. At the time of this writing, in addition to various standard HTML 2.0 tags, Internet Assistant for Word also supports various HTML enhancements such as tables, table cell colors, TrueType fonts, and font colors.

Internet Assistant is not part of Microsoft Word. Before using it to create content for the Web, Internet Assistant for Microsoft Word has to be downloaded from Microsoft's Web site.

URL

Microsoft Internet Assistant for Word download site:

`http://www.microsoft.com/msword/internet/ia/ia95/chcklist.htm`

Installing Internet Assistant for Word

After downloading the Internet Assistant for Word from Microsoft's Web site, simply execute the executable file and specify a directory where IA for Word should be installed. Note that it is recommended you close all applications before installing IA for Word, because the installation program might need to copy several shared .DLL files. When IA for Word is installed, you might get a few message boxes similar to the one shown in Figure 13.1. Simply press the Ignore button to proceed installing IA for Word. Later, if you encounter problems running IA for Word, remove applications from the Windows NT start folder, reboot NT, and then install IA for Word soon after logging in.

FIGURE 13.1.

Shared .DLL *files that are open and being used by other applications cannot be replaced by the Internet Assistant for Word installation program.*

After IA for Word is installed, you will see a message box similar to the one shown in Figure 13.2. At this point, you can launch MS Word and begin creating documents for the Web using MS Word.

FIGURE 13.2.

Immediately after IA for Word is installed, MS Word is capable of creating content for the Web.

Creating an HTML Document with Word

Once IA for Word is installed, creating HTML documents is as easy as creating Word documents. This section demonstrates how various features of IA for Word can be used to create an HTML document with TrueType fonts, inline images, a table, and various other HTML attributes. In order to begin creating an HTML document, select File and New from the main menu. You will be presented with a dialog box similar to the one shown in Figure 13.3. Note the HTML document template that has been added by the IA for Word installation program.

FIGURE 13.3.

The HTML document template can be used to create HTML files with Internet Assistant.

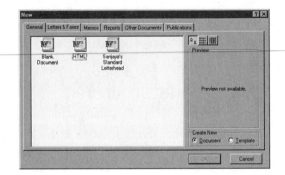

From the dialog box shown in Figure 13.3, select the HTML document template and press the OK button. You are now ready to start creating an HTML document using MS Word. Before continuing to create a document, you might want to select Tools | Customize from the main menu to customize the tool bar. Because you will be shown how to add TrueType fonts to HTML files shortly, you might want to make sure the Font button shown in Figure 13.4 is added to your toolbar.

FIGURE 13.4.

The MS Word tool bar can be customized with useful HTML attributes such as TrueType fonts.

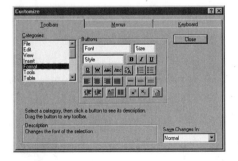

Background Images and Text Colors

HTML documents created with Word can be customized with a background image and various text attribute colors. This can be done by selecting Format | Background and Links from the main menu. By using a dialog box similar to the one shown in Figure 13.5, you will be able to specify various text attributes, colors, and a background image.

When using background images and special text colors, always use either a light-colored background and dark colored text, or light-colored text with a dark background. Otherwise, users browsing your document will not be able to read the text. Before putting a document created with MS Word on the Internet, use a Web browser to preview the documents to ensure they are legible.

FIGURE 13.5.

Background and Link attribute specification dialog box.

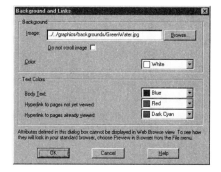

If you wish to specify a background image, click the Browse button to bring up the Insert Picture dialog box shown in Figure 13.6. This dialog box is handy for selecting backgrounds because it displays a preview of the background image on the right column. After selecting the image you wish to use, click the OK button. It is recommended that you work with a directory structure identical to that of the production Web server to make sure directory path names are compatible between the production server and the development environment in which you work.

FIGURE 13.6.

Insert Picture dialog box can be used to add a background image to an HTML document.

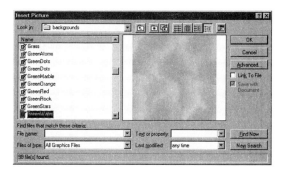

Using TrueType Fonts

MS Word supports TrueType fonts in HTML documents. In order to change the font of some text, select the text and select Format | Font from the menu bar. You will then be able to specify a TrueType font typeface for the selected text using a dialog box similar to the one shown in Figure 13.7. This dialog box can also be used to specify the size and color of the selected typeface. Note that not all Web browsers support TrueType fonts.

FIGURE 13.7.
*Font specification
dialog box.*

Inserting Tables

HTML documents created with Word can also have tables. Inserting a table into an HTML document is as easy as inserting a table into a Word document. Simply select Table | Insert Table, and you will see the dialog box shown in Figure 13.8. This dialog box can be used to specify the number of rows and columns the table should have. Table columns and rows can be inserted, deleted, and merged if it becomes necessary to make changes to a table after it is created.

FIGURE 13.8.
Insert Table dialog box.

Inserting Inline Images and Video

Inline images and video clips can be inserted to an HTML document by selecting Insert | Picture from the main menu. The dialog box shown in Figure 13.9 can then be used to select an image or video clip to insert into a Word HTML document. When adding an image, use the data entry field for Alternative Text to describe the image. Web browsers such as Internet Explorer show this text in a balloon if a user rests the mouse pointer on the image. If you click the Browse button shown in Figure 13.9, a dialog box similar to the one in Figure 13.6 can be used to select an image.

FIGURE 13.9.
*Inline picture insertion
dialog box.*

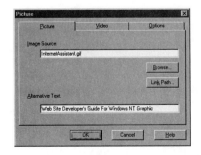

Formatting Table Cells

It is easy to format table cells of an HTML document. Simply select the cell(s) you wish to format and click the right mouse button. You will then see a pop-up menu similar to the one shown in Figure 13.10. This menu can be used to specify various cell formatting attributes. For example, if you wish to change the background of a cell, select it and click the Background Color option of the pop-up menu shown in Figure 13.10. You will then be able to define a background color for the selected cell using a Background Color dialog box similar to the one in Figure 13.11.

FIGURE 13.10.

The right mouse button can be used to format cells in a table.

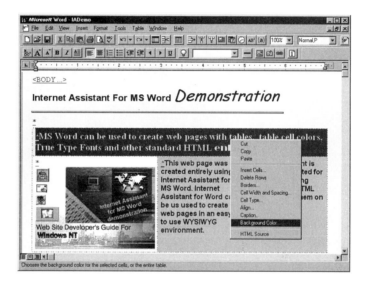

FIGURE 13.11.

The Background Color dialog box can be used to assign a color to one or more selected table cells.

Publishing an HTML Document with MS Word

Attractive HTML documents can be created with MS Word using various tips and procedures discussed earlier. An example of an HTML document created with various standard HTML 2.0 extensions such as tables and TrueType fonts is shown in Figure 13.12. After creating an HTML document with Word, publishing it on the Internet is as easy as saving the document as an HTML file.

HTML documents created with MS Word can be viewed with any Web browser. The HTML document shown in Figure 13.12 looks similar to the Web page in Figure 13.13 when it is viewed with Internet Explorer. As you can see in Figure 13.13, the inline image and text in the table is appropriately formatted by IA for Word. As demonstrated in previous sections, IA for Word is a powerful Web publishing tool that can be used to leverage the power of Word to the Internet and create richly formatted Web pages.

FIGURE 13.12.

An HTML document created with MS Word.

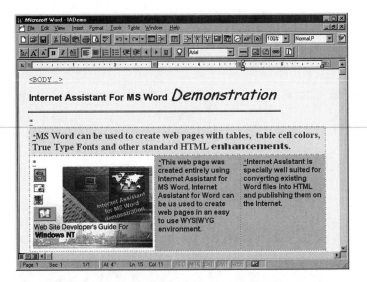

FIGURE 13.13.

A Web browser, such as Internet Explorer, can be used to view HTML documents created with MS Word.

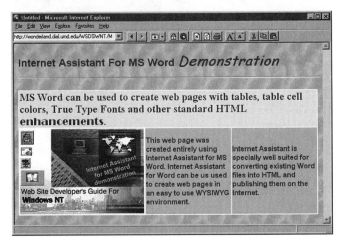

Publishing on the Web with Microsoft Excel

Internet Assistant for Excel can be used to effortlessly convert Excel spreadsheets into HTML documents so they can be published on the Web. You might want to visit the MS Excel Web page to obtain the most up-to-date information about Excel and how it can be used to create content for the Web. The next few sections illustrate how the Excel spreadsheet shown in Figure 13.14 can be converted into HTML and published on the Web.

FIGURE 13.14.

Shortly, you will be shown how to convert this spreadsheet into HTML.

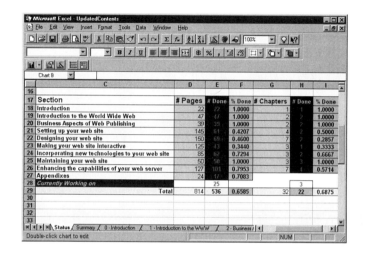

Section	# Pages	# Done	% Done	# Chapters	# Done	% Done
Introduction	22	22	1.0000	1	1	1.0000
Introduction to the World Wide Web	47	47	1.0000	2	2	1.0000
Business Aspects of Web Publishing	39	39	1.0000	2	2	1.0000
Setting up your web site	145	61	0.4207	4	2	0.5000
Designing your web site	150	69	0.4600	7	2	0.2857
Making your web site interactive	125	43	0.3440	3	1	0.3333
Incorporating new technologies to your web site	85	62	0.7294	3	2	0.6667
Maintaining your web site	50	50	1.0000	3	3	1.0000
Enhancing the capabilities of your web server	127	101	0.7953	7	4	0.5714
Appendixes	24	17	0.7083			
Currently Working on		25			3	
Total	814	536	0.6585	32	22	0.6875

Incidentally, the spreadsheet shown in Figure 13.14 was actually used when this book was being written. Internet Assistant for Excel was used to regularly update the contents of the spreadsheet in Figure 13.14 to an HTML file so my acquisitions editor could monitor the progress of the book. The HTML file was stored in a secure Web server directory protected with a password. This is an example of how IA for Excel can be used to share information with selected users using a secure Web server.

URL

Use the following URL to reach the Microsoft Excel home page:

`http://www.microsoft.com/msexcel/default.htm`

Installing Internet Assistant for Excel

Internet Assistant for Excel can be installed by following a few simple steps after downloading it from Microsoft's Web site.

URL

Internet Assistant for Microsoft Excel download site:

`http://www.microsoft.com/msexcel/Internet/IA/default.htm`

The steps you need to follow to install Internet Assistant for Excel are as follows:

1. Download Internet Assistant for Excel. This file is named HTML.XLA.

2. After downloading it, place it in the \EXCEL\LIBRARY directory if you are running a stand-alone version of Excel, and \MSOFFICE\EXCEL\LIBRARY if you are running the MS Office version of Excel 7.0.

3. Start MS Excel and select Tools | Add-Ins from the main menu. You will then be presented with a dialog box similar to the one shown in Figure 13.15.

FIGURE 13.15.
MS Excel tool Add-Ins
dialog box.

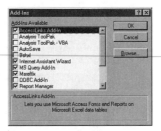

4. Locate the tool Internet Assistant Wizard and place a check mark beside it and click the OK button.

Internet Assistant for MS Excel is now installed and ready for use.

Publishing a Spreadsheet on the Web with Excel

Internet Assistant for Excel can be used to effortlessly convert a spreadsheet into HTML. As shown in Figure 13.16, simply highlight the area of a spreadsheet you wish to convert into HTML and select Tools | Internet Assistant Wizard from the main menu.

FIGURE 13.16.
The selected area of a
spreadsheet can be
converted into HTML
using Internet Assistant for
Excel.

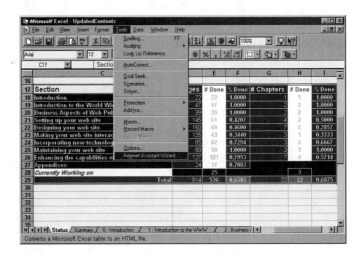

After the Internet Assistant Wizard menu option is selected, a dialog box similar to the one shown in Figure 13.17 will be displayed to confirm the area selected in Figure 13.16. At this point, you can change the area selected to be converted into HTML.

FIGURE 13.17.

Step 1 of Internet Assistant Wizard for Excel confirms the area selected in Figure 13.16.

The next dialog box (Figure 13.18) will ask if you'd like to create a new HTML file or would like the data to be inserted into an existing HTML document. Note that if you select to have the data inserted into an exiting file, the file should contain the string `<!--##Table##-->`. Internet Assistant for Excel will then insert the data from the spreadsheet where it encounters the string `<!--##Table##-->`.

FIGURE 13.18.

Target HTML file selection dialog box.

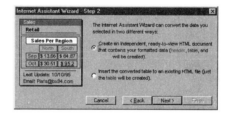

If you selected the option to create a new HTML file, a dialog box similar to the one shown in Figure 13.19 will be presented to you. This dialog box can be used to customize the HTML file created by IA for Excel.

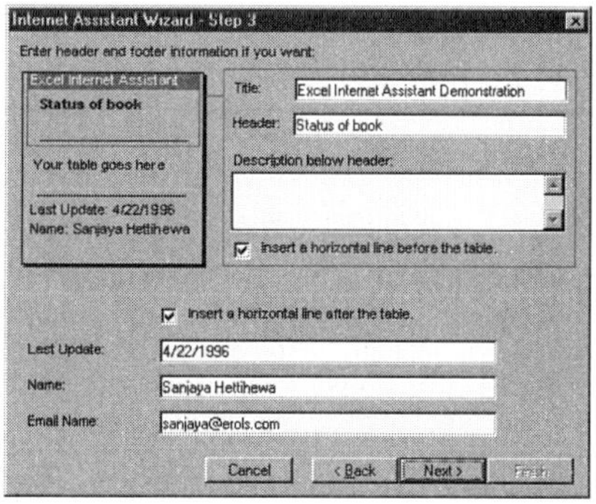

FIGURE 13.19.

HTML file customizing dialog box.

The next dialog box will ask if you'd like to preserve as much formatting as possible. Select this option if you'd like the HTML file created by IA for Excel to resemble the original Excel spreadsheet as much as possible. Use the other option only if you notice other browsers having problems with some of the enhanced HTML tags used by IA for Excel. If your users use Internet Explorer or Netscape, using the option to preserve as much formatting as possible will produce the best results. Afterwards, provide the HTML filename of the new file and the spreadsheet you selected in Figure 13.16 will be saved as an HTML file. After the HTML file is saved, it can be viewed with a Web browser as shown in Figure 13.20. Compare the HTML document in Figure 13.20 with the Excel spreadsheet in Figure 13.14 and note how they closely resemble each other. As illustrated in this example, it is quite easy to publish Excel spreadsheets on the Web using Internet Assistant for Excel.

FIGURE 13.20.

Spreadsheet in Figure 13.14 after it is converted into HTML.

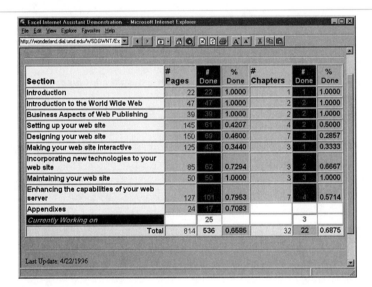

Publishing on the Web with Microsoft PowerPoint

PowerPoint is a powerful presentation tool that can be used to create slide show presentations on the Internet using Internet Assistant for PowerPoint. The next few sections illustrate how easy it is to create a PowerPoint presentation and save it as an HTML file. For the purpose of this demonstration, you will be shown how to convert the slides in Figure 13.21 into HTML. Visit the Microsoft PowerPoint Web page for the most up-to-date information about PowerPoint and Internet Assistant for PowerPoint.

URL

Microsoft PowerPoint Web page:

`http://www.microsoft.com/mspowerpoint/default.htm`

FIGURE 13.21.

You will learn shortly how to convert these two slides into HTML.

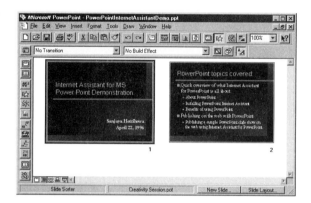

Installing PowerPoint Internet Assistant

Internet Assistant for PowerPoint can be downloaded from Microsoft's Web site. After downloading it, copy it to a temporary directory and execute the executable file. This will decompress the PowerPoint distribution file. Once the distribution file is decompressed, execute the file IA4PPT95.EXE to install Internet Assistant for PowerPoint. Before executing this file, make sure PowerPoint is not running. The installation program will then install IA for PowerPoint and terminate with a message similar to the one shown in Figure 13.22.

URL

Internet Assistant for Microsoft PowerPoint download site:

`http://www.microsoft.com/mspowerpoint/Internet/ia/default.htm`

FIGURE 13.22.

PowerPoint Internet Assistant installation program.

Converting a PowerPoint Slide Show into HTML

PowerPoint slides can be easily converted into HTML by selecting File | Export as HTML from the main menu. After selecting Export as HTML, a dialog box similar to the one shown in Figure 13.23 will be presented to obtain information about the output that should be generated by IA for PowerPoint.

FIGURE 13.23.

*HTML Export options
dialog box.*

The "Output style" radio button is used to specify if IA for PowerPoint should output the slides in color or grayscale format. It is recommended that you select slides to be exported in color unless your slides contain only a limited number of colors and you are concerned about the size of slide files.

The next radio button is used to specify the file format of the exported PowerPoint slides. Generally, use the JPEG format for natural photograph-looking slides that do not have too many sharp edges; use the GIF format for all other slides. Refer to Chapter 11, "Adding Multimedia to Your Web Site," for a more in-depth discussion of when to use the GIF format and the JPEG format.

If you are using the JPEG format, the slide bar in Figure 13.23 can be used to define the image quality of JPEG files. Higher image quality results in larger files and lower image quality results in smaller files. You might want to experiment with various settings to determine the ideal level of quality for your slide presentation if you are concerned about bandwidth and file sizes. Note that this is not an issue in an intranet environment where there is usually an abundance of available network bandwidth.

Finally, specify the folder that will contain the HTML version of the PowerPoint presentation and click the OK button to begin the conversion. IA for PowerPoint will then export the slide show presentation and display a message similar to the one shown in Figure 13.24.

FIGURE 13.24.

*HTML conversion
dialog box.*

The PowerPoint presentation can now be viewed using a Web browser as shown in Figure 13.25. Note that the first page contains an index of all slides of the presentation.

FIGURE 13.25.

HTML slide presentation index.

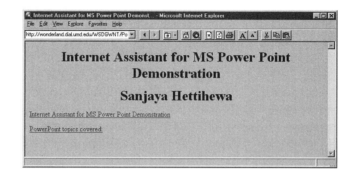

The index shown in Figure 13.25 can be used to view individual PowerPoint slides as shown in Figure 13.26. Note the navigation aids at the bottom of the slide. These navigation aids are automatically created by IA for PowerPoint to make it easier for users to browse a PowerPoint presentation using a Web browser.

FIGURE 13.26.

PowerPoint slides exported as HTML files can be viewed with a Web browser.

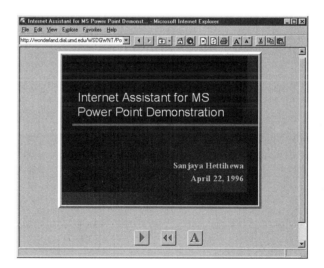

Publishing on the Web with Microsoft Access

An Internet Assistant is also available for Microsoft Access. As you will be shown shortly, information in a Microsoft Access database can be easily published on the Web using Internet Assistant for Access. Visit the Microsoft Access Internet tools Web page for the most up-to-date information about publishing Access databases on the Internet.

URL

The Microsoft Access Internet tools Web page:

`http://www.microsoft.com/msaccess/it_acc.htm`

Installing Internet Assistant for Access

Internet Assistant for MS Access can be downloaded from Microsoft's Web site. After downloading it, execute the executable file and allow the installation program to detect the Microsoft Access directory. After it detects the directory Access is installed in, click the large Install button to install IA for Access.

URL

Microsoft Internet Assistant for Access download site:

`http://www.microsoft.com/msaccess/internet/ia/default.htm`

Publishing a Database on the Web with Access

The next few sections illustrate how a Microsoft Access database can be published on the Web using IA for Access. In order to publish an Access database, load the database into Access and select Tools | Add-ins | Internet Assistant from the main menu (see Figure 13.27). Internet Assistant for Access will then begin a welcome message. Click the Next button, and a dialog box similar to the one shown in Figure 13.28 will be displayed.

FIGURE 13.27.

The Internet Assistant for Access can be invoked from the tools menu.

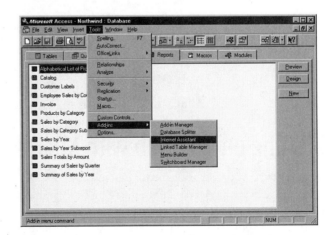

Internet Assistant for Access can be used to export any combination of MS Access tables, queries, reports, and forms into HTML. This is done by selecting the object type and names of objects in that type using a dialog box similar to the one shown in Figure 13.28. Note that one or more object types and object names can be selected. For example, you might want to select several reports and several tables.

FIGURE 13.28.

Various MS Access objects can be selected to be exported into HTML.

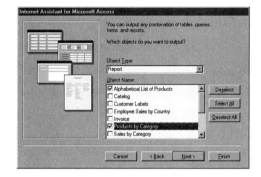

After selecting various objects to export as HTML files, click the Next button to continue. IA for Access will then present you with a dialog box similar to the one in Figure 13.29 and ask you for a template. A template can be used to enhance the appearance of data exported by IA for Access by adding a background image, navigation buttons, and various graphics to its output. Various templates included with IA for access can be browsed by clicking the browse button. Note that templates with filenames ending with the suffix _r are used for reports and those without _r for data sheets. When several object types are selected, select the template without the _r suffix and IA for Access will apply the correct template based on its filename.

FIGURE 13.29.

A template can be used to format HTML output generated by Internet Assistant for Access.

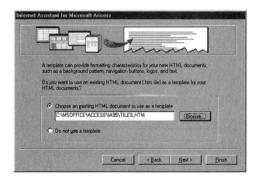

After selecting a template, type in a directory that will contain the exported HTML files. After typing in the directory, click the Finish button to export selected objects as HTML files. IA for Access will then export selected objects and let you know when it has finished creating the HTML files. The exported data can then be viewed using a Web browser as shown in Figure 13.30.

FIGURE 13.30.

Data exported by IA for Access can be viewed with a Web browser.

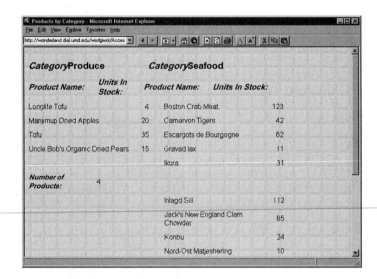

Note that IA for Microsoft Access might not always copy all the graphic files that are part of the HTML files it creates into the target HTML directory. Use a Web browser to look at HTML files that IA for Access creates. If you see any broken images, look at the source code to locate graphic files it refers to and copy them to the target HTML directory. These graphics files are located in the \MSOFFICE\ACCESS\IA95 directory (assuming you installed Office 95 into the \MSOFFICE directory). If you do not feel like doing this, you might want to copy all the graphic files from the \MSOFFICE\ACCESS\IA95 directory to the target HTML directory.

Summary

Microsoft Office is a powerful suite of productivity applications. Various Internet Assistants available for Microsoft Office can be used to effortlessly publish content for the Internet. These Internet assistants are especially useful for converting large amounts of MS Office files into HTML so they can be published on the global Internet or a local intranet.

What's Next?

FutureTense Texture is a Java-based Web publishing system that can be used to create multi-media–rich, interactive content for the Internet. FutureTense uses the power and platform neutral capabilities of Java to publish content for the Web. The next chapter covers the various capabilities of FutureTense and demonstrates how it can be used to create visually appealing and highly interactive Web pages.

14

Designing Web Pages with FutureTense Texture

FutureTense Texture is a unique Web content development application. It can be used to create visually rich, highly interactive Web publications in a short period of time. Publications created with Texture can be viewed on any platform that supports Java. Texture is a unique Web content development application because it relies on a Java applet. Content created with the Texture editor is read by the Texture Java applet and is formatted on the browser. This is a innovative solution to document formatting limitations of HTML. As you will learn shortly, Texture is a powerful tool for formatting documents. Content developers have complete control over various objects of a document created with Texture. Although Texture offers many benefits over other Web content development applications, there are a few drawbacks in taking this route. Subsequent sections will explore these drawbacks and suggest ways in which you can deal with them. Be sure to visit the FutureTense Web site for the most up-to-date information about Texture.

URL

The FutureTense Web site:

`http://www.futuretense.com/`

Applications of FutureTense Texture

Texture is ideal for creating high-impact Web publications that are interactive and easy to update. This is because Texture encourages the separation between content and formatting, and gives Web content designers complete control over the layout of a publication.

On the other hand, Texture is ideal for formatting the contents of an online magazine or newsletter. In addition to these publications, Texture is ideal for creating other Web-based publications such as online sales presentations and product catalogs that can benefit from advanced document layout features of Texture. Any publication that can use powerful document formatting capabilities of Texture can benefit from it. Refer to Figure 14.1 for an example of an online newspaper created with Texture. As you can see, publications created with Texture can be highly formatted and made interactive with the use of various controls in a page. For example, the up and down buttons you see on Figure 14.1 are actually two graphics images. These graphics images have been turned into interactive controls by assigning *actions* and *triggers* to them. Shortly, you will learn how Texture can be used to create a publication like the one shown in Figure 14.1 in a matter of minutes.

FIGURE 14.1.

*Interactive Web publica-
tion created with Texture.*

Compatibility Issues and Drawbacks

Publications created with Texture require a Java compatible Web browser. This means users who do not have a Java compatible Web browser will not be able to view content created with Texture. However, this restriction might not apply to you. The two most commonly used Web browsers, Internet Explorer and Netscape Navigator, both support Java. Therefore, most users will be able to view Texture publications. Because Microsoft Internet Explorer is free for all Windows 95, Windows NT, and Macintosh users, a majority of these users will switch to Internet Explorer in the near future. Therefore, although the fact that Texture relies on Java places a restriction on who can view Texture publications, this restriction might not apply to you if most of your users use Internet Explorer or Netscape Navigator. In the near future, Spyglass Mosaic users also should be able to view Texture publications.

Another drawback of Texture is the fact that it depends on a Java applet. If a user has not installed the Texture viewer, the user's browser has to download the Texture viewer each time it encounters a Texture publication. Although in a corporate/intranet environment, due to high-speed Internet connections, this is not a major issue; it becomes an issue for users navigating a Web site with relatively slow POTS links to the Internet. FutureTense is aware of this drawback. By the time you read this, you might expect to see a solution to this problem. Again, visit the FutureTense Web site for the most up-to-date information about Texture.

Installing Netscape Plug-In for FutureTense Texture

Before experimenting with Texture, it is highly recommended that you install the Netscape plug-in for Texture. This will make sure you do not have to download the Texture Java applet each time you view a Texture publication. The Texture viewer for Netscape Navigator can be downloaded from the following URL. By the time you read this, it is likely that FutureTense also will have a similar solution for MS Internet Explorer.

URL

The FutureTense Texture viewer download site:

```
http://www.futuretense.com/viewdown.htm
```

HTML Tags Supported by Texture

As you will learn shortly, contents of a Texture text box can be dynamically retrieved using a URL when a user browses a Web page with a Texture publication. This is a powerful feature, because changes made to various documents of a Texture publication can be immediately made available to users browsing a Web site without having to worry about the layout of the publication.

The FutureTense Texture viewer supports a number of HTML tags. These tags can be used to format text displayed on Texture publications. It is recommended that you only use the following HTML tags, because HTML tags not understood by the Texture viewer will be ignored regardless of the Web browser used to view the Texture publication.

Controlling Fonts and Attributes of Text

The following HTML tags can be used to control font sizes. Use these tags to control the appearance of text appearing inside a Texture publication text box:

```
<H1> This text will appear in a very large font </H1>
<H2> This text will appear in a large font </H2>
<H3> This text will appear in a medium font </H3>
<H4> This text will appear in a small font </H4>
<H5> This text will appear in a very small font </H5>
<H6> This text will appear in a tiny font </H6>

<FONT FACE=[Name of Typeface]>
This text appears in the typeface specified in the FONT tag
</FONT>

<FONT COLOR=#RRGGBB>
This text appears in the RGB value specified in the FONT tag.
```

```
RR=Red value, GG=Green value, BB=Blue value.
</FONT>

<FONT SIZE=[Size of font]>
This text appears in the font size specified in the FONT tag
Note that font sizes are specified in pixels.
</FONT>
```

The following character styles also are supported by Texture. Use these styles to highlight text appearing inside a Texture publication text box:

```
<EM> This text appears emphasized (usually italicized) </EM>
<STRONG> This text is typically rendered in bold </STRONG>
<I> This text appears italicized </I>
<B> This text appears in bold </B>
<PRE> Reformatted text </PRE>
```

Formatting Paragraphs

Paragraphs of text appearing in a Texture text box also can be formatting using the following HTML tags:

```
<P ALIGN=Center>
Text in this paragraph will appear centered
</P>

<P ALIGN=Left>
Text in this paragraph will appear left justified
</P>

<P ALIGN=Right>
Text in this paragraph will appear right justified
</P>

<P ALIGN=Justify>
Text in this paragraph will appear full justified
</P>
```

Lists

Lists can be used to format a list of items. The following HTML tags are supported by Texture to format a list of items:

```
<DL>
<DT> First Term </DT>
<DD> This is the definition of the first term. </DD>
<DT> Second Term </DT>
<DD> This is the definition of the second term. </DD>
</DL>

<OL>
<LI> Ordered List item one.</LI>
<LI> Ordered List item two.</LI>
<LI> Ordered List item three.</LI>
</OL>
```

```
<UL>
<LI> Unordered List item one.</LI>
<LI> Unordered List item two.</LI>
<LI> Unordered List item three.</LI>
</UL>
```

Text Spacing

You are probably familiar with the HTML tag used for line breaks. The line break tag is supported by the Texture viewer and can be used as follows:

```
First line of text<BR>
Second line of text<BR>
```

The BLOCKQUOTE element usually is used to format text quoted from another source. The BLOCKQUOTE HTML tag usually inserts space above and below the quote. The syntax of the BLOCKQUOTE tag is as follows:

```
<BLOCKQUOTE>
This line of text was typed in the wee hours of the morning.
</BLOCKQUOTE>
```

Special Characters

The Texture viewer supports special characters that can be specified using an *entity reference* (&#lt;) or a *character reference* (<). Refer to Appendix C for an example of a list of useful entity and character reference codes for generating special HTML characters.

Commenting HTML Code

In addition to the above tags, Texture also respects the HTML tag used to comment Web pages. Web pages can be commented using the following HTML tags. Text appearing inside the HTML comment tag is ignored by the Texture viewer:

```
<!--
This text will not appear inside a Texture text box because
it is used to comment HTML code.
-->
```

Hello World, FutureTense Texture!

It is easy to create publications with Texture. The following example will help you become familiar with various capabilities of Texture and learn how various Texture controls can be used to make a publication interactive. The following publication uses several powerful document formatting features of Texture. It is recommended that you experiment with the Hello World publication before reading how it was put together. You then will be able to easily understand how various *controls, actions,* and *triggers* can be used to make a Texture publication interactive. Assuming you've already installed the Texture viewer, you can view the Hello World publication by opening the Texture publication using Netscape. If you have not already installed the Texture viewer, please do so now. The Hello World Texture publication is included in the CD-ROM that accompanies the book (`\Chapter-14\HelloWorld\HelloWorld.html`). Note that the Texture viewer does not have to be installed to view Texture publications. At the end of this chapter, you will be shown how to publish Texture publications so users can view them by dynamically downloading the Texture viewer Java applet.

Note that a few user interface dialog boxes might be different in the released version of Texture. This chapter is based on a pre-release beta version of Texture. However, for the most part, you will not have any difficulty following steps in this chapter to create Texture publications.

Beginning to Create a Texture Publication

In order to begin creating a Texture publication, select File | New to bring up the Project Manager dialog box shown in Figure 14.2. This dialog box is used to specify the project folder and name of the publication. When specifying a page name, please leave the extension `.ftl` as it is because it will help you easily identify the Texture project file.

URL

FutureTense Texture can be obtained by visiting the following URL and filling in and submitting a form. Instructions for downloading Texture will be e-mailed once the form is submitted.

`http://www.futuretense.com/contact.htm`

FIGURE 14.2.

The Project Manager dialog box can be used to specify the filename and folder of a new publication.

After typing in a filename and folder, click the Next button to continue. You then will see a Page Properties dialog box similar to the one shown in Figure 14.3. This dialog box can be used to specify the dimensions of a Texture publication. If you are not absolutely sure of the dimensions of your publication, simply type in a reasonable value, such as 400 × 300, and select a background color for the publication. You can change these values later by selecting Edit | Page Properties from the main menu.

FIGURE 14.3.
Page Properties dialog box.

The dialog box in Figure 14.3 also can be used to specify the background color of the Texture publication. When the Color button in Figure 14.3 is pressed, a standard color selection dialog box will be displayed. As shown in Figure 14.4, this dialog box can be used to select a color using a number of ways. After specifying the dimensions of the publication, and selecting a background color, click the OK button to continue.

FIGURE 14.4.
Color selection dialog box.

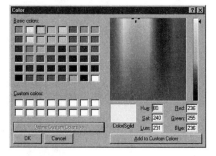

Creating a Manual Image Animation

The Hello World Texture publication contains a manual graphics animation. What is a manual graphics animation? A graphic will be displayed by default. When a user clicks the graphic, another graphic will be displayed. This sequence will continue each time a user clicks the graphic.

It is easy to create a manual graphics animation with Texture. First, select Objects | New | Image from the main menu. Draw a graphics image box as shown in Figure 14.5. Then, select the image box and click the right mouse button. Using the pop-up menu that appears when the right mouse button is clicked, select the Object Properties option as shown in Figure 14.5.

FIGURE 14.5.

The right mouse button can be used to invoke the Object Properties dialog box of an image box.

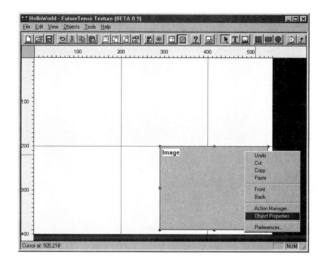

You then will see the Object Properties dialog box shown in Figure 14.6. The Object Properties dialog box is a tabbed dialog box. Use the Name data entry field to give the image box a name. Be sure to give descriptive names to all objects of a Texture publication. It is also a good idea to specify the type of object in its name. For example, because we are naming an image box, the name given to the image box in Figure 14.6 ends with "graphic." Although this may seem trivial at the moment, once you have a dozen or so objects in a publication, you will realize the benefit of using descriptive names and specifying the type of object in its name.

The Object Properties dialog box also can be used to specify its position as well as dimensions. Click the Initially Shown checkbox to make sure the image box is visible when the publication is first displayed. The Color button can be used to assign a background color to the image box. If you do not want the color to show up, simply click the transparent check box.

The data entry field for Tip can be used to specify the contents of the balloon that pops up when a user rests the mouse pointer on the graphic. As shown in Figure 14.6, this data entry field can be used to let the user know what would happen if he or she clicks the graphic.

FIGURE 14.6.

General tab of the Object Properties dialog box.

The "Actions" and "Targets" tabs are covered in a later section. The Content tab is used to specify the contents of the image box. There are two ways to specify the contents of an image box. You can type in its URL if the image is located on a Web server. The image then will be dynamically loaded from a Web server when the publication is viewed. Because we are creating an animation, more than one graphic has to be added to the text box. This can be done by selecting several graphics files as shown in Figure 14.7. Note that only the first graphic will be initially displayed. Soon, you will learn how to get Texture to display other graphics specified in the Content tab of the Object Properties dialog box.

FIGURE 14.7.

Content tab of the Object Properties dialog box.

A local graphic also can be specified by clicking the Grab button and selecting a content file from a dialog box identical to the one shown in Figure 14.8. Note that when a file is selected using this dialog box, it is copied to the Texture project directory. Before beginning to create a Texture publication, you might want to copy all the graphics files to a directory. You then can select graphics files without roaming all over your directories and hard drives.

The Image tab of the Object Properties dialog box (see Figure 14.9) is useful for specifying the appearance of a graphic inside the image box. This dialog can be used to fit the graphic to the image box or fit the image box to the graphic. It also can be used to specify the placement of a graphic and whether it should be *tiled*. After making your selection, click the OK button to continue.

FIGURE 14.8.

Content file selection dialog box.

FIGURE 14.9.

Image tab of the Object Properties dialog box.

You now will see the first graphic specified in Figure 14.7 (see Figure 14.10). Note how the name of the image box, specified in Figure 14.6, is displayed to the upper-left corner of the image box. It is now required to set up *actions* and *triggers* for the manual graphics animation. This is done by selecting the image box, clicking the right mouse button, and selecting Action Manager as shown in Figure 14.10.

FIGURE 14.10.

The right mouse button pop-up menu of an image box can be used to invoke the Action Manager dialog box.

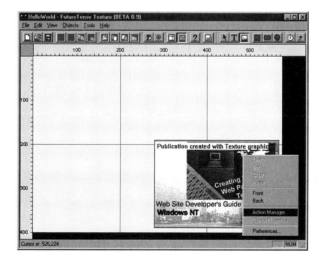

The Action Manager dialog box is used to specify actions related to the object selected when the Action Manager was invoked and what object should trigger the action selected. This is somewhat tricky. However, after you learn how it works, it will seem very natural and easy to use. As mentioned earlier, we need to set up our manual graphics animation so that if a user clicks the graphic, Texture will display another graphic. When Action Manager was invoked, the image box containing the first graphic of the animation was selected. As shown in Figure 14.7, the image box selected before invoking the Action Manager contains two graphics. As far as Texture is concerned, these graphics are URLs. Therefore, use the scroll-down list and select the Next URL action as shown in Figure 14.11. Afterward, click the Trigger button and the mouse pointer will change into a different icon (a hand with a pointing finger). Next, click the image box selected earlier to create a trigger / action event.

FIGURE 14.11.

*Action Manager
dialog box.*

Texture then will display a dialog box similar to the one shown in Figure 14.12 to confirm the Action/Trigger creation was a success. Realize what just happened. When a user clicks the image box, a mouse click action is fired. This mouse click in turn triggers the action selected in the Action Manager. Because the image box in Figure 14.10 was selected before invoking the Action Manager, actions selected in the Action Manager apply to the image box shown in Figure 14.10. In this case, the mouse click action triggers an event (Next URL) in the same object. Note that this event could have been triggered just as easily by another object. At this moment if you select View | Preview Page from the main menu, you will see the first graphic specified in Figure 14.7. If you click this graphic, Texture will display the next graphic. Note that at the end of the list of URLs (graphics) in Figure 14.7, Texture reverts back to the first graphic. By default, Texture publications are displayed using Sun's Applet Viewer. View | Preferences can be selected from the menu bar to choose a different Texture publication viewer, such as Netscape Navigator.

FIGURE 14.12.

*Action / Trigger creation
confirmation dialog box.*

Creating a Manual Text Animation

A manual text animation can be created as easily as a manual graphics animation. In order to create a text animation, select Objects | New | Text from the menu bar. Then, draw a text box using the mouse, select it, and click the right mouse button. A pop-up menu then will be displayed next to the text box. Use this menu to select Object Properties as shown in Figure 14.13.

FIGURE 14.13.

The right mouse button pop-up menu of a text box can be used to invoke the Object Properties dialog box.

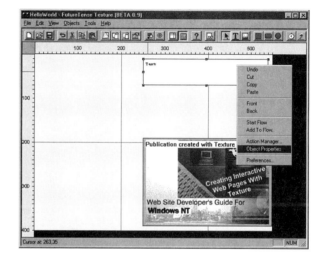

You will now see an Object Properties dialog box similar to the one shown in Figure 14.14. This dialog box is similar to the one in Figure 14.6. Use it to label the text box and specify the tip that will be displayed when a user rests the mouse pointer on the text box. Again, note how the name of the text box ends with "text box" to make it easier to identify it as a text box in Object Manager. You will learn about Object Manager shortly. After customizing the text box as shown in Figure 14.14, click the Content tab to continue.

FIGURE 14.14.

General tab of the Object Properties dialog box.

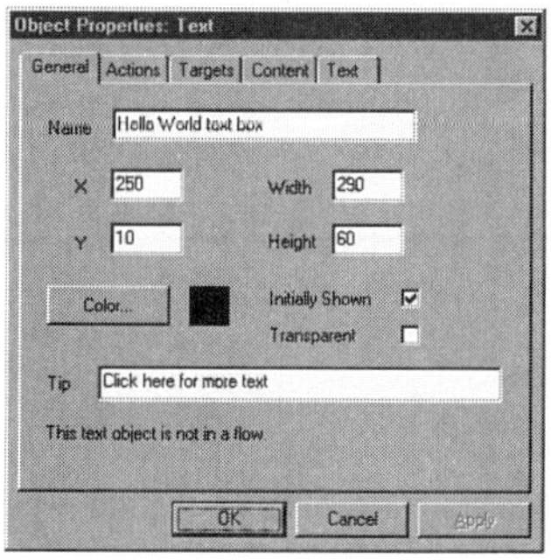

The Content tab is used to specify the contents of the text box. There are three ways to specify the contents of a text box. Just like image boxes, you can either give a local filename or an HTTP URL. There is a third way to specify the contents of a text box. If you precede a URL name with an exponent symbol, the text after the exponent will be interpreted as the contents of the text box. For example, if you would like to specify the string "Hello World!" in a text box, you would simply type in the string "!Hello World!" as a URL name. This is a powerful feature for creating text boxes that do not contain paragraphs of text. As you can see in Figure 14.15, the exponent is used to insert three strings, as URLs, to the text box in Figure 14.13. By default, only the first string will be displayed. After typing in the contents of the text box, click the Text tab to continue.

FIGURE 14.15.

Content tab of the Object Properties dialog box.

The Text tab, shown in Figure 14.16, is handy for formatting text in a text box. The Text Justification radio buttons can be used to format the justification of text in the text box. The Face Color button can be used to assign a color to text displayed in the text box. One of the most sophisticated features of Texture is hidden beneath the Font button.

FIGURE 14.16.

Text tab of the Object Properties dialog box.

Texture enables Web content developers to use whatever fonts installed on the system they are working on without having to worry about fonts installed on the user's computer. This means if you use a special TrueType font in a Texture publication and if a Macintosh user looks at the publication, the Macintosh user will see the publication in the font the text was meant to be viewed in. This works thanks to the technology of a font recording and playback technology licensed from Bitstream Inc.

> **NOTE**
>
> When a Texture publication is saved, Texture uses Bitstream's technology to *record* fonts used in a Texture document in a proprietary and portable format called "Portable Font Resource." When a Texture publication is being displayed by the Texture viewer, it checks the Texture publication for various fonts that are used in the publication. If a font is locally found on the user's system, that font is used. Otherwise, the *font resource* is dynamically downloaded from the Web server. All this happens seamlessly depending on the operating system the user is using. For example, if a user is using Windows NT, the font resource for Arial will never be downloaded, because it is locally installed on virtually all Windows NT computers. If most of your users use Windows NT or Windows 95, it's best to use default Windows fonts such as Arial and Times Roman as much as possible.

After selecting a font for the text box (see Figure 14.17), press OK to continue. You then can bring up the Action Manager dialog box and create an Action/Trigger for the text box the same way one was created for the image box. Once the Action/Trigger is created, you will see a confirmation dialog box similar to the one shown in Figure 14.18.

FIGURE 14.17.
Font selection dialog box.

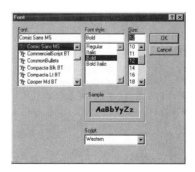

FIGURE 14.18.
Trigger / Action confirmation dialog box for the manual text animation.

Displaying Contents of a URL in a Texture Publication

At this point, we have a pretty interesting publication with two manual animations. That's very nice, but our publication really does not do anything yet. You now will be shown how to display the contents of a URL in a text box. By default, Texture does not automatically create scroll bars in text boxes. This means if text in a text box does not fit the text box, users have no way of viewing that text. This can be fixed by adding a *previous* and *next* graphic to the publication. Actions and Triggers then can be used to display text that does not fit in the text box. You will be shown how to do this shortly. In order to set this, you first need to create two graphics and a text box as shown in Figure 14.19. The text box will be used to display the contents of a Web page and the two graphics will be used as "page up" and "page down" buttons for the text box.

FIGURE 14.19.

Contents of a URL can be displayed in a text box.

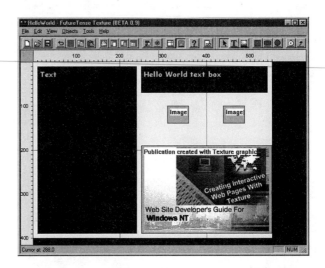

After creating the two graphics and the text box, select the text box and click the right mouse button. Use the pop up menu displayed when the right mouse button is clicked to select the Object Properties dialog box. You then will see the General tab of the Object properties dialog box shown in Figure 14.20. Use it to assign a name to the text box and specify a tip that will be shown when a user rests the mouse pointer on the text box. Afterward, click the Content tab.

FIGURE 14.20.

General tab of the Object Properties dialog box.

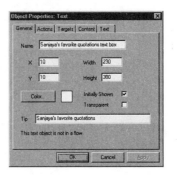

The Content tab can be used to specify the contents of a text box. As discussed earlier, a URL, filename, or a text label can be the contents of a text box. For the purpose of this example, as shown in Figure 14.21, a filename is used as the contents of the text box. Click the OK button after typing in a filename. The filename specified in Figure 14.21 is incidentally my favorite quotations collection file. (If you would like to share one of your favorite quotations with me, e-mail it to me!)

FIGURE 14.21.

Content tab of the Object Properties dialog box can be used to specify the contents of a text box.

After the text box is assigned content and two appropriate images are assigned to the two image boxes, the Texture publication will look similar to the one shown in Figure 14.22. It now is required to assign a Page Up and Page Down action to the two image boxes. To do this, select each text box as shown in Figure 14.22 and click the right mouse button. Then, use the pop-up menu to select Action Manager.

FIGURE 14.22.

After the text box is assigned content and two images are added to the publication.

As shown in Figure 14.23, use the Action Manager dialog box to select the Scroll Down action and assign it to the appropriate graphic using the Trigger button. Do the same to the other graphic by assigning the Scroll Up action to it.

FIGURE 14.23.

Action Manager dialog box of the text box.

When actions and triggers are created, you will see a dialog box similar to the one shown in Figure 14.24 to confirm the Action/Trigger creation. Note how descriptive object names are helpful when working with Texture publications.

FIGURE 14.24.

Action/Trigger creation confirmation dialog box.

Using the Timer Object

The Timer object is handy for triggering actions after a certain time period. This example will demonstrate how the Timer object can be used to create an "automatic" animation. Unlike the previous animation, this animation does not require any user intervention. Instead, after a certain time period, the animation will automatically advance to the next frame. In order to create this animation, create a simple text box with about two lines of text as shown in Figure 14.25. Note how the exponent is used to define literal strings. After typing in the contents, click the OK button to continue.

FIGURE 14.25.

Content tab of the simple text animation text box.

Afterwards, a Timer object has to be added to control the animation. A Timer object can be added by selecting Objects | New | Timer from the main menu. Note that the Timer object is an *invisible* object. It is never displayed in Texture publications. Therefore, as shown in Figure 14.26, feel free to draw the Timer object anywhere in the publication. After creating the Timer object, use its Object Properties dialog box to give it a name, specify a time delay interval, and click the OK button to continue.

FIGURE 14.26.

Texture publication after inserting a Timer object.

The last two animations used the mouse click event to trigger the next URL action. Because this animation does not require any user intervention, the animation is triggered by the Timer object. In order to use the Timer object to control the animation, select the text box and click the right mouse button. As shown in Figure 14.27, then use the dialog box that pops up to invoke the Action Manager dialog box of the text box selected.

Use the Action Manager dialog box to specify the Timer object to trigger the next URL event. This is done by selecting Next URL, clicking the Trigger button, and selecting the Timer object. You then will see a message box to confirm the Action/Trigger creation.

That is all there is to creating a relatively sophisticated Texture publication. This publication now can be viewed with any Web browser, such as Internet Explorer and Netscape Navigator, that supports Java. Select View | Preview Page to view the publication and it will be shown in Applet Viewer as shown in Figure 14.28.

FIGURE 14.27.

Invoking Action Manager of the animation text box after creating a Timer object.

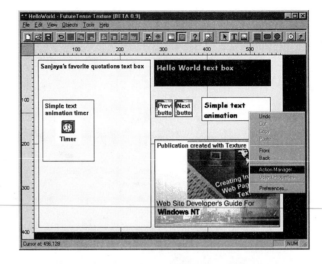

FIGURE 14.28.

Publication viewed with Applet Viewer.

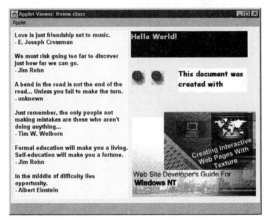

At this time, if a user clicks the Next button, Texture will display the next page of quotations. Refer to Figure 14.29 for an example of what the publication in Figure 14.28 looks like after a few user interactions. As you can see, Texture can be used to create high-impact, *active* publications quite easily. As you become more familiar with Texture, you will find yourself using it to create various innovative Web publications that are impossible to create with standard HTML.

FIGURE 14.29.

Publication after a few user interactions with Applet viewer.

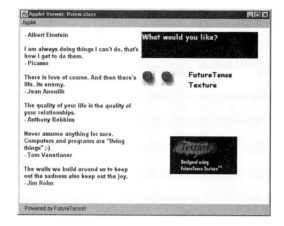

Publishing Texture Publications on the Internet

When a Texture publication is saved, you will see an HTML file in the project directory. The HTML file created with Texture can be immediately published on the Web. There are a few things you should be aware of when publishing Texture publications on the Internet. Texture publications are stored in project directories. It is highly recommended that you leave the directory structures of Texture project directories the way they are. In other words, if you wish to publish a Texture publication, simply copy the *entire* project folder to a child of your Web server's root directory. Then, users can view the Texture publication by looking up the HTML file created by Texture. If you take a look at Figure 14.30, you will notice that the URL of the Texture publication is `file:///H%7C/Publish/WWW/WSDGWNT/Texture/HelloWorld/HelloWorld.html`. This is because the publication directory (HelloWorld) was copied in its entirety to the `H:\Publish\WWW\WSDGWNT\Texture` directory.

By default, Texture publications require users to download and install a special Netscape plug-in. (FutureTense will have a similar solution for Internet Explorer and possibly Mosaic by the time you read this.) Although it is highly recommended that you get users to download and install the Texture viewer, because it will save a great deal of time in the long run, the Texture viewer can be made available dynamically. In order to make it available dynamically, locate the file `Futurew32.zip` in the `\Texture\classes` directory and decompress it. Be sure to use a 32-bit file decompression utility such as WinZip to ensure long filenames and directory names are preserved when the file `Futurew32.zip` is decompressed. Also be sure to turn on any *switches* in the file decompression program to preserve *embedded* directory names in compressed file. When the file is decompressed, it will create the following directory structure:

```
\—Classes
   +—bitstream
   +—Future
   |   +—Agent
   |   +—Content
   |   +—Fable
   |   +—Interfaces
   |   +—Native
   |   +—Parser
   |   +—Read
   |   +—Util
   |   \—Viewer
   \—sun
       \—awt
           \—win32
```

Copy this entire directory structure to the document root directory of your Web server and locate the HelloWorld.html file in the project directory. By default, in this file, you will see an applet definition similar to the one shown next.

```
<applet code=ftview.class width=575 height=400 codebase=>
<param name=ft value=HelloWorld.ftl>
<param name=ver value=3>
</applet>
```

Note that it does not have a value defined for the codebase= tag. As it is, the publication can be viewed only if a user has installed the Netscape (or Internet Explorer) plug-in. In order to make sure users can view Texture publications with any Java-compatible browser without having to install a special plug-in, simply change the above code listing as follows. Note how the codebase tag now refers to the Classes directory that was copied to the document root directory of the Web server. That's all there is to publishing a Texture publication on the Web! Again, encourage users to download and install the browser plug-in since it will save them a great deal of time in the long run.

```
<applet code=ftview.class width=575 height=400
        codebase=/Classes>
<param name=ft value=HelloWorld.ftl>
<param name=ver value=3>
</applet>
```

FIGURE 14.30.
Hello World publication viewed with Netscape.

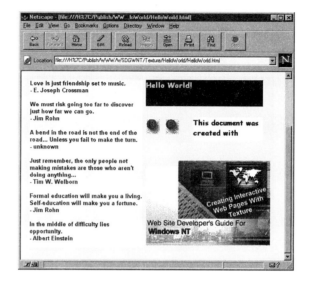

Summary

Texture is a powerful Java-based Web content development application. It can be used to create publications that are highly interactive and exciting to browse. Texture also provides Web content developers better control over publications they create. For example, fonts used in a Texture publication are portable across all platforms that support Java. This is a major advantage because finally, with Texture, Web content developers do not have to be bound with using only one or two standard typefaces. In addition to this, Texture also includes a collection of powerful objects that can be used with various actions and triggers to create *active publications*. FutureTense Texture is an ideal solution for creating high-impact Web publications that require complete control over the layout, typefaces, and interactive behavior of the publication.

If you have any questions about using Texture to create Web applications, join the beta-interest mailing list. To subscribe, send an e-mail message to list@futuretense.com. In the first line of the message type **JOIN BETA-INTEREST**.

What's Next?

As you add more information to your Web site, it is going to be increasingly difficult for users to locate the information they need. This is why you should set up a search engine at your Web site and enable users to search your Web site for various key words. The next chapter demonstrates how a Web site can be made searchable by setting up a search engine.

15

Making Your Web Site Searchable

Users browsing a Web site should able to locate the information they need in just a few minutes. Information at a Web site is of little use to anyone if it is hard to reach. For a moment, think what the World Wide Web would be if not for various Web site cataloging databases. If not for these cataloging and search databases, the Internet community would be unable to locate the information it needs. The same concept applies to your Web site on a smaller scale.

In this chapter, you learn how you can make your Web site searchable by setting up a Web search engine. Several search engines are available for Windows NT. The first section discusses how you can use the Verity topicSEARCH engine to make a Web site searchable. This search engine is an Internet Server Application Programming Interface (ISAPI) application that is designed to take advantage of features of Internet Information Server (IIS) and make a Web site searchable while conserving system resources.

In the other sections, you learn how you can use the built-in search engines of WebSite and the Netscape server to make a Web site searchable. After reading this chapter, you will be able to make a Web site hosted with IIS, WebSite, and Netscape searchable in a matter of minutes.

Purveyor also is shipped with Verity's search engine. Although you do not specifically learn how a Web site hosted with Purveyor can be made searchable in the following section, you do get an idea how to do so. Refer to Purveyor documentation for additional information about setting up and using the Verity search engine.

Setting Up and Using the Verity topicSEARCH Engine

In this section, you learn how you can make a Web site hosted with IIS searchable using the Verity topicSEARCH engine. You can download the topicSEARCH engine from Verity's Web site. Note that you might need to fill in a form and submit it before you are given a username and a password to download the search engine.

URL

Verity topicSEARCH engine download site:

```
http://www.verity.com/products/topicSEARCH.html
```

Installing the Verity topicSEARCH Engine

After you download the Verity search engine, copy it to a temporary directory and decompress it. Then run the file `setup.exe` to begin installing the Verity search engine. The installation program first gathers some information from you, such as your name and company name. Then a dialog box similar to the one shown in Figure 15.1 appears. In the Choose Destination Location dialog box, you specify the target directory of the Verity search engine. After you select a directory, click the Next button to continue. In the next dialog box that appears, you select an NT Start Menu program folder for the search engine. Either select an existing folder or type in the name of a new folder, and click the Next button to continue.

FIGURE 15.1.

Choosing a destination location of topicSEARCH.

SECURITY

The Verity search engine should be installed on an NTFS partition. If it is installed on a FAT partition, unauthorized users can access the search engine's administration menu and potentially abuse its functionality.

The installation program then installs the topicSEARCH search engine and displays a Setup Complete dialog box like the one shown in Figure 15.2. Checking both checkboxes in this dialog box is a good idea. You then can learn more about the search engine and immediately begin using it with Internet Explorer. Note that before you can use the search engine, you need to configure it with Internet Explorer by indexing your Web site.

FIGURE 15.2.

The Setup Complete dialog box.

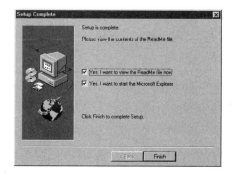

After you install the search engine, you can test the search engine installation by looking up the URL `http://<your server name>/topic/admin/qstart.htm`, as shown in Figure 15.3. Replace `<your server name>` with the Internet address of your server. Note that you might need to stop and restart IIS before you can look up this URL. It is not a very good idea to allow users browsing your Web site to configure your search engine if they stumble onto the Web page shown in Figure 15.3. Refer to Chapter 6, "Installing and Using Microsoft Internet Information Server," for more information about how you can restrict access to certain parts of a Web site with a username and a password. Note that you can restrict access to certain parts of a Web site only if the search engine is installed in an NTFS partition.

FIGURE 15.3.
The topicSEARCH welcome page.

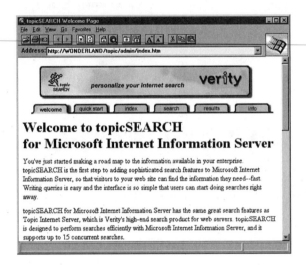

Configuring the Verity topicSEARCH Engine

The Verity search engine is easy to configure. As you learn later in this section, you can make a Web site searchable in just a few minutes by using the Web page shown in Figure 15.4. You invoke this Web page by clicking the quick start tab of the Web page. Before you continue to build a search index, you should test the search engine to make sure that it is properly installed. To do so, click option 1, Diagnose your system.

When the Web page shown in Figure 15.5 appears, you can diagnose the topicSEARCH installation by clicking the diagnose button. The Verity search engine then diagnoses the topicSEARCH installation and displays a Web page similar to the one shown in Figure 15.6.

If the Verity search engine is installed properly, a Web page similar to the one shown in Figure 15.6 appears. If no errors are found, proceed to create a new search index by clicking option 2, Index your local Web site.

FIGURE 15.4.

The topicSEARCH Quick Start page.

FIGURE 15.5.

The topicSEARCH diagnostics Web page.

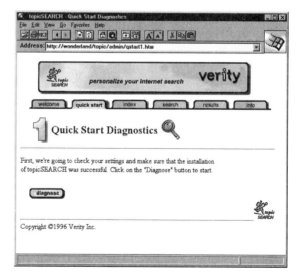

FIGURE 15.6.

*The topicSEARCH
diagnostics completed
Web page.*

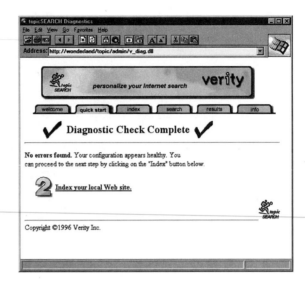

Before you can search a Web site, you have to index it using the Web page shown in Figure 15.7. Indexing your entire Web site is generally a good idea. Users browsing the Web site then can easily locate information they need by executing a search. After you type the URL indicating where topicSEARCH should begin indexing, click the index button. topicSEARCH then begins with the URL specified and creates a search index indexing all local Web pages linked to that URL.

FIGURE 15.7.

Creating a search index.

After you click the index button on this page, topicSEARCH indexes the specified URL and then displays a Web page identical to the one shown in Figure 15.8. Depending on the number of documents at your Web site, indexing the entire Web site might take a while. You can click the terminate button to cancel indexing.

FIGURE 15.8.

The indexing status Web page.

You can click the recent button on this Web page to check the status of indexing the URL specified earlier. After you click this button, the last few Web pages indexed by topicSEARCH are displayed, as shown in Figure 15.9. After you index the Web site, you can search it by clicking the search tab.

FIGURE 15.9.

Viewing the status of indexing a Web site.

Searching a Web Site with the topicSEARCH Engine

You can use the search tab in the Web page shown in Figure 15.10 to test the topicSEARCH engine by executing a search. Click the Power Search link to initiate a search.

FIGURE 15.10.

Selecting a search form.

You can use the Web page shown in Figure 15.11 to initiate a search. For the purpose of this example, search the Web site indexed earlier for the string `"Great Falls"`. Great Falls is a national park in West Virginia, and several Web pages contain this string.

The results of the search initiated in Figure 15.11 are displayed in Figure 15.12. As you can see, topicSEARCH has successfully indexed the Web site and matched the string `"Great Falls"` with several personal Web pages. When search results are displayed, topicSEARCH assigns a score to each document based on the number of matches and other criteria. Refer to topicSEARCH documentation for additional information about customizing searches.

As I mentioned previously, You should use URLs containing the directory `/topic/admin/` only for administration purposes. Users browsing a Web site can use the URL `http://<your.server.com>/topic/docs/search3.htm` to search for various keywords. Be sure to create several links to this Web page from various Web pages at your site.

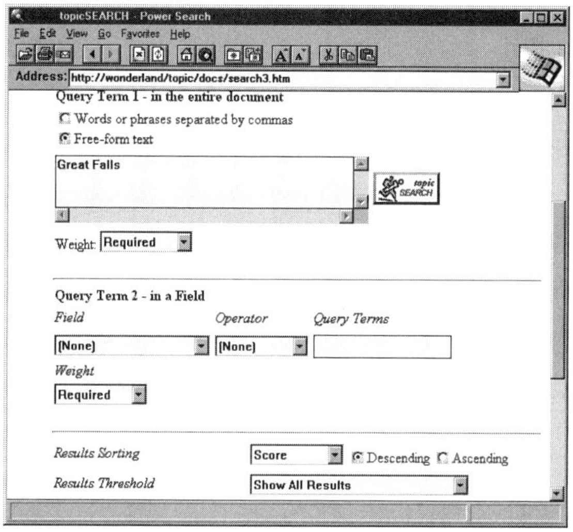

FIGURE 15.11.
Initiating a search.

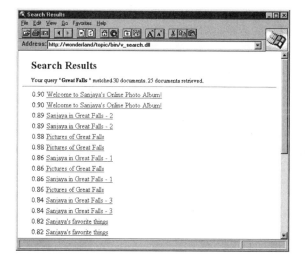

FIGURE 15.12.
The search results.

It is a good idea to create a standard button bar and include it in all your Web pages. You can map one of these buttons to the URL just mentioned. The other buttons can be used to provide feedback, return to the main Web page, and so on.

Securing topicSEARCH Engine Administration Pages

Limiting access to the \Verity\topic\admin directory is crucial so that unauthorized users cannot access Web pages in this directory to configure the search engine. Users with malicious intent can potentially abuse various search engine configuration settings and bring about un-desired results.

Because IIS uses NTFS file permissions, you can use the File Manager to restrict access to the `Verity\topic\admin` directory. To do so, first invoke the File Manager and select the `Verity\topic\admin` directory. Then choose Security|Permissions from the main menu to invoke the Directory Permissions dialog box, as shown in Figure 15.13. In this dialog box, you can restrict access to the Internet guest account that is used by IIS. Assign "No Access" to the Internet guest account and "Full Control" to the Administrators group. Next, check the two checkboxes to replace permissions of subdirectories and existing files; then click the OK button.

FIGURE 15.13.

File Manager's Directory Permissions dialog box.

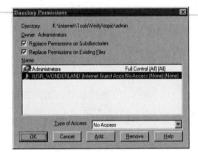

The Verity topicSEARCH engine administration menu is now accessible only to members of the Administrators group. At this time, if you restart your Web browser and try to connect to `http://<your.server.com>/topic/admin/search.htm`, you are asked for a username and a pass-word. A username and password of a user who is part of the Administrators group are now required to access files in the `Verity\topic\admin` directory. To make sure that users of the Administrators group can log on, you should check the Basic (Clear Text) checkbox of the IIS properties dialog box.

You also can check the Windows NT Challenge/Response checkbox to enable users of the Administrators group to log on and configure the search engine. The Windows NT Challenge/Response authentication mechanism automatically encrypts usernames and passwords. Only Internet Explorer version 2.0 and later, however, support this password authentication scheme. Refer to Chapter 6 for more information about securing a Web site hosted with IIS.

Configuring Netscape's Built-In Search Engine

In a matter of minutes, you can make a Web site hosted with the Netscape Enterprise Server searchable. Netscape Enterprise Server ships with the Verity topicSEARCH engine, and you can configure it using the Web page shown in Figure 15.14. Refer to Chapter 7, "Publishing on the Web with WebSite, Purveyor, and Netscape," for more information about installing the Netscape Enterprise Server and accessing the configuration Web page shown in the figure.

FIGURE 15.14.

The Netscape search engine configuration Web page.

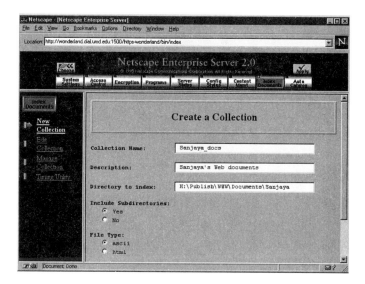

Using the Create a Collection Web page shown in Figure 15.14, you can create a collection by specifying a collection name, description, and directory. A *collection* is a collection of documents that can be searched. A Web site, for example, might have a directory for technical support and another directory for sales reports. A user executing a search for technical support is probably not interested in documents in the sales reports directory. You can use collections to refine searches by indexing similar documents. You can create, for example, a collection (or search index) for the sales reports directory and the technical support directory. After you type in the information requested, click the On button to index the Web site. Click the Help button at the end of the page if additional help is needed.

After you create a search index, the Netscape server displays a Web page similar to the one shown in Figure 15.15. As described in this Web page, the directory that was indexed is now searchable. All that you need to do is copy the HTML code in this page to another Web page and enable users to use the form in the HTML code to search the directory that was indexed. Users also can search the Web site by looking up the URL http://<your.server.com>/search/ iaquery.exe as shown in Figure 15.16.

FIGURE 15.15.

Results of successful search index creation.

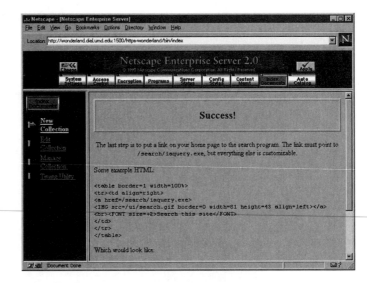

Searching a Web Site with Netscape's Search Engine

Using the Web page shown in Figure 15.16, you can initiate a search by typing in several keywords and selecting a subject. Subjects correspond to search indexes created using the Web page shown in Figure 15.14. After you type in the search criteria, click on the Search button to initiate the search.

After Netscape's search engine performs the search, Web pages matching the search criteria are displayed in a Web page similar to the one shown in Figure 15.17. This Web page lists titles of Web pages matched along with their URLs. Depending on the contents of the Web page, a score also is given to each Web page to make it easier to locate the most relevant Web pages. You can use the input controls in the search results page either to refine the search by typing in additional keywords or to perform a new search altogether.

FIGURE 15.16.
Initiating a search.

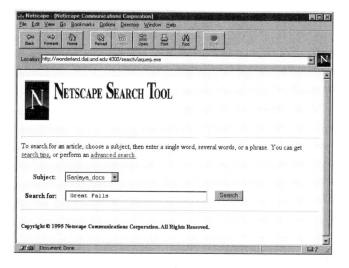

FIGURE 15.17.
Search results Web page.

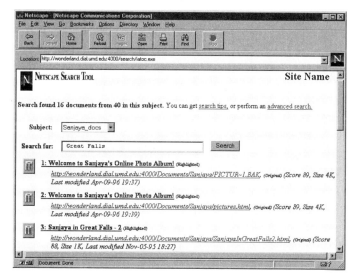

Configuring WebSite's Built-In Search Engine

A search engine also is included with WebSite. Refer to Chapter 7 for more information about installing WebSite and accessing the WebIndex dialog box shown in Figure 15.18. To invoke the WebIndex dialog box, double-click on the WebIndex icon in the WebSite applications folder. In this dialog box, you can select Web pages to index.

FIGURE 15.18.

Selecting Web pages to index.

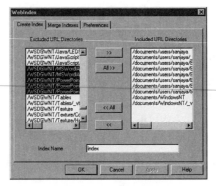

On the Merge Indexes tab of the WebIndex dialog box, you can merge search indexes to create larger search indexes. As shown in the dialog box in Figure 15.19, you can merge several search indexes by selecting them and giving a name to the new search index by typing it in the Merged Index Name text box.

FIGURE 15.19.

Merging search indexes.

After you select Web pages on the Create Index tab, you can configure search index settings on the Preferences tab of the WebIndex dialog box, as shown in Figure 15.20. Then click the OK button to create a search index. After creating a search index, users browsing the Web site can use the Web page shown in Figure 15.21 to search and locate Web pages in which they are interested.

FIGURE 15.20.

Configuring search index settings.

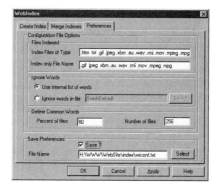

Searching a Web Site with WebSite's Search Engine

Using the Web page shown in Figure 15.21, you can search a Web site indexed with WebIndex. You can use this Web page to select an index and initiate a search for several keywords. After you generate a search index, create links to the URL `http://<your.server.com>/cgi-bin/WebFind.exe` from other Web pages to enable users browsing the Web site to search for various keywords. Because index names are exposed to users, giving descriptive names to search indexes is a good idea. This way, users can easily locate Web pages they are interested in without being confused about various index names.

FIGURE 15.21.

Initiating a search.

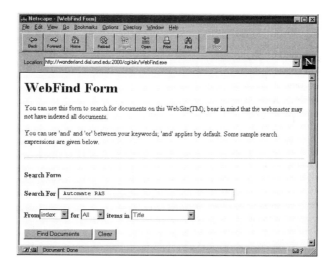

After it searches for the search criteria specified in Figure 15.21, WebIndex displays Web pages that match the search criteria, as shown in Figure 15.22.

FIGURE 15.22.
Search results Web page.

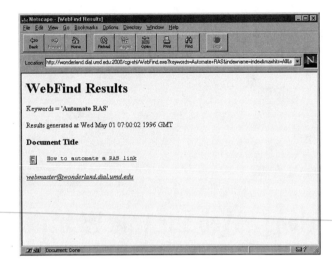

Summary

Making your Web site searchable is very important so that users browsing it can search and locate information they need without unnecessarily browsing hierarchies of Web pages. As you learned in this chapter, you can make a Web site searchable in a matter of minutes. As demonstrated, search engines are available for all four Web servers covered in this book—Internet Information Server, WebSite, Purveyor, and Netscape Enterprise Server.

What's Next?

Although in this and preceding chapters you learned how you can set up a Web server to publish information, none of these chapters discussed how to make it provide dynamic content based on various needs of users browsing a Web site. The next chapter introduces you to Windows NT CGI programming and demonstrates how you can make your Web site interactive with the use of CGI programs.

One of the best things about the World Wide Web is how it can be used to distribute information to millions of people. CGI enables you to interact with this large audience of people. The next chapter covers all the fundamentals of CGI programming. First, you learn various aspects of adding CGI applications to a Web site and then how you can write CGI applications in PERL (Practical Extraction Report Language) and C/C++.

After you read the next chapter, be sure to read Chapter 17, "Advanced Windows NT CGI Applications," to learn how you can use various CGI programs to create innovative server-side applications to provide dynamic content to users browsing a Web site. The next few chapters demonstrate how you can exploit various capabilities of CGI to create information-rich, active Web sites that are interesting and easy to navigate.

V

Making Your Web Site Interactive

16

Introduction to Windows NT CGI Programming

One of the best things about the World Wide Web is that you can use it to interact with potentially millions of users to obtain and provide different information. Due to the dynamic nature of this information, static HTML pages alone are not enough. There has to be a way to display dynamic information to those surfing your Web site based on what they need. CGI is a mechanism that enables you to do just that. *CGI* stands for *Common Gateway Interface.* After you have your Web site all set up and have created some Web pages, it's time to think about making your Web site dynamic by setting up CGI scripts on your Web server. By utilizing CGI, you can exploit the World Wide Web to its fullest potential because it allows you to interact with browsers of your Web site.

Feedback forms, e-mail forms, database query interfaces, database update mechanisms, Web page counters, and search engines are all applications of CGI. Thanks to the user-friendly development environment of Windows NT, by the end of this chapter you will be able to develop CGI scripts, experiment with them, and harness the power of interactive Web interfaces. This chapter first provides you with an introduction to CGI and explains how CGI works. Then you are shown practical applications of CGI and how CGI scripts can be utilized to enhance your Web site. Next, you are shown how to develop CGI programs. C and Perl are used to illustrate how CGI programs can be created to perform various tasks. At the end of this chapter, you will be able to utilize CGI to interact with your Web site browsers. The next chapter, "Advanced Windows NT CGI Applications," covers advanced CGI programming and builds on material covered in this chapter. Among other things, it demonstrates how databases on your Web server can be queried and updated by using a Web front end.

Introduction to CGI

Before going any further, an introduction to CGI is in order. CGI is a standard for various programs at your Web site that you can use to interact with users surfing your site. Because CGI is a standard, it is not browser- or server-dependent and can be moved from one Web server to another while still retaining its full functionality.

Just like application programs, CGI programs can be written in almost any programming language that will let you either create an executable program or let you interpret it in real time with another program (as in the case of AWK and Perl). The following lists a few languages that you can utilize to create CGI applications under Windows NT:

- AWK
- C/C++
- FORTRAN
- Pascal
- Perl

■ Visual Basic

■ NT Batch scripts

Depending on your expertise, what's available, and the nature of your CGI projects, you will have to choose the best language to suit your needs. Customarily, CGI scripts are stored in the CGI-BIN directory of the Web server's document root directory. All files and pathnames of a Web site are relative to this directory.

Benefits of an Interactive Web Site

Plain text HTML files retrieved by Web clients are static. The information contained in these files never changes unless you manually edit them to make changes. However, by utilizing CGI scripts, your Web pages can be created dynamically each time a client accesses them. To the client, it will look as if the page has been specially created for him or her based on the information needed. Obviously, this is a very powerful tool for interacting with Web surfers. You should utilize CGI to make your Web site interactive so that you can provide customized content and enable those browsing your Web site to interact with the information you provide.

Benefits of CGI are invaluable to any Web site. These benefits range from having a customized input form for feedback to allowing someone browsing your Web site to update and retrieve information from a database on your server. By setting up a customized e-mail feedback form, you can make sure you are provided with all the information you need. Furthermore, you can be sure that your e-mail feedback form will always work because it does not depend on how the e-mail capability of your client's Web browser is set up (in case it is not set up correctly for e-mail). In the "Setting Up a Feedback Form" section, you will be shown how to utilize CGI to set up an e-mail feedback page. Furthermore, if you want to set up a database that collects data from users browsing your Web site, you can use a CGI script to update information provided by these users to a database. With the aid of CGI, it is possible to update a database on your server without your direct human intervention. As you can see, the possibilities and applications of CGI are endless.

One of CGI's best features is its capability to let Web surfers interact with databases on your server. For example, you might have a Microsoft Access database on your server that needs to be updated with information provided by users surfing your Web site. You might also need to make parts of this database available to authenticated users for querying. Although you can use plain old e-mail to correspond with people, and manually perform database queries and updates, this is not very practical after you start getting more and more visitors. Eventually, you will end up spending the whole day answering and responding to e-mail. (Maybe you do this already, but just imagine how much worse it will be!) By setting up a simple form, you can perform updates to your database by utilizing a CGI script. Keep on reading, and soon you will find out how easy it is to use CGI to interact with people browsing your Web site.

Dynamic content that is output by CGI programs can be made portable across other Web servers. For example, if in the output of a CGI script, a hypertext link has to be created to the main homepage of a Web server, you can use the CGI environment variable SERVER_NAME. By using this CGI variable as opposed to hard coding the homepage in the CGI program, the CGI script will be portable across various Web servers.

> **TIP**
>
> Whenever possible, you should make use of such CGI variables to make moving scripts from one Web server to another as effortless as possible.

By utilizing CGI to make your Web site interactive, users visiting your Web site will be able to easily find the information they need. Because your Web site is easy to navigate, these users will visit it again and again for more information. CGI also enables you to customize what people see when browsing your Web site by providing dynamic content. Furthermore, you can use a CGI script to provide content that's customized for the Web browser being used to access the information.

Applications of CGI

Many organizations and individuals are using CGI for a variety of tasks, from having a simple counter on a Web page to counting the number of accesses to a CGI script managing an entire store front-end. This CGI script can allow users visiting a Web site to look at various merchandise being sold and even place orders. In addition to this, various Web sites offer search capabilities of the site to make finding information easier.

You can use CGI whenever you want to interact with those browsing your Web site, to get feedback from those browsing your Web site, or to provide dynamic content. The following lists a few applications of CGI that you can use to enhance the capabilities of your Web site:

- Setting up a guest book
- Setting up a feedback form
- Adding a counter to a Web page
- Designing a database front-end for the Web
- Allowing Web surfers to visit various Web pages via a pull-down list
- Enabling those browsing your Web site to e-mail comments
- Providing customized Web pages based on Web browsers being used by a client
- Enabling those browsing your Web site to search your Web site

This chapter and the following chapter demonstrate how to add most of these capabilities to your Web site. Before moving on to more advanced topics, it's time to cover the basics of CGI.

CGI Basics

A CGI script is typically used to provide dynamic content to the client that called the CGI script. CGI scripts communicate with Web browsers, as shown in Figure 16.1. If the CGI script is an interactive script, typically a form with various input controls is sent to the Web client. After filling in the form, the user submits it to the Web server. The Web server then uses CGI to call the CGI script with data from the Web client. The CGI script processes the data, possibly accessing a database on the server, and sends a message to the client that made the request. If the CGI script is a noninteractive CGI script, the output of the script is sent directly to the client that called the CGI script with its URL.

FIGURE 16.1.

Architecture of a typical Web server with CGI scripts.

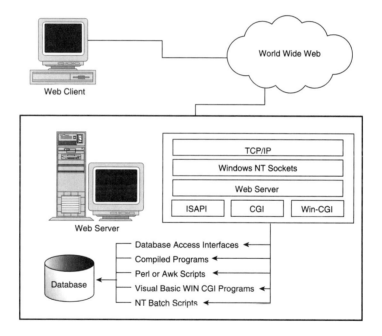

When a CGI script is called, the Web server first examines the REQUEST_METHOD used to call the CGI script to determine how the Web client is sending data to the CGI script. This process is shown in Figure 16.2. If the REQUEST_METHOD used to call the CGI script is GET, any data supplied by the Web client for the CGI script is found immediately following the URL name of the CGI script. Therefore, this information will be stored in the environment variable QUERY_STRING. On the other hand, if the REQUEST_METHOD used was POST or PUT, the size of input for the CGI script is stored in CONTENT_LENGTH. CONTENT_LENGTH contains the size of data supplied to the CGI script in bytes. The CGI script can then read from standard input the number of bytes returned by `CONTENT_LENGTH` to find out data given to the CGI script. If you are confused about all these strange environmental variables, don't worry—they are all discussed in the "CGI Environment Variables" section.

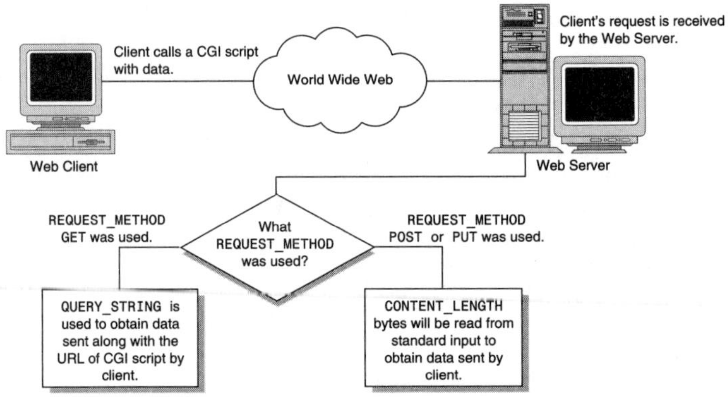

FIGURE 16.2.

How Web servers determine and handle the `REQUEST_METHOD`, *which calls the CGI scripts.*

How CGI Works

Although a major use of CGI is to provide dynamic content to those browsing your Web site, CGI programs do not always need to be interactive. You can use noninteractive CGI scripts to provide dynamic information that does not need user input to be created. For example, in order to take advantage of various features offered by Web browsers such as Netscape Navigator and Microsoft Internet Explorer, it is relatively simple to write a CGI program to determine the browser being used by a client and send a page specially designed to take advantage of that browser's capabilities. In the "Using CGI to Provide Customized Content" section, you will see how easy it is to write a CGI script to provide customized content based on the browser being used to access a page. In such an event, the CGI script will not need to interact with the person browsing the Web site. The CGI script can be executed transparently to the user without any user intervention. For example, if the default Web page of a Web server is `welcome.html`, the main Web page of the Web server can be mapped to a CGI script by creating a URL-CGI mapping, as shown in Figure 16.3. Such a script can determine the browser being used by the client and display a page with dynamic content optimized for the browser being used by the client. Please refer to your Web server's documentation for more information on creating URL-CGI mappings.

If a CGI script—such as the one described previously—does not make use of user input, what happens when a client accesses the page is very simple. First, the client connects to the Web server and requests a Web page. Because the document requested is linked to a CGI script, the Web server executes the CGI program that the page is linked to. Output of the CGI program is then sent to the client that requested the page. Afterward, the connection between the Web server and the Web client is closed. This interaction is shown in Figure 16.4.

FIGURE 16.3.

You can map a Web page URL to a CGI script to provide dynamic content.

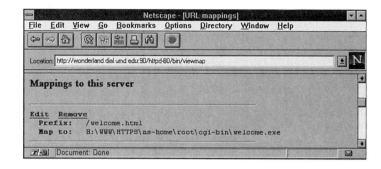

FIGURE 16.4.

You can use a noninteractive CGI script to provide dynamic content.

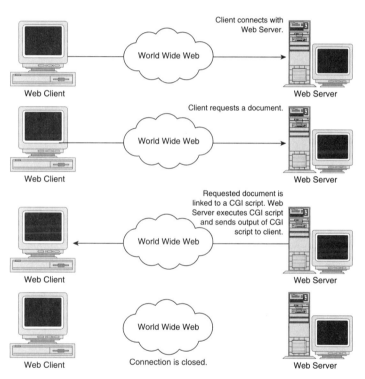

One of the greatest aspects of CGI is its capability to interact with those browsing your Web site. You can ask a user to fill in a form and then submit the form. The CGI script can then validate the user's input, ask the user to complete any incomplete information, and process the user's input, as shown in Figure 16.5.

In the case of a CGI script interacting with a Web client to display dynamic content, first a Web page with various controls is sent to the Web browser. After the user fills in the form, the form is submitted to the Web server to be processed. Depending on the REQUEST_METHOD used to communicate with the CGI script, the CGI script obtains data sent from the client, processes the data, and displays its output to *standard output*. Everything written to standard output by the CGI script will be visible to the client that called the CGI script.

FIGURE 16.5.

You can use an interactive CGI script to provide dynamic content.

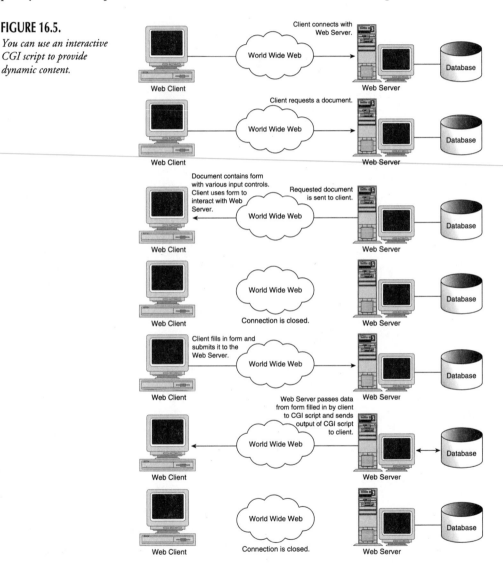

CGI Issues

When setting up CGI scripts, there are a few things you should be concerned with. Each time you allow a CGI script to be executed by someone surfing your Web site, you are allowing someone to execute a program on your server. This can potentially lead to security breaches. Although this might sound a little perilous, it's not as bad as it sounds, provided that you follow a few guidelines. As long as it is utilized properly, CGI is very safe.

Processing Time

Another issue is the time it takes for a CGI script to fulfill a client's request. If you will be providing the data to those browsing your Web site in real time, you should ensure that, at most, no one has to wait longer than about five to ten seconds. If it's going to take longer to process a request, you should obtain the e-mail address of the person requesting the information and simply e-mail the information when the data is processed. If it takes longer than about ten seconds to process a request, a person waiting at the other end might think there is something wrong and simply stop waiting.

> **PERFORMANCE**
>
> If you need to provide data in real time and CGI scripts take longer than about ten seconds to execute, it's a very good indication that you are outgrowing your server and need more processing power and/or RAM. This might also be an indication of a bottleneck, such as an inefficient database access driver or a poorly written CGI script.

Multiple Instances of the Same Script

Due to the nature of HTTP, it's possible that two or more clients will call the same CGI script at the same time. If the CGI script locks various files or databases when it is processing data, this can cause problems, potentially causing loss of data. CGI scripts should be capable of handling such a situation without any problem. This can be done by making sure the CGI application does not lock databases or files that might potentially be accessed by another instance of the same application.

Security

Although CGI is a very powerful tool for making information available to those browsing your Web site, you need to be aware of certain things. The first thing you should be concerned about is security. You should be particularly careful about CGI scripts that take input from a Web client and use that data (without checking) as a command line argument. An example of this would be using an e-mail address supplied by a Web client to call Blat, a command line e-mail program. When using such an e-mail address, make sure there is no possibility of it being interpreted as a command-line command. Your CGI scripts should always check for special control characters to avoid potential security breaches. If you have various sections of your Web site protected with a password, you might want to disable directory browsing of your Web server.

By disabling directory browsing, you're preventing someone from "snooping around" your Web site by browsing various directories and their contents, unless that person knows the URL of a certain page or is transferred to a page from one of your own pages.

Controlling Access to CGI Directory

You should be cautious about who has access to your Web server's CGI directory. It's very dangerous to allow users who upload files to your Web site via FTP to have access to your CGI directory. It doesn't take much knowledge in programming to write a potentially malicious program, upload it to the CGI directory, and execute it with a Web browser. Therefore, you should control who has access to your CGI directory via FTP or any other method.

Transmitting Sensitive Data

You should never set up CGI applications to distribute potentially harmful personal information unless the Web server is configured to encrypt the data before it is transmitted over the Internet. If you will be distributing financial information or credit card numbers, you should not use CGI unless you have configured your Web server to encrypt data before it is transmitted over the Internet. If you need to transmit sensitive data and your Web server does not encrypt data before transmitting, you should consider a medium such as *PGP (Pretty Good Privacy)* protected e-mail to transmit such data.

Validating Users

If you validate users who access parts of your Web site, you should never use the IP address returned by the Web server as the real IP address of the Web client. It's possible to trick the Web server into believing the client making the HTTP request is requesting the data from a site other than the site the Web client is connecting from. Even if you protect a certain area of your Web server with a password and a user ID, this data might be intercepted by a third party. Someone might be able to intercept a valid user ID and password when a legitimate user uses it to access your Web site. If the Web server being used supports data encryption, this won't be a problem; however, it will be a problem if you are not using any Web server-based encryption. In such a case, you should use an *OTP (One Time Password)* mechanism to validate users. An OTP authorizing mechanism works by making sure a password used once cannot be used again. Such a mechanism typically sends a "challenge string" to the client who wants to gain access. The client then uses a special program to find out the correct "response string" for the "challenge string" supplied by the server. This is done by typing the user's secret password and the challenge string and obtaining a response string generated by this special program. The response string is then sent to the server. The server validates the user and remembers the response string so that it can't be used again. The next time the user wants to gain access, the server will send a different challenge string to the client that can be decoded only with the user's secret password. Because the user's secret password never travels across the Internet, this is a safe way of authorizing users. However, unless an encryption technology is used, the content being accessed by a client might still be intercepted by a clever person with too much free time. For more information on such an OTP mechanism, you might want to visit

```
http://www.yahoo.com/Computers_and_Internet/Security_and_Encryption/S_KEY/
```

CGI Environment Variables

Each time the Web server executes a CGI script, it creates a number of environment variables to pass information to the CGI script. These variables inform the CGI script how the script is being invoked as well as provide information about the server and the Web browser being used by the client. Depending on how the CGI script is invoked, some environment variables may not be available in some cases.

Environment variables supplied to CGI scripts are always all uppercase. When they are being accessed by a C Program or Perl script, or whichever language you are using, be sure to use all uppercase letters.

This section discusses the environment variables available to CGI scripts. By accessing these variables, CGI scripts can obtain certain information, such as the browser used to invoke the script. After the following discussion about environment variables, you learn how to access these variables from a Perl script, as well as a C program via CGI.

AUTH_TYPE

Some Web servers can be configured to authenticate users. If the server has authenticated a user, the authentication type used to validate the user is stored in the AUTH_TYPE variable. The authentication type is determined by examining the Authorization Header the Web server might receive with an HTTP request.

CONTENT_LENGTH

Sometimes CGI scripts are invoked with additional information. This information is typically input for the CGI program. The length of this additional information is specified by the number of bytes taken up by the additional information in this variable. If a CGI script is called with the PUT or POST method, CONTENT_LENGTH is used to determine the length of the input.

CONTENT_TYPE

MIME content types are used to label various types of objects (HTML files, Microsoft Word files, GIF files, etc.). The MIME content-type for data being submitted to a CGI script is stored in CONTENT_TYPE. For example, if data is submitted to a CGI script using the GET method, this variable will contain the value application/x-www-form-urlencoded. This is because responses to the form are encoded according to URL specifications.

GATEWAY_INTERFACE

The CGI specification revision number is stored in the GATEWAY_INTERFACE environment variable. The format of this variable is CGI/revision. By examining this variable, a CGI script can determine the version of CGI that the Web server is using.

HTTP_ACCEPT

Various Web clients can handle different MIME types. These MIME types are described in the HTTP_ACCEPT variable. MIME types accepted by the Web client calling the CGI script will be a list separated by commas. This list takes the format type/subtype, type/subtype. For example, if the Web client supports the two image formats GIF and JPEG, the HTTP_ACCEPT list will contain the two items image/gif, image/jpeg.

HTTP_USER_AGENT

By looking at this value, the Web browser used by the client can be determined. For example, if Netscape 2.0 beta 4 is being used by the client, the HTTP_USER_AGENT variable will contain the value Mozilla/2.0b4 (WinNT; I). The general format of this variable is software/version library/version.

PATH_INFO

The PATH_INFO variable is usually used to pass various options to a CGI program. These options follow the script's URL. Clients may access CGI scripts with additional information after the URL of the CGI script. PATH_INFO will always contain the string that was used to call the CGI script after the name of the CGI script. For example, PATH_INFO will have the value /These/Are/The/Arguments if the CGI script FunWithNT.EXE is called with the following URL:

http://your_server.your_domain/cgi-bin/FunWithNT.EXE/These/Are/The/Arguments

PATH_TRANSLATED

In the event the CGI script needs to know the absolute path name of itself, the CGI script can obtain this information from PATH_TRANSLATED. For example, if the CGI script being invoked is HelloNTWorld.EXE, all CGI scripts are stored in H:\www\http\ns-home\root\cgi-bin, and the CGI script is accessed with the URL http://your_server.your_domain/root/cgi-bin/HelloNTWorld.EXE, PATH_TRANSLATED will contain the value H:\www\http\ns-home\root\cgi-bin\HelloNTWorld.EXE. If the CGI program needs to save or access any temporary files in its home directory, it can use PATH_TRANSLATED to determine its absolute location by examining this CGI variable.

QUERY_STRING

You may have noticed that when you submit some forms, there is a string of characters after a question mark, followed by the URL name of the script being called. This string of characters is referred to as the *query string* and contains everything after the question mark. When a CGI script is called with the GET method, QUERY_STRING typically contains variables and their values as entered by the person who filled in the form. QUERY_STRING is sometimes used by various search engines to examine the input when a form is submitted for a keyword search. For example, if a CGI application is executed using the URL, `http://www.server.com/cgi-bin/application.exe?WindowsNT=Fun`, QUERY_STRING will contain the string "WindowsNT=Fun."

REMOTE_ADDR

The IP address of the client that called the CGI program is stored in the REMOTE_ADDR environment variable. Due to security reasons, the value of this variable should never be used for user authentication purposes. It's not very hard to trick your Web server into believing a client is connecting to your Web server from a different IP address.

REMOTE_HOST

If the Web server can do a DNS lookup of the client's IP address and finds the alias of the IP address, the REMOTE_HOST variable will contain the alias name of the client's IP address. Some Web servers allow DNS lookups to be turned on or off. If you will be using this variable to find the IP address alias of clients, be sure the DNS lookup option is turned on. The Web server can find the IP address aliases of most clients, but it might not be capable of getting the aliases of some clients. In such an event, the REMOTE_HOST variable will not be assigned the client's DNS alias value; it will just contain the client's IP address. This value should never be used for user authentication purposes.

REMOTE_IDENT

If the Web server being used supports RFC 931 identification, this variable will contain the user name retrieved from the server. Unfortunately, this value cannot be trusted when transmitting sensitive data. Typically, a Web server obtains this value by contacting the client that initiated the HTTP request and speaking with the client's authentication server. Visit `http://www.pmg.lcs.mit.edu/cgi-bin/rfc/view?number=931` for additional information about RFC 931 and the Authentication Server Protocol.

REMOTE_USER

Some Web servers support user authentication. If a user is authenticated, the CGI script can find out the username of the person browsing the Web site by looking at the value of the REMOTE_USER environment variable. The REMOTE_USER CGI variable is available only if the user has been authenticated using an authentication mechanism.

REQUEST_METHOD

A client can call a CGI script in a number of ways. The method used by the client to call the CGI script is in the REQUEST_METHOD variable. This variable can have a value like HEAD, POST, GET, or PUT. CGI scripts use the value of this variable to find where to obtain data passed to the CGI script.

SCRIPT_NAME

All files on a Web server are usually referenced relative to its document root directory. SCRIPT_NAME contains the virtual path name of the script called relative to the document root directory. For example, if the document root directory is c:\www\http\ns-home\root, all CGI scripts are stored in c:\www\http\ns-home\root\cgi-bin\ and the CGI script HelloNTWorld.EXE is called, the SCRIPT_NAME variable will contain the value \cgi-bin\HelloWorld.EXE. The advantage of this variable is that it allows the CGI script to refer to itself. This is handy if somewhere in the output, the script's URL needs to be made into a hypertext link.

SERVER_NAME

The domain name of the Web server that invoked the CGI script is stored in this variable. This domain name can either be an IP address or DNS alias.

SERVER_PORT

Typically, Web servers listen to HTTP requests on port 80. However, a Web server can listen to any port that's not in use by another application. A CGI program can find out the port the Web server is serving HTTP requests by looking at the value of the SERVER_PORT environment variable. When displaying self-referencing hypertext links at runtime by examining the contents of SERVER_NAME, be sure to append the port number of the Web server (typically port 80) by concatenating it with the value of SERVER_PORT.

SERVER_PROTOCOL

Web servers speak the *HyperText Transport Protocol (HTTP)*. The version of HTTP the Web server is using can be determined by examining the SERVER_PROTOCOL environment variable. The SERVER_PROTOCOL variable contains the name and revision data of the protocol being used. This information is in the format protocol/revision. For example, if the server speaks HTTP 1.0, this variable will have the value HTTP/1.0.

SERVER_SOFTWARE

The name of the Web server that invoked the CGI script is stored in the SERVER_SOFTWARE environment variable. This environment variable is in the format name/version. If a CGI script is designed to make use of various special capabilities of a Web server, the CGI script can determine the Web server being used by examining this variable before those special capabilities are used.

CGI Perl Scripts

This section introduces you to Perl and how you can set up CGI Perl scripts on Windows NT Web servers. The Internet contains many CGI Perl scripts written by various people. By utilizing these scripts and customizing them to suit your needs, you can easily improve a Web site. A comprehensive tutorial of Perl is beyond the scope of this book, so this chapter discusses only the basics of writing CGI Perl scripts.

Perl stands for *Practical Extraction and Report Language.* With the growth of the World Wide Web, Perl is being used increasingly to write CGI programs. Most of the best features of C, sed, awk, and sh are incorporated in Perl. This allows Perl scripts to be developed in the least amount of time possible by avoiding reinventing the wheel for fundamental tasks such as string manipulation. The expression syntax of Perl corresponds quite closely to the expression syntax of C programs. This makes Perl an easy language to learn for those who are already familiar with C. One of the best things about Perl is its portability. Perl is an interpreted language that is available for a number of hardware platforms including PCs, Macs, and various flavors of UNIX. Unlike most languages, and utilities, Perl does not impose limits on the size of data. As long as you have enough system resources, Perl will happily read the contents of an entire file into a string. Thanks to various optimizing algorithms built into Perl, scripts written in Perl are robust and fast.

Before proceeding any further, you need to obtain Perl for Windows NT and install Perl on your Web server. Perl for Windows NT is provided free of charge on the Internet. You can obtain it from `http://info.hip.com/ntperl/`. After obtaining Perl for NT, create a directory for Perl and copy the Perl distribution file to this directory. Then uncompress the distribution file. When uncompressing the distribution file, be sure to use the option to use stored directory names in the archive. If this option is not used, all files will be extracted to the Perl directory you created, and you'll find yourself in a mess! After the archive is uncompressed, run install.bat to install Perl on your server. Then you need to copy `Perl.EXE` to the root CGI directory of your Web server, which enables your Web server to execute Perl CGI scripts.

> **NOTE**
>
> When uncompressing the ZIP file, be sure to use a 32-bit unzipping program that supports long filenames. Otherwise, the distribution files may not be properly installed. WinZip is a fine file uncompressing program that supports long filenames and a variety of file compression formats. You can obtain WinZip from
>
> `http://www.winzip.com/WinZip/download.html`

After installing Perl, you need to reboot your server for the installation directory paths to become effective. Failure to do this will cause Perl to greet you with an `Unable to locate DLL` message. (Yes, I was naïve and tried it!) If you don't feel like rebooting your server, there is another alternative (and I found a way around the problem!). You can simply copy all files in the `Perl\bin` directory to the CGI directory of your Web server. However, this is *not* recommended in a production Web server. Doing this opens several security holes.

Before creating CGI applications, it is recommended that you check your Web server settings and find out the name of its CGI directory. The remainder of this chapter assumes this directory to be `CGI-BIN`.

Perl Resources on the Internet

After you're comfortable with CGI and using CGI Perl scripts, for more information about Perl and sample CGI Perl scripts, you might want to give the following URLs a click:

Yahoo—Computers and Internet:Internet:World Wide Web:Programming:Perl Scripts

```
http://www.yahoo.com/Computers_and_Internet/Internet/World_Wide_Web/
➥Programming/Perl_Scripts/
```

Yahoo—Computers and Internet:Languages:Perl

```
http://www.yahoo.com/Computers_and_Internet/Languages/Perl/
```

To keep up-to-date with the latest news on Perl for Windows NT, you might also want to consider joining the following mailing lists:

Perl-Win32—Perl discussion list

To subscribe, send e-mail to:

```
majordomo@mail.hip.com
```

Include the following in the message body:

```
subscribe Perl-Win32
```

Perl-Win32_announce—Perl announcements

To subscribe, send e-mail to:

```
majordomo@mail.hip.com
```

Include the following in the message body:

```
subscribe Perl-Win32_announce
```

The Perl discussion list is a relatively high-volume mailing list. However, this list is read by many Windows NT Perl programmers and will answer any questions you might have when starting out with Perl.

CGI C Scripts

Because you're reading this book, chances are that you have at least heard of C and possibly know how to program in C. Therefore, an introduction to the C programming language will not be provided. For more information, please refer to one of the many fine books that have been written about programming in C.

C is a general purpose language with very few restrictions imposed on the programmer. It is also a portable language that can be moved from one computer to another as long as only standard POSIX/ANSI C function calls are used. There are many CGI programs written in C on the Internet that you can use to enhance the capabilities of your Web site. For more information on C CGI programs, please look up

```
http://www.yahoo.com/Computers_and_Internet/Internet/World_Wide_Web/Programming/
```

By using various Windows API calls from C programs, you can further exploit the capabilities of C and Windows NT. Although a command line C compiler for Windows NT can be obtained from `ftp://ftp.cygnus.com/pub/sac/gnu-win32/`, it is recommended that you invest in a C compiler with a GUI development environment such as Microsoft Visual C++ or Borland C++.

"Content Type" Returned by CGI Applications

All CGI scripts have one thing in common: the first two lines displayed by all CGI programs that display text output are the same. The first line displayed by all CGI programs that display text is `Content-type: text/html`. This line of text is always followed by two blank lines. Typically, ASCII character 10 is used twice, immediately after this line of text to create the blank lines.

For example, the first line of output for all CGI C programs with text output is

```
printf("Content-type: text/html%c%c",10,10) ;
```

The first line of output for all CGI Perl scripts with text output is

```
print "Content-type: text/html\n\n";
```

A Few Things to Note about Developing CGI Applications

A small note about programming in CGI is in order before moving into writing CGI programs. Sooner or later, when you write your own programs or try out examples, you'll get error messages generated by your Web server when you call the CGI script. Although things might get somewhat frustrating for you, don't give up! Most likely, the error message you receive from your Web server is due to a small oversight on your behalf. After a while, if you're still not getting anywhere with debugging your CGI script, it's time for you to start printing everything you can think of to standard output. Perhaps a variable you thought contained a value contains nothing but a NULL string. Perhaps an environmental variable you thought would be available to your script is not available. It's also possible that you left out the most important thing of all: the first line of all CGI scripts, as mentioned in the preceding section.

Rather than trying to debug CGI scripts by executing them on your Web server, you can execute them from the command prompt as well. It is possible to execute CGI programs by running them from the command prompt to find out what really happens. In order to do this, you need to manually set various CGI environment variables to make the CGI program believe that it's really being invoked by a Web server. Environmental variables can be defined by using the SET command, with the following syntax:

```
SET VARIABLE_NAME=VARIABLE_VALUE
```

For example, you can create a batch file with the following variable declarations to test CGI programs when running them from the command prompt. Please note that you may need to change the value of QUERY_STRING if your CGI script makes use of arguments.

```
SET SERVER_SOFTWARE=Netscape-Communications/1.12
SET SERVER_NAME=your.host.name
SET GATEWAY_INTERFACE=CGI/1.1
SET SERVER_PROTOCOL=HTTP/1.0
SET SERVER_PORT=80
SET REQUEST_METHOD=GET
SET SCRIPT_NAME =/cgi-bin/ScriptName.exe
SET QUERY_STRING=ArgumentsToCGIScript
SET REMOTE_HOST =000.000.000.000
SET REMOTE_ADDR =000.000.000.000
SET CONTENT_TYPE=application/x-www-form-urlencoded
SET HTTP_ACCEPT=image/gif, image/x-xbitmap, image/jpeg, image/pjpeg, */*
SET HTTP_USER_AGENT=Mozilla/2.0b4 (WinNT; I)
```

Hello World!, CGI

It's customary for the first program written in a new language or programming interface to display the string Hello World! Although this is a very simple application of CGI, it will teach you the basics of CGI scripts as well as how CGI scripts are called by Web browsers. The Hello World! script is demonstrated in Perl as well as C to make you more familiar with both languages and syntaxes of calling Perl and CGI scripts.

The Hello World! CGI script will simply display the current day, time, arguments passed in, and the browser being used by the client to access the CGI script. And of course, the string Hello World! will also be displayed!

Hello World! CGI Script in Perl

The script that displays Hello World! and the additional information is very simple to write in Perl. The code for this Perl script is listed next. The output of the Perl script appears in Figure 16.6.

SECURITY

Do not place PERL.EXE in your CGI directory. A user with malicious intent can potentially use PERL.EXE to execute commands on your NT Server. Rather than place PERL.EXE in your CGI directory, create a CGI extension mapping and place PERL.EXE in a directory that's not accessible via your Web server. Refer to your Web server documentation for information about creating CGI extension mappings.

```perl
# Sanjaya Hettihewa, http://wonderland.dial.umd.edu/
# December 31, 1995
# "Hello World" CGI Script in Perl
# Display content type being outputted by CGI script
print "Content-type: text/html\n\n";

# Label title of contents being outputted
print "<TITLE>Perl CGI Script Demonstration</TITLE>\n";

# Display text
print "<H1>Hello World!</H1>\n";
print "<H3>Welcome to the fun filled world of<BR>\n";
print "Windows NT CGI programming with Perl!</H3><BR><BR>\n";
print "The Web browser you are using is:";

# Display value of the environmental variable HTTP_USER_AGENT
print $ENV{"HTTP_USER_AGENT"} , "<BR>\n" ;
print "Arguments passed in: ";

# Display value of the environmental variable QUERY_STRING
print $ENV{"QUERY_STRING"} , "<BR>\n" ;

# Obtain date and time from the system
($sec, $min, $hour, $mday, $mon, $year, $wday, $yday, $isdst) = localtime(time);

# display time
print "\nThe current time is: ";
print  $hour, ":", $min, ":", $sec , "<BR>\n";

# display date
print "\nThe current date is: ";
print $mon + 1 , "/", $mday , "/", $year, "<BR>\n";
```

FIGURE 16.6.

Output of Hello World!
CGI Perl script.

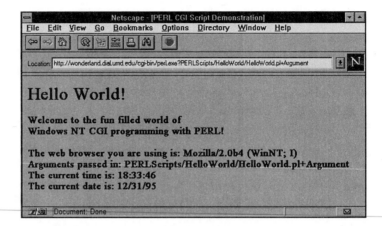

Pay particular attention to how the Perl CGI script is invoked. In the case of this example, the URL used to invoke the CGI script is

```
http://wonderland.dial.umd.edu/cgi-bin/perl.exe?PERLScripts/HelloWorld/
➥HelloWorld.pl+Argument
```

When calling a Perl script on a Windows NT Web server, the general syntax of the URL is

```
http://A/B?C+D
```

where

A is the host name of the Web server; in this example, it is `wonderland.dial.umd.edu`.

B is the relative path to PERL.EXE; in this example, it is `cgi-bin/perl.exe`.

C is the location of the Perl script. This path is relative to the location of PERL.EXE.

D contains any arguments passed into the Perl script. These arguments can be obtained by examining the contents of the CGI environment variable `QUERY_STRING`.

As you can see from the preceding example, when Perl scripts are called with arguments, the length of URLs can become quite long. You can avoid this by creating aliases for Perl scripts on your Web server. (Please consult your Web server's documentation for more information on creating aliases for URLs.) For example, if an alias called `Hello` was created for

```
http://wonderland.dial.umd.edu/cgi-bin/perl.exe?PERLScripts/HelloWorld/
➥HelloWorld.pl
```

the URL to call the preceding Perl CGI script will be reduced to

```
http://wonderland.dial.umd.edu/Hello+Argument
```

Whenever you have complex URLs for CGI scripts, create an alias for the CGI script. By hiding gory details such as long and complicated URL paths, your Web site will actually look "friendlier" to someone browsing your Web site. It will also save you time whenever you refer to such CGI scripts from one of your Web pages because you will have to do less typing. If you're still not convinced, it's much easier to remember

```
http://wonderland.dial.umd.edu/Hello+Argument
```

as opposed to

```
http://wonderland.dial.umd.edu/cgi-bin/perl.exe?PERLScripts/HelloWorld/
HelloWorld.pl+Argument
```

Hello World! CGI Script in C

The following code lists the C program that displays the same information as the preceding Perl example. The output of the C script appears in Figure 16.7.

```c
/* Sanjaya Hettihewa, http://wonderland.dial.umd.edu/
 * December 31, 1995
 * "Hello World" CGI Script in C
 */

/* Libraries containing special functions used in program */
#include <stdio.h>
#include <stdlib.h>
#include <time.h>

main ( )
{
/* Obtain current time */
  time_t        currentTime ;
  struct tm     *timeObject ;
  char          stringTime[128] ;
  currentTime = time ((time_t *) NULL )  ;
  timeObject  = localtime (&currentTime) ;

/* Display content type being outputted by CGI script */
  printf ("Content-type: text/html\n\n");

/* Displaying simple text output */
  printf ("<TITLE>C CGI Script Demonstration</TITLE>\n");
  printf ("<H1>Hello World!</H1>\n");
  printf ("<H3>Welcome to the fun filled world of<BR>\n");
  printf ("Windows NT CGI programming with C!</H3><BR><BR>\n");

/* Display value of the environmental variable HTTP_USER_AGENT */
  printf ("The Web browser you are using is: ");
  if ( getenv ( "HTTP_USER_AGENT" ) != NULL )
    printf ( "%s%s" , getenv ( "HTTP_USER_AGENT" ) ,"<BR>\n") ;

/* Display value of the environmental variable QUERY_STRING */
  printf ("Arguments passed in: ");
  if ( getenv ( "QUERY_STRING" ) != NULL )
    printf ( "%s%s", getenv ( "QUERY_STRING" ) ,"<BR>\n") ;
```

```
/* Display date and time using strftime() to format the date */
  strftime ( stringTime, 128, "%H:%M:%S", timeObject ) ;
  printf   ("\nThe current time is: %s<BR>\n", stringTime );
  strftime ( stringTime, 128, "%m/%d/%y", timeObject ) ;
  printf   ("\nThe current date is: %s\n", stringTime );

  return   ( 0 ) ;
}
```

FIGURE 16.7.

Output of Hello World!
CGI C script.

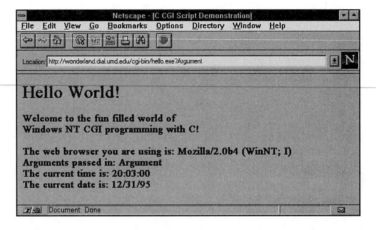

CGI C programs are accessed differently than Perl CGI scripts. C Programs can be directly executed by the Web server. However, Perl scripts have to be interpreted using the Perl interpreter. After compiling the C program into an executable program, it should be placed either in the CGI directory of your Web server or in a directory that's a child of the CGI directory. In this example, the executable program was placed in the cgi-bin directory, and the URL used to invoke the CGI script is

`http://wonderland.dial.umd.edu/cgi-bin/hello.exe?Argument`

When a CGI program on a Windows NT Web server is called, the general syntax of the URL is

`http://A/B?C`

where

A is the host name of the Web server. In this example, it is wonderland.dial.umd.edu.

B is the relative path to the executable program from the Web server's document root directory. In this example, it is cgi-bin/hello.exe.

C contains any arguments passed into the C program. You can obtain these arguments by examining the contents of the CGI environment variable QUERY_STRING.

Accessing Environment Variables Available to CGI Scripts

A thorough introduction to various programming languages and how you can utilize them to develop CGI applications is beyond the scope of this book. Therefore, most CGI applications developed in this chapter are developed by using the C programming language. However, to give you a feel for how various programming languages can be used to write CGI applications, you are shown how various environmental variables can be accessed by using Perl and C.

Accessing CGI Environment Variables from a C Program

The following C program displays all CGI variables that have been set by the Web server. Note that all environmental variables may not be defined depending on how the script is called. The following CGI program will display all CGI variables that have been defined by the Web server before invoking the CGI script:

```c
/* C Program to display CGI environment variable values defined by the Web server
before the CGI program is invoked */

#include <stdio.h>
#include <stdlib.h>
#define  NUM_ENVIRONMENT_VARIABLES 19

main ( )
{

/* Define the data structure that stores all the CGI variable
   names   */
  char* environmentVariables[] =
        { "SERVER_SOFTWARE",    "SERVER_NAME",
          "GATEWAY_INTERFACE", "SERVER_PROTOCOL",
          "SERVER_PORT",         "REQUEST_METHOD",
          "PATH_INFO",           "PATH_TRANSLATED",
          "SCRIPT_NAME",         "QUERY_STRING",
          "REMOTE_HOST",         "REMOTE_ADDR",
          "AUTH_TYPE",           "REMOTE_USER",
          "REMOTE_IDENT",        "CONTENT_TYPE",
          "CONTENT_LENGTH",      "HTTP_ACCEPT",
          "HTTP_USER_AGENT" } ;
  int  count ;

  printf("Content-type: text/html%c%c",10,10) ;
  printf("%s%s" ,
        "<PRE>\n",
        "<TITLE>CGI Environmental Variables Demonstration</TITLE>\n") ;

/* Loop through all CGI variables that were defined earlier */
  for (count = 0; count < NUM_ENVIRONMENT_VARIABLES; count++)
/* Check if a certain CGI variable has been defined by the Web server
   and print its value if the CGI variable has been defined */
```

```
   if ( getenv ( environmentVariables[count] ) != NULL )
     printf   ( "%17s = %s\n" , environmentVariables[count] ,
                  getenv ( environmentVariables[count] ) ) ;

  printf("</PRE>\n") ;
  return   ( 0 ) ;
}
```

The output of the preceding CGI script appears in Figure 16.8. As you can see from the URL, the URL of the CGI script is followed by additional arguments to the CGI script. Notice how the Web server has passed the arguments following the URL to the CGI script by using an environment variable.

FIGURE 16.8.

Output of a CGI program written in C when called with an argument after the URL of the CGI program.

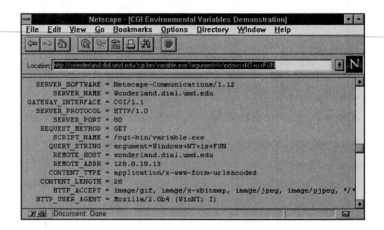

Accessing CGI Environment Variables from a Perl Script

Similarly, CGI scripts can be accessed very easily from a Perl script. The CGI Perl script that displays values of various CGI variables follows:

```
# Print the first line of all CGI scripts
print "Content-type: text/html\n\n";
print "<TITLE>PERL CGI Variable Demonstration</TITLE>\n";

printf( "<PRE>\n" );

foreach $EnvVar ( SERVER_SOFTWARE, SERVER_NAME, GATEWAY_INTERFACE,
                  SERVER_PROTOCOL, SERVER_PORT, REQUEST_METHOD,
                  PATH_INFO, PATH_TRANSLATED, SCRIPT_NAME, QUERY_STRING,
                  REMOTE_HOST, REMOTE_ADDR, AUTH_TYPE, REMOTE_USER,
                  REMOTE_IDENT, CONTENT_TYPE, CONTENT_LENGTH, HTTP_ACCEPT,
                  HTTP_USER_AGENT )

# Loop through all environment variables and display the values of all
  CGI variables that have been defined by the Web server.

{
```

```
  if ( $ENV{"$EnvVar"} ) {
    printf( "%17s = %s\n",  $EnvVar, $ENV{"$EnvVar"} );
  }
}

printf( "</PRE>\n" );
exit( 0 );
```

The output of the preceding Perl script appears in Figure 16.9. Note again how the Perl script is being called. The URL of the Perl script is made up of the URL of PERL.EXE and the location of the Perl script with respect to the location of PERL.EXE.

FIGURE 16.9.

Output of CGI script written in Perl to display CGI variables.

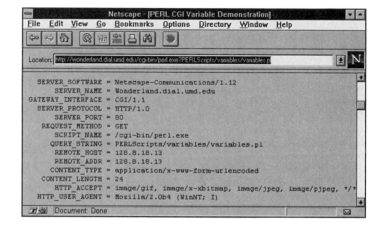

Using CGI to Provide Customized Content

With the expansion of the World Wide Web, more and more Web browsers are being invented. Although there are many Web browsers available for Windows NT, their capabilities differ greatly. Although at the time this book was written, Netscape roughly accounted for about 70 percent of all Web browsers being used. In all likelihood, with the release of Internet Explorer 3.0, this will change when Microsoft's Internet Explorer becomes more widely used. If the appearance of your Web site is very important to you, you might want to consider setting up a CGI script to provide a customized Web page, depending on the browser being used. Clearly, this is not practical for a very large Web site. However, by setting up a very simple CGI script as shown next, you can find out which Web browser is being used by the user browsing your Web site. If the browser being used is Netscape Navigator or Microsoft's Internet Explorer, you can provide a richly formatted Web page with various HTML enhancements, or otherwise provide a basic page with the same content.

Most Web pages that make use of special HTML tags (such as Netscape enhancements to HTML) look very attractive when viewed with a browser that supports the special HTML tags used. However, these pages tend to look less attractive when viewed with browsers that do not support the enhancements. The percentage of people with Web browsers that do not support various enhancements to HTML can be as much as 40 percent. For these Web browsers, it's possible to set up a CGI script that will display the same content that's formatted by using standard HTML. Such a CGI script can display customized content, as shown in Figure 16.10, based on the CGI variable HTTP_USER_AGENT.

FIGURE 16.10.

Using a CGI program to provide customized content based on the Web browser being used.

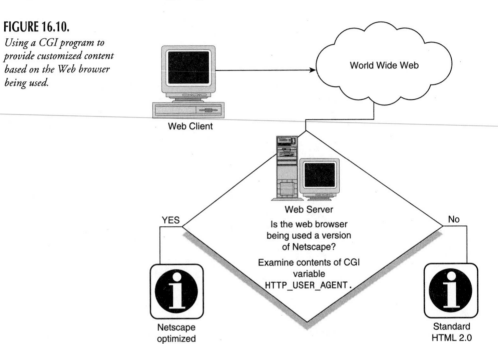

The CGI script in the following code listing is very simple. It first determines the Web server being used by looking at the environment variable HTTP_USER_AGENT. Depending on the value of this variable, a page with Netscape enhancements to HTML can be displayed if the browser being used is Netscape. On the other hand, a page that contains only standard HTML 2.0 can be displayed if the browser used by a Web surfer is not Netscape. By modifying the script, you can always add more customized pages for other browsers. Such a script can be used for important pages like the main home page of your organization. By utilizing CGI to provide dynamic content, you will give a good impression to someone browsing the contents of your Web site. You can ensure that a user with an advanced Web browser will see richly formatted Web pages. It is not feasible to support more than two custom Web pages. Both Internet Explorer and Netscape Navigator interpret HTML tags more or less the same way. You might want to create one page with Netscape and Internet Explorer extensions and another that uses only standard HTML 2.0.

PERFORMANCE

Please note that the following program is not optimized for speed of processing but for ease of reading. Because it is written to demonstrate how a CGI program can be written to provide customized content, it focuses on teaching CGI fundamentals and not on optimizing the code. You can make it more efficient by reading chunks of the file at a time rather than reading and outputting the file character by character.

```c
/* (C) 1995 Sanjaya Hettihewa http://wonderland.dial.umd.edu/
 * January 1, 1996
 * Program to output a customized Web page based on
   Web browser being used.
 */

/* Special function libraries being used by this program */
#include <stdio.h>
#include <stdlib.h>
#include <string.h>

/* Please note the use of double quotes. This is because a single quote is
   used to quote the next character */

/* If you provide content specialy formatted for a different browser, please
   change the following */
#define  SPECIAL_BROWSER_SUB_STRING "Mozilla"

/* Please change the following to the full path name of the HTML file that's
     specially formatted */
#define  SPECIAL_BROWSER_PAGE "H:\\www\\https\\ns-
home\\root\\documents\\WSDGNT\\special.htm"

/* Please change the following to the full path name of the HTML file that's
   formatted using standard HTML */
#define  OTHER_BROWSER_PAGE   "H:\\www\\https\\ns-
home\\root\\documents\\WSDGNT\\regular.htm"

/* Please change the following to the e-mail address of your Web site
   administrator */
#define  WEBMASTER            "mailto:Webmaster@wonderland.dial.umd.edu"

static int DisplayPage ( char *pageName ) ;

main ( )
{

/* The "First Line" of all CGI scripts... */
  printf("Content-type: text/html%c%c",10,10) ;

/* Find out what Web browser is being used */
  if ( getenv ( "HTTP_USER_AGENT" ) == NULL ) {
    printf("FATAL ERROR: HTTP_USER_AGENT CGI variable undefined!\n") ;
    return   ( 0 ) ;
  }
```

```
/* Display appropriate page based on browser being used by client */
  if (strstr (getenv ("HTTP_USER_AGENT" ), SPECIAL_BROWSER_SUB_STRING)!=NULL)
    DisplayPage ( SPECIAL_BROWSER_PAGE ) ;
  else
    DisplayPage ( OTHER_BROWSER_PAGE ) ;
  return   ( 0 ) ;

}

/* Contents of file passed into this function will be displayed to standard
    output. The Web server will transmit what's displayed to standard output
    by this CGI script to the client that called the CGI script */
int DisplayPage ( char *pageName )
{

  FILE *inFile   ;
  char character ;

/* Check to ensure a valid file name is given */
  if ((inFile = fopen(pageName, "r")) == NULL) {
      printf ( "FATAL ERROR: Content file can't be opened! %s<BR>", pageName);
      printf ( "Please contact the  <A HREF=%s>Webmaster.</A><BR>",
             WEBMASTER );
      return ( 0 ) ;
  }

/* Displaying contents of file to standard output
    Please note that this can be done more efficiently by reading chunks of the
    file at a time */
  fscanf ( inFile  , "%c" , &character ) ;
  while ( !feof(inFile) ) {
     printf ( "%c" , character ) ;
     fscanf ( inFile  , "%c" , &character ) ;
  }
  fclose(inFile);
  return ( 1 ) ;

}
```

Because the purpose of this program is to provide customized content based on the browser being used to browse your Web site, you need to create two separate Web pages. The first Web page is sent to any non-Netscape browser, assuming it does not parse various HTML-enhanced tags as does Netscape. This Web page can be very simple. For the purpose of this demonstration, assume that you need to display a number of options inside a table. Because browsers that do not support the <TABLE> tag might interpret this tag differently, you will have no control over what your Web site will look like when viewed with a different browser. To remedy this situation, you can use the preceding CGI program. For Web browsers that do not support enhanced HTML tags, you can create a non-table version of the same page using only standard HTML. By doing this, the appearance of your Web site can be controlled no matter what browser is being used to access your Web pages.

The following is the standard HTML Web page designed for non-Netscape browsers. In case you're interested in knowing where this Web page is referenced in the CGI program, this file will be saved at

```
H:\\www\\https\\ns-home\\root\\documents\\WSDGNT\\regular.htm
```

The location of the preceding file is defined in the C program so that its contents can be displayed for non-Netscape browsers. In the C program, the location of the preceding file is defined in OTHER_BROWSER_PAGE.

```
<TITLE>Standard HTML page</TITLE>
<BODY>
Welcome to the standard HTML page for technically challenged Web browsers.
<P>
Option One<BR>
Option Two<BR>
Option Three<BR>
</BODY>
```

The following is the Netscape-enhanced HTML Web page that is specially designed for those browsing your Web site with Netscape. The following HTML code displays the same three options that are displayed by the standard HTML page. However, the options are displayed inside a table with some additional Netscape enhancements. Because the C program needs to know the location of this file for the purpose of this example, the following page is located at

```
H:\\www\\https\\ns-home\\root\\documents\\WSDGNT\\special.htm
```

In the C program, the full path name of the preceding file is stored in SPECIAL_BROWSER_PAGE. The contents of this file are displayed by the CGI program whenever Netscape Navigator is used. You will need to change this variable depending on where you store the Netscape-enhanced Web page.

```
<TITLE>Netscape Enhanced page</TITLE>
<BODY>
<CENTER>
<TABLE BORDER=15 CELLPADDING=10 CELLSPACING=10 >
<TR>
<TD >
Welcome to the
<FONT SIZE=4>Ne</FONT><FONT SIZE=5>ts</FONT><FONT SIZE=6>ca</FONT><FONT SIZE=7>pe</
FONT>
<FONT SIZE=6>En</FONT><FONT SIZE=5>ha</FONT><FONT SIZE=4>nc</FONT><FONT SIZE=3>ed
</FONT>
 Web page!
</TD>
<TD >Option One<BR></TD >
<TD >Option Two<BR></TD >
<TD >Option Three<BR></TD >
</TR>
</TABLE>
</CENTER>
</BODY>
```

After compiling the preceding program and placing it in your Web server's CGI directory, depending on the browser being used to call the CGI script, the appropriate page will be displayed. When compiling the C program, please be sure to change SPECIAL_BROWSER_PAGE, OTHER_BROWSER_PAGE, and WEBMASTER. The output of the CGI program to provide customized content appears in Figures 16.11 and 16.12. For the purpose of this example, the two Web browsers Netscape and Mosaic were used. Note how the enhanced HTML page is displayed when accessing the script with Netscape, and the standard HTML page is displayed when accessing the script with Mosaic.

FIGURE 16.11.

Output of a CGI program when it is invoked by using Netscape.

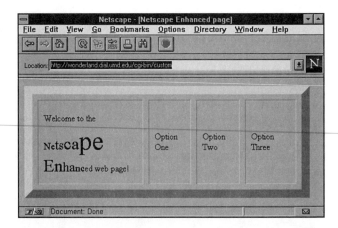

FIGURE 16.12.

Output of a CGI program when invoked with a non-Netscape browser such as Mosaic.

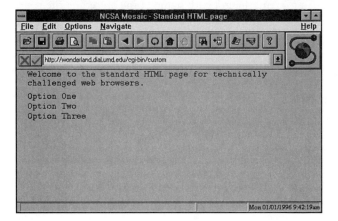

Setting Up a Feedback Form

One of the best things about CGI is that it lets you interact with people browsing your Web site. What better way is there to interact with them than ask for their feedback? By using a Windows NT command line mail utility called Blat and another CGI program that can be used to e-mail the contents of a form, you can set up a feedback form at your Web site in just a few minutes. Please refer to Chapter 26, "Setting Up Mail Server," to learn how to set up Blat on your system.

After setting up Blat, you need to create a feedback form. This feedback form will be used by users who want to e-mail their feedback to you. Before setting up the form, you need to download the program that will process the contents of the form after it's submitted. The program you need to download is wwwmail.exe, and you can download it from

```
http://www.esf.c-strasbourg.fr/misc/amsoft.exe?www
```

After downloading wwwmail.exe, you need to copy it to the CGI directory of your Web server. Then you need to create a page that displays after the user submits his or her feedback. This page can then thank the user for the feedback and allow the user to choose another link to follow.

Now all that's left to do is to create a feedback form and a response page that will display after the form is submitted. Refer to the following code listing for a simple feedback page. You can utilize a similar page to set up a feedback form at your Web site. There are a few values that you need to change to customize the feedback form, depending on how your Web site is organized. These values are

```
name="mailto"          value="user_ID@your.site"
name="WWWMail-Page"    value="<Full Path of page to display after submitting the
form">
action="<your CGI Directory>/wwwmail.exe/cgi-bin/feedback.hfo">
```

TIP

In order to provide the user with a set of predefined selections, you can have a pull-down list using the <SELECT/OPTION> tag, as shown in the following listing.

```
<HTML>
<HEAD>
<title>Feedback Form Demonstration</title>
</HEAD>

<BODY>
<FORM  method=POST
       action="/cgi-bin/wwwmail.exe/cgi-bin/feedback.hfo">
<INPUT TYPE=hidden name="mailto"
       value="Webmaster@wonderland.dial.umd.edu">
<INPUT TYPE=hidden name="WWWMail-Page" value="H:\www\netscape_commerce\ns-
home\root\documents\feedback\ThanksForFeedback.html">

<PRE>
<b>Subject:</b> <SELECT name="subject">
  <OPTION> I have some Feedback
  <OPTION> I have a comment...
  <OPTION> I have a suggestion...
  <OPTION> I need assistance with...
  <OPTION> Other
</SELECT>
```

```
<B>Your E-mail address please:</B>     <INPUT name="sender" SIZE=30>
<b>Your name Please:</b>               <INPUT name="name" SIZE=30 >
<b>Your phone # (If you wish)</b>   <INPUT name="phoneno" SIZE=20 >
<b>Would you like a reply from me?</b> <SELECT name="Reply">
  <OPTION> If you wish
  <OPTION> Yes, please
  <OPTION> No thanks
</SELECT>
<b>Is this message urgent?</b>         <SELECT name="Urgency">
  <OPTION> Not particularly
  <OPTION> Yes, very urgent
  <OPTION> Not at all
</SELECT>

<b>Please type your message and press the submit button:</b>
<TEXTAREA name="comments" cols=65 rows=3> </TEXTAREA>
<input type=submit value="Please click here to send message">
</FORM>
</PRE>
</BODY>
</HTML>
```

After setting up a form similar to the one in the preceding listing, you will have a feedback form that looks like the form shown in Figure 16.13.

FIGURE 16.13.

A generic feedback form.

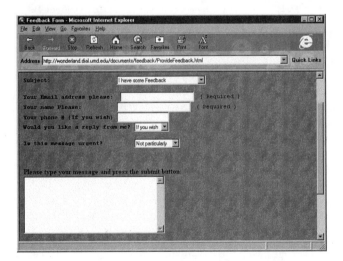

Now you need to create a page like the one shown in Figure 16.14. After the feedback form is submitted, this page will be displayed by the CGI script to thank the user for the feedback. The location of this page is defined in the variable WWWMail-Page of the HTML form. After the form is filled in and submitted, the page defined in WWWMail-Page should let the user know that you received the feedback and will get in touch with the user soon. It will also be helpful if you can let users know how soon you will be able to get in touch with them. Also, this page should provide a hypertext link to another page at your Web site so the user can continue to browse your Web site with ease.

FIGURE 16.14.

After the feedback form is submitted, the user will see a "thank you" page defined in hidden CGI variable WWWMail-Page.

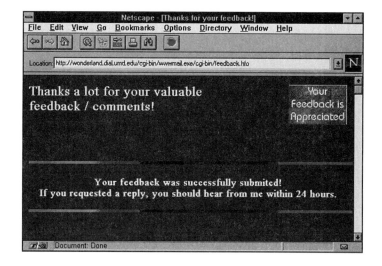

Summary

One of the best things about the World Wide Web is how you can use it to distribute information to millions of people. CGI allows you to interact with this large audience of people. This chapter was an introduction to using CGI to enhance the capabilities of your Web site as well as how to write CGI scripts in Perl and C. Various aspects of setting up CGI scripts, such as security, were also covered in this chapter so that the CGI scripts you develop and set up will not be a threat to the security of your Web server. Various practical applications of CGI were illustrated along with the source code so that you can modify examples presented to enhance your Web site.

In order to become more familiar with the topics covered in this chapter, you need to spend some time with either C or Perl. After writing some CGI programs and experimenting with the effects of making changes to them, you will discover how CGI scripts work as well as gain more experience in debugging and developing CGI scripts. Afterward, you will be able to create various CGI applets to perform many specialized tasks. As you gain more experience, CGI programs you once thought to be very complicated will be easy for you. By utilizing CGI and unleashing its potential to make the contents of your Web site easier to navigate, you will have an outstanding Web site with many repeat visitors.

What's Next?

With the knowledge gained by reading this chapter, you're now ready to move on to the more advanced applications of CGI in the next chapter. Chapter 17, "Advanced Windows NT CGI Applications," shows you how to retrieve data from feedback forms and process them. It also covers a number of tools that you can use to create forms and dynamic Web pages.

17

Advanced Windows NT CGI Applications

The preceding chapter discussed how you can develop CGI applications using Perl and C/C++. In this chapter, you learn how you can use PolyForm, a powerful CGI form utility, and iBasic, a server-side scripting language, to provide dynamic content to users browsing a Web site. The purpose of this chapter is not to cover all aspects of these two applications comprehensively. Instead, you learn how you can use various capabilities of these two applications to provide dynamic content and make a Web site interactive in a matter of minutes.

Creating Interactive Web Pages with PolyForm

PolyForm, from O'Reilly & Associates (ORA), is a useful CGI application that you can use to make a Web site interactive in a matter of minutes. As the name suggests, PolyForm is ideal for creating forms for users to fill in and submit. You can create a typical form application, such as a guest book or e-mail feedback form, with PolyForm in less than five minutes. PolyForm works with both Windows CGI (WinCGI) and Internet Server API (ISAPI) Web servers. At the time of this writing, PolyForm supports the following Web servers:

- WebSite from O'Reilly & Associates
- Microsoft Internet Information Server (IIS) and other ISAPI-compliant Web servers
- Netscape Commerce Server and Communications Server
- Web Commander
- AliBaba from CSM
- FolkWeb from Ilar Concepts
- ZBServer from ZBSoft
- Quarterdeck WebSTAR
- Commerce Builder and Communications Builder from Internet Factory

URL

Visit the following Web site for the most up-to-date information about PolyForm:
`http://polyform.ora.com/`

Installing PolyForm

Using the PolyForm Installation Wizard, you can install PolyForm in just a few minutes.

URL

You can download an evaluation copy of PolyForm from the following Web page:
`http://software.ora.com/download/`

After you download the PolyForm distribution file, copy it to a temporary directory and de-compress it. After you decompress the distribution file, execute the file `setup.exe` to begin installing PolyForm. The PolyForm Installation Wizard then pops up and guides you through the installation. The first dialog box asks you to quit all Windows applications before continuing. You click the Next button in this dialog box to acknowledge the warning and proceed to the next dialog box. Before doing so, however, make sure that all Windows applications you can afford to quit are terminated. When you install PolyForm, the installation program needs to copy several shared DLL files to the Windows NT System directory. The PolyForm Install Wizard is unable to do so if other applications are using the shared DLL files that have to be replaced. In this case, you can select to ignore certain DLL files. Doing so, however, may bring about certain undesired results.

Using the Server Software dialog box shown in Figure 17.1, you can select the Web server you are running. PolyForm supports WinCGI- and ISAPI-compliant Web servers. For the purpose of this example, install PolyForm on the MS Internet Information Server, an ISAPI-compliant Web server. After you select your server software, click the Next button to proceed to the next dialog box.

FIGURE 17.1.

The Web Server Software selection dialog box.

The Mail Settings dialog box asks for the Web server's domain name, as shown in Figure 17.2. Type in the domain name (`www.server.com`) and click the Next button to continue. Use the next dialog box to specify the location of the Web server's CGI directory (`H:\Publish\WWW\cgi-bin`) and click the Next button. You then are asked for the URL of the CGI directory, which is usually `http://www.server.com/cgi-bin`.

FIGURE 17.2.

The Mail Settings dialog box. Type in the domain name of the mail server and e-mail address of the PolyForm administrator.

After obtaining information discussed previously, the PolyForm Installation Wizard installs PolyForm and configures it with the data supplied. Then the installation program displays PolyForm release notes in a dialog box. You should read the release notes to find out more about PolyForm and whether you need to do anything special to get PolyForm to function with your Web server. The PolyForm installation program also creates a new Windows NT Start Menu folder similar to the one shown in Figure 17.3. PolyForm is now fully installed and ready for use.

FIGURE 17.3.

The PolyForm Start Menu folder.

Understanding Components of PolyForm

PolyForm consists of two applications. Figure 17.4 shows the first application, which you invoke by selecting the PolyForm CGI icon shown in Figure 17.3. Although the PolyForm CGI application has limited functionality, it is convenient for determining how many forms were submitted to the PolyForm CGI application for processing. The box next to POSTs contains the number of form submissions. You can reset this value by double-clicking it.

FIGURE 17.4.

The PolyForm CGI Application.

You use the PolyForm Control Panel application, shown in Figure 17.5, to create and edit PolyForm forms. You can invoke it either by selecting the PolyForm Control Panel icon in Figure 17.3 or by choosing Control | Control Panel from the dialog box shown in Figure 17.4.

FIGURE 17.5.
PolyForm Control Panel.

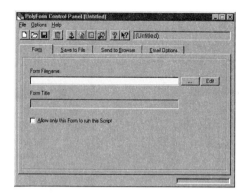

Creating a Feedback Form with PolyForm

Creating a feedback form with PolyForm is easy. To begin creating a feedback form, invoke the PolyForm Control Panel by double-clicking on the PolyForm Control Panel icon. You then see a dialog box similar to the one shown in Figure 17.5. You can create forms with PolyForm in two ways. You can either use the PolyForm Wizard or the PolyForm Control Panel shown in Figure 17.5. Either way, you can customize the form using the PolyForm Control Panel. I recommend that you first use the PolyForm Wizard to create a form and then use the PolyForm Control Panel to customize it. Choose File | Script Wizard (or click the blue wizard hat icon) to invoke the PolyForm Script Wizard shown in Figure 17.6.

FIGURE 17.6.
The PolyForm Script Wizard.

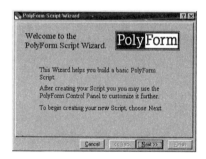

In the PolyForm Script Wizard, click the Next button to advance to the next dialog box. Using the dialog box shown in Figure 17.7, you can select the type of form to create from several different form types. Select Feedback Form from the drop-down list, and click the Next button to advance to the next dialog box.

In this dialog box, you can save the contents of the form in one of three ways. You can save the contents as a text file, a data file, or not at all. The option to save the form contents as data is useful if the data in the form is to be exported to an application such as MS Access or Excel at a later time. Because the feedback form is going to be e-mailed, the Don't Save option is selected in the dialog box shown in Figure 17.8. Press the Next button to continue creating the feedback form.

FIGURE 17.7.
Selecting the type of form.

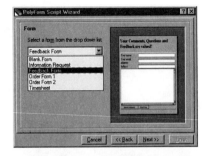

FIGURE 17.8.
Options for saving form contents.

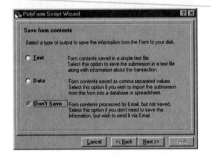

After the form is submitted, you can use the dialog box shown in Figure 17.9 to send a customized Web page to the browser. For the purpose of this example, send a standard conformation message to the user. After selecting an option, click the Next button. Note that you can modify this setting to send a customized Web page, at a later time, by using the PolyForm Control Panel.

FIGURE 17.9.
Selecting a response to browser.

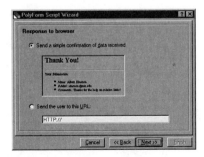

Using the dialog box shown in Figure 17.10, you can specify various e-mail options. When the form is e-mailed by PolyForm, information in this dialog box is used to customize the e-mail message. Make sure that the Copy Form Contents to check box is checked before proceeding to the next dialog box.

FIGURE 17.10.
E-mailing options.

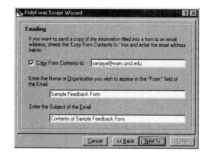

Use the dialog box shown in Figure 17.11 to name the PolyForm script. This name identifies the PolyForm script that you will create shortly. Give a descriptive name so that you won't have any trouble locating it at a later time. Note that PolyForm script names cannot contain any spaces.

FIGURE 17.11.
Naming the PolyForm script.

After all the data is entered, PolyForm displays a data confirmation dialog box, as shown in Figure 17.12. Use this opportunity to make sure that data supplied to the PolyForm Script Wizard is accurate. After you verify the information, click the Next button to create the PolyForm form.

FIGURE 17.12.
Script settings confirmation dialog box.

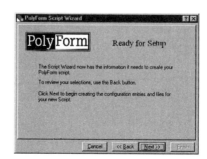

After it creates the script, PolyForm displays a dialog box identical to the one shown in Figure 17.13. Click the Finish button to exit the PolyForm Script Wizard and return to the PolyForm

Control Panel. After you exit the PolyForm Script Wizard, you can use the PolyForm Control Panel to customize various script settings. If you make any changes to the script, be sure to choose File | Save from the main menu to save the changes.

FIGURE 17.13.

The feedback form is now ready for use.

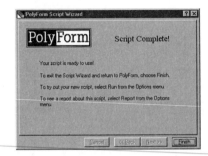

Customizing PolyForm Scripts

On the Forms tab of the PolyForm Control Panel shown in Figure 17.14, you can customize and create PolyForm scripts. I recommend that you place a checkmark next to the Allow only this Form to run this Script check box. If this check box is not checked, a user can potentially make a copy of one of your forms, make changes to it, fill it with some data, and submit it. This action can lead to undesired consequences because the order and existence of various fields can no longer be guaranteed when a form is tampered with.

FIGURE 17.14.

You can use the PolyForm Control Panel to customize PolyForm scripts.

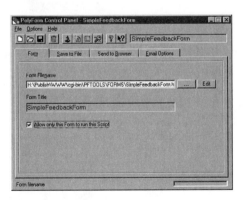

On the Save to File tab of the PolyForm Control Panel shown in Figure 17.15, you can configure how data submitted with a form is saved. You can save the data as a text file, data file (for exporting to a database), or a template (for exporting to an application such as MS Word). If you're using a feedback form, and its contents will be e-mailed by PolyForm, you can select to discard the data, as shown in Figure 17.15.

FIGURE 17.15.

Configuring how data submitted is saved to a file or discarded.

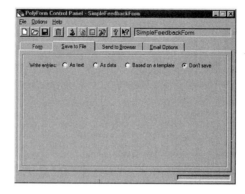

You can send a customized Web page to the user who submitted the Form using the Send to Browser tab of the PolyForm Control Panel, as shown in Figure 17.16. I recommend that you use this feature to send a customized Web page to the user. Be sure to include a link in the customized Web page so that the user can select to continue navigating your Web site. Don't let users use the Web browser's back arrow button to go back to a previous page after the form is submitted. This gives the impression that your Web site was not put together in a thoughtful manner.

FIGURE 17.16.

Specifying that a Web page be sent to a browser after the form is processed.

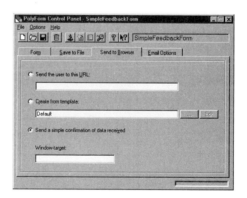

Using the Email Options tab of the PolyForm Control Panel, you can customize e-mail messages sent by PolyForm. (See Figure 17.17.) In addition to sending the contents to a certain user, you also can send a copy of the e-mail message to the user who submitted the Form by placing a checkmark on the Letter to user check box. Note that if this check box is checked, the Form should have an `<INPUT NAME="E-Mail">` field; this field is case-sensitive.

FIGURE 17.17.

Customizing e-mail options.

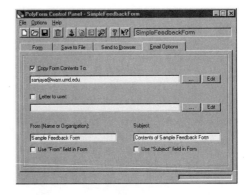

Testing Feedback Forms Created with PolyForm

Refer to PolyForm documentation for more information about using various advanced features of PolyForm to create interactive Web pages. You can access the feedback form that you just created by using a Web browser by looking up the URL http://wonderland.dial.umd.edu/cgi-bin/PolyForm.dll/SimpleFeedbackForm. Note that if your Web server does not support ISAPI, the URL contains PolyForm.exe instead of PolyForm.dll. The form created by the PolyForm Script Wizard is shown in Figure 17.18. PolyForm forms are located in the directory PFTOOLS\forms and can be customized to suit your needs. You might want to add a few extra fields, and perhaps, a graphic or two.

FIGURE 17.18.

The completed feedback form.

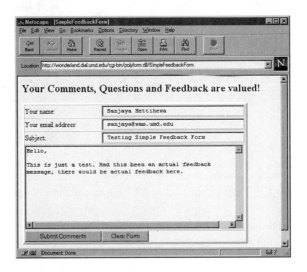

After the feedback form is submitted, because a simple confirmation message is selected in the Send to Browser tab of the PolyForm Control Panel (see Figure 17.16), PolyForm echoes the contents of the form back to the browser, as shown in Figure 17.19.

FIGURE 17.19.
The feedback confirmation message.

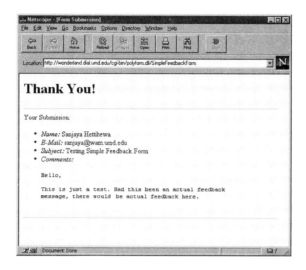

The e-mail message sent by PolyForm to the address specified in the Email Options tab (see Figure 17.17) is shown in Figure 17.20. Note how information typed into the form in Figure 17.18 is formatted by PolyForm. As just demonstrated, PolyForm can be used to create interactive Web pages effortlessly without spending hours or even days creating forms with a programming language such as C or Perl.

FIGURE 17.20.
Contents of the e-mail messages mailed by PolyForm. Note how information submitted using the Web page in Figure 17.18 is formatted by PolyForm.

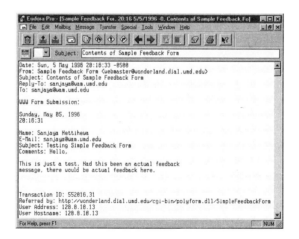

Creating a URL Selector with PolyForm

You might have noticed how some Web pages use a drop-down list from which you can select various URLs. After selecting a URL and clicking on a button, you are automatically transferred to the URL that you selected. You can implement such a drop-down list with PolyForm in a couple of minutes. When you create a drop-down list of URLs, you do not have to specify a script name. The drop-down list of URLs created with the HTML code in Listing 17.1 is shown in Figure 17.21.

Listing 17.1. Drop-down URL list demonstration.

```
<HTML>
<TITLE>Drop down URL list demonstration</TITLE>

<BODY BGCOLOR=FFFFFF>

<HR>
It is very easy to implement a drop-down list of URLs with
PolyForm. Please select a URL from the list below and
click on the "Please take me there" button.<P>
<HR>
<FORM METHOD="POST" ACTION="/cgi-bin/polyform.dll">
<select name="URL" size=1>
<option value="http://www.NetInnovation.com"> NetInnovation.COM
<option value="http://www.Microsoft.com"> Microsoft Web site.
<option value="http://www.mcp.com"> Macmillan Web site.
<option value="http://polyform.ora.com"> PolyForm Web site.
</select>
<input type="submit" value="Please take me there!">
</FORM>
<HR>

</BODY>
</HTML>
```

FIGURE 17.21.

You can use PolyForm to implement a drop-down list of URLs.

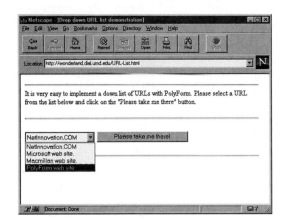

Where to Go from Here

In the preceding sections, you learned some of PolyForm's functionality and how you can use it to create interactive Web pages. Take some time to go over the PolyForm documentation to learn more about its features. PolyForm is a general-purpose CGI application that you can use for a wide variety of tasks, in addition to creating feedback forms. Take the time to learn some of its advanced features such as the capability to export data into MS Access, Excel, and other spreadsheet or database applications. You then make your Web site interactive, and automate various tasks that would otherwise have to be done manually.

Creating Dynamic Web Pages with iBasic

Although you can use C and C++ to create custom CGI applications, these programming languages were not designed to be used for CGI programming applications. iBasic is a powerful scripting language that is ideal for creating CGI applications. The purpose of this section is not to cover all aspects of the iBasic language comprehensively. Instead, it is to provide you with an overview of iBasic and some of its capabilities. Refer to the iBasic documentation for additional information about iBasic.

> **URL**
>
> Visit the following Web site for the most up-to-date information about iBasic:
> `http://www.ibasic.com/`

Installing iBasic

Installing iBasic on your system is easy as long as your Web server supports ISAPI or CGI. The iBasic scripting language and server extensions are contained in two files.

> **URL**
>
> The iBasic (server-side scripting tool) download Web page:
> `http://www.ibasic.com/Download.html`

After you download both files, create two temporary directories and copy each file to its own directory. Before you proceed to install iBasic, note the temporary evaluation key given at the Web site from which iBasic was downloaded. This key is required to install iBasic on your system.

Installing the iBasic Scripting Language

After you copy the iBasic scripting language distribution file to a temporary directory, execute it to decompress the distribution file. Then execute the file `setup.exe` to begin installing iBasic. The installation program first presents you with a license agreement. Read it and proceed to the next dialog box. This dialog box asks for the product key. Type in the temporary evalua-tion key obtained from the Web page from which iBasic was downloaded to continue installing iBasic. You can select various iBasic components to be installed using the Select Components dialog box shown in Figure 17.22. I strongly recommend that you select all com-ponents in this dialog box before moving on to the next dialog box.

FIGURE 17.22.

The iBasic component selection dialog box.

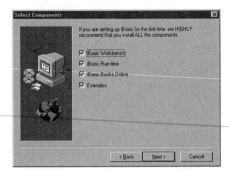

Using the Choose Destination Directory dialog box shown in Figure 17.23, you can select the destination directory of iBasic. Note that this directory does not have to be a child of your Web server's document root directory. After you select a destination directory, proceed to the next dialog box.

FIGURE 17.23.

Selecting destination directory of iBasic.

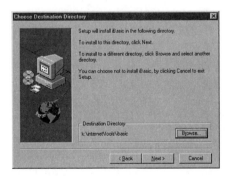

The iBasic installation program uses the information from the Web Server Selection dialog box shown in Figure 17.24 to find out the Web server you will be using with iBasic. As you can see, iBasic supports several Windows NT Web servers, including all four Web servers covered in this book. Select your Web server from the list of supported Web servers and proceed to the next dialog box.

FIGURE 17.24.
Selecting the type of Web server.

The installation program uses the information from the Web Server Settings dialog box to obtain the document root directory, the CGI directory, and the domain name of your Web server. Type in the requested information, as shown in Figure 17.25, and proceed to the next dialog box to begin installing iBasic.

FIGURE 17.25
The Web Server Settings dialog box.

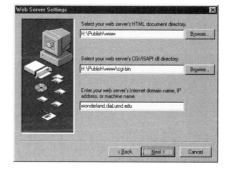

After it installs the iBasic scripting language, the installation program insists that you reboot your server before using iBasic. I recommended that you follow this advice and reboot your server before continuing. By rebooting, you can ensure that iBasic is fully installed on your system.

Installing iBasic Extensions

After you install the iBasic scripting language, log on to the temporary directory to which the iBasic extensions file is copied. Then execute the distribution file to decompress it and execute the file setup.exe to begin installing iBasic. First, you are presented with a dialog box displaying the iBasic license agreement; read it and proceed to the next dialog box. Using the Select Components dialog box shown in Figure 17.26, you can select various iBasic Server Extensions' components to install. I recommend that you select all components in this dialog box before continuing to make maximum use of various iBasic features.

FIGURE 17.26.

iBasic Server Extensions'
component selection dialog
box.

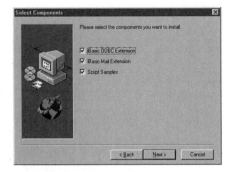

In the Choose Destination Directory dialog box, displayed in Figure 17.27, you can select the destination directory of iBasic Server Extensions. After you type in the destination directory, the installation program installs iBasic server extensions on your system.

FIGURE 17.27.

iBasic Server Extensions'
destination directory
selection dialog box.

After it installs iBasic, the installation program adds an iBasic application icon to the Windows NT Start Menu, as shown in Figure 17.28. Proceed to the next section to learn how you can use iBasic to provide dynamic content to users browsing your Web site. Reboot your server and then make sure that it is functioning normally before you proceed to the next section.

FIGURE 17.28.

After iBasic is installed, an
iBasic application icon is
added to the Windows NT
Start Menu folder.

Using the iBasic Development Environment

The iBasic development environment is thoughtfully laid out. Using it, you can easily create iBasic applications. You can execute the iBasic application, hereafter called the *iBasic Work-bench*, by selecting it from the Windows NT Start Menu. As shown in Figure 17.29, the iBasic

Workbench comprises two panes. The left pane displays various files and directories, and the right pane displays the file selected.

FIGURE 17.29.

The iBasic Workbench.

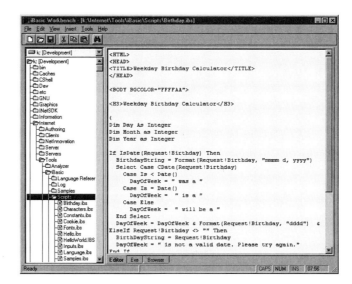

Notice the three tabs at the bottom of the right pane of the iBasic Workbench. These tabs are useful when creating iBasic applications. You can use the Editor tab to edit iBasic applications, as shown in Figure 17.29. Figure 17.30 demonstrates how you can use the Exe tab to view Basic source code of iBasic applications. If you compare Figure 17.29 to Figure 17.30, you will notice that the iBasic application in Figure 17.29 has been translated into a Basic application in Figure 17.30. iBasic is compatible with Visual Basic for Applications (VBA).

FIGURE 17.30.

Exe tab of the iBasic Workbench.

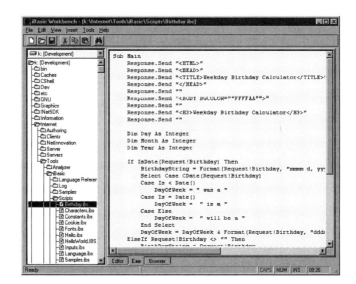

A Web browser also is included with iBasic. Because it is integrated with the iBasic Workbench, you can use the Web browser included with iBasic to test iBasic applications. You do so by selecting the application in the left pane and clicking the Browser tab. Figure 17.31 demonstrates how you can test the Birthday application included with iBasic using the built-in Web browser.

FIGURE 17.31.

The Web Browser tab of the iBasic Workbench.

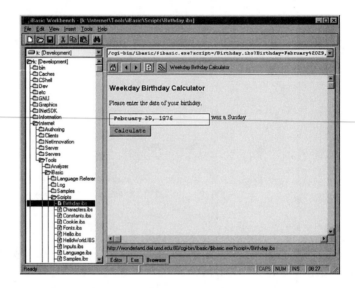

Hello World, iBasic!

If you are familiar with Visual Basic, the iBasic code in Listing 17.2 should look familiar to you. If not, spend some time with the iBasic documentation to become more familiar with it. You can access iBasic documentation by choosing Help|Contents from the iBasic Workbench main menu.

Listing 17.2. "Hello World" iBasic script.

```
<HTML>
<TITLE>
Hello World, iBasic!
</TITLE>

<BODY BGCOLOR=FFFFFF>
<H1>
Hello World!
</H1>

<HR>

<P>Welcome to the fun filled and dynamic world
of iBasic programming!
```

```
<P>Today is %Format(Date(), "mmmm d, yyyy")%,
and time is now %Time()% EDT.

{
For count = 1 To 10
  For countTwo = 1 To count
    Response.Send "*"
  Next countTwo
  Response.Send "<BR>"
Next count
}

<HR>

</BODY>

</HTML>
```

Refer to Figure 17.32 for the output of the Hello World application. It simply displays the string "Hello World" and the current time of the Web server. In addition, it uses a simple loop to draw a triangle of asterisks. If you look at the iBasic code listing, you will notice that it looks similar to HTML code. The only difference is the loop structure enclosed with curly braces, and time and date functions enclosed within two percentage signs. As demonstrated in this simple example, iBasic functions can be used to create dynamic Web pages by enclosing them with percentage signs. You can enclose longer iBasic code listings, like the one that draws the triangle, within a pair of curly braces.

FIGURE 17.32.

The output of the Hello World application.

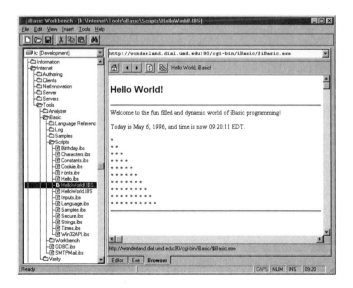

A More Useful iBasic Application

The preceding section described how you can create a simple iBasic application and publish it on the Web. Of course, the Hello World application is not very useful; the iBasic application presented next is more useful. In fact, you might want to incorporate it into your Web site.

The next application demonstrates how to create an iBasic application that uses *cookies*. Cookies have been implemented to make it easier for a server and client to remember previous transactions. Because HTTP is a stateless protocol, cookies are very important. The application shown in Listing 17.3 uses cookies to keep track of the last date and time a user visited a Web page. It also uses cookies to determine whether a user is visiting the Web page for the first time. If so, the iBasic application displays the Web page shown in Figure 17.33.

FIGURE 17.33.

The Web page displayed by the iBasic application the first time a user visits the page.

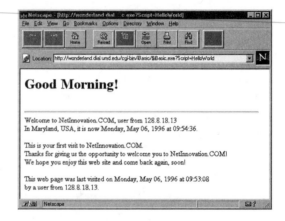

If a user has already visited the Web page, the iBasic application displays a Web page similar to the one shown in Figure 17.34.

URL

Visit the following Web site for more information about client-side state HTTP cookies:

`http://www.netscape.com/newsref/std/cookie_spec.html`

The iBasic application in Listing 17.3 is very simple. Lines 1–7 define variables used by the iBasic application. Lines 9–24 use cookies to determine the last day and time a user visited the Web page. Depending on whether a user has visited the Web page earlier, the Boolean variable NewUser is either set to True or False. The following application also keeps track of the host name and time someone last accessed the Web page. This information is saved in a file. Lines 26–42 process this information. Then, depending on the time of the Web server, the iBasic application displays a suitable message to the user. The remainder of the application is similar to the preceding Hello World application. Refer to the iBasic documentation for additional information about various functions used in the following code listing (Listing 17.3).

FIGURE 17.34.

The Web page displayed by the iBasic application each subsequent time a user visits the page.

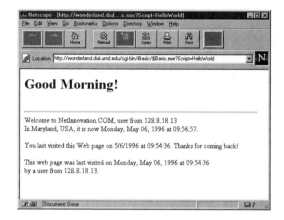

Listing 17.3. A more advanced iBasic program.

```
1: {
2: Sub Main
3:   Dim LastLogon As Cookie,  _
4:       NewUser   As Boolean, _
5:       LogDate   As Variant, _
6:       LastUser  As Variant, _
7:       LastTime  As Variant
8:
9:   Set LastLogon = Cookies![Last Visit]
10:
11:   If LastLogon Is Nothing Then
12:     Set LastLogon = Cookies.Add("Last Visit")
13:     NewUser = True
14:   Else
15:     LogDate  = LastLogon
16:     NewUser  = False
17:   End If
18:
19:   With LastLogon
20:     .Value = Format(Now, "ddddd") + " at " + _
21:             Format(Now, "Long Time")
22:     .Expires = Now + 365
23:   End With
24: }
25:
26: {
27: Open "LastAccess.TMP" For Output As #1
28: Print #1, Env!REMOTE_ADDR
29: Print #1, Now
30: Close #1
31:
32: If (Dir("LastAccess") = "LastAccess" )Then
```

continues

Listing 17.3. continued

```
33:    Open "LastAccess" For Input As #1
34:    Line Input #1, LastUser
35:    Line Input #1, LastTime
36:    Close #1
37:    Kill "LastAccess"
38: End If
39:
40: Name "LastAccess.TMP" As "LastAccess"
41:
42: }
43:
44: <HTML>
45:
46: <BODY BGCOLOR="FFFFFF">
47:
48: <H1>
49: {If Hour(Time()) >= 18 Then}
50:    Good Evening!<P>
51: {ElseIf Hour(Time()) >= 12 Then}
52:    Good Afternoon!<P>
53: {Else}
54:    Good Morning!<P>
55: {End If}
56: </H1>
57:
58: <HR>
59:
60: Welcome to NetInnovation.COM, user from
61: %Env!REMOTE_ADDR% <BR>
62: In Maryland, USA, it is now %Format(Now, "Long Date")%
63: at %Format(Now, "Long Time")%.<P>
64:
65: {If Not NewUser Then}
66:    You last visited this Web page on %LogDate%.
67:    Thanks for coming back!<P>
68: {Else}
69:    This is your first visit to NetInnovation.COM.<BR>
70:    Thanks for giving us the opportunity to welcome
71:    you to NetInnovation.COM!<BR>
72:    We hope you enjoy this Web site and
73:    come back again, soon!<P>
74: {End If}
75:
76: This Web page was last visited on
77:    %Format(LastTime, "Long Date")% at
78:    %Format(LastTime, "Long Time")%<BR>
79:    by a user from %LastUser%.
80:
81: </BODY>
82: </HTML>
83: {End Sub}
```

Where to Go from Here

The preceding sections were meant to be a brief introduction to iBasic and some of its capabilities. As you will learn when you go over iBasic documentation, iBasic is a powerful scripting language that you can use for a variety of tasks. Take some time to go over iBasic documentation and learn some of its capabilities. You can use iBasic, for example, to access powerful Win32 API functions and create sophisticated Web pages.

Summary

PolyForm and iBasic are two useful CGI applications that you can use to create interactive and dynamic Web pages. Although these two applications are not distributed free of charge or included with Windows NT, they can potentially save days or even weeks of CGI application development time. I recommended that you download both these applications and use them to make your Web site dynamic and interactive.

What's Next?

The next chapter discusses how you can publish databases on the WWW. Several powerful database publishing applications are available for Windows NT. You can use these applications to publish databases effortlessly on the Web in a matter of minutes. The next chapter also demonstrates how you can make information in a database available to users browsing a Web site.

18

Publishing Databases on the Web

Information in a database can be made available to users for searching and updating. Several Web publishing applications are available for Windows NT. You can use these applications to publish databases on the Web in just a few minutes. In this chapter, you learn how you can use Cold Fusion and the Internet Database Connector to publish databases. Note that Internet Information Server (IIS) is required to publish databases on the Web with the Internet Database Connector.

Publishing Databases on the Web with Cold Fusion

Cold Fusion is a sophisticated database publishing application. Using it, you can effortlessly publish various Open Database Connectivity (ODBC) compliant databases on the Web. In this section, you learn how to install Cold Fusion and use it to publish databases. The purpose of this section is to provide an overview of how you can use Cold Fusion to create Web/database interfaces. Refer to the Cold Fusion documentation to learn about various advanced capabilities not discussed in this section. I guide you through the installation of Cold Fusion and then show you how you can use it to update and query ODBC data sources. Cold Fusion supports several Web servers, including all four Web servers covered in this book. Visit the following Web site for the most up-to-date information about Cold Fusion.

> **URL**
>
> Cold Fusion (Web database tool) home page:
> `http://www.allaire.com/`

Installing Cold Fusion

You can download Cold Fusion from the following Web site. After you do so, copy it to a temporary directory and decompress the distribution file.

> **URL**
>
> Cold Fusion download Web page:
> `http://www.allaire.com/cgi-shl/dbml.exe?template=/allaire/downloads/`
> `download.dbm`

Then locate the file `setup.exe`, and execute it to begin installing Cold Fusion. The first installation dialog box displays a software license agreement. Click the OK button to acknowledge it. The next dialog box recommends that you exit all Windows NT applications before installing Cold Fusion. I recommend that you follow this advice. The Cold Fusion installation program is unable to copy certain DLL files if they are being used by other applications. Acknowledge the recommendation and proceed to the next dialog box. In the Choose Destination Directory dialog box shown in Figure 18.1, you can select the destination directory of Cold Fusion. This directory should not be a child of the Web server's document root directory due to security reasons. Click Next and proceed to the dialog box in Figure 18.2.

FIGURE 18.1.

Cold Fusion destination directory selection dialog box.

In the Select Components dialog box, you select which Cold Fusion components should be installed by the Cold Fusion installation program. I recommend that you make sure that all components except the ODBC component are selected. If the version of ODBC installed on your system is the same as the one shown in the dialog box in Figure 18.2, you can skip installing the ODBC Desktop drivers. If you do not have ODBC installed on your system, however, or if the version of ODBC installed is older than the one shown in Figure 18.2, select to install the ODBC component. After you select the Cold Fusion components, click Next and proceed to the next dialog box to select a Web server.

FIGURE 18.2.

Cold Fusion component selection dialog box.

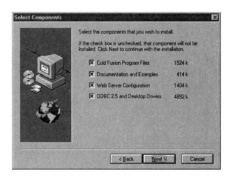

The dialog box shown in Figure 18.3 lists various Web servers supported by Cold Fusion. In this dialog box, you can select the Web server you want to use with Cold Fusion. If your Web server is not listed, select the Other Server radio button. Click the Next button to proceed to the next dialog box.

FIGURE 18.3.
Cold Fusion Web server
selection dialog box.

Use the input controls shown in the dialog box in Figure 18.4 to specify various Web server settings. For Cold Fusion to be installed properly, it needs the path of your Web server's document root directory, CGI directory, and the alias of the CGI directory. Cold Fusion attempts to locate these settings for you. If the settings are correct, click the Next button. If they are not, change the settings, verify them with your Web server's configuration settings, and click the Next button.

FIGURE 18.4.
Web server settings
dialog box.

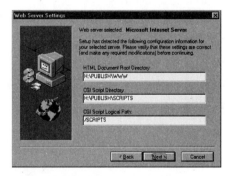

If you selected to install ODBC drivers in the Select Components dialog box (refer to Figure 18.2), the installation program displays the dialog box shown in Figure 18.5. Before you install the ODBC drivers, make sure that no other applications are using various shared DLL files that will be replaced by the ODBC installation program. If the ODBC installation program fails to install because other applications are still using various shared DLL files it should replace, reboot your system and execute the ODBC Setup icon shown in Figure 18.6.

FIGURE 18.5.
Quit other applications
before attempting to install
ODBC drivers.

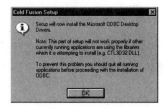

FIGURE 18.6.

Cold Fusion Windows NT
Start Menu folder.

After the installation program installs Cold Fusion, it creates a Windows NT Start Menu folder similar to the one shown in Figure 18.6. After this Start Menu folder is created, Cold Fusion is completely installed and ready for use.

The Cold Fusion Setup dialog box, shown in Figure 18.7, gives you the chance to verify that the Cold Fusion installation is working properly. I recommend that you select the Yes button to verify the Cold Fusion installation. You can also verify it at a later time by executing the Getting Started icon in the Start Menu folder (refer to Figure 18.6).

FIGURE 18.7.

Cold Fusion installation
complete dialog box.

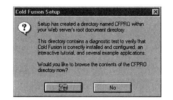

Verifying Cold Fusion Installation

After you install Cold Fusion, you should verify that it is installed properly before using it. Use the Getting Started with Cold Fusion Web page (see Figure 18.8) to verify correct installation. You can invoke this Web page either by answering Yes to the Cold Fusion Setup dialog box (refer to Figure 18.7) or by executing the Getting Started icon in the Start Menu folder (refer to Figure 18.6).

To verify successful installation of Cold Fusion, select the Verify Installation and Configuration link on the Web page. You then see a Web page identical to the one shown in Figure 18.9. Use this Web page to submit a query and verify that Cold Fusion has been set up properly. Use the drop-down list to select a department and then click the Submit Query button.

After you click on the Submit Query button, if Cold Fusion is installed properly, you see a Web page similar to the one shown in Figure 18.10. If you do not see a similar Web page, chances are, ODBC is not set up properly on your system. When you install the ODBC drivers, if you encounter any error messages, you might have to reboot your system and reinstall the ODBC drivers included with Cold Fusion.

FIGURE 18.8.

Using the Getting Started with Cold Fusion Web page, you can verify that Cold Fusion is installed properly.

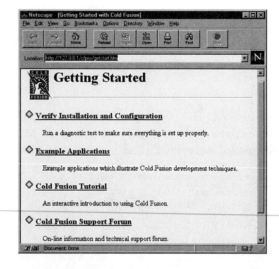

FIGURE 18.9.

The Cold Fusion Test Query Web page.

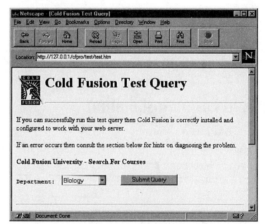

FIGURE 18.10.

The Test Query results Web page.

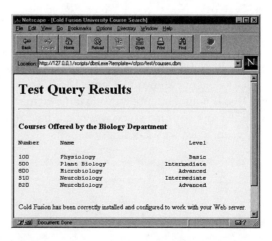

Inserting Data to an ODBC Data Source Using Cold Fusion

Inserting data into an ODBC data source with Cold Fusion is easy. In this section, you learn how you can insert information in a form into the table of an ODBC-compliant data source. The following example is meant to provide you with an overview of some of Cold Fusion's capabilities. Refer to the Cold Fusion documentation for additional information about inserting data into ODBC data sources.

Cold Fusion is made up of a CGI executable program (DBML.EXE). Data in ODBC data sources is manipulated with Cold Fusion using Database Markup Language (DBML) template files. Cold Fusion functions by manipulating data in ODBC data sources as predefined in a template file. The Cold Fusion executable program (DBML.EXE) is called with a template containing information about how data in an ODBC data source should be manipulated. For example, the URL `dbml.exe?template=/cfpro/tutorial/step2b.dbm` calls Cold Fusion with the template step2b.dbm. Cold Fusion then accesses an ODBC data source as specified in the template file and returns the results.

After you install Cold Fusion, if you look up the URL `http://127.0.0.1/cfpro/tutorial/step1a.htm`, you see a Web page similar to the one shown in Figure 18.11. Note that 127.0.0.1 is the address of the local host. Your Web server has to be functioning to access the URL given earlier. The source code of this Web page is shown in Listing 18.1 (line numbers have been added to make it easier to refer to various statements). In line 16, notice that the contents of the form are submitted to Cold Fusion along with the name of a template. Cold Fusion uses this template to determine what to do with the data submitted. The Web page containing the form merely collects information and forwards it to Cold Fusion. Note that names of input controls in the following form correspond with various data fields in the database.

Listing 18.1. The Web page source code.

```
 1: <HTML>
 2: <HEAD>
 3: <TITLE>Lesson 1 - Inserting Data</TITLE>
 4:
 5:
 6: </HEAD>
 7:
 8: <BODY>
 9: <H1><a href="/cfpro/tutorial/tutorial.htm">
     ➥<img src="../cfusion.gif" height=72 width=59 border=0 align=left></a>
Lesson 1 - Inserting Data </H1>
10: <HR>
11:
12: <P>Displayed below is a standard HTML Form.
13: If you enter data into the form and press the &quot;Enter Course
     ➥Information&quot; button the
14: data will be automatically appended to the <I>CourseList</I> table of the
     ➥database:
15:
```

continues

Listing 18.1. continued

```
16: <FORM ACTION="/scripts/dbml.exe?Template=/cfpro/tutorial/step1b.dbm"
    ➥METHOD="POST">
17:
18: <PRE>
19:   Course Name: <INPUT TYPE="text" NAME="CourseName" SIZE=38>
20:    Department: <SELECT NAME="Department_ID">
21:         <OPTION VALUE="BIOL"> Biology
22:         <OPTION VALUE="CHEM"> Chemistry
23:         <OPTION VALUE="ECON"> Economics
24:         <OPTION VALUE="MATH"> Mathematics
25:         </SELECT>   Level: <SELECT NAME="CourseLevel">
26:             <OPTION VALUE="Basic"> Basic
27:             <OPTION VALUE="Intermediate"> Intermediate
28:             <OPTION VALUE="Advanced"> Advanced
29:             </SELECT>
30:     Course No: <INPUT TYPE="text" NAME="CourseNumber" SIZE=3>
31:
32:   Course Description:
33:   <TEXTAREA COLS=48 ROWS=3 NAME="CourseDescription"></TEXTAREA>
34:
35:   <INPUT TYPE="submit" VALUE="Enter Course Information">
36: </PRE>
37: </FORM>
```

FIGURE 18.11.

Inserting data into an ODBC data source.

The contents of the template referred to in line 16 of Listing 18.1 are shown in Listing 18.2. Cold Fusion uses this template to determine what to do with the data contents of the form. Cold Fusion uses line 3 of this code listing to determine the data source and the table where the contents of the form should be inserted. In this particular example, the data is inserted into the table CourseList in data source CF Examples. After the data is inserted, Cold Fusion displays the HTML statements shown in lines 8-29 of Listing 18.2. Refer to the Cold Fusion documentation for information about various statements that you can insert into the template files to manipulate data submitted with a form.

Listing 18.2. Inserting data into an ODBC data source table.

```
 1: <!-- Insert the data into the table 'CourseList' -->
 2:
 3: <DBINSERT DATASOURCE="CF Examples" TABLENAME="CourseList">
 4:
 5: <!-- Show the user a brief message indicating that the
 6:       insert was successful -->
 7:
 8: <HTML>
 9: <HEAD>
10: <TITLE>Lesson 1 - Inserting Data</TITLE>
11: </HEAD>
12:
13: <BODY>
14:
15: <H2>New Course Entered into Database</H2>
16:
17: <P>You just entered a new course into the <I>CourseList</I> table.
18: The fields CourseName, Department_ID, CourseLevel, CourseNumber
19: and CourseDescription were populated by data you entered in the form.
20:
21: <P>
22:
23: <A HREF="/cfpro/tutorial/step1a.htm">
24:     Go Back to Lesson 1 - Inserting Data</A>
25: <P>
26: <HR>
27:
28: </BODY>
29: </HTML>
```

After the data in Figure 18.11 is inserted into the ODBC data source, Cold Fusion displays a message similar to the one shown in Figure 18.12.

FIGURE 18.12.

The message displayed after data is successfully inserted into an ODBC data source.

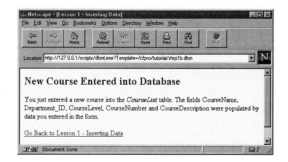

Viewing Data in an ODBC Data Source Using Cold Fusion

Viewing data with Cold Fusion is as easy as inserting data. After you insert data using the form shown in Figure 18.11, enter the URL http://127.0.0.1/scripts/dbml.exe?template=/cfpro/tutorial/step2b.dbm to obtain the contents of the database, as shown in Figure 18.13. Note how the data inserted into the form has been inserted into the database. The information in Figure 18.13 was created with the template (tep2b.dbm) defined in the URL just mentioned.

FIGURE 18.13.

Contents of ODBC data source after inserting the record in Figure 18.11.

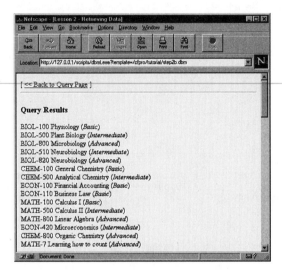

Refer to Listing 18.3 for the contents of this template file (line numbers have been added to make it easier to refer to various statements). The first line of the template file uses a Structured Query Language (SQL) statement to obtain data from the data source CF Examples. The statements in lines 12–14 display the contents of the table.

Listing 18.3. Displaying contents of an ODBC data source.

```
 1: <DBQUERY NAME="GetAllCourses" DATASOURCE="CF Examples"
 2:     SQL="SELECT * FROM CourseList" >
 3:
 4: <HTML><HEAD>
 5:         <TITLE>Step2 - Retrieving Data (template)</TITLE>
 6: </HEAD>
 7:
 8: <BODY>
 9:
10: <B>AVAILABLE COURSES</B>
11:
12: <DBOUTPUT QUERY="GetAllCourses">
13:     #Department_ID#-#CourseNumber# #CourseName# (#CourseLevel#)
14: </DBOUTPUT>
15:
16: </BODY></HTML>
```

Where to Go from Here

In the preceding sections, you learned how you can use Cold Fusion to update and query information in an ODBC data source. Refer to the Cold Fusion documentation for additional information about how you can use it to publish databases on the Internet. Cold Fusion also ships with many sample applications that demonstrate various capabilities of Cold Fusion and how you can use it to provide dynamic content to users browsing a Web site. Go over these examples by executing the Getting Started icon in the Start Menu folder.

Publishing Databases on the Web with the Internet Database Connector

Using the Internet Database Connector (IDC), you can publish databases on the Web. IDC is a .DLL file (HTTPODBC.DLL) that is included with Internet Information Server (IIS). In this section, you find out how you can publish a database by using the IDC.

To create a Web interface to a database, you have to create two files. The first file is called the *Internet Database Connector* file and ends with an .IDC extension. This file contains information for accessing an ODBC data source and executing an SQL statement. After the SQL statement is executed, the HTML file defined in the IDC file is used to format the results of the SQL statement. The other file is called the *HTML extension* file and ends with an .HTX extension.

Creating a Guest Book with Internet Database Connector

In the following sections, you learn how you can use IIS and IDC to create a guest book and interface it with the Web. Creating a guest book is a three-stage process composed of the following steps:

1. Create a data source.
2. Make the data source a System Data Source Name (DSN) for using ODBC with Microsoft Internet Information Server's IDC.
3. Create the necessary files: an HTML file for data input, an .IDC file, and an .HTX file for processing input and formatting it.

Creating a Data Source

You can create a data source by using any application that has an ODBC driver installed. The guest book in this exercise uses a Microsoft Access database. Before you proceed any further, run Microsoft Access Setup and make sure that the Microsoft Access ODBC driver is installed on your system.

Then open Microsoft Access and create a table similar to the one shown in Figure 18.14. It does not have to be a complicated table. Simply create an Access database that you can use to store guest book entries. The database can have fields for the user's name, e-mail address, and comments. After you create the table, make a note of its name and save it as a Microsoft Access file. Also be sure to make a note of the location of the Access file and names of various data fields.

FIGURE 18.14.

Creating the guest book data source by using Microsoft Access.

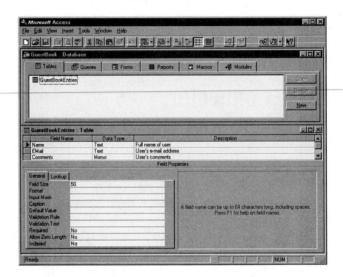

Creating a System DSN for the Access Database

After you save the Access file, invoke the Control Panel and locate the ODBC icon, as shown in Figure 18.15. If the ODBC icon is not visible in the Control Panel, no ODBC drivers are installed on your system. In that case, run either Microsoft Access or Office Setup, and select to install the Microsoft Access ODBC driver.

FIGURE 18.15.

Locate the ODBC icon in the Control Panel.

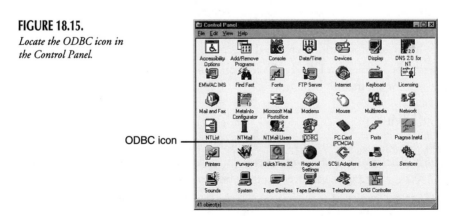

After you locate the ODBC icon, execute it to open the Data Sources dialog box shown in Figure 18.16. In this dialog box, you create System DSNs for databases with ODBC drivers. Click on the System DSN button to create a System DSN for the Microsoft Access database created earlier. Note that IDC works only with System DSNs.

FIGURE 18.16.
The Data Sources
dialog box.

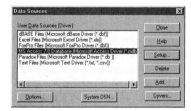

After you select the System DSN button, a dialog box similar to the one shown in Figure 18.17 appears. In the System Data Sources dialog box, click the Add button to create a System DSN for the Microsoft Access database. After a System DSN is created for the Microsoft Access guest book, it will be visible in this dialog box (look ahead to Figure 18.20).

FIGURE 18.17.
The System Data Sources
dialog box.

After you click the Add button, the Add Data Source dialog box appears, as shown in Figure 18.18. Use this dialog box to select the Microsoft Access ODBC driver and then click the OK button. If the Microsoft Access ODBC driver is not visible, reboot your system and reinstall the Microsoft Access ODBC driver.

FIGURE 18.18.
Selecting an ODBC driver
for a new System DSN.

Using the dialog box shown in Figure 18.19, you can create a System DSN by specifying a data source name and a description for it. Then click the Select button to select an ODBC database that will become an alias for the System DSN. Use this dialog box to select the Microsoft Access database created earlier. Then click the OK button to create a System DSN for the Microsoft Access guest book.

FIGURE 18.19.

Creating a System DSN for the Microsoft Access guest book.

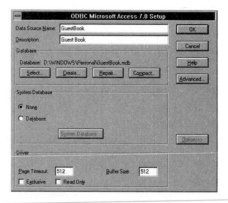

Next, verify that a System DSN has been created for the Microsoft Access guest book application. You can do so by invoking the Data Sources dialog box (refer to Figure 18.16) and clicking the System DSN button. If a System DSN was successfully created for the Microsoft Access guest book, you see it in the window of the dialog box, as shown in Figure 18.20.

This completes the information you need for creating a System DSN for a database. You are not done yet, however; you can follow the preceding steps to create various database applications and interface them with the Web using the IDC.

FIGURE 18.20.

Verifying creation of a System DSN for the Microsoft Access guest book.

Using IDC to Interface a System DSN with the Web

You need to create three files to insert data from a form to a System DSN. Listing 18.4 contains the HTML code used to gather data for the Microsoft Access guest book System DSN. Pay particular attention to line 17, which refers to an .IDC file. IIS maps .IDC files to a .DLL file (HTTPODBC.DLL) that is essentially the Internet Database Connector. Refer to Figure 18.21 for an example of how you can use the HTML code in Listing 18.4 to submit a guest book entry.

Listing 18.4. Guest book using Internet Database Connector.

```
1: <html>
2: <title>Guestbook - Using Internet Database Connector</title>
3: <BODY BGCOLOR="FFFFFF">
4: <TABLE>
```

```
 5: <TR>
 6:
 7: <h2>
 8: Guestbook - Using Internet Database Connector
 9: </h2>
10:
11: <HR>
12: Please enter the following information and press the SUBMIT button<BR>
13: <HR>
14:
15: <P>
16:
17: <form action="/scripts/samples/GuestBookInsert.idc" method=get>
18:
19: <B>Please enter your name </B>
20: <input type="text" name="Name" value="" size=35 maxlength=40>
21: <P>
22:
23: <B>Please enter your e-mail address</B>
24: <input type="text" name="EMail" value="" size=45 maxlength=50>
25: <P>
26:
27: <B>Please enter your comments below</B>
28: <textarea name="Comments" cols=70 rows=4 ></textarea>
29: <P>
30:
31: <input type="submit" value="SUBMIT Guest Book Entry">
32: <input type="reset" value="Reset Form">
33:
34: </form>
35: <P>
36:
37: <HR>
38: <a HREF="/scripts/samples/GuestBookView.idc?">View Guest Book</a>
39: <HR>
40:
41: </body>
42: </html>
```

Recall that line 17 of Listing 18.4 contains the statement `action="/scripts/samples/GuestBookInsert.idc"`. The contents of the file GuestBookInsert.idc are shown in Listing 18.5. Note how line 1 of this code listing refers to the guest book System DSN you created in the dialog box shown in Figure 18.19. It also declares `Name` and `Email` to be required parameters in line 4. These parameters prevent a user from submitting a guest book entry that does not contain a name or an e-mail address. Lines 6–8 contain the SQL statement that inserts data submitted by the form shown in Figure 18.21 to the Microsoft Access guest book System DSN. Line 6 specifies the table of the guest book database to which the data should be inserted. Finally, lines 7 and 8 insert the three form fields to their corresponding table fields.

FIGURE 18.21.

The form used to gather data for a Microsoft Access guest book.

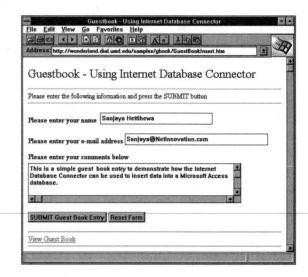

Listing 18.5. Inserting data to an ODBC data source.

```
1: Datasource: GuestBook
2: Username: sa
3: Template: GuestBookInsert.htx
4: RequiredParameters: Name, EMail
5: SQLStatement:
6: +  INSERT INTO GuestBookEntries
7: +  (Name, Email, Comments)
8: +  VALUES('%Name%', '%Email%', '%Comments%');
```

Refer to line 3 of Listing 18.5; it defines the file GuestBookInsert.htx as a template. This file is used to format the message returned to the user after the form is submitted. The message in Figure 18.22 was created with Listing 18.6. Note how the message is personalized to include the user's name in line 10. The expression `<%idc.[Field Name]%>` can be used to echo information filled in by the user. `[Field Name]` refers to the name of a form input control.

Listing 18.6 Internet Database Connector HTML Extensions file (GuestBookInsert.htx).

```
1: <html>
2: <title>Thanks for the guest book entry!</title>
3: <BODY BGCOLOR="FFFFFF">
4:
5: <h1>Guest Book entry added to Microsoft Access database.</h1>
6:
7: <HR>
8:
9: <h2>
10: Hello <%idc.Name%>,
11: </h2>
12:
```

```
13: Thanks very much for visiting this Web site and signing the guest
14: book. We hope you visit this Web site again, soon.
15:
16: </body>
17: </html>
```

FIGURE 18.22.

The message displayed after successful insertion of a guest book entry into the Microsoft Access database.

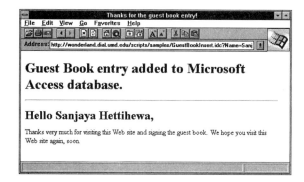

You can use the URL `http://your.server.com/scripts/samples/GuestBookView.idc?` to obtain the contents of the Microsoft Access guest book database, assuming that the two files GuestBookView.idc and GuestBookView.htx are stored in the /scripts/samples/ directory. The contents of the GuestBookView.idc file are shown in Listing 18.7. The contents of this file are similar to that of GuestBookInsert.idc. The only difference is the fact that Listing 18.7 selects data from the GuestBook System DSN instead of inserting it.

Listing 18.7. Selecting data from an ODBC data source.

```
1: Datasource: GuestBook
2: Username: sa
3: Expires: 2
4: Template: GuestBookView.htx
5: SQLStatement:
6: +SELECT Name, EMail, Comments
7: +FROM GuestBookEntries
```

The contents of the file `GuestBookView.htx` are shown in Listing 18.8. (Also see Figure 18.23.) This file formats results of the SQL statements in lines 5–7 of Listing 18.7. Pay particular attention to lines 9–15. The two keywords `<%begindetail%>` and `<%enddetail%>` surround HTML code that formats data from an SQL statement consisting of multiple records in response to an SQL query. The HTML code defined between the two tags `<%begindetail%>` and `<%enddetail%>` format and merge each record returned by the SQL query.

Listing 18.8. The contents of `GuestBookView.htx`.

```
 1: <html>
 2: <title>Contents of Guest Book</title>
 3: <BODY BGCOLOR="FFFFFF">
 4:
 5: <h1>Contents of Guest Book</h1>
 6:
 7: <HR><P>
 8:
 9: <%begindetail%>
10: <B>Name: </B><%Name%><BR>
11: <B>EMail: </B><%EMail%><BR>
12: <B>Comments: </B><%Comments%><BR>
13: <p>
14: <HR><P>
15: <%enddetail%>
16:
17: <hr>
18: <a href="/samples/gbook/GuestBookInsert.htm">Sign the Guest Book</a>
19: <hr>
20:
21: </body>
22: </html>
```

FIGURE 18.23.

Contents of guest book.

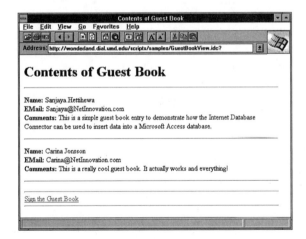

Figure 18.24 displays contents of the Microsoft Access guest book database after two records are inserted to it using the HTML form shown in Figure 18.21. Note how the two records shown in Figure 18.23 are stored in the Microsoft Access database.

FIGURE 18.24.

Contents of the Microsoft Access guest book database.

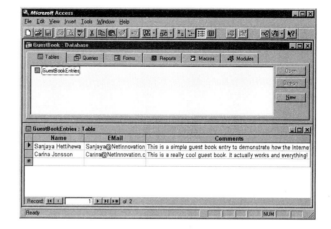

Summary

Using Cold Fusion and IDC, you can effortlessly publish databases on the Internet. IDC is included free of charge with IIS and can be used to create Web interfaces to ODBC data sources. Cold Fusion works with several Windows NT Web servers, including IIS, and offers many powerful features that you can use to create sophisticated Web or database applications.

In this chapter, you learned how you can use Cold Fusion to insert data to an ODBC database. You also learned how you can view data inserted into an ODBC database by using Cold Fusion. In the final sections, you found out how you can use the Internet Database Connector to set up a guest book.

What's Next?

Java is a powerful programming language that you can use to create applications for the WWW. Java is an ideal programming language for the Internet because you can use it to create applications that are platform neutral and secure. Using Java applets, you can make Web pages interactive and more interesting to browse. In the next chapter, you learn how you can develop and add Java applets to a Web site.

VI

Incorporating Technologies into Your Web Site

19

Adding Java to Your Web Site

Java is a platform-neutral programming language developed for the Internet by Sun Microsystems. Unlike other programming languages, applications created with Java work on any computer platform as long as an applet viewer is available for that platform.

Except for a few differences, Java is a programming language that is similar to C++. Therefore, comprehensively covering programming with Java is beyond the scope of this book. This chapter will demonstrate how you can add Java applets to your Web site and introduce you to Java programming by demonstrating how to write a simple Java applet. The first few sections will discuss various capabilities and applications of Java. Afterwards, you will be shown how Java applets can be downloaded and added to your Web site. The next few sections briefly cover Java programming fundamentals and demonstrate how to create a simple Java applet. You also will be shown how to download and install the Java developer's kit so you can start experimenting with creating Java applets. The final section of this chapter lists various Java resources on the Internet. Visit Web sites listed in this section to obtain more information about Java and find interesting Java applets that can be added to your Web site.

Benefits of Java

There are numerous benefits in using Java to make a Web site more interesting to navigate. Unlike some other technologies that need a special plug-in or helper application, Java applications are executed on the browser. This is convenient for users, because all they have to do is use a Java-compatible Web browser.

Java is a secure programming language. This is an important aspect of Java. A Java applet in a Web page is essentially an application that can be downloaded from anywhere on the Internet and executed on a user's Web browser. The Java language has been implemented with security in mind to make sure Java applets cannot be used for malicious intent (such as to format a user's hard drive). Computer security is never perfect. Sooner or later someone with a lot of free time is going to discover a way to defeat various security mechanisms that have been put in place to enforce security. However, Java is reasonably safe to be used on the Internet and the Internet community has accepted it as a reasonably secure programming language. Browse the Java security FAQ to obtain more information about Java security.

URL

The Java security FAQ:

`http://java.sun.com/sfaq/`

Drawbacks of Java

At the moment, most Java applets are nothing more than eye candy for Web pages. However, this is likely to change in the near future as Java developers realize various capabilities of Java and begin creating useful applications that solve real-world tasks. FutureTense Texture, covered in Chapter 14, is an excellent example of such an application. Although Java is a powerful language, Java applications are somewhat plagued with bandwidth limitations. This is holding back some of its potential, because it's often hard to write sophisticated applications that can be transmitted through a slow modem link in a few seconds. As high bandwidth connection lines find their way to more users, Java developers will be able to create more sophisticated applications that perform various useful real-world tasks.

How Does Java Work?

Java is similar to traditional object-oriented programming languages except for one difference. Usually when a program is compiled, an executable binary file is created. This file can be executed on the computer the binary file was created. On the other hand, when Java source code is compiled, a Java *bytecode* file is created. Bytecode is an intermediary state between source code and binary executable code. Although bytecode is slower than binary executable code—because it has to go through another layer of processing before it can be executed—Java bytecode is platform neutral. This is a major advantage for using Java to create applications for the Web, because the Internet is made up of many different kinds of computers. Figure 19.1 illustrates how Java applets are created. As shown in Figure 19.1, Java source code can be converted into platform neutral bytecode using a Java compiler. Due to this reason, Java applets run on a variety of operating systems including Windows NT, Windows 95, Macintosh, and various flavors of UNIX.

FIGURE 19.1.
How Java applets are created.

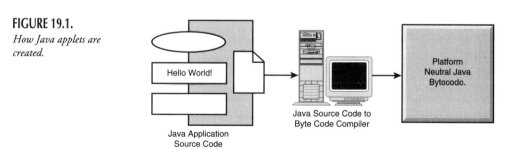

Hello World!

Java Application
Source Code

Java Source Code to
Byte Code Compiler

Platform
Neutral Java
Bytecode.

Java applets in Web pages are downloaded and executed by Web browsers that support Java. This process is shown in Figure 19.2. After a Web browser downloads a Java applet, it is executed using a Java bytecode interpreter.

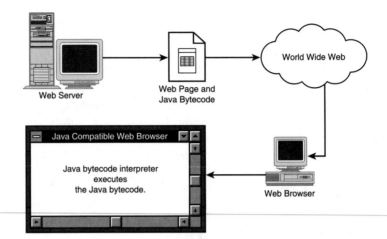

FIGURE 19.2.
How Java applets are executed.

Adding Java Applets to Your Web Site

Adding a Java applet to a Web page is as easy as adding an inline image to a Web page. The only difference is rather than specifying the URL of an image, you will be specifying the URL of a Java applet. Before adding Java to a Web site, it helps to know various parameters that can be used to insert Java applets to a Web page. The following HTML tags can be used to insert a Java applet into a Web page and pass information to it using <param> tags. Note that data fields enclosed in two square brackets should be replaced with values specific to the applet being inserted.

```
<applet
  code=["JavaApplet.class"]
  width=[Width of applet] height=[Height of applet]
  alt=["Description of Java applet"]
  align=["alignment of applet"]
  vspace=[vertical space around applet]
  hspace=[horizontal space around applet]
  codebase=["/Java/AppletDirectory"]>
<param name=[ParameterName] value=[ParameterValue]>
</applet>
```

When adding a Java applet to a Web page code, width, and height are required HTML tags. Refer to Table 19.1 for a list of applet definition parameters.

Table 19.1. Java applet definition parameters.

HTML Tag	Description
code	Filename of Java applet. The Java applet's location will be calculated relative to the codebase element if it is specified in the applet definition.
width	Width of applet window in number of pixels.

HTML Tag	Description
height	Height of applet window in number of pixels.
alt	Text displayed by Web browsers that do not support Java.
align	Alignment of Java applet. This parameter is used the same way the align attribute is used in the <IMG> tag.
vspace	Vertical space around the applet.
hspace	Horizontal space around the applet.
codebase	URL of directory containing the Java applet's code.

Adding an LED Message Display

A Java applet that can be used to display messages in an LED display has been written by Darrick Brown. This applet can be downloaded from the URL listed next. After downloading it, decompress the distribution file using a file decompression utility such as WinZip.

URL

The LED sign Java applet:

```
http://www.cs.hope.edu/~dbrown/java/LEDSign/WWW/LED.html
```

A directory by the name of LEDSign will be created when the distribution file is decompressed. It is recommended that you move this entire directory to the root directory of your Web server. Or, if you would like to keep things more organized, create a directory under your Web server's root directory called Java. You then can use this directory to store Java applets and copy the LEDSign directory structure into the Java directory that you just created. Afterwards, open a Web page where you would like to insert the Java applet, and insert the following code where you would like the Java applet to appear. The following example assumes you copied the LEDSign directory structure into the root directory of your Web server. After the following code is inserted into a Web page and it is viewed with a Java-compatible Web browser, the LED sign applet will be visible in the Web page as shown in Figure 19.3. Note that you do not have to have a Web server installed to view Java applets using a Web browser. If a Java applet and its corresponding HTML file is in the same directory, simply open the HTML file locally and you will be able to see the Java applet.

```
<applet codebase="/LEDSign/LED" code="LED.class"
  width=405 height=40 >
  <param name="script" value="/LEDSign/scripts/Demo.led">
  <param name="border" value="1">
  <param name="bordercolor" value="100,130,130">
  <param name="spacewidth" value="3">
```

```
    <param name="wth" value="100">
    <param name="font" value="/LEDSign/fonts/default.font">
</applet>
```

FIGURE 19.3.
LED sign Java applet.

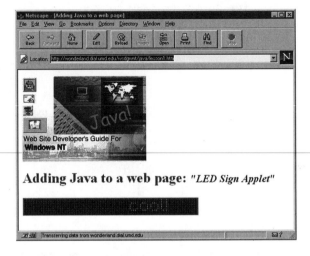

Adding a Digital Java Clock to a Web Page

John Criswick has created a digital Java clock that can be inserted into a Web page to display the current time. It is easy to download and insert this Java applet into a Web page.

URL

The digital clock can be downloaded from the Java LED clock Web site:

```
http://www.conveyor.com/digital-clock.html
```

After visiting the digital clock Web site, you might want to download the raw Java class file and save it into a local directory rather than downloading a compressed version of the Java applet. The applet is so small that its not worth the trouble of downloading a compressed version and decompressing it using another program. After downloading the class file, save it into a local directory. If you are adding the digital clock into a page at your Web site, you might want to create a directory called /Java/Classes and store all your Java class files in that directory. Assuming you downloaded the class file into the /Java/classes directory, the following HTML code can be used to add a digital Java clock to a Web page. Additional configuration information pertaining to the digital clock applet can be obtained from the same Web site from which you downloaded the Java applet. The Web page in Figure 19.4 uses the following HTML code to display the digital Java clock:

```
<applet codebase="/Java/Classes/"
   code="BigTime10b2.class" width=120 height=36>
   <param name=ledcolor value=green>
   <param name=framecolor value=lightgray>
   <param name=backcolor value=black>
   <param name=mode value=12>
</applet>
```

FIGURE 19.4.
Digital clock Java applet.

As shown in the previous two examples, it is easy to add Java applets to a Web page. Visit Yahoo!'s Java information Web page (the URL is given at the end of this chapter) to locate and download useful Java applets. When adding Java applets, be considerate toward users browsing your Web with relatively slow POTS connections to the Internet. As a rule of thumb, avoid using Java applets that take longer than 30 seconds to load over a relatively slow POTS link to the Internet.

Installing the Java Developer's Kit

The Java developer's kit has to be installed from the CD-ROM that came with this book before it can be used to develop Java applications.

To install the Java SDK, copy it to the parent directory of the directory in which you plan to install the Java developer's kit. For example, if you would like to install the Java developer's kit in the directory K:\Internet\Authoring\Java, copy the Java developer's kit distribution file to the K:\Internet\Authoring directory. Afterwards, simply execute the distribution file and it will create a directory called Java and install the developer's kit into this directory.

Afterwards you need to set two Windows NT environment variables. To do this, invoke Control panel and double-click the System icon. This will bring up the system configuration dialog box shown in Figure 19.5. This dialog box can be used to create two required Windows NT environment variables as shown in Figure 19.5.

Update the PATH variable to contain the location of your java\bin directory. For example, if you installed the Java developer's kit into the K:\Internet\Authoring\Java directory, add K:\Internet\Authoring\Java\bin to the PATH variable. Note that semicolons are used to separate directories in the PATH variable.

After updating the PATH variable, a new environment variable called CLASSPATH has to be created. The value of CLASSPATH should point to the java\classes directory. For example, if the Java developer's kit was installed into the K:\Internet\Authoring\Java directory, assign the value K:\Internet\Authoring\Java\classes to the CLASSPATH variable as shown in Figure 19.5. Note that you need to log out and log back in for the environment variable changes to take effect.

FIGURE 19.5.

Windows NT System configuration dialog box can be used to add and modify NT environment variables.

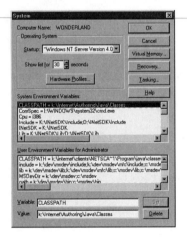

Creating a Simple Java Applet

It is easy to create Java applets using the Java developer's kit. If you are already familiar with C++ or C, Java programs will look somewhat familiar to you. You might want to obtain a copy of *Teach Yourself Java in 21 Days* by Sams.net publishing to learn more about creating Java applications. It is an excellent book and has been written so that even if you do not have a background in C or C++, you can still follow the text and learn how to create Java applications. The following example is meant to get you started with creating Java applets and demonstrate how a Java application can be developed and compiled using the Windows NT Java developer's kit.

Browse the Java resources in the next section to find out more about the Java language and how it can be used to create applications for the Internet. The following Java program can be used to display the string "Hello World." When naming Java applications, use the applet's class name and add a .java extension to it. For example, the following application will be saved as HelloWorld.java.

```
// Java Hello World Application (HelloWorld.java)

import java.awt.Graphics;
import java.awt.Font;
import java.awt.Color;

public class HelloWorld extends java.applet.Applet {

  Font textFont = new Font ("TimesRoman",Font.BOLD,48) ;

  public void paint(Graphics g) {
    g.setColor      (Color.blue) ;
    g.setFont       (textFont) ;
    g.drawString ("Hello world!", 10,60) ;
  }

}
```

The Hello World application can be compiled using the command `javac HelloWorld.java`.
This command invokes the Java compiler, checks the file `HelloWorld.java` for any syntax errors, and creates a bytecode file with the extension `.class`. Upon successful compilation of the
Hello World application, the Java compiler will create a bytecode file named `HelloWorld.class`.
The following HTML code can be used to insert the Hello World Java applet into a Web page.
The Hello World Java applet created in this exercise is shown in Figure 19.6.

```
<applet
  code="/Java/Classes/HelloWorld.class"
  width=300 height=100>
</applet>
```

FIGURE 19.6.

*Java Hello World
application.*

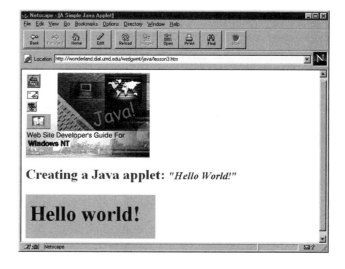

Java Resources on the Internet

Numerous Java resources are available on the Internet. Visit the following Web sites to locate useful Java applications you can add to your Web site. By visiting these Web sites, you also will be able to learn how to write Java applications by examining the source code of applications and tutorials.

Sun Microsystems's Java Overview Web Page

Visit Sun Microsystems's Java overview Web page to obtain official information about Java. This Web page contains many white papers and information that is useful for creating Java applets.

URL

Sun Microsystems's Java overview Web page:

```
http://java.sun.com/doc/overviews.html
```

The Java Tutorial Web Page

The Java Tutorial Web page provides a quick overview of the Java language specification and demonstrates how Java can be used to create applications for the Internet. Visit this URL to learn how to write programs with Java by experimenting with source code samples found at this Web site.

URL

The Java Tutorial Web page:

```
http://java.sun.com/tutorial/
```

EarthWeb's Gamelan

Visit EarthWeb's Gamelan Web site to find out how Java can be used to make a Web site more interesting to navigate. This Web site also contains many Java resources for developing Java applications. Many Java programming resources also can be found at this Web site.

URL

EarthWeb's Gamelan Web site:

`http://www.gamelan.com/`

Yahoo!'s Java Information Web Page

Yahoo!'s Java information Web page is a comprehensive source for locating Java-related Web sites on the Internet. It is highly recommended that you add this site to your Internet bookmark list and visit it periodically to find out new and innovative ways of using Java to make Web pages interactive and more interesting to navigate.

URL

Yahoo!'s Java information Web site:

`http://www.yahoo.com/Computers_and_Internet/Languages/Java/`

Java Mail List Archives

When learning a new language, it is often helpful to learn about problems and solutions encountered by others. Visit the Java mail list archives for issues related to Java encountered by other Java developers. By browsing this archive, you will not only be able to find problems encountered by other Java developers, but also solutions to those problems recommended by others.

URL

The Java mail list archives:

`http://java.sun.com/archives/`

Java Newsgroup

If you have a question about using Java, you should visit the Java newsgroup `comp.lang.java`. Many Java programmers read this newsgroup frequently to discuss issues related to creating Java applets.

Summary

Java is a powerful programming language that can be used to create applications for the Web. Java is an ideal programming language for the Internet because it can be used to create applications that are platform neutral and secure. In fact, FutureTense Texture, covered in Chapter 14, actually relies on a Java applet to format objects in a Web page.

It is easy to add Java applets to a Web page. In fact, it's as easy as adding an inline image to a Web page. Java applets can be used to make Web pages interactive and more interesting to browse.

The Java developer's kit can be used to create Java applets. It can be downloaded free of charge from Sun Microsystems's Web site. The Java developer's kit can be used to compile Java source code files into Java bytecode files. Java bytecode files are platform neutral and can be viewed on any platform supported by Java.

What's Next?

Prior to client-side scripting languages, making a Web page interactive meant using a CGI program along with HTML input controls. Although this is quite effective in some cases, it is a waste of network bandwidth, time, and server processing power. This created the phenomenon known as the *thin client* syndrome. Thin client syndrome refers to Pentium and 486 computers used to browse the Web, essentially doing nothing more than fetching an HTML page from a Web server and displaying it. After the page is displayed, its CPU is idle, doing nothing, in most cases. This is a waste of client-side resources.

JavaScript is a powerful scripting language that can be used to combat the thin client syndrome and create interactive Web pages. Because JavaScript applications do not need to interact with a Web server, they are capable of validating information users enter into various forms before the data is sent to a Web browser for processing. This saves time, resources of the Web server, and also network bandwidth. JavaScript also can be used to make a Web site easier to navigate by providing additional information to users browsing a Web site. For example, when a user moves the mouse pointer over an HTML link, JavaScript can be used to display a message on the status bar of the Web browser and give more information about the link.

20

Creating Interactive Web Pages with JavaScript

JavaScript is a powerful scripting language for the World Wide Web. You can use it to create interactive Web pages and make a Web site easier and more interesting to navigate. Traditionally (over the past few years), Web site developers have relied on CGI to make Web sites interactive. Although it may work well in some cases, it is a waste of resources in other cases. If a user in Sweden makes a mistake when filling out a form at a Web site in the United States, for example, the user will not know about it until the entire form is filled in and submitted to the Web server via transcontinental network lines. After the form is submitted, the server performs a series of error checks, detects the mistake, and returns an error message to the user in Sweden. This process is clearly a waste of resources. It wastes Internet bandwidth and unnecessarily burdens the Web server because the error check could have been performed on the browser. This phenomenon is known as the *thin client syndrome.* Although Web browsers are increasingly becoming more and more sophisticated, resources of most computers used to browse the Web are underutilized. Using JavaScript, you can make use of these resources and create highly interactive Web sites.

The purpose of this chapter is not to provide you with a comprehensive overview of JavaScript. Such an overview is beyond the scope of this book. Refer to *Teach Yourself JavaScript in One Week,* published by Sams.net for additional information about JavaScript. The next few sections, however, do provide an overview of JavaScript and discuss how you can use it to make a Web site interactive and exciting to navigate. Before you get to the overview of JavaScript, the next section demonstrates how easy it is to create a simple application with JavaScript by showing you how to create the classic "Hello World" application.

In later sections, you learn various aspects of the JavaScript language and examine a few examples of simple JavaScript applications. Because you can find these examples on the CD-ROM, I recommend that you spend some time experimenting with them as you read this chapter. Several informative JavaScript resources on the Internet that you can use to obtain the most up-to-date information about JavaScript also are presented at the end of this chapter.

JavaScript "Hello World" Application

The "Hello World" application shown in Figure 20.1 was created with the following HTML code. This HTML code does not have the `<SCRIPT>` tag. Instead, as you can see in line 25, it uses a JavaScript *event* to invoke a JavaScript function and display a message box. The message box created by the `alert` function in line 25 is shown in Figure 20.2.

```
1:  <!--
2:    (c)1996 Sanjaya Hettihewa (http://wonderland.dial.umd.edu)
3:    All Rights Reserved.
4:        Permission is hereby given to modify and distribute this code as you wish
5:    provided that this block of text remains unchanged.
6:  !-->
7:
8:  <HTML>
9:  <HEAD>
```

```
10: <TITLE>JavaScript Tutorial: Hello World!</TITLE>
11: </HEAD>
12:
13: <BODY BGCOLOR="#FFFFFF" TEXT="#0000FF"
14:     LINK="#B864FF" VLINK="#670000" ALINK="#FF0000">
15:
16: <IMG SRC="JavaScript.gif"><P>
17:
18: <B><FONT FACE="Comic Sans MS" SIZE=6 COLOR=RED>
19: JavaScript Tutorial: </FONT></B>
20: <I><FONT FACE="Comic Sans MS" SIZE=5 COLOR=BLUE>
21: "Hello World!" </I><P></FONT>
22:
23: <FORM>
24:
25: <INPUT onClick="alert('Hello World')"
26:   TYPE=BUTTON VALUE="Please click here for message box">
27:
28: </FORM>
29:
30: </BODY>
31:
32: </HTML>
```

FIGURE 20.1.

The JavaScript "Hello World" application.

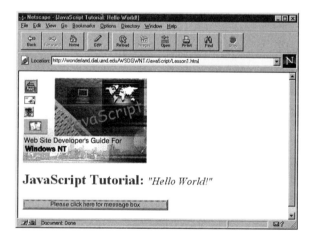

FIGURE 20.2.

The Message box created by the alert function when the command button in Figure 20.1 is clicked.

Benefits of JavaScript

Using JavaScript, you can accomplish a variety of tasks at the client side without interacting with a Web server. The following sections list a few tasks that you can accomplish with JavaScript.

You also can find various JavaScript examples presented in this chapter on the CD-ROM that accompanies this book in the directory Chapter-20. I recommend that you experiment with various JavaScript programs in the CD-ROM as you read about them.

Client-Side Data Validation

JavaScript is ideal for validating user input and making sure that data entered by users is valid. Prior to client-side scripting languages such as JavaScript, when a user filled in a form with information, it had to be sent to the server to be processed via a CGI script to validate user input. This process was time-consuming and a waste of network and Web server resources. A better way of handling this process would be to set up a JavaScript application to check user input before it is submitted to a Web server for processing.

Managing Browser Objects

You can easily manipulate various browser objects with JavaScript. When a user moves the mouse pointer over a hypertext link, for example, you can use JavaScript to display the URL's description on the status bar of the browser. Later in this chapter, you learn how easy it is to use JavaScript to display messages on the status bar of Web browsers.

Conserving Bandwidth

Although some people might argue that JavaScript-enhanced pages take up more bandwidth, this is not really the case if JavaScript is used intelligently to conserve bandwidth. Before invalid data in a form is sent to a Web server for processing, for example, JavaScript can validate the data.

Conserving Resources of the Web Server

JavaScript supports distributed processing by enabling various tasks to be performed on the client rather than on the server. Although you can perform various tasks using CGI programs, a client-side scripting language such as JavaScript is ideal for performing simple operations that do not require access to information on a remote server.

Basics of JavaScript

As shown in the following code listing, JavaScript code is enclosed in the two HTML tags <SCRIPT LANGUAGE="JavaScript"> and </SCRIPT>. Browsers that do not understand certain HTML tags sometimes display text defined between the two unknown tags as they appear. This is not desirable for JavaScript programs because it will most likely confuse users browsing a JavaScript-enhanced Web page with a Web browser that does not support JavaScript. As shown in lines 2 and 4 of the code listing, JavaScript code can be hidden from browsers that do not support it by commenting out JavaScript programs using the two HTML tags used to comment HTML code (<!-- and -->).

```
1: <SCRIPT LANGUAGE="JavaScript">
2: <!-- Hide JavaScript from technologically challenged Web browsers
3: … JavaScript Code …
4: // Hide JavaScript from technologically challenged Web browsers -->
5: </SCRIPT>
```

Defining all JavaScript code in the HEAD section of a Web page is recommended. This way, you can make sure that any JavaScript code that should be evaluated before users are given the chance to manipulate various objects of a Web page. For example, a Web page might have an input control whose default value is set by a JavaScript subroutine. This input control should be updated with an appropriate value before the user is given a chance to manipulate the input control.

JavaScript Data Type Values

JavaScript supports the manipulation of a number of data type values. Various types of data supported by JavaScript are listed next. These data types can be manipulated with operators and expressions covered in the next two sections.

Numbers such as 1234 and 123.456.

Boolean expressions such as true and false.

Literals such as 1234, 123.456, and "Hello".

Strings of characters such as "Windows NT". Note that strings and literals can be concatenated with the + operator.

Floating-point numbers such as 123, 123.456, -123.1E12, and .1e23.

Special character sequences such as \b for backspace, \n for new line character, \r for carriage return, and \t for tab character.

Escape characters such as \" used to represent the quoted character literally.

Useful JavaScript Operators

The operators presented next are supported by JavaScript to manipulate expressions and objects of various data types supported by JavaScript.

String Operators

Strings can be concatenated with the two operators + and +=. For example, "Windows " + "NT" returns the string "Windows NT". The += operator is handy for adding a string expression to a string variable. For example, if the string stringVariable contains the string "Windows ", stringVariable += "NT" results in the string "Windows NT" being assigned to stringVariable.

Comparison and Logical Operators

Expressions of similar data types can be compared with various comparison operators. If you use a string expression, comparison operators compare the two expressions based on the standard lexicographic ordering. After the comparison is performed, a Boolean expression is returned by the comparison operators shown in Table 20.1.

Table 20.1. Comparison operators.

Operator	Description
= =	If both operands are equal, true is returned.
!=	If both operands are not equal, true is returned.
>	If the left operand is greater than the right operand, true is returned.
>=	If the left operand is greater than or equal to the right operand, true is returned.
<	If the right operand is greater than the left operand, true is returned.
<=	If the right operand is greater than or equal to the left operand, true is returned.
&&	If both left and right operands evaluate to true, true is returned.
¦¦	If either the left or right operand evaluates to true, true is returned.

Mathematical Operators

You can use the mathematical operators shown in Table 20.2 to evaluate various numerical expressions.

Table 20.2. Mathematical operators.

Operator	Description
+=	Adds left operand to right operand and assigns the result to the left operand.
-=	Subtracts left operand from the right operand and assigns the result to the left operand.
%=	Calculates the value of the left operand modulo right operand and assigns it to the left operand.
/=	Calculates the value of the left operand divided by the right operand and assigns it to the left operand.
++	Increments the operand.

Operator	Description
- -	Decrements the operand.
!	Negates the operand. (If operand is false, `true` is returned.)

JavaScript Expressions

The simplest JavaScript expression is `<VariableName>` = `<expression>` where the value of the `<expression>` is assigned to the `<VariableName>`. JavaScript also supports *conditional expressions.* You can use conditional expressions to selectively assign a value to a variable based on a certain condition according to the following syntax:

```
<Variable Name> = (<Boolean expression) ? "<value if expression is true>" : "<value
if expression is false>"
```

JavaScript Events

Table 20.3 lists various events supported by JavaScript. *Events* are actions associated with various objects of a Web page. When a user clicks on a button, for example, the `onClick` event is triggered. JavaScript programs can respond to various user interactions by monitoring and responding to the various events listed in this table.

Table 20.3. JavaScript events.

JavaScript Event Name	Event Description
onBlur	An object loses focus.
onClick	An object is clicked on.
onChange	The value of an input object is changed.
onFocus	An object receives focus.
onLoad	A Web page is loaded.
onMouseOver	The mouse pointer is moved over an object.
onSelect	The user selects the form element's input field.
onSubmit	A form is submitted.
onUnload	The user leaves the current Web page.

Sample JavaScript Applications

Creating JavaScript applications is easy after you grasp the basics of JavaScript. Before you create your own JavaScript applications, I recommend that you study the JavaScript language by visiting various JavaScript Internet resources given at the end of this chapter. It is also a good idea to experiment with the following JavaScript examples and study how various JavaScript functions, operators, and expressions are used.

Labeling URLs on the Status Bar

The following code listing demonstrates how you can use JavaScript to label hypertext links of a Web page. When the mouse pointer is moved over a Web page, its description is displayed on the Web browser's status bar. As shown in the following code listing, the JavaScript event onMouseOver is used to determine whether the mouse pointer is over a hypertext link. If it is, the window.status object is used to display a message on the Web browser's status bar. Note how the status bar of the Web browser shown in Figure 20.3 displays the message defined in line 26 of this code listing.

```
 1: <!--
 2:    (c)1996 Sanjaya Hettihewa (http://wonderland.dial.umd.edu)
 3:    All Rights Reserved.
 4:    Permission is hereby given to modify and distribute this code as
 5:    you wish provided that this block of text remains unchanged.
 6: !-->
 7:
 8: <HTML>
 9: <HEAD>
10: <TITLE>JavaScript Tutorial: Labeling URLs</TITLE>
11: </HEAD>
12: <BODY BGCOLOR="#FFFFFF" TEXT="#0000FF"
13:            LINK="#B864FF" VLINK="#670000" ALINK="#FF0000">
14:
15: <TABLE COLSPEC="L20 L20 L20" BORDER=2 WIDTH=100%>
16: <CAPTION ALIGN=top>Labeling URLs with JavaScript</CAPTION>
17: <TR><TD>
18: <IMG SRC="JavaScript.gif">
19: <TD>
20:
21: <TABLE BORDER=2 width=100%>
22: <CAPTION ALIGN=top>URLs</CAPTION>
23: <TR><TD>
24: <A HREF="http://www.microsoft.com/"
25:    onMouseOver="window.status=
26:    'Status bar description = Microsoft Web site';
27:    return true">URL # 01</A>
28: </TD><TD>
29: <A HREF="http://home.nestcape.com/"
30:    onMouseOver="window.status=
31:    'Status bar description = Netscape Web site';
32:    return true"">URL # 02</A>
33: </TD></TR>
34: <TR><TD>
35: <A HREF="http://www.mcp.com/"
36:    onMouseOver="window.status=
37:    'Status bar description = Macmillan Web site';
38:    return true"">URL # 03</A>
39: </TD><TD>
40: <A HREF="http://www.yahoo.com/"
```

```
41:    onMouseOver="window.status=
42:    'Status bar description = Yahoo Web site';
43:    return true"">URL # 04</A>
44: </TD></TR>
45: </TABLE>
46: </TR>
47: </TABLE>
48:
49: <B><FONT FACE="Comic Sans MS" SIZE=6 COLOR=RED>
50: JavaScript Tutorial: </FONT></B>
51: <I><FONT FACE="Comic Sans MS" SIZE=5 COLOR=BLUE>
52: Labeling URLs with JavaScript</I><P></FONT>
53:
54: </BODY>
55: </HTML>
```

FIGURE 20.3.

You can use JavaScript to label hypertext links of a Web page.

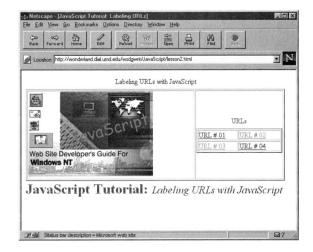

Displaying the Last Modification Date of Web Pages

The last modified date of a Web page is often useful to users browsing a Web site—specifically, if the Web page contains time-sensitive information. Although you can add the time and date manually whenever a Web page is modified, doing so just adds an extra step to the Web page development process. You can automate this process by using a JavaScript program. The date and time of the last Web page modification shown in Figure 20.4 was generated with the following code listing. The line numbers are for reference purposes only, and are not part of the HTML code.

```
1: <!--
2: (c)1996 Sanjaya Hettihewa (http://wonderland.dial.umd.edu)
3: All Rights Reserved.
4: Permission is hereby given to modify and distribute this code
5: as you wish provided that this block of text remains unchanged.
6: !-->
7:
8: <HTML>
```

```
 9: <HEAD>
10: <TITLE>JavaScript Tutorial: Displaying Date of Modification</TITLE>
11: </HEAD>
12:
13: <BODY BGCOLOR="#FFFFFF" TEXT="#0000FF"
14:            LINK="#B864FF" VLINK="#670000" ALINK="#FF0000">
15:
16: <TABLE COLSPEC="L20 L20 L20" BORDER=2>
17: <CAPTION ALIGN=top>Displaying Date of Modification</CAPTION>
18: <TR><TD>
19: <IMG SRC="JavaScript.gif">
20: </TD><TD>
21: This Web page was last modified on: <BR>
22: <SCRIPT LANGUAGE="JavaScript">
23:  lastModifiedDate = document.lastModified
24:  document.write(lastModifiedDate);
25: </SCRIPT>
26: </TD></TR></TABLE>
27:
28: <B><FONT FACE="Comic Sans MS" SIZE=6 COLOR=RED>
29: JavaScript Tutorial: </FONT></B>
30: <I><FONT FACE="Comic Sans MS" SIZE=5 COLOR=BLUE>
31: Dating Web pages</I><P></FONT>
32:
33: </BODY>
34:
35: </HTML>
```

FIGURE 20.4.

You can use JavaScript to automatically display the date and time a Web page was last modified.

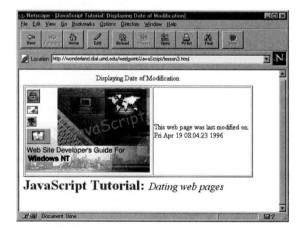

JavaScript Resources on the Internet

Numerous JavaScript resources are available on the Internet. Visit the following URLs to obtain additional information about JavaScript. Because JavaScript is a relatively new and evolving language, you should visit the following Web sites for the most up-to-date information about the language and various innovative applications of it. A number of Web sites listed in the following sections also contain sample JavaScript applications that demonstrate various capabilities of the language.

Netscape's JavaScript Authoring Guide

Netscape's JavaScript authoring guide is a comprehensive source of information about JavaScript. Visit it to obtain extensive information about various JavaScript functions and language concepts.

> **URL**
>
> Netscape's JavaScript authoring guide:
>
> ```
> http://home.netscape.com/eng/mozilla/2.0/handbook/javascript/index.html
> ```

JavaScript Snippet Library

The JavaScript Snippet Library contains many useful JavaScript applications. Applications at this Web site are broken down into various sections. Visit the URL listed next to learn more about JavaScript and how you can use it to create interactive Web pages.

> **URL**
>
> JavaScript Snippet Library:
>
> ```
> http://www.freqgrafx.com/411/library.html
> ```

Java Message Exchange

When you program with JavaScript, knowing various tips and tricks that can potentially save time and frustration is often valuable. A good way to avoid commonly made mistakes is to read about them.

> **URL**
>
> The Java Message Exchange Web site contains an index of questions and answers related to JavaScript:
>
> ```
> http://porthos.phoenixat.com/~warreng/WWWBoard/wwwboard.html
> ```

JavaScript Color Center

The JavaScript Color Center is a good example of how you can use JavaScript to create sophisticated, multiframe applications.

> **URL**
>
> See the JavaScript Color Center Web site to learn more about JavaScript and to find RGB color codes:
>
> `http://www.hidaho.com/c3/`

Summary

JavaScript is a powerful scripting language that you can use to combat the *thin client syndrome* and create interactive Web pages. Because JavaScript applications do not need to interact with a Web server, they are capable of validating information that users enter into various forms before it is sent to a Web browser for processing. This capability saves both resources of the Web server and also network bandwidth.

You also can use JavaScript to make a Web site easier to navigate by providing additional information to users browsing the site. When a user moves the mouse pointer over an HTML link, for example, JavaScript can display a message on the status bar of the Web browser and give more information about the link.

As you learned in various examples in this chapter, you can use JavaScript to make a Web site interactive and more interesting to navigate by making use of resources at the client side that are often underutilized. Using JavaScript and VBScript, which is covered in the following chapter, you can add a new level of interaction to a Web site without using CGI.

What's Next?

VBScript is similar to JavaScript in many ways. It was designed by Microsoft to make it easier for Web site developers to create compelling Web sites and incorporate various ActiveX controls to a Web page. You can use VBScript, which is a subset of Visual Basic, to create "Active" Web pages. In the next chapter, you get a thorough overview of VBScript and learn how you can create VBScript applications and add them to a Web page. To get you started with VBScript, you can use the several sample applications given in the chapter.

21

Unleashing the Power of VBScript

VBScript is Microsoft's scripting language for the Internet. Similar in functionality to JavaScript, VBScript has been designed to leverage the skills of millions of Visual Basic programmers to the Internet. Although JavaScript is a powerful scripting language, it is not as easy to learn and use as VBScript. VBScript can be used to easily create active Web pages. Since VBScript is supported by Microsoft, in the near future you will also see a great deal of VBScript/Windows NT/95/MSOffice Backoffice integration, unlike JavaScript. VBScript code is lightweight, fast, and has been optimized to be transmitted via the Internet. You should spend some time with VBScript and learn how it can be used to enhance a Web site by making it easier and more exciting to navigate. By the time you read this, you can expect to see VBScript supported by several other Web browsers in addition to Internet Explorer—specifically, browsers from Oracle, Spyglass, and NetManage.

Introduction to VBScript

VBScript is a subset of Microsoft Visual Basic and is upwardly compatible with Visual Basic for Applications (VBA). VBA is shipped with MS Office applications to make it easier for developers to build custom solutions using MS Office applications. The ability to provide scripting, automation, and customization capabilities for Web browsers is a major feature of VBScript. If you are already familiar with Visual Basic, very shortly you will be able to leverage your skills to the Internet using VBScript. Even if you are not familiar with another programming language, after reading this chapter you will be able to create active Web pages using VBScript. However, familiarity with a programming language will make it easier for you to grasp various concepts such as recursion, type casting, and Boolean arithmetic. Several VBScript applications are included in the CD-ROM; experiment with them to become more familiar with VBScript. Visit the Microsoft VBScript home page for the most up-to-date information about VBScript.

URL

Visit the Microsoft VBScript information Web site for the latest information about VBScript.

```
http://www.microsoft.com/VBScript
```

How VBScript Works

VBScript programs are defined between two HTML tags. Browsers that support VBScript read the VBScript program contained between the two HTML tags and execute it after checking for any syntax errors. VBScript works as shown in Figure 21.1.

FIGURE 21.1.
How VBScript works.

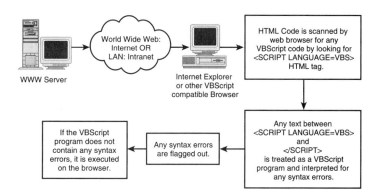

As you can see in Figure 21.1, a VBScript program is part of a regular HTML file and is enclosed between two HTML tags, `<SCRIPT LANGUAGE=VBS>` and `</SCRIPT>`. When a Web browser that supports VBScript encounters the `<SCRIPT LANGUAGE=VBS>` HTML tag, all text between that tag and `</SCRIPT>` is treated as a VBScript program and is interpreted for syntax errors. If any syntax errors are detected, they are flagged by the VBScript interpreter as shown in Figure 21.2.

FIGURE 21.2.
Syntax errors in VBScript programs are flagged by the VBScript interpreter.

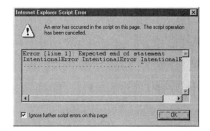

If the code does not contain any syntax errors, it is executed on the Web browser. In order to hide VBScript code from "technologically challenged" Web browsers, VBScript code can be enclosed in two HTML comment tags as shown below.

```
<SCRIPT LANGUAGE=VBS>
<!-- To hide VBScript code from technologically challenged browsers
… VBScript code …
!-->
</SCRIPT>
```

Hello World!

Writing the classic Hello World! application with VBScript is very easy. For the purpose of this example, you will be shown how to create a Web page similar to the one in Figure 21.3. This Web page will have three buttons. The first button will display a message box with a greeting, the second button will display the current time, and the third button will display today's date.

FIGURE 21.3.

The classic Hello World! application written with VBScript.

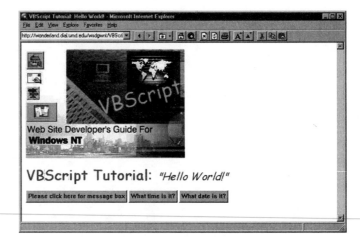

If you would like to experiment with the VBScript application shown in Figure 21.3, it can be found in the CD-ROM that accompanies this book in the directory \Chapter-21\Hello.htm. Various key elements of the Hello World! VBScript program are outlined next.

The Hello World! Dialog Box

As shown in Figure 21.4, the Hello World! dialog box is shown each time a user clicks on the Please click here for message box button in Figure 21.3. If you look at the HTML page the VBScript program is in, you will see that the command button associated with the Hello World! dialog box is named BtnHello (NAME="BtnHello"). As you can see from the following listing, the OnClick event is associated with the BtnHello subroutine. Each time a user clicks on the Please click here for message box button in Figure 21.3, the Web browser invokes the BtnHello_OnClick subroutine and any VBScript code defined in that subroutine is executed.

The BtnHello_OnClick subroutine is a very simple VBScript subroutine. The first three lines create strings displayed by the dialog box in Figure 21.4. Note how the string concatenation operator (&) is used in line 4 to merge two strings into one and assign the result to a variable. The result is then displayed in a message box, as shown in Figure 21.4.

> **NOTE**
>
> Line numbers in various code segments are not part of the VBScript code. The line numbers are only there for reference purposes.

```
1: Sub BtnHello_OnClick
2:   titleString = "Web Site Developer's Guide for Windows NT"
3:   helloString = "Hello world! Welcome to the fun filled "
```

```
4:  helloString = helloString & "world of VBScript programming!"
5:  MsgBox helloString, 0, titleString
6: End Sub
```

FIGURE 21.4.

The Hello World! dialog box.

Time Dialog Box

The `BtnTime_OnClick` subroutine is very similar to the `BtnHello_OnClick` subroutine. The only difference is the fact that rather than concatenating two strings, it concatenates a string with the result of a function. The time function returns the current time. As shown in Figure 21.5, line 3 of the following program listing displays the current time in a dialog box.

```
1: Sub BtnTime_OnClick
2:  timeString = "So, you want to know the time? The time is " & time
3:  MsgBox  timeString , 0, "Time Dialog Box"
4: End Sub
```

FIGURE 21.5.

Time dialog box.

Date Dialog Box

The date dialog box displays the current date in a dialog box, as shown in Figure 21.6. As you can see in line 2 of the following code listing, the result of one function (`date`) can be used as an argument of another function (`DateValue`).

```
1: Sub BtnDate_OnClick
2:  dateString = "Today's date is " & DateValue(date)
3:  MsgBox  dateString , 0, "Date Dialog Box"
4: End Sub
```

FIGURE 21.6.

Date dialog box.

For your reference, the full source code of the Hello World! application is listed next.

Listing 21.1. The Hello World! Web page.

```
<!--
(C) 1996 Sanjaya Hettihewa (http://wonderland.dial.umd.edu)
All Rights Reserved.
```

continues

Listing 21.1. continued

```
!-->

<HTML>
<HEAD>
<TITLE>VBScript Tutorial: Hello World!</TITLE>
</HEAD>

<BODY BGCOLOR="#FFFFFF" TEXT="#0000FF"
      LINK="#B864FF" VLINK="#670000" ALINK="#FF0000">

<IMG SRC="vbscript.jpg"><P>

<B><FONT FACE="Comic Sans MS" SIZE=6 COLOR=RED>
VBScript Tutorial: <FONT></B>
<I><FONT FACE="Comic Sans MS" SIZE=5 COLOR=BLUE>
 "Hello World!" </I><P><FONT>

<form>
<INPUT TYPE=BUTTON VALUE="Please click here for message box"
      NAME="BtnHello">
<INPUT TYPE=BUTTON VALUE="What time is it?"
      NAME="BtnTime">
<INPUT TYPE=BUTTON VALUE="What date is it?"
      NAME="BtnDate">
</form>
<SCRIPT LANGUAGE=VBS>
<!-- To hide VBScript code from technologically challenged browsers

Sub BtnHello_OnClick
 titleString = "Web Site Developer's Guide for Windows NT"
 helloString = "Hello world! Welcome to the fun filled "
 helloString = helloString & "world of VBScript programming!"
 MsgBox helloString, 0, titleString
End Sub

Sub BtnTime_OnClick
 timeString = "So, you want to know the time? The time is " & time
 MsgBox  timeString , 0, "Time Dialog Box"
End Sub

Sub BtnDate_OnClick
 dateString = "Today's date is " & DateValue(date)
 MsgBox  dateString , 0, "Date Dialog Box"
End Sub
!-->
</SCRIPT>

</BODY>

</HTML>
```

VBScript Operators

VBScript supports several operators for various string, Boolean, and number-manipulation tasks. Various operators supported by VBScript are listed next.

Addition Operator

Syntax: `<operand1> + <operand2>`

The addition operator can be used to add two operands together. If both operands are numeric, the result of the addition operator will also be numeric. However, if they are strings, VBScript will instead do a string concatenation instead of a numeric addition. To avoid ambiguity, it is recommended that you use the string concatenation operator (&) when joining strings, and use the addition operator (+) when adding numeric expressions.

Subtraction Operator

Syntax: `<operand1> - <operand2>`
Syntax: `-<OperandToNegate>`

The subtraction operator is used as a unary minus and the binary subtraction operator. When used as the binary subtraction operator, it subtracts `<operand2>` from `<operand1>` and returns the resulting value. When used as the unary minus, it negates the numeric operand it is used with.

Multiplication Operator

Syntax: `<operand1> ^ <operand2>`

The multiplication operator takes two numeric operands, multiplies them, and returns the resulting value.

Exponential Operator

Syntax: `<operand1> ^ <operand2>`

Returns the resulting value of `<operand1>` raised to the `<operand2>` power.

Floating-Point Division Operator

Syntax: `<operand1> / <operand2>`

The division operator is used to divide `<operand1>` from `<operand2>`. Both `<operand1>` and `<operand2>` have to be numeric expressions, and the resulting value is a floating-point number.

Integer-Division Operator

Syntax: `<operand1> \ <operand2>`

The integer-division operator is somewhat similar to the floating-point division operator. The integer-division operator returns an integer number after dividing `<operand1>` from `<operand2>`. If you wish to experiment with this operator, refer to `\Chapter-21\Int.htm` in the CD-ROM. A few examples of the integer division operator are listed next.

```
( 23 \ 4 ) = 5
( 4 \ 23 ) = 0
( 4 \ 2 ) = 2
( 5 \ 2 ) = 2
```

String-Concatenation Operator

Syntax: `<operand1> & <operand2>`

The string-concatenation operator can be used to join `<operand1>` and `<operand2>` together.

MOD Operator

Syntax: `<operand1> MOD <operand2>`

The MOD operator is somewhat similar to the integer-division operator. The only difference is the fact that it returns the remainder of `<operand1>` divided by `<operand2>`. If you wish to experiment with this operator, refer to `\Chapter-21\Mod.htm` in the CD-ROM. A few examples of the MOD operator are listed next.

```
( 23 MOD 4 ) = 3
( 4 MOD 23 ) = 4
( 4 MOD 2 ) = 0
( 5 MOD 2 ) = 1
```

Boolean Operators

VBScript supports a number of Boolean operators. The best way to explain how Boolean operators work is with a truth table. Refer to Figure 21.7 for truth tables of a number of useful VBScript Boolean operators. Various useful VBScript Boolean operators are listed next, along with how they can be used in VBScript programs.

AND Operator

Syntax: `<operand1> AND <operand2>`

The AND operator returns TRUE if both `<operand1>` and `<operand2>` are true. If not, it returns FALSE. The AND operator can be used with expressions and functions that return a Boolean value.

FIGURE 21.7.
Truth tables of VBScript Boolean operators.

AND				
TRUE	AND	TRUE	=	TRUE
TRUE	AND	FALSE	=	FALSE
FALSE	AND	TRUE	=	FALSE
FALSE	AND	FALSE	=	FALSE

OR				
TRUE	OR	TRUE	=	TRUE
TRUE	OR	FALSE	=	TRUE
FALSE	OR	TRUE	=	TRUE
FALSE	OR	FALSE	=	FALSE

XOR				
TRUE	XOR	TRUE	=	FALSE
TRUE	XOR	FALSE	=	TRUE
FALSE	XOR	TRUE	=	TRUE
FALSE	XOR	FALSE	=	FALSE

NOT				
	NOT	TRUE	=	FALSE
	NOT	FALSE	=	TRUE

OR **Operator**

Syntax: `<operand1> OR <operand2>`

The OR operator returns TRUE if either <operand1> or <operand2> is true. The OR operator can be used with expressions and functions that return a Boolean value.

NOT **Operator**

Syntax: `NOT <operand>`

The NOT operator can be used to negate a Boolean value. The NOT operator can be used with expressions and functions that return a Boolean value.

XOR **Operator**

Syntax: `<operand1> XOR <operand2>`

The XOR operator is very similar to the OR operator. The only difference is the fact that in order for the XOR operator to return TRUE, <operand1> or <operand2> has to be true. However, they both can't be true at the same time. The NOT operator can be used with expressions and functions that return a Boolean value.

Equivalence Operator

Syntax: `<operand1> Eqv <operand2>`

The equivalence operator can be used to determine if `<operand1>` is equal to `<operand2>`. If either `<operand1>` or `<operand2>` is NULL, then the resulting value will also be NULL. The truth table of the equivalence operator is listed next.

```
TRUE Eqv TRUE = TRUE
FALSE Eqv TRUE = FALSE
TRUE Eqv FALSE = FALSE
FALSE Eqv FALSE = TRUE
```

*(*TRUE *may be replaced with binary 1 and* FALSE *may be replaced with binary 0.)*

Object-Reference Operator

Syntax: `<operand1> IS <operand2>`

The object-reference operator is used to compare two object reference variables. If `<operand1>` refers to the same object as `<operand2>`, the object-reference operator returns TRUE. Otherwise, it returns FALSE.

Comparison Operators

VBScript supports several comparison operators. These comparison operators can be used to compare strings as well as numbers. Various comparison operators that can be used in VBScript programs are listed next.

Equal Operator

Syntax: `<operand1> = <operand2>`

Returns TRUE if both `<operand1>` and `<operand2>` are equal to each other. However, if either `<operand1>` or `<operand2>` is NULL, the equal operator will return NULL.

Unequal Operator

Syntax: `<operand1> <> <operand2>`

Returns TRUE if both `<operand1>` and `<operand2>` are unequal to each other. However, if either `<operand1>` or `<operand2>` is NULL, the unequal operator will return NULL.

Less Than Operator

Syntax: `<operand1> < <operand2>`

Returns TRUE if `<operand1>` is less than `<operand2>`. However, if either `<operand1>` or `<operand2>` is NULL, the less than operator will return NULL.

Less Than or Equal to Operator

Syntax: <operand1> <= <operand2>

Returns TRUE if <operand1> is less than or equal to <operand2>. However, if either <operand1> or <operand2> is NULL, the less than or equal to operator will return NULL.

Greater Than Operator

Syntax: <operand1> > <operand2>

Returns TRUE if <operand1> is greater than <operand2>. However, if either <operand1> or <operand2> is NULL, the greater than operator will return NULL.

Greater Than or Equal to Operator

Syntax: <operand1> >= <operand2>

Returns TRUE if <operand1> is greater than or equal to <operand2>. However, if either <operand1> or <operand2> is NULL, the greater than or equal to operator will return NULL.

VBScript Control Structures

Control structures are an important part of any language. They give a language "life" by allowing programmers to add intelligence to programs with conditional and iterative statements. Various VBScript control structures are listed next, along with how they can be used in VBScript programs.

Call

Call is used to transfer program control to another VBScript subroutine. Note that when Call is used to transfer control to another subroutine, if that subroutine has any parameters, they should be enclosed in parentheses. However, if Call is omitted, subroutine arguments do not need to be enclosed in parentheses. Return values of functions are ignored when they are invoked with the Call statement.

Dim

The Dim statement is used to declare variables, such as arrays, and assign them storage space. When variables are declared with Dim, if they are numeric variables, they are initialized with the value zero. Otherwise, they are assigned an empty string. The Dim statement can be used to declare several types of variables. Various types of variables that can be created with the Dim statement are listed next.

Declaring Variant Variables

`Syntax: Dim <VariableName1> , <VariableName2>`

This statement can be used to declare variables of variant type. As shown here, several variables can be defined at the same time by separating them with commas.

Multiple Variables Declarations

`Syntax: Dim <VariableName1> As Integer, <VariableName2>`

One `Dim` statement can be used to declare several variables of more than one type. As in the case of the previous `Dim` command, `<VariableName1>` is declared as an integer variable and `<VariableName2>` is declared as a variant variable.

Declaring Static Arrays

`Single Dimension Array Syntax: Dim <NameOfArray>(50)`

The `Dim` statement can be used to define arrays. In this example, an array of 50 storage locations of type variant is created using the `Dim` statement. If an index range is not specified for an array, VBScript will index the array starting at zero. For example, in this case, `<NameOfArray>` is indexed from 0 to 49.

`Multi Dimension Array Syntax: Dim <NameOfArray>(5,1 To 5)`

The `Dim` statement can also be used to declare multidimensional arrays. For example, the preceding statement can be used to declare a two-dimensional array by the name of `<NameOfArray>`. As shown in this example, the index range of an array can be customized by using a number range (`1 To 5`). By adding an `As <VariableType>` command to an array declaration, it is possible to define an array of a certain data type.

Declaring Dynamic Arrays

If you are unsure about the size of an array when it is first declared, VBScript allows the creation of dynamic arrays. Dynamic arrays can be expanded or reduced as needed. Dynamic arrays can be created using the following syntax.

`Dim <NameOfArray>()`

Storage space for additional elements can be allocated for a dynamic array using the `ReDim` statement, as shown next. (Simply indicate, in parentheses, the number of elements the array should have.)

`ReDim <NameOfArray>(10)`

As an added incentive, VBScript dynamic arrays can be expanded while preserving existing array values. As shown in the next example, this is done by adding a `Preserve` statement in between the `ReDim` statement and the array name.

```
ReDim Preserve <NameOfArray>(20)
```

Note that if a data type was defined for a dynamic array using the As statement, the array's data type cannot be changed using the ReDim statement. Also, if a dynamic array is reduced in size, using the ReDim statement, any data stored in the portion of the array that was deleted is permanently lost.

Do/While/Until/Loop

The Do/Loop control structure can be used to iterate a group of statements until a certain Boolean expression becomes TRUE. The syntax of the Do/Loop control structure is listed next. As shown in the following example, the Boolean expression of a Do/Loop structure can be placed either at the beginning or the end.

```
Do <condition> <BooleanExpression>
… VBScript statements …
Loop
```

As shown next, the Boolean expression of a Do/Loop structure can also be placed at the end of the control structure.

```
Do
… VBScript statements …
Loop <condition> <BooleanExpression>
```

The preceding two examples will repeatedly execute VBScript statements enclosed in the loop structure until <BooleanExpression> becomes TRUE. In the examples, <condition> may be replaced with either While or Until. As the name implies, if While is used, the loop will iterate while <BooleanExpression> is TRUE. In the like manner, if Until is used, the loop will iterate until <BooleanExpression> is TRUE. Note that within a Do/Loop structure, it is possible to transfer control out of the loop using an Exit Do statement.

Erase

Syntax: Erase <NameOfArray>

The Erase statement is used to free memory used by dynamic arrays and reinitialize elements of static arrays. If the array is a dynamic array, all space taken up by the array is freed. Dynamic arrays then need to be reallocated using the ReDim statement before they can be used again. If the array is a static array, all array elements are initialized with zero if its elements are numeric or empty strings otherwise.

Exit

The Exit statement causes program control to be transferred out of the control structure it is used in. The control structure can be a loop or a subroutine. Various forms of the Exit command are listed next.

```
Exit Do—Exits a Do loop.
Exit For—Exits a For loop.
Exit Function—Exits a function.
Exit Sub—Exits a procedure.
```

For/Next

The For/Next control structure can be used to iterate a group of VBScript statements a certain number of times. The syntax of the For/Next control structure is listed next.

```
For <LoopCount> = <BeginLoop> To <EndLoop> Step <StepCount>
… VBScript statements …
Next
```

The previous definition can be used to iterate a group of VBScript statements a certain number of times by replacing various labels (enclosed in pointed braces) of the definition, as follows:

<LoopCount>—Name of variable used to keep track of the number of iterations. It's best that your VBScript statements do not alter the value of this variable, because it can easily complicate your code and make it harder to debug.

<BeginLoop>—The first value of the iteration sequence.

<EndLoop>—The last value of the iteration sequence.

Step <StepCount>—<StepCount> can be replaced with the <LoopCount>, which will be incremented after each iteration of the loop. The Step statement is optional; by default, <LoopCount> will be incremented by one.

Note that the Exit For statement can be used to exit a For loop.

For Each/Next

The For Each/Next control structure is useful for iterating VBScript statements for each object in a *collection* or each element in an array. The syntax of the For Each/Next loop is listed next.

```
For Each <LoopIndex> In <ArrayOrCollection>
… VBScript statements …
Next <LoopIndex>
```

A For Each/Next loop can be added to a VBScript program by substituting various labels of the preceding example, as follows.

<LoopIndex>—Name of variable that's used to traverse through the elements of an array or objects in a *collection*.

<ArrayOrCollection>—Name of an array or collection of objects.

Note that the Exit For statement can be used to exit a For Each loop. Also note that <LoopIndex> can be omitted in the Next <LoopIndex> statement. However, this is not recommended; it can complicate things and cause errors if a For Each loop is nested inside another For Each loop.

Function

New functions can be defined using the Function statement. The syntax of the Function statement is as follows:

```
<FunctionType> Function <NameOfFunction> <ArgumentsOfFunction>
… VBScript statements …
<NameOfFunction> = <ReturnValueOfFunction>
End Function
```

A function can be created by replacing various labels of the above definition with the values listed next.

> <FunctionType>—The <FunctionType> can be left out if it is not needed. By replacing <FunctionType> with Static, it is possible to preserve values of local variables in between function calls. Unless you have a reason for doing so, Static functions are usually not suitable for recursion (a function calling itself).
>
> <NameOfFunction>—Used to specify the name of the function.
>
> <ArgumentsOfFunction>—Arguments of a function can be specified soon after <NameOfFunction>. By using commas, more than one argument can be specified. An argument can be passed either by value or reference. In order to make an argument *pass by value*, precede the argument name with ByVal; to *pass by reference*, precede the argument name with ByRef. When an argument is passed by value, its original value cannot be changed from within the function. However, when it is passed by reference, the variable used in the function is merely a pointer to the original variable. Therefore, any changes made to the value of a variable passed by reference are actually made to the original variable.

Note that the Exit Function statement can be used to exit a function. VBScript procedures created with the Function statement are very similar to procedures created with the SUB statement. The only difference is that procedures created with the Function statement can return values, whereas procedures created with the Sub statement cannot.

If/Then/Else

The If/Then/Else statement can be used to execute various VBScript statements based on Boolean expressions. The syntax of the If/Then/Else control structure is as follows:

```
IF <BooleanExpression> THEN
… VBScript statement …
ELSE IF <BooleanExpression> THEN
```

```
… VBScript statement …
ELSE
… VBScript statement …
END IF
```

As shown in the previous example, various VBScript statements can be made to execute using an If/Then/Else statement based on various Boolean expressions.

Let

The Let command can be used to assign values to variables. The Let command is not required to assign a value to a variable. The syntax of the Let command is as follows:

```
Let <variableName> = <ValueOfVariable>
```

LSet

LSet is used to copy a variable of one user-defined type to a variable of another user-defined type. When a variable is copied with the LSet command, it is *left-aligned.* The syntax of the LSet statement is listed next.

```
LSet <Variable> = <ValueOfVariable>
```

If the length of <Variable> is longer than that of <ValueOfVariable>, after copying <ValueOfVariable> to <Variable> the remaining space will be filled in with white spaces. In the like manner, if the length of <Variable> is less than that of <ValueOfVariable>, <ValueOfVariable> will be truncated to fit in the space allocated for <Variable>. For example, if <Variable> can hold only four characters, and <ValueOfVariable> contains the string "ABCDEFG", after it is copied to <Variable> with the LSet command, <Variable> will have the value "ABCD."

Mid

Mid is a very handy statement for replacing one or more characters of a string with characters from another string. The syntax of the Mid statement is listed next.

```
Mid (<Variable>, <Begin>, <NumCharactersToReplace>) = <Replacement>
```

The Mid statement can be used by replacing various labels of the preceding example, as follows:

<Variable>—Name of variable containing the string that will be modified.

<Begin>—The position to begin replacing text. For example, if <Variable> contained the string "1234" and you would like "34" to be replaced with "67", <Begin> will be replaced with "3" because the sub string "34" begins at the third position.

<NumCharactersToReplace>—Lists the number of characters that should be replaced by <Replacement>. This value can be left out if you wish, in which case the entire <Replacement> string will be copied over.

<Replacement>—Contains string that will be copied over to <Variable>.

On Error

Usually, when a runtime error occurs in a VBScript program, it halts execution of the VBScript program. Using the `On Error Resume Next` statement, however, it is possible to ignore the error and continue with the program.

Private

By preceding a variable declaration with the `Private` keyword, it is possible to limit its scope to the script it was declared in.

Public

By preceding a variable declaration with the `Public` keyword, the scope of a variable can be extended to other scripts.

Randomize

Can be used to initialize the random-number generator. `Randomize` can be used either with or without a numeric argument. If it is used with a numeric argument, the numeric argument is used to *seed* the random-number generator. If `Randomize` is used without an argument, a number from the system clock is used to *seed* the random-number generator.

Rem

The `Rem` command is used to document VBScript code. The syntax of the `Rem` command is listed next.

```
Rem This is a comment
```

Note that the apostrophe (') is equivalent in functionality to the `Rem` command. The only difference between the `Rem` statement and the apostrophe is the fact that if `Rem` is used in the same line with a VBScript statement, it needs to be separated from the VBScript statement with a colon.

RSet

The syntax of the `RSet` command is listed next.

```
RSet <Variable> = <StringToCopy>
```

The `RSet` command is similar in functionality to the `LSet` command. The only difference is the fact that when a variable is assigned a string using the `RSet` command, it is assigned to the variable *right-aligned*.

Set

The `Set` command can be used to assign an object reference to a variable or property. The syntax of the `Set` command is as follows.

```
Set <ObjectVariable> = <Object>
```

When the keyword `Nothing` is assigned to `<ObjectVariable>`, system resources consumed by the object are freed when no other variables refer to the `<Object>`.

Static

By preceding variable and procedure declarations with the keyword `Static`, it is possible to retain values of variables. When a procedure is declared as a static procedure, all variables in that procedure retain values assigned to them throughout the life of the program. Precede variable declarations of *nonstatic procedures* with the `Static` keyword to preserve their values. (Variable values of static procedures are automatically preserved.)

Sub

The `Sub` statement can be used to create VBScript procedures and is identical to the `Function` statement except for one difference. Procedures created with the `Function` statement can return values; procedures created with the `Sub` statement cannot. The syntax of the `Sub` statement is listed next. Note that the `Exit Sub` statement can be used to transfer control out of a procedure. The syntax of the `Sub` statement is listed next.

```
<ProcedureType> Sub <NameOfProcedure> <ArgumentsOfProcedure>
… VBScript statements …
End Sub
```

A procedure can be created by replacing various labels of the preceding definition with the values listed next:

> `<ProcedureType>`—The `<ProcedureType>` can be left out if it is not needed. By replacing `<ProcedureType>` with `Static`, it is possible to preserve values of local variables in between procedure calls. Unless you have a reason for doing so, `Static` functions are usually not suitable for recursion (a function calling itself).

> `<NameOfProcedure>`—Used to specify the name of the procedure.

> `<ArgumentsOfProcedure>`—Arguments of a procedure can be specified soon after `<NameOfProcedure>`. By using commas, more than one argument can be specified. An argument can be passed either by value or reference. In order to make an argument *pass by value*, precede the argument name with `ByVal`, and to *pass by reference*, precede the argument name with `ByRef`. When an argument is passed by value, its original value cannot be changed from within the procedure. However, when it is passed by

reference, the variable used in the procedure is merely a pointer to the original variable. Therefore, any changes made to the value of a variable passed by reference is actually made to the original variable.

While/Wend

The While/Wend control structure can be used to iterate a group of VBScript statements while a certain Boolean expression is true. The syntax of the While/Wend command is listed next.

```
While <BooleanExpression>
… VBScript statements …
Wend
```

VBScript Functions

Various functions supported by VBScript are listed next. The following functions can be used to add a new level of interactivity to a Web site by creating active Web pages. Shortly, you will be shown how these functions can be used to develop various VBScript programs.

Abs

The Abs function can be used to obtain the absolute value of a number. For example, Abs(-30) = 30 = Abs(30).

Array

The Array function can be used to quickly create an array because it returns a variant containing an array. An example of how the Array function can be used is given next. The following two commands create an array with three elements. After the two commands are executed, Colors(2) will equal "Blue."

```
Dim Colors As Variant
Colors = Array ( "Red", "Blue", "Green" )
```

Asc

Returns the ASCII character code of a character or the first character of a string. For example, Asc ("A") returns 65 and so does Asc ("America").

Atn

Returns the arctangent of a number.

CBool

Returns the Boolean value of an expression passed into the function. For example, CBool (A = B) will return TRUE if both A and B contain the same value.

CByte

Converts a number passed into the function into a number of type byte and returns it. For example, if CByte is called with the number 123.678, it will return 123.

CDate

If a valid date expression is passed into the function, it is converted into date type and returned. Before passing an expression to the CDate function, it is possible to determine if it can be converted by CDate into date type by using the IsDate function.

CDbl

Converts an expression passed into the function into a variant of subtype double.

Chr

Returns the ASCII character of an ASCII code. For example, Chr(65) returns the character A.

CInt

Converts an expression into a variant of subtype Integer. For example, CInt (1234.567) returns 1235.

CLng

Returns a variant of subtype long after the expression passed into the function is converted into long. For example, CLng (12345.67) returns 12346.

Cos

Returns the cosine of an angle passed into the function.

CSng

Converts a numerical expression passed into the function into a variant of subtype single. For example, CSng (12.123456) returns 12.12346.

CStr

Converts an expression passed into CStr into a string and returns it. For example, CStr(123.456) returns the value "123.456".

CVErr

Used to return a user-specified error code. The syntax of CVErr is CVErr(ErrorNumber).

Date

Returns the date from the system clock. The value returned by the Date command at the time of this writing is 4/1/1996.

DateSerial

DateSerial is a handy function that can be used to calculate various days. By using numerical expressions and using the DateSerial function, it is possible to count backward and forward from a date simply by adding and subtracting numbers. The syntax of the DateSerial function is as follows:

```
DateSerial (<Year>, <Month>, <Day>)
```

If the current date is 4/1/1996, for example, DateSerial(1996,4-2,1+28) returns the value 2/29/1996. (Of course, if the year was 1997 (not a leap year), the result would have been 3/1/1996.)

DateValue

Converts an expression passed into the function into a variant of subtype date and returns it. For example, DateValue("February 29, 1976") returns 2/29/1976. If the year is left out, it will be obtained from the system clock.

Day

The Day function returns a value between 1 and 31 and can be used to find the day of a date. For example, Day("4/1/1996") returns 1.

Exp

Returns the value of e raised to a power. For example Exp(1) returns 2.71828182845905.

Hex

Returns the hexadecimal (base 16) value of a numerical expression. For example, Hex(10) returns A.

Hour

Returns the number of hours of a time expression. For example, Hour("12:25:34") returns 12.

InputBox

The InputBox function is used to obtain input from the user by presenting a dialog box. The syntax of the InputBox command is as follows:

```
InputBox(<Prompt>,<Title>,<Default>,<X>,<Y>)
```

Various arguments of the above command enclosed in pointed brackets can be replaced with the following values:

■ <Prompt>—Dialog-box prompt

■ <Title>—Title of dialog box

■ <Default>—Default input value

■ <X>—Horizontal position, in number of twips, from the left side of the screen. A twip is 1/20 of a printer's point, which is 1/1,440 of an inch.

■ <Y>: Vertical position, in number of twips, from the top of the screen

InStr

Returns the location of one string in another string. The syntax of InStr is as follows:

```
InStr (<BeginPosition>, <String1>, <String2>, <ComparisonType>)
```

■ <BeginPosition>—This argument is optional and specifies the starting position of search.

■ <String1>—String being searched

■ <String2>—String to locate

■ <ComparisonType>—This argument is optional. Use 0 for a binary search and 1 for a case- insensitive search. The default value is 0.

Int, Fix

Both Int and Fix convert numerical expressions into integers. The only difference is the fact that Int converts a negative number with a fraction into a smaller integer, and Fix converts a negative number with a fraction into a larger integer. The following examples illustrate how `Int` and `Fix` handle numbers with fractions.

```
Int(11.75) = 11
Fix(11.75) = 11
Int(12.45) = 12
Fix(12.45) = 12
Int(-17.75) = -18
Fix(-17.75) = -17
Int(-7.25) = -8
Fix(-7.25) = -7
```

IsArray

Returns TRUE if a variable is an array and FALSE otherwise.

IsDate

Returns TRUE if an expression can be converted to a valid date and FALSE otherwise.

IsEmpty

Returns TRUE if a variable has been initialized and FALSE otherwise.

IsError

Returns TRUE if an expression is an error code and FALSE otherwise.

IsNull

Returns TRUE if an expression is NULL and FALSE otherwise.

IsNumeric

Returns TRUE if an expression is numeric and FALSE otherwise.

IsObject

Returns TRUE if an expression references an OLE Automation Object and FALSE otherwise.

LBound

`LBound` can be used to find the minimum index of an array dimension. For example, if `ArrayVariable` is a three-dimensional array declared with the statement `Dim ArrayVariable(5 To 100, 10 To 200, 20 To 300)`, `UBound(ArrayVariable,1)` returns 5, `LBound(ArrayVariable,2)` returns 10, and of course `LBound(ArrayVariable,3)` returns 20.

LCase

Converts a string expression to lowercase and returns it.

Left

Returns a certain number of characters from the left side of a string. For example, `Left("Windows NT", 7)` returns "Windows."

Len

Returns the number of characters of a string expression.

Log

Returns the natural logarithm of a nonnegative, numerical expression.

LTrim, RTrim, Trim

Eliminates spaces from a string and returns it. `LTrim` eliminates preceding spaces, `RTrim` eliminates trailing spaces, and `Trim` eliminates both trailing and preceding spaces.

Mid

Returns a certain number of characters from a string. For example `Mid("Windows NT", 0, 7)` returns "Windows."

Minute

Returns the number of minutes when called with the time. For example, `Minute("23:50:45")` returns `50`.

Month

Returns the month when called with a date. For example, `Month("4/1/1996")` returns `4`.

MsgBox

A message box can be displayed using the `MsgBox` command. The syntax of the `MsgBox` command is as follows:

```
MsgBox <MessageBoxPrompt>,<ButtonStyle>,<Title>
```

By replacing `<ButtonStyle>` with various values shown in Table 21.1, a message box can be customized using the following table. For example, an OK dialog box with a warning message icon can be created by replacing `<ButtonStyle>` with `48`.

Table 21.1. Message Box codes.

Button Type	Button Description
0	OK
1	OK and Cancel
2	Abort, Retry, and Ignore
3	Yes, No, and Cancel
4	Yes and No
5	Retry and Cancel
16	Critical Message icon (Figure 21.8)
32	Warning Query icon (Figure 21.9)
48	Warning Message icon (Figure 21.10)
64	Information Message icon (Figure 21.11)
256	Second button is default
512	Third button is default
4096	All applications are stopped until the user responds to the message box

FIGURE 21.8.
The Critical Message box.

FIGURE 21.9.
The Warning Query box.

FIGURE 21.10.
The Warning Message box.

FIGURE 21.11.
The Information Message box.

Now

Returns the current date and time from the system clock. The return value is followed by the date and then the time. For example, the `Now` command returned the string `4/1/1996 23:08:31` at the time of this writing.

Oct

Returns the octal value (base 8) of a numerical expression. For example, `Oct(10)` returns `12`.

Right

Returns a certain number of characters from the right side of a string. For example, `Right("Windows NT", 2)` returns `NT`.

Rnd

Returns a random number between 1 and 0. Be sure to *seed* the random number generator by calling `Randomize` before using the `Rnd` function.

Second

Returns the number of seconds of a date expression. For example, `Second("18:23:57")` returns `57`.

Sgn

Returns the sign of a numerical expression. If the expression is `0`, `0` is returned. If it is less than `0`, `-1` is returned. Otherwise, `1` is returned.

Sin

Returns the sine of an angle. For example, `Sin (Pi)` returns `0`.

Sqr

Returns the square root of a nonnegative, numerical expression.

Str

Converts a numeric expression into a string and returns it.

StrComp

The syntax of the StrComp function is as follows.

```
StrComp (<String1>, <String2>, <ComparisonMethod>)
```

After StrComp compares both strings, it returns 0 if both strings are identical, -1 if <String1> is less than <STRING2>, and 1 otherwise. The <ComparisonMethod> argument is optional. If it is 0, a binary comparison is performed, and if it is 1, a case-insensitive comparison is performed. If <ComparisonMethod> is left out, a binary comparison is performed.

String

The String function is handy for repeating a character a certain number of times. For example, String(5,"*") can be used to create a string of five asterisks.

Tan

The Tan function can be used to calculate the tangent of an angle. For example, Tan (0) returns 0.

Time

Returns the current time from the system clock. For example, the value 01:23:48 was returned by the Time function at the time of this writing.

TimeSerial

This is a very handy function that can be used to perform various time calculations. For example, if the current time is 12:30, TimeSerial can be used to calculate the time 25 minutes ago. For example, TimeSerial(12,30-25, 0) returns 12:05:00.

TimeValue

Returns an expression passed into the function after converting it into a variant of subtype Date. For example, TimeValue ("2:35:17pm") returns 14:35:17.

UBound

UBound can be used to determine the maximum size of an array dimension. For example, if ArrayVariable is a three-dimensional array defined with the statement Dim ArrayVariable(100,200,300), UBound(ArrayVariable,1) returns 100, UBound(ArrayVariable,2) returns 200, and, of course, UBound(ArrayVariable,3) returns 300.

UCase

Converts strings passed into the function into uppercase and returns them. For example, UCase("Windows NT") returns WINDOWS NT.

Val

The Val function can be used to obtain a number contained in a string. The function scans the string until it encounters a character that is not part of a number. For example, Val(" 1234 567 in a string") returns the number 1234567.

VarType

The type of a variable can be determined using the VarType function. For example, if IntVariable was an Integer variable, VarType(IntVariable) will return 2. The type of a variable can be determined by examining the return value of VarType according to Table 21.2.

Table 21.2. Variable type codes.

Value Returned	Type of Variable
0	Empty
1	Null
2	Integer
3	Long integer
4	Single-precision, floating-point number
5	Double-precision, floating-point number
6	Currency
7	Date
8	String
9	OLE Automation object
10	Error
11	Boolean
12	Variant
13	Non-OLE Automation object
8192	Array

Weekday

The Weekday function returns a number between 1 and 7. The numbers returned by the Weekday function correspond to the days of the week, as shown in Table 21.3.

Table 21.3. Day codes.

Day Code	Day of Week
1	Sunday
2	Monday
3	Tuesday
4	Wednesday
5	Thursday
6	Friday
7	Saturday

For example, Weekday("April 2, 1996") returns 3—which is, indeed, a Tuesday.

Year

Returns the year of the expression. For example, Year("February 29, 1976") returns 1976.

Applications of VBScript

Various control structures and commands that can be used to create VBScript programs were outlined in preceding sections. The last few sections will be devoted to applications of these commands and control structures to demonstrate how VBScript can be used create active Web pages.

Simple Calculator

Using various functions and control structures described earlier, a simple calculator can be created using VBScript. If you wish to experiment with the source code of the calculator program, it is included on the CD-ROM (\Chapter-21\Lesson2.htm). Shortly, you will learn how to create a calculator similar to the one shown in Figure 21.12.

FIGURE 21.12.

The Simple Calculator application.

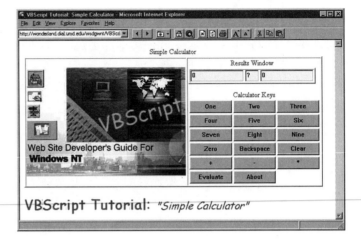

Operators and numbers can be entered into the calculator either by using numeric buttons shown in Figure 21.12 or simply typing them into one of the three text boxes. Before proceeding any further, it is recommended that you experiment with the calculator program and find out how it works. When the Simple Calculator Web page is first invoked and numbers are typed in using various command buttons, they appear in the left-hand text box. After a valid operator is entered into the operator text box, numbers entered next appear on the right-hand text box. At this point, if the Evaluate button is clicked, the VBScript program will evaluate the expression entered and return its value in a dialog box, as shown in Figure 21.13.

FIGURE 21.13.

When the Evaluate button is pressed, the VBScript program calculates the expression entered and returns its value in a dialog box.

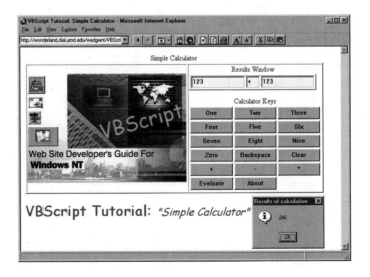

After the OK button in the dialog box shown in Figure 21.13 is pressed, the result of the calculation will be copied to the first text box, as shown in Figure 21.14. The user can then keep on performing calculations using the results of previous calculations.

FIGURE 21.14.
The result of a calculation is copied to the first text box so that it can be used as part of another calculation.

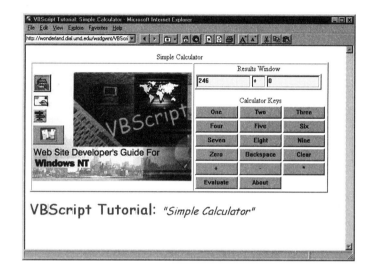

Let's now examine the calculator program in detail and learn how it works. The following VBScript subroutine displays a dialog box similar to the one shown in Figure 21.15 when a user clicks on the About button. Note how the string-concatenation operator is used in line 4 to merge two strings.

```
1: Sub BtnAbout_OnClick
2:   titleString = "Web Site Developer's Guide for Windows NT"
3:   helloString = "Simple VBScript calculator by "
4:   helloString = helloString & "Sanjaya Hettihewa."
5:   MsgBox helloString, 64, titleString
6: End Sub
```

FIGURE 21.15.
The About dialog box.

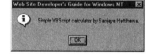

Error checking is an important part of any application. One of VBScript's strengths is its ability to perform various error checks when users enter data into a form. By using the OnChange event, it is possible to check the value of a text box that was recently changed by the user. The subroutine shown next makes sure the user entered a valid number into a text box that is used to obtain an operand from the user. The error-checking subroutine of the second operand is similar to the one shown next. Note how Chr(10) is used to create a multiline string. As you can see in Figure 21.16, when a user enters an invalid number, the following subroutine informs the user and resets the text box.

```
 1: Sub Operand1Box_OnChange
 2:  IF (NOT IsNumeric(Operand1Box.Value)) THEN
 3:     MsgBoxString = "Do not type invalid characters "
 4:     MsgBoxString = MsgBoxString & "into the Results Window! "
 5:     MsgBoxString = MsgBoxString & chr(10)
 6:     MsgBoxString = MsgBoxString & "Results Window will now be reset."
 7:     MsgBox MsgBoxString , 48 , "Invalid input detected!"
 8:     Operand1Box.Value = 0
 9:  END IF
10: End Sub
```

FIGURE 21.16.
Invalid numbers entered by users are detected by the Operand1Box_OnChange *subroutine.*

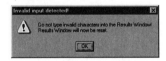

A similar subroutine is used to check that operators entered into the operator text box are valid. The following code listing verifies that operators entered into the operator text box are valid. Note how the underline character (_) is used to join a long expression that spans several lines. If an invalid operator is entered, it is detected by OperatorBox_OnChange subroutine, the text box is reset, and the user is informed of the invalid input, as shown in Figure 21.17.

```
 1: Sub OperatorBox_OnChange
 2:  IF (NOT((OperatorBox.Value = "+" ) OR _
 3:      (OperatorBox.Value = "-" ) OR _
 4:      (OperatorBox.Value = "^" ) OR _
 5:      (OperatorBox.Value = "?" ))) THEN
 6:     MsgString = "Do not type invalid characters "
 7:     MsgString = MsgString & "into the operator text box! "
 8:     MsgString = MsgString & chr(10)
 9:     MsgString = MsgString & "The operator text box will now be reset."
10:     MsgString = MsgString & chr(10) & chr(10)
11:     MsgString = MsgString & "Valid input: +, -, *"
12:     MsgBox MsgString , 48 , "Invalid input detected!"
13:     OperatorBox.Value = "?"
14:  END IF
15: End Sub
```

FIGURE 21.17.
Invalid operators entered into the operator text box are detected by the OperatorBox_OnChange *subroutine.*

The Delete button is used to delete characters entered into one of the operand text boxes. The subroutine associated with the Delete button, BtnDelete_OnClick, is a smart function subroutine. As shown in line 2 of the following code listing, the subroutine first examines the operator text box and determines if a calculation has already been performed. If so, it knows that any numbers added appear on the text box to the right and deletes a digit from that text box. If not, a digit from the left text box is deleted.

```
1: Sub BtnDelete_OnClick
2:   IF (OperatorBox.Value = "?") THEN
3:       IF ((Len (Operand1Box.Value) > 0) AND (Operand1Box.Value <> 0)) THEN
4:           Operand1Box.Value = Left (Operand1Box.Value,  Len (Operand1Box.Value) -
            ➥1)
5:       IF (Len (Operand1Box.Value) = 0) THEN
6:           Operand1Box.Value = 0
7:       END IF
8:       END IF
9:   ELSE
10:       IF ((Len (Operand2Box.Value) > 0) AND (Operand2Box.Value <> 0)) THEN
11:           Operand2Box.Value = Left (Operand2Box.Value,  Len (Operand2Box.Value) -
            ➥1)
12:       IF (Len (Operand2Box.Value) = 0) THEN
13:           Operand2Box.Value = 0
14:       END IF
15:       END IF
16:   END IF
17: End Sub
```

The Evaluate button calculates two operands using an operator and returns a value as shown in Figure 21.13. As you can see in line 2 of the following program listing, the BtnEvaluate_OnClick subroutine first checks the Operator text box. If a valid operator is found, it performs a calculation and displays it using a dialog box. If not, a dialog box similar to the one shown in Figure 21.18 is displayed. Afterwards, as shown in lines 17 and 18, the operand text boxes are reset so that additional calculations can be performed. Note that the result of the calculation is copied in line 17 to the left operand box so that the result of the calculation can be used as part of another calculation.

```
1: Sub BtnEvaluate_OnClick
2:   IF (OperatorBox.Value = "?") THEN
3:       MsgBoxString = "A valid operator is required to carry out "
4:       MsgBoxString = MsgBoxString & "an evaluation."
5:       MsgBoxString = MsgBoxString & chr(10)
6:       MsgBoxString = MsgBoxString & "Valid operators are: +, -, *"
7:       MsgBox MsgBoxString , 48 , "Invalid operator!"
8:   ELSE
9:       IF (OperatorBox.Value = "+")  THEN
10:          answer = CDbl(Operand1Box.Value) + CDbl(Operand2Box.Value)
11:      ELSEIF (OperatorBox.Value = "-")  THEN
12:          answer = CDbl(Operand1Box.Value) - CDbl(Operand2Box.Value)
13:      ELSEIF (OperatorBox.Value = "*")  THEN
14:          answer = CDbl(Operand1Box.Value) * CDbl(Operand2Box.Value)
15:      End IF
16:      MsgBox answer , 64 , "Results of calculation"
```

```
17:      Operand1Box.Value = answer
18:      Operand2Box.Value = 0
19:   END IF
20: End Sub
```

FIGURE 21.18.

The operands are evaluated only if a valid operator is found.

The AddDigit subroutine adds a digit selected via one of the calculator buttons into one of the operand text boxes. As shown in line 4 of the following program listing, if a valid operator is not present, digits are added to the left text box. However, if a valid operator is present, this means that the user has either entered a valid number to the left text box or that it contains the result of a previous calculation (in which case, the digit selected by the user is added to the right text box). When adding digits, there is a possibility that the user will try to add too many digits. This is taken care of in lines 9 and 16, where a separate subroutine is used to inform the reader by displaying a dialog box similar to the one shown in Figure 21.19.

```
1: Sub AddDigit ( digit )
2:   REM Just in case there are any preceding zeros or spaces
3:   Operand1Box.Value = CDbl (Operand1Box.Value)
4:   IF ( OperatorBox.Value = "?") THEN
5:      IF ( Len ( Operand1Box.Value ) < 14 ) THEN
6:         Operand1Box.Value = Operand1Box.Value & digit
7:         Operand1Box.Value = CDbl (Operand1Box.Value)
8:      ELSE
9:         TooManyDigits
10:      END IF
11:   ELSE
12:      IF ( Len ( Operand2Box.Value ) < 14 ) THEN
13:         Operand2Box.Value = Operand2Box.Value & digit
14:         Operand2Box.Value = CDbl (Operand2Box.Value)
15:      ELSE
16:         TooManyDigits
17:      END IF
18:   END IF
19: End Sub
```

FIGURE 21.19.

The AddDigit subroutine prevents users from entering too many digits into a text box.

For your reference, the full source code of the Calculator application is given in Listing 21.2.

Listing 21.2. The Calculator Web page.

```
<!--
(C) 1996 Sanjaya Hettihewa (http://wonderland.dial.umd.edu)
All Rights Reserved.
Permission is hereby given to modify and distribute this code
as you wish provided that this block of text remains unchanged.
!-->

<HTML>
<HEAD>
<TITLE>VBScript Tutorial: Simple Calculator</TITLE>
</HEAD>

<TABLE COLSPEC="L20 L20 L20" BORDER=2 WIDTH=10 HEIGHT=10>
<CAPTION ALIGN=top>Simple Calculator</CAPTION>
<TR><TD>
<BODY BGCOLOR="#FFFFFF" TEXT="#0000FF"
      LINK="#B864FF" VLINK="#670000" ALINK="#FF0000">
<IMG ALIGN=TOP SRC="vbscript.jpg">
<TD>

<TABLE BORDER=2 >
<CAPTION ALIGN=top>Results Window</CAPTION>
 <TD>
 <input type=text size=14 maxlength=14 name="Operand1Box" value="0">
 <input type=text size=1 maxlength=1 name="OperatorBox" value="?">
 <input type=text size=14 maxlength=14 name="Operand2Box" value="0">
 </TD>
</TABLE>

<TABLE COLSPEC="L20 L20 L20" >

<CAPTION ALIGN=top>Calculator Keys</CAPTION>
<TR>
 <TD><INPUT TYPE=BUTTON VALUE="One" NAME="BtnOne"></TD>
 <TD><INPUT TYPE=BUTTON VALUE="Two" NAME="BtnTwo"></TD>
 <TD><INPUT TYPE=BUTTON VALUE="Three" NAME="BtnThree"></TD>
</TR>
<TR>
 <TD><INPUT TYPE=BUTTON VALUE="Four" NAME="BtnFour"></TD>
 <TD><INPUT TYPE=BUTTON VALUE="Five" NAME="BtnFive"></TD>
 <TD><INPUT TYPE=BUTTON VALUE="Six" NAME="BtnSix"></TD>
</TR>
<TR>
 <TD><INPUT TYPE=BUTTON VALUE="Seven" NAME="BtnSeven"></TD>
 <TD><INPUT TYPE=BUTTON VALUE="Eight" NAME="BtnEight"></TD>
 <TD><INPUT TYPE=BUTTON VALUE="Nine" NAME="BtnNine"></TD>
</TR>
<TR>
 <TD><INPUT TYPE=BUTTON VALUE="Zero" NAME="BtnZero"></TD>
 <TD><INPUT TYPE=BUTTON VALUE="Backspace" NAME="BtnDelete></TD>
 <TD><INPUT TYPE=BUTTON VALUE="Clear" NAME="BtnClear"></TD>
</TR>
```

continues

Listing 21.2. continued

```
<TR>
 <TD><INPUT TYPE=BUTTON VALUE="+" NAME="BtnPlus"></TD>
 <TD><INPUT TYPE=BUTTON VALUE="-" NAME="BtnMinus"></TD>
 <TD><INPUT TYPE=BUTTON VALUE="*" NAME="BtnMultiply"></TD>
</TR>

<TR>
 <TD><INPUT TYPE=BUTTON VALUE="Evaluate" NAME="BtnEvaluate"></TD>
 <TD><INPUT TYPE=BUTTON VALUE="About" NAME="BtnAbout"></TD>
</TR>

</TABLE>

</TR>
</TABLE>

<P>

<B><FONT FACE="Comic Sans MS" SIZE=6 COLOR=RED>
VBScript Tutorial: <FONT></B>
<I><FONT FACE="Comic Sans MS" SIZE=5 COLOR=BLUE>
 "Simple Calculator" </I><P><FONT>


<SCRIPT LANGUAGE=VBS>
<!-- To hide VBScript code from technologically challenged browsers

Sub BtnAbout_OnClick
 titleString = "Web Site Developer's Guide for Windows NT"
 helloString = "Simple VBScript calculator by "
 helloString = helloString & "Sanjaya Hettihewa."
 MsgBox helloString, 64, titleString
End Sub

Sub Operand1Box_OnChange
 IF (NOT IsNumeric(Operand1Box.Value)) THEN
    MsgBoxString = "Do not type invalid characters "
    MsgBoxString = MsgBoxString & "into the Results Window! "
    MsgBoxString = MsgBoxString & chr(10)
    MsgBoxString = MsgBoxString & "Results Window will now be reset."
    MsgBox MsgBoxString , 48 , "Invalid input detected!"
    Operand1Box.Value = 0
 END IF
End Sub

Sub Operand2Box_OnChange
 IF (NOT IsNumeric(Operand2Box.Value)) THEN
    MsgBoxString = "Do not type invalid characters "
    MsgBoxString = MsgBoxString & "into the Results Window! "
    MsgBoxString = MsgBoxString & chr(10)
    MsgBoxString = MsgBoxString & "Results Window will now be reset."
    MsgBox MsgBoxString , 48 , "Invalid input detected!"
    Operand2Box.Value = 0
 END IF
End Sub
```

```vbscript
Sub OperatorBox_OnChange
  IF (NOT((OperatorBox.Value = "+" ) OR _
     (OperatorBox.Value = "-" ) OR _
     (OperatorBox.Value = "*" ) OR _
     (OperatorBox.Value = "?" ))) THEN
     MsgString = "Do not type invalid characters "
     MsgString = MsgString & "into the operator text box! "
     MsgString = MsgString & chr(10)
     MsgString = MsgString & "The operator text box will now be reset."
     MsgString = MsgString & chr(10) & chr(10)
     MsgString = MsgString & "Valid input: +, -, *"
     MsgBox MsgString , 48 , "Invalid input detected!"
     OperatorBox.Value = "?"
  END IF
End Sub


Sub BtnOne_OnClick
  IF (IsNumeric(Operand1Box.Value)) THEN
     AddDigit ( 1 )
  ELSE
     ResetResultsWindow
  END IF
End Sub
Sub BtnTwo_OnClick
  IF (IsNumeric(Operand1Box.Value)) THEN
     AddDigit ( 2 )
  ELSE
     ResetResultsWindow
  END IF
End Sub
Sub BtnThree_OnClick
  IF (IsNumeric(Operand1Box.Value)) THEN
     AddDigit ( 3 )
  ELSE
     ResetResultsWindow
  END IF
End Sub
Sub BtnFour_OnClick
  IF (IsNumeric(Operand1Box.Value)) THEN
     AddDigit ( 4 )
  ELSE
     ResetResultsWindow
  END IF
End Sub
Sub BtnFive_OnClick
  IF (IsNumeric(Operand1Box.Value)) THEN
     AddDigit ( 5 )
  ELSE
     ResetResultsWindow
  END IF
End Sub
Sub BtnSix_OnClick
  IF (IsNumeric(Operand1Box.Value)) THEN
     AddDigit ( 6 )
  ELSE
     ResetResultsWindow
  END IF
End Sub
```

continues

Listing 21.2. continued

```
Sub BtnSeven_OnClick
 IF (IsNumeric(Operand1Box.Value)) THEN
    AddDigit ( 7 )
 ELSE
    ResetResultsWindow
 END IF
End Sub
Sub BtnEight_OnClick
 IF (IsNumeric(Operand1Box.Value)) THEN
    AddDigit ( 8 )
 ELSE
    ResetResultsWindow
 END IF
End Sub
Sub BtnNine_OnClick
 IF (IsNumeric(Operand1Box.Value)) THEN
    AddDigit ( 9 )
 ELSE
    ResetResultsWindow
 END IF
End Sub
Sub BtnZero_OnClick
 IF (IsNumeric(Operand1Box.Value)) THEN
    AddDigit ( 0 )
 ELSE
    ResetResultsWindow
 END IF
End Sub

Sub BtnDelete_OnClick
 IF (OperatorBox.Value = "?") THEN
    IF ((Len (Operand1Box.Value) > 0) AND (Operand1Box.Value <> 0)) THEN
       Operand1Box.Value = Left (Operand1Box.Value,  Len (Operand1Box.Value) - 1)
    IF (Len (Operand1Box.Value) = 0) THEN
       Operand1Box.Value = 0
    END IF
    END IF
 ELSE
    IF ((Len (Operand2Box.Value) > 0) AND (Operand2Box.Value <> 0)) THEN
       Operand2Box.Value = Left (Operand2Box.Value,  Len (Operand2Box.Value) - 1)
    IF (Len (Operand2Box.Value) = 0) THEN
       Operand2Box.Value = 0
    END IF
    END IF
 END IF
End Sub

Sub BtnClear_OnClick
 Operand1Box.Value = 0
 Operand2Box.Value = 0
 OperatorBox.Value = "?"
End Sub

Sub BtnPlus_OnClick
 OperatorBox.Value = "+"
End Sub
```

```
Sub BtnMinus_OnClick
 OperatorBox.Value = "-"
End Sub

Sub BtnMultiply_OnClick
 OperatorBox.Value = "*"
End Sub

Sub BtnEvaluate_OnClick
 IF (OperatorBox.Value = "?") THEN
    MsgBoxString = "A valid operator is required to carry out "
    MsgBoxString = MsgBoxString & "an evaluation."
    MsgBoxString = MsgBoxString & chr(10)
    MsgBoxString = MsgBoxString & "Valid operators are: +, -, *"
    MsgBox MsgBoxString , 48 , "Invalid operator!"
 ELSE
    IF (OperatorBox.Value = "+")  THEN
       answer = CDbl(Operand1Box.Value) + CDbl(Operand2Box.Value)
    ELSEIF (OperatorBox.Value = "-")  THEN
       answer = CDbl(Operand1Box.Value) - CDbl(Operand2Box.Value)
    ELSEIF (OperatorBox.Value = "*")  THEN
       answer = CDbl(Operand1Box.Value) * CDbl(Operand2Box.Value)
    End IF
    MsgBox answer , 64 , "Results of calculation"
    Operand1Box.Value = answer
    Operand2Box.Value = 0
 END IF
End Sub

Sub AddDigit ( digit )
 REM Just in case there are any preceeding zeros or spaces
 Operand1Box.Value = CDbl (Operand1Box.Value)
 IF ( OperatorBox.Value = "?") THEN
    IF ( Len ( Operand1Box.Value ) < 14 ) THEN
       Operand1Box.Value = Operand1Box.Value & digit
       Operand1Box.Value = CDbl (Operand1Box.Value)
    ELSE
       TooManyDigits
    END IF
 ELSE
    IF ( Len ( Operand2Box.Value ) < 14 ) THEN
       Operand2Box.Value = Operand2Box.Value & digit
       Operand2Box.Value = CDbl (Operand2Box.Value)
    ELSE
       TooManyDigits
    END IF
 END IF
End Sub

Sub ResetResultsWindow
 MsgBoxString = "Do not type invalid characters "
 MsgBoxString = MsgBoxString & "into the Results Window! "
 MsgBoxString = MsgBoxString & chr(10)
 MsgBoxString = MsgBoxString & "Use Calculator keys instead. "
 MsgBoxString = MsgBoxString & "Results Window will now be reset."
 MsgBox MsgBoxString , 48 , "Invalid input detected!"
 Operand1Box.Value = 0
```

continues

Listing 21.2. continued

```
 Operand2Box.Value = 0
 OperatorBox.Value = "?"
End Sub

Sub TooManyDigits
 MsgBoxString = "The number of digits you have typed "
 MsgBoxString = MsgBoxString & "exceed the maximum"
 MsgBoxString = MsgBoxString & chr(10)
 MsgBoxString = MsgBoxString & "number of digits allowed. "
 MsgBoxString = MsgBoxString & "The digit you selected will "
 MsgBoxString = MsgBoxString & "not be added. Sorry!"
 MsgBox MsgBoxString , 48 , "Too many digits!"
End Sub

!-->
</SCRIPT>

</BODY>
</HTML>
```

Labeling an Image

VBScript can be used to label a graphic when the mouse is moved over it. The VBScript program listed shortly can be used to label an image. When the Web page containing the VBScript program is first invoked, it looks similar to Figure 21.20. Note the string `Hello! Select a link, please.` is contained in the description text box.

FIGURE 21.20.

Text box contains the string Hello! Select a link, please. *when the VBScript Web page is first invoked.*

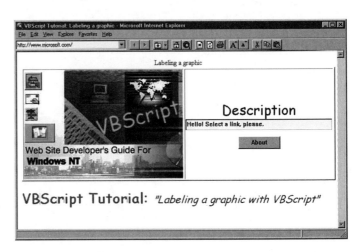

At this point, if the mouse is moved over the graphic in Figure 21.20, the value of the text box changes.

FIGURE 21.21.

When the mouse is moved over the graphic, the value of the text box changes to No link selected. Please select a link!.

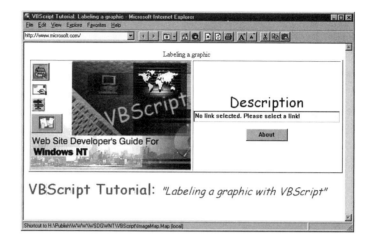

As you can see in Figure 21.22, there are four icons in the graphic to the left of the browser window. When the mouse is moved over any of these icons, the text box will list the description of the text box. For example, when the mouse is over the bulletin-board icon, the value of the text box in Figure 21.21 changes to Post messages on an online discussion forum. Various key subroutines of the label-image program will be discussed next.

FIGURE 21.22.

When the mouse is over one of the icons of the image, the value of the text box changes the icon's description.

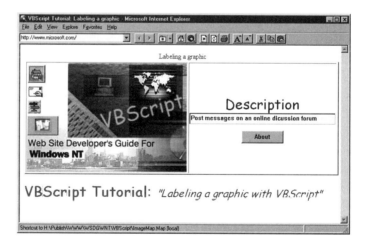

In order to detect mouse movement over the graphic in Figure 21.22, a special identification code needs to be assigned to the graphic. This is done in line 1 of the following code listing:

```
1: <A ID="ImageMapGraphic" HREF="ImageMap.Map">
2: <IMG  ALIGN=TOP SRC="vbscript.jpg" ALT="Sample Graphic" ISMAP BORDER=0>
3: </A>
```

The `ImageMapGraphic_MouseMove` is the heart of the VBScript shown in Figure 21.22. When the mouse is moved over the graphic, the following subroutine is activated. When the mouse pointer falls in a predetermined region of the graphic, the text box is updated with the description of the region the mouse pointer is over, as shown in line 4 of the following program listing. The `HotSpot` subroutine simply returns `TRUE` if the mouse coordinates passed into the `HotSpot` subroutine fall within a certain region of the graphic.

```
 1: Sub ImageMapGraphic_MouseMove(keyboard,mouse,xPosition,yPosition)
 2:
 3: IF (HotSpot(xPosition, yPosition,  2, 5, 70, 41)) THEN
 4:   Description.Value = "Main Homepage"
 5: ELSE IF (HotSpot(xPosition, yPosition,  2, 49, 70, 82)) THEN
 6:   Description.Value = "Send Feedback"
 7: ELSE IF (HotSpot(xPosition, yPosition,  2, 84, 70, 117)) THEN
 8:   Description.Value = "Site Map"
 9: ELSE IF (HotSpot(xPosition, yPosition,  2, 119, 70, 164)) THEN
10:   Description.Value = "Post messages on an online discussion forum"
11: ELSE
12:   Description.Value = "No link selected. Please select a link!"
13: END IF
14: END IF
15: END IF
16: END IF
```

If you would like to experiment with the VBScript program listed next, it can be found on the CD-ROM (\Chapter-21\Lesson3.htm) that accompanies this book. For your reference, the full source code of the Label Image application is given in Listing 21.3.

Listing 21.3. Labeling a graphic.

```
<!--
(C) 1996 Sanjaya Hettihewa (http://wonderland.dial.umd.edu)
All Rights Reserved.
       Permission is hereby given to modify and distribute this code as you wish
provided that this block of text remains unchanged.
!-->

<HTML>
<HEAD>
<TITLE>VBScript Tutorial: Labeling a graphic</TITLE>
</HEAD>

<BODY BGCOLOR="#FFFFFF" TEXT="#0000FF"
            LINK="#B864FF" VLINK="#670000" ALINK="#FF0000">

<TABLE COLSPEC="L20 L20 L20" BORDER=2 WIDTH=10 HEIGHT=10>
<CAPTION ALIGN=top>Labeling a graphic</CAPTION>
<TR><TD>

<A ID="ImageMapGraphic" HREF="ImageMap.Map">
<IMG  ALIGN=TOP SRC="vbscript.jpg" ALT="Sample Graphic" ISMAP BORDER=0>
</A>

</TD><TD>
```

```
<CENTER><FONT FACE="Comic Sans MS" SIZE=6 COLOR=Black>
Description<FONT></CENTER>
<input type="text" name="Description"
       Value="Hello! Select a link, please." size=45><P>

<CENTER><INPUT TYPE=BUTTON VALUE="About" NAME="BtnAbout"></CENTER>

</TD><TD>

</TR>
</TABLE>

<P>

<B><FONT FACE="Comic Sans MS" SIZE=6 COLOR=RED>
VBScript Tutorial: <FONT></B>
<I><FONT FACE="Comic Sans MS" SIZE=5 COLOR=BLUE>
 "Labeling a graphic with VBScript" </I><P><FONT>
</TD></TR>
</TABLE>

<SCRIPT LANGUAGE="VBS">
<!-- To hide VBScript code from  technologically challenged browsers

Sub BtnAbout_OnClick
  titleString = "Web Site Developer's Guide for Windows NT"
  helloString = "Labeling a graphic with VBScript by "
  helloString = helloString & "Sanjaya Hettihewa."
  MsgBox helloString, 64, titleString
End Sub

Sub ImageMapGraphic_MouseMove(keyboard,mouse,xPosition,yPosition)

IF (HotSpot(xPosition, yPosition,  2, 5, 70, 41)) THEN
  Description.Value = "Main Homepage"
ELSE IF (HotSpot(xPosition, yPosition,  2, 49, 70, 82)) THEN
  Description.Value = "Send Feedback"
ELSE IF (HotSpot(xPosition, yPosition,  2, 84, 70, 117)) THEN
  Description.Value = "Site Map"
ELSE IF (HotSpot(xPosition, yPosition,  2, 119, 70, 164)) THEN
  Description.Value = "Post messages on an online dicussion forum"
ELSE
  Description.Value = "No link selected. Please select a link!"
END IF
END IF
END IF
END IF

End Sub

Function HotSpot ( mouseX, mouseY, TopX , TopY, BottomX, BottomY)
 HotSpot = (mouseX >= TopX) AND _
           (mouseX <= BottomX) AND _
           (mouseY >= topY) AND _
           (mouseY<=bottomY)
End Function
```

continues

Listing 21.3. continued

```
!-->
</SCRIPT>

</BODY>
</HTML>
```

Summary

VBScript, a subset of Visual Basic, is an easy-to-use scripting language that can be used to create active Web pages. It enables Web-site developers to create various client-side solutions and make a Web site easier and more interesting to navigate.

What's Next?

A Web site's success depends on how well it is publicized on the Internet. The next chapter will discuss various ways of publicizing a Web site on the Internet to attract more visitors to it. As you will learn shortly, in addition to traditional information-distribution mediums such as newspapers, newsletters, television, magazines, and so on, a Web site can be publicized on the Internet using newsgroups, mail lists, and various Web-site cataloging databases.

VII

Maintaining Your Web Site

22

Publicizing Your Web Site

In 1995, more than 150,000 Web servers were in use. This number is expected to be as high as around 2,000,000 by 1998. Your Web site is going to be just one of many other Web sites on the Internet. If you followed the tips presented in earlier chapters and incorporated various technologies into your Web site to make it easier and more interesting to navigate, you should now have an interesting and user-friendly Web site. However, the success of a Web site depends on how well it's publicized. Unlike other mediums of information distribution, such as television, you can't take information at a Web site to your customers; instead, they have to come in search of information and visit your Web site. The next few sections discuss how you can publicize a Web site on the Internet.

Depending on your success in publicizing your Web site, you might want to consult a commercial Web promoting service to promote your Web site. However, if you follow the suggestions and tips presented in this chapter, you should be able to significantly increase the number of *hits* served by your Web site. On the Internet, sometimes there is some confusion as to what exactly a Web site hit is. Because HTTP is a connectionless protocol, a new connection has to be made for every object on a Web page (image, background sound, Java applet, and so on), including the Web page itself. For example, if a Web page contains a background sound file, a background image file, and two other icons, this Web page will generate five hits each time a user accesses it. This is because a new connection has to be made for each object, and each object transmitted by the Web server is counted as a hit.

It's very important that you keep a pulse on your Web site by analyzing its access log file. The Web server access log file logs every HTTP request received by the server and how the request was handled (success, invalid URL, and so on). The success of your efforts in publicizing a Web site can be determined by analyzing the Web server's access log file. It's impossible to determine the effectiveness of various efforts to publicize a Web site without analyzing this file. Therefore, make sure that your Web server is configured to log Web server accesses and that you have necessary tools to analyze the Web server access log file. Refer to Chapter 24, "Utility Applications for Your Server," to find out about various Web server log analyzing programs.

Newsgroups

Internet newsgroups are read by thousands of users each day. Because a newsgroup has been set up for virtually every topic imaginable, you can use newsgroups to publicize your Web site. As shown in Figure 22.1, you can use a news reading program such as Netscape Navigator to browse newsgroups and post messages.

Before posting a message, you should first determine relevant newsgroups to post your message by using the search option of your news reading program. This can be done by using a dialog box similar to the one shown in Figure 22.2. If you are not using the Netscape news reading application, the dialog box you see will be different. After making a list of newsgroups to post your message, you should be aware of a few things before posting a message. Some

Internet users don't welcome commercial announcements on public discussion forums. When posting a message, to avoid any undesired reactions to it, try to make the post as informative as you can.

FIGURE 22.1.

Internet newsgroups.

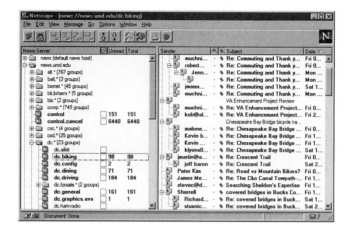

FIGURE 22.2.

You can use a news reading program to search for newsgroups.

Internet Mail Lists

You also can use Internet mail lists to publicize a Web site. However, depending on what your Web site is about, finding an Internet mail list might prove to be a rather challenging task. By using several Internet search engines, you should be able to find a few mail lists that discuss a topic covered at your Web site. Just as when posting to a newsgroup, when posting a message to a mail list to publicize your Web site, emphasize information at your Web site and how users can benefit from it.

NOTE

Some mail lists require users to join before messages can be posted.

Registering with Web Search Engines

Registering your Web site with Internet search engines is perhaps the most effective thing you can do to publicize your Web site. Millions of users use Internet search engines to locate information they need. After registering URLs at your Web site with various Web site cataloging databases, users will visit your Web site when they need information. A few Web site cataloging databases you can use to register URLs free of charge are listed in the following sections.

In addition to providing a brief overview of different Web site cataloging databases, the next few sections also include screen captures of them. The screen captures are meant to give you a better understanding of the Web site cataloging database being discussed and how they enable various URLs to be added by using a form.

When registering URLs with various Web site indexes, register all informative URLs at your Web site. However, avoid registering temporary URLs that will cease to exist after a certain time period. Keep in mind that most Web site cataloging databases take up to a few weeks to add a URL to its index. Therefore, Web site cataloging databases are not suitable for publicizing a temporary URL. Instead, use newsgroups and mail lists to publicize such URLs.

Alta Vista

The Alta Vista Web page shown in Figure 22.3 can be used to add URLs to its database. In order to add URLs to Alta Vista, simply type them in the space provided and press the Submit New URL button. It is not possible to delete or change URLs submitted to Alta Vista. However, inactive and invalid URLs will be deleted from Alta Vista's database.

> **URL**
>
> The Alta Vista Web site cataloging database:
> `http://altavista.digital.com/cgi-bin/query?pg=addurl`

BizWiz

You should submit only business-related URLs to the BizWiz Web site cataloging database. Unlike most search engines discussed in this chapter, BizWiz catalogs only business-related Web sites. You can add URLs to BizWiz by using a form similar to the one shown in Figure 22.4.

> **URL**
>
> The BizWiz Web site cataloging database:
> `http://www.bizwiz.com/bizwiz/`

FIGURE 22.3.
Alta Vista URL submit service.

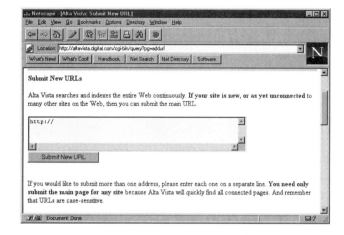

FIGURE 22.4.
BizWiz URL submit service.

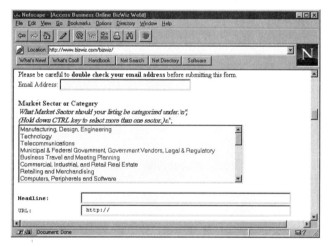

Galaxy

Galaxy is a searchable index of various kinds of Web sites. By visiting Galaxy's Web site, filling in a form similar to the one shown in Figure 22.5, and clicking on the Send to Galaxy button, you can add URLs to its database.

URL

The Galaxy Web site cataloging database:
`http://galaxy.einet.net/cgi-bin/annotate?Other`

FIGURE 22.5.

Galaxy URL submit service.

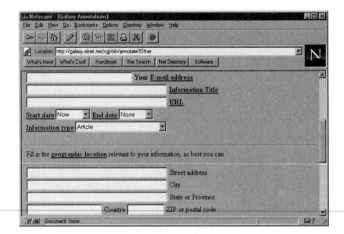

InfoSeek

InfoSeek is a comprehensive Web site cataloging database that enables URLs to be added to it in two ways. If you're familiar with how Yahoo! and WebCrawler index URLs, InfoSeek is like a mix of them. Visit InfoSeek's Web page for more information about customizing various aspects of URLs added to its database.

URL

The InfoSeek Web site cataloging database:

`http://guide.infoseek.com/AddUrl?pg=DCaddurl.html`

As shown in Figure 22.6, URLs can be added to InfoSeek's index of Web pages. This index is not broken down into various categories. When a user initiates a search, URLs that match various search criteria are returned to the user.

FIGURE 22.6.

InfoSeek index URL submit service.

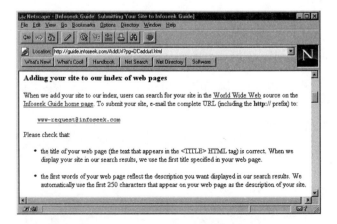

InfoSeek Select Web pages are reviewed by InfoSeek staff and are placed in various categories. Web pages can be added to InfoSeek Select by using a form similar to the one in Figure 22.7.

FIGURE 22.7.
InfoSeek Select URL submit service.

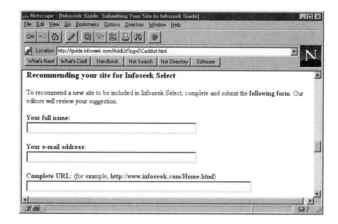

Lycos

Lycos is a widely used Web search index. URLs can be added or deleted from Lycos by using its URL registration page. Refer to Figure 22.8 for an example of how a URL can be added to Lycos.

> **URL**
>
> The Lycos Web site cataloging database:
>
> `http://www.lycos.com/register.html`

FIGURE 22.8.
Lycos URL submit service.

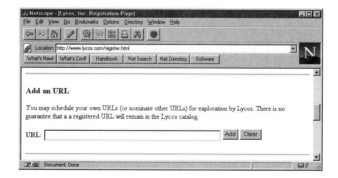

Nerd World Media

You can add Web pages to Nerd World Media by using a form similar to the one in Figure 22.9. Web sites added to Nerd World Media are categorized to make it easier for users to find Web sites they're interested in.

URL

The Nerd World Media Web site cataloging database:

`http://www.nerdworld.com/nwadd.html`

FIGURE 22.9.
Nerd World Media URL submit service.

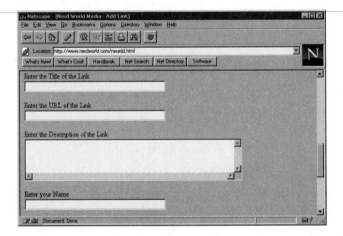

New Riders' World Wide Web Yellow Pages

You can add URLs to New Riders' World Wide Web Yellow Pages by filling in a form and submitting it, as shown in Figure 22.10. If your URL is selected, it will be added to the next edition of World Wide Web Yellow Pages published by Macmillan Publishing.

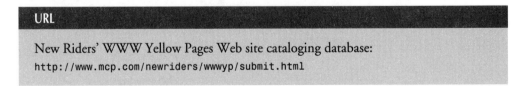

URL

New Riders' WWW Yellow Pages Web site cataloging database:

`http://www.mcp.com/newriders/wwwyp/submit.html`

FIGURE 22.10.
*New Riders' WWW Yellow
Pages URL submit service.*

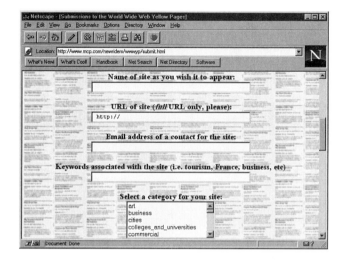

WebCrawler

WebCrawler is a very comprehensive and widely used Web site cataloging database. You can
add URLs to WebCrawler by using a form similar to the one shown in Figure 22.11.

URL

The WebCrawler Web site cataloging database:
`http://Webcrawler.com/WebCrawler/SubmitURLS.html`

FIGURE 22.11.
*WebCrawler URL
submit service.*

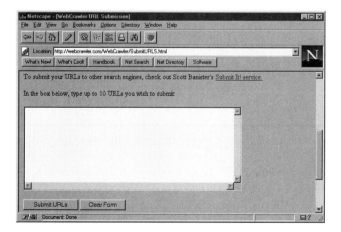

Yahoo!

Yahoo! is an extensively used Web search engine. Web sites in Yahoo!'s database are grouped into various categories. This makes it easier for users to navigate Yahoo!'s Web site and find Web sites they are interested in.

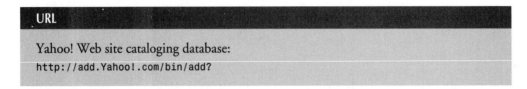

> **URL**
>
> Yahoo! Web site cataloging database:
> `http://add.Yahoo!.com/bin/add?`

Before adding a URL to Yahoo!, a category has to be selected for it. This can be done by browsing Yahoo!'s Web site, as shown in Figure 22.12. After making a note of one or more categories for the URL you wish to add to Yahoo!, proceed to its URL registration page.

FIGURE 22.12.

Various Yahoo! categories.

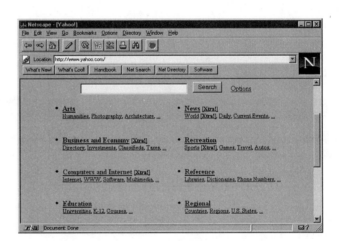

You can add a URL to Yahoo!'s Web site by using a form similar to the one in Figure 22.13. After a URL is submitted, it will be reviewed by Yahoo! staff and added to one or more Yahoo! categories.

Submit It!

As shown in Figure 22.14, Scott Banister's Submit It! is an easy-to-use Web site indexing tool you can use to submit URLs to several Web cataloging databases at the same time. If you're short of time and don't want to individually visit the Web sites discussed earlier to submit URLs, use Submit It! However, due to the diversity of various Web cataloging databases, you might not be able to have access to various customization features offered by various Web cataloging databases when using Submit It!

FIGURE 22.13.

Yahoo! URL submit Web page.

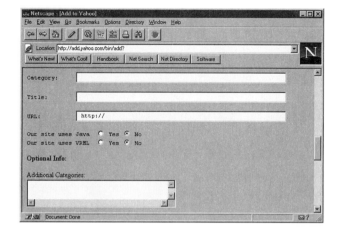

URL

Submit It! URL submit service:

`http://www.submit-it.com/all.html`

FIGURE 22.14.

Submit It! URL submit service.

Other Web Site Cataloging Databases

Listed next are several additional Web site cataloging databases you can use to promote your Web site. Register your Web site with as many Web site cataloging databases as possible to attract many users to your site.

URL

The Excite Web site cataloging database:
`http://www.excite.com/cgi/comsubhelp.cgi?display=excite;path=/`
`query.html;section=search;Suggest+Link=Suggest+Link`
The Open Text Index Web site cataloging database:
`http://www.opentext.com:8080/omw/xsubmit_c.html`
The Magellan Web site cataloging database:
`Magellan: http://www.mckinley.com/feature.cgi?add_bd`

Other Ways of Publicizing a Web Site

You should be careful if you intend to announce a Web site's URL on the radio. Unless the URL is easy to pronounce, even seasoned Internet users will have trouble remembering a URL such as `http://www.idyllmtn.com/`. When announcing a URL on a medium such as radio, you may want to omit `http://` from the name of the URL. Instead, let them know the address is a World Wide Web site.

Unlike the radio, printed advertisements are ideal for publicizing a Web site. After setting up your Web site, you should include its URL in all corporate documents and letterheads so that customers will be able to access your Web site for more information.

In addition to using newsgroups, mail lists, and Web site cataloging databases, by using traditional advertising mediums such as newsletters, radio, television, and so on, you will be able to effectively publicize your Web site and attract more users to it.

Summary

This chapter outlined various ways of publicizing a Web site on the Internet to attract more visitors to it. Before publicizing a Web site, the Web server should be set up to log Web server accesses to a log file so that Web server access information can be analyzed with a log analyzing program. In addition to traditional information distribution mediums such as newspapers, newsletters, television, and magazines, you can publish a Web site on the Internet by using newsgroups, mail lists, and Web site cataloging databases.

What's Next?

The next chapter discusses various design and maintenance issues related to hosting a Web site. After setting up a Web site and using it for some time, it needs to be maintained to make sure everything functions properly and at maximum efficiency. Tips provided in the next chapter will help you maintain an efficient Windows NT system on the Internet.

23

Design and Maintenance Issues

There is more to creating a Web site than adding some HTML files to a Web server and perhaps setting up a Web database interface. The design and presentation of a Web site is very important. Poorly designed Web sites are hard to navigate and maintain. The tips presented in this chapter will help you design a user-friendly Web site that is easy to manage.

Web Site Design Issues

A few tips and ideas that are helpful when designing a Web site are listed next. If you follow these guidelines, you will have a Web site that's easy to maintain and administer.

Creating a Logical Directory Structure

Creating a logical directory structure is very important. As shown in Figure 23.1, a logical directory structure makes it easy to maintain a Web site and to assign file permissions to various users based on directory hierarchies. Although it's possible to store all objects of a Web page in the same directory, this can turn into a mess after more directories and files are added. For example, if you have about ten directories with a few dozen Web pages and suddenly decide to make a change to an icon that's used in several Web pages, you'll likely have to browse each directory and locate the graphic you wish to modify. This can be time consuming and error prone. On the other hand, if all images are stored in a separate directory, it's easy to locate a graphic you want to change and make the modifications. After the changes are saved, all Web pages that refer to the graphic will automatically refer to the updated graphic. Also, when adding various graphics to a Web site, it's recommended that you use directories to organize them. For example, I've got hundreds of graphics at my Web site. If all the graphics were in the same directory, finding a graphic would be very time consuming. To make matters easier, the graphics directory is broken down into various sections such as Animations, Icons, Bullets, Lines, and so on, as shown in Figure 23.1 This makes it very easy to locate graphics to add to a Web page.

URL Naming Issues

When adding Web pages, especially ones that will be manually entered by many users, try to keep them as short as possible. (Have you ever had to retype a long URL a half dozen times to get it right?) Short URLs are easy to advertise, easy to remember, and easier to refer to when creating links from other Web pages.

URL Short Cuts

If you have Web pages at your Web site with hard-to-remember URLs, you should create URLs for them as shown in Figure 23.2. Although you're probably intimately familiar with the directory structure of your Web site, your users probably don't know it that well. For example, it's much easier to remember http://wonderland.dial.umd.edu/~sanjaya than http://wonderland.dial.umd.edu/documents/sanjaya/sanjaya.html.

FIGURE 23.1.

A logical directory structure makes it easy to maintain a Web site.

FIGURE 23.2.

Create easy-to-remember URL shortcuts for pages that are most frequently accessed.

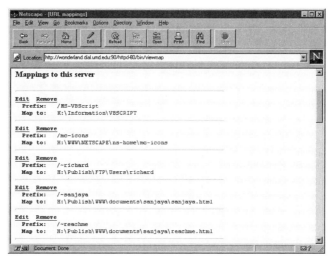

Using a Revision Control System

A *revision control system (RCS)* makes it easier for several people to work on a project without stepping on each other's toes. In case a mistake is made, when RCS is used, it's very easy to *roll back* a file (restore the contents of a file to a previous state) to what it was before the mistake was made.

Slightly Change the Layout of the Web Site Periodically

If possible, slightly change the layout of the Web site at least once every two months to make sure it looks new and attractive to users who visit it frequently. This does not mean that you should make dramatic changes to all the Web pages at your Web site. Instead, slightly change the appearance of a few selected Web pages (such as the main Web page of a Web site) that act as an index to various informative Web pages.

Dos and Don'ts for Your Web Site

A few dos and don'ts for a Web site are listed next. By following these guidelines, you can avoid common mistakes made by Webmasters of various Web sites. Each of these guidelines is discussed in detail in the following sections.

- **Do** respond to feedback promptly.
- **Do** monitor Web server's access log file.
- **Don't** use large graphics.
- **Do** optimize graphics at your Web site.
- **Do** browse your Web site with multiple browsers.
- **Do** check for invalid or broken links.
- **Don't** use large background images.
- **Do** remove outdated Web pages.
- **Do** use graphic thumbnails.
- **Do** make the best use of browser space.
- **Do** keep URLs consistent.
- **Do** register URLs with search engines.
- **Don't** use complex background images.
- **Do** create URL shortcuts.
- **Do** use the <ALT> tag when adding graphics.
- **Do** use tables.

Do Respond to Feedback Promptly

Promptly responding to feedback is the key to the success of a Web site. A user might detect a broken link and mail you about it or want to point out a mistake you've made in one of your Web pages.

Do Monitor Web Server's Access Log File

Monitoring your Web server's access log file is very crucial for determining who accessed what from your Web site. By keeping an eye on your Web server's access log file, it's possible to find out various sections of a Web site that are widely used and also those sections that are not so popular. Refer to Chapter 24, "Utility Applications for Your Server," for more information about analyzing your Web server's access log file.

Don't Use Large Graphics

Avoid adding very large graphics to your Web site. They take longer for a page to load, especially over low-bandwidth phone lines, and can be frustrating for a user browsing your Web site. Make an effort to reduce file sizes of graphics as much as possible while keeping their appearance the same. Chapter 11, "Adding Multimedia to Your Web Site," contains numerous tips for optimizing graphics for the Internet.

Do Optimize Graphics at Your Web Site

It's very important that graphics at your Web site be optimized for the Internet. By judiciously using various graphics formats, it's possible to exploit the capabilities of the graphics formats and optimize graphics for the Internet. The key to optimizing graphics for the Internet is experimenting with various graphics formats and trying to reduce the file size of the graphic as much as possible while keeping the appearance of the graphic the same.

Do Browse Your Web Site with Multiple Browsers

Browse your Web site with at least two Web browsers after creating a page. Although a page might look attractive with one browser, it might not look so attractive when viewed with another browser. Because Internet Explorer and Netscape Navigator are two of the most widely used Web browsers, it's recommended that you view new Web pages with both of these browsers before adding them to a Web site. Note that this does not apply to Web pages done in standard HTML (HTML 2.0) because virtually all browsers handle standard HTML the same way.

Do Check for Invalid or Broken Links

Navigate your Web site every now and then to find invalid and broken links, especially after adding a new Web page to your Web site. Although some links might work locally, on a development machine—due to different directory structures—they might fail to work after a Web page is transferred to the production server.

Don't Use Large Background Images

Try to keep background images as small as possible. A large background image might take a few seconds to load and make it hard for a user browsing your Web site to view the contents of a page. This is especially true for users browsing your Web site with Web browsers such as Netscape Navigator. Netscape first displays the text of a Web page before loading the background image. Depending on the background color of the Web browser, text on a Web page might look almost invisible. For example, if the default background color of Netscape is gray and you created a Web page with a dark background with white text, because white doesn't stand out very well against a gray background, the contents of the Web page will look unattractive and hard to read until the background image is loaded and displayed by Netscape.

Do Remove Outdated Web Pages

It's not very attractive to have outdated information at a Web site. (Have you ever come across a URL with a NEW icon attached to it that points to a page modified six months ago?) Make a note of time-sensitive information at a Web site and remove outdated items to keep a Web site's information up-to-date.

Do Use Graphic Thumbnails

Use graphic thumbnails whenever large images are added to a Web page. Set up the graphic thumbnail so that users can see the full image by clicking on the thumbnail.

Do Make the Best Use of Browser Space

Vertical space of a Web browser is golden. Try to design Web pages so that Web browser space is efficiently used. This makes it easy for users to navigate a Web site without extensively relying on scroll bars.

Do Keep URLs Consistent

Keep URL names consistent as much as possible, especially those that have been added to various Web search engines. After a Web page is added to a Web site, its URL should not be changed unless it's going to be removed from the Web site.

Do Register URLs with Search Engines

Register informative URLs at your Web site with various search engines. This makes it easier for users to locate your Web site. Generally, you should register URLs at your Web site with as many search engines as possible. Refer to Chapter 22, "Publicizing Your Web Site," for more information about registering URLs with Internet search engines.

Don't Use Complex Background Images

When adding background images, keep in mind that the purpose of a background image is to make the text of a Web page easier and more pleasing to read. Complex background images make it hard to read the contents of a Web page. As a rule of thumb, always use background images that are either light or dark in color and use text that is of opposite color. For example, use white text in a Web page that has a dark blue background. Avoid using background images with both light and dark colors.

Do Create URL Shortcuts

Create URL shortcuts to shorten long URLs and make it easier to remember and advertise them.

Do Use the <ALT> Tag When Adding Graphics

Web browsers such as Internet Explorer use text defined in the <ALT> tag of a graphic to describe the graphic when the mouse is moved over it by using *balloon text.* You might have noticed when you rest the mouse pointer on the tool bar of some applications, you see some text appear that describes the purpose of the button the mouse pointer is on. This text is referred to as balloon text. When adding graphics to a Web page, use the <ALT> tag to take advantage of this feature.

Do Use Tables

Tables are very useful for formatting the contents of a Web page. Without tables, it would be impossible to use various multimedia formats and make the maximum use of Web browser space. Most Web browsers that are being used on the Internet support tables. Use tables to make the best use of browser space when using several multimedia objects on the same page.

Tips for Creating a User-Friendly Web Site

It's important that you make your Web site a *user-friendly* Web site. Compared to the effort it takes to create a Web site, design Web pages, and publish them on the Internet, it takes very little effort to make a Web site user-friendly and easy to navigate. The following sections discuss a few tips for creating a user-friendly Web site.

Compatibility with 640×480 Monitors

When designing Web pages, be sure to look at them with a Web browser sized to 640×480. Most Web surfers use this size of monitor to surf the Web. Although a page might look very attractive on a monitor with a higher resolution, it might not look as attractive on a 640×480 monitor. With a little effort, you can create *640×480 friendly* Web pages. This can be done by browsing your Web site after resizing the Web browser window to 640×480.

Avoid Long URLs

Whenever possible, you should avoid unnecessarily long URLs. They are hard to remember and type, and are also difficult to advertise in various documents such as newsletters.

Create a Standard Button Bar

It's a good idea to create a standardized button bar for your Web site. Users will then be able to provide feedback and return to the main Web page of a Web site whenever they want to, no matter where they are. Of course, be sure to include a link to the main Web page of your Web site as well as a link to a page that can be used to submit feedback.

Create a Map of Your Web Site

A map of a Web site is often quite helpful to users navigating it. Users will then be able to directly go to a Web page they're interested in by looking at various Web pages at your Web site all at once. When adding a Web site map, use title names of pages and perhaps even a short description of each page to make it easy for users to find Web pages they're interested in.

Add a What's New Page

A What's New page is a very important part of any Web site; however, most Web sites don't have one. A What's New page enables a user browsing a Web site to quickly locate the most up-to-date information.

Create Links to Helper Apps

There are many multimedia file formats in use on the Internet, and not everyone has helper applications for most of these multimedia file formats. Some require the setup of special helper applications and others require users to download and install various *plug ins*. Plug ins are downloadable software that is capable of enhancing the capabilities of a Web browser by handling special object formats not originally supported by the Web browser. When using various multimedia formats, be sure to create links that can be used to download necessary helper applications.

Use Frames

When used properly, frames can make a Web site easier to navigate. Refer to Chapter 9, "Advanced HTML Techniques," to learn how to use frames to make a Web site easier to navigate.

Easy Access to a Feedback Form

You can make it easy for users to provide you feedback by creating a standard button bar to be included in all Web pages and by adding a feedback button to it.

Legalities

When setting up a Web site, you should be aware of certain legalities. By following a few guidelines, you can avoid unnecessary legal problems. The first thing to remember is that normal copyright laws do indeed apply to the Web. Copyright laws do not change just because the medium of information distribution changes. If you own a copyright on something, you can "publish" it on the Web; if others misuse your work, you can take legal action, and they're as guilty as if they'd done the same thing in a non-electronic medium.

You should be concerned about copyright law when designing your Web site and making information available to the Internet community. The goal of the World Wide Web and the Internet is to make information readily available to those who need it. On the other hand, copyright law is designed to restrict access and use of information to a certain degree. Therefore, there's a conflict between the intentions of copyright law and the spirit of the Internet. However, copyright law is part of the law, and the spirit of the Internet isn't. Therefore, you should make sure your Web site complies with copyright law.

Creating a Disclaimer Page

It's also a good idea to have a link to a *disclaimer page* at your Web site, which states that your company (or client) is not endorsing any product or other company; instead, the links are meant for informational purposes and to explore the Web. Therefore, if someone doesn't like what you've linked to (even though you're not responsible for the content at the other end of the link), he or she can't complain to you about it or take legal action against you.

Using Graphics from Other Web Sites

You should also be careful about using graphics that are trademarks of various organizations. If you want to use such a graphic, make sure you get permission first. You can get permission to use a graphic simply by asking permission from the Webmaster of the Web site containing the graphics you wish to use.

> **NOTE**
>
> If you're concerned about your work, you can register it with the copyright office for a minimal price. Furthermore, you should also include a copyright symbol © on your work. You can insert the copyright symbol by using © in your Web pages.

"Obtaining" graphics from other sites and adding them to your own pages can also get you into trouble. If you'd like to have something, you should first send some e-mail and ask for permission. If not, you can simply visit one of the public graphics icon archives and get all the graphics you need.

URL

Various icon collections on the Internet:

`http://www.infi.net/~rdralph/icons/`

`http://www.meat.com/textures/`

`http://www.cs.yale.edu/homes/sjl/clipart.html`

`http://www.yahoo.com/Computers/World_Wide_Web/Programming/Icons`

`http://www.sfsu.edu/~jtolson/textures/textures.htm`

`http://www.stars.com/Vlib/Providers/Images_and_Icons.html`

TIP

Ask nicely! If you would like to use information or a graphic at another Web site, ask for permission to use it beforehand. As long as the information is not too proprietary, chances are that you will be given permission to use it.

Of course, you should also avoid issues that are illegal in the real world, such as slander, libel, and child pornography. Even though the electronic medium of the Web might seem different from the real world, keep in mind that some things are illegal no matter what medium you're using. For more information about copyright law, please visit the following URL.

URL

Visit the WWW Virtual Law Library for information about various legal issues, categorized by subject, related to publishing information on the Internet:

`http://www.law.indiana.edu/law/lawindex.html`

Communications Decency Act

The Communications Decency Act (CDA) is a controversial law that affects the very existence of the Internet; this is because it assumes criminal liability on online access providers whose customers might publish content on the Internet that someone decides are "obscene, lewd, lascivious, filthy, or indecent." Due to various restrictions placed by the CDA on the freedom of speech, it's unlikely that it will be fully enforced by the government. Legally, however, you could get into a lot of trouble for violating the restrictions. Therefore, at a minimum, refrain from publishing "adult" content at your Web site. I will not mention everything the CDA prohibits you from doing because the list is too long. However, visit the URL listed next for a full text description of the CDA.

URL

A full text listing of the CDA can be found at the following Web site:

```
http://www.ganson.com/jganson/cda.html
```

Many Web sites wear a *blue ribbon* as a symbol of protesting the CDA. If you believe the CDA is unconstitutional, you can obtain a blue ribbon for your Web site from the Blue Ribbon Campaign for Online Free Speech Web site.

URL

Blue ribbons that have become a symbol of protest toward the CDA can be obtained from the Blue Ribbon Campaign for Online Free Speech Web site:

```
http://www.eff.org/blueribbon.html
```

Summary

There are various design and maintenance issues that you should take into consideration when designing a Web site. You can create a user-friendly Web site that's easy to manage by following the tips and ideas presented in this chapter.

What's Next?

The next chapter discusses various applications that you can use to maintain and make it easier to perform various tasks on your NT server.

24

Utility Applications for Your Server

Numerous utility applications are available to make Windows NT easier to use and to perform various system-administration tasks. The following sections discuss several applications that make it easier to administer an NT Web site.

Monitoring Web-Server Accesses

Monitoring the access log file is the key to determining who accessed what from a Web server. Several Web-server, log-analyzing applications are available for Windows NT. Most of these applications are either freeware or shareware applications. Listed next are a few Web-server, log-analyzing applications that run on Windows NT.

> AccessWatch
> http://netpresence.com/accesswatch/
>
> getstats
> http://www.eit.com/software/getstats/getstats.html
>
> Intersé market focus
> http://www.interse.com/marketfocus/
>
> WebTrends
> http://www.webtrends.com/

The remainder of this section is devoted to WebTrends. Although it is a commercial program, WebTrends is a very feature-rich application that can be used to obtain various statistics about a Web site.

Using WebTrends

As you will be shown shortly, WebTrends can be used to obtain a variety of access statistics for a Web site. The WebTrends application looks similar to Figure 24.1.

FIGURE 24.1.
A WebTrends application.

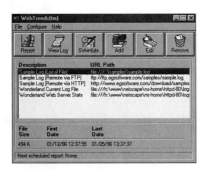

WebTrends originally comes preconfigured to analyze a few Web-server access log files. A new log file can be analyzed by clicking the Add button. This will bring up a dialog box similar to the one shown in Figure 24.2.

FIGURE 24.2.

Adding/editing WebTrends log files.

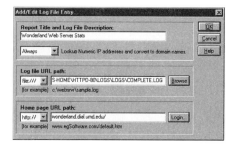

Using the dialog box in Figure 24.2, WebTrends can be configured to analyze a log file using a local filename, FTP, or HTTP. The last two options are particularly handy for analyzing the access log file of a remote Web server. By clicking the Schedule button in Figure 24.1, it is possible to configure WebTrends to analyze a log file at a preset time and generate a statistics report. A dialog box similar to the one in Figure 24.3 is displayed when the Schedule button is pressed.

FIGURE 24.3.

The Scheduler can be used to analyze a log file at a certain preset time.

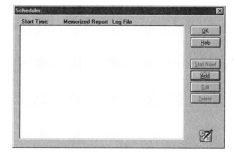

A log file can be scheduled to be analyzed by pressing the Add button in Figure 24.3. When the Add button is pressed, a dialog box similar to the one shown in Figure 24.4 is displayed to obtain various information.

FIGURE 24.4.

Log files can be added to the WebTrends scheduler.

As shown in Figure 24.4, WebTrends can be configured to analyze a log file at a certain date and time and repeat the process a preset number of minutes, hours, or days later.

The access log file of a Web server can easily be a few dozen megabytes in size. This makes it hard to view a certain section of the log file using a text editor. WebTrends can be used to solve this problem. When the View Log button in Figure 24.1 is pressed, a dialog box similar to the one in Figure 24.5 is displayed. This dialog box can be used to specify the section of the log file you are interested in viewing.

FIGURE 24.5.

WebTrends can be used to view a certain section of a Web-server access log file.

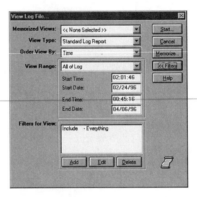

Sometimes, you might not be interested in certain Web-server accesses. For example, you might want to exclude local accesses when WebTrends generates a statistics report. This can be done by clicking Filters in the dialog box shown in Figure 24.5 and clicking the Add button. A dialog box then asks you if you would like to include or exclude various records. For example, in order to exclude yourself, click the Exclude button, and a dialog box similar to the one in Figure 24.6 is displayed to gather various information.

FIGURE 24.6.

Filters can be added to reports generated by WebTrends.

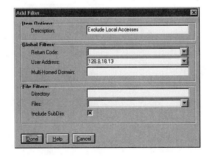

As shown in Figure 24.6, your IP address can be typed in the space provided for User Address in order to exclude yourself from the report generated by WebTrends. After clicking on Done in the dialog box shown in Figure 24.6, and Start in the dialog box in Figure 24.5, the section of the log file you selected is displayed as shown in Figure 24.7.

FIGURE 24.7.

WebTrends can be used to view the contents of a log file.

WebTrends also can be used to generate a comprehensive statistics report of a Web-server access log file by clicking on the Report button in Figure 24.1, and using two dialog boxes similar to those shown in Figures 24.5 and 24.6. By selecting a predefined template or creating a new template using Figure 24.8, the statistics report generated by WebTrends can be customized.

FIGURE 24.8.

Reports generated by WebTrends can be customized using templates.

Refer to Figures 24.9 through 24.15 for examples of various statistics graphs generated by WebTrends.

FIGURE 24.9.
User profile by regions.

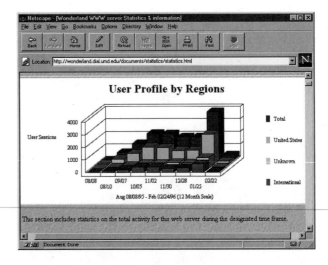

FIGURE 24.10.
User breakdown by organizations.

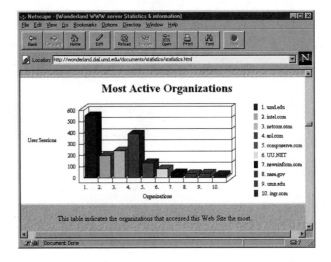

FIGURE 24.11.

User breakdown by countries.

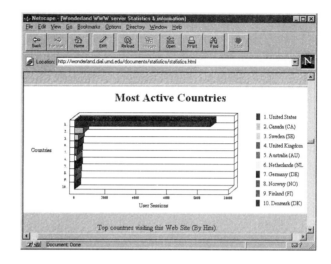

FIGURE 24.12.

Activity by day of the week.

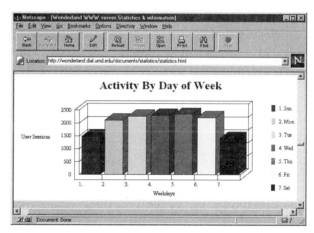

FIGURE 24.13.

Activity by hour.

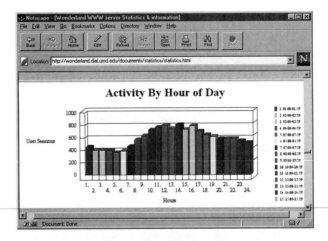

FIGURE 24.14.

Domestic breakdown by states.

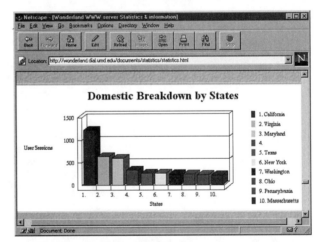

FIGURE 24.15.

Domestic breakdown by cities.

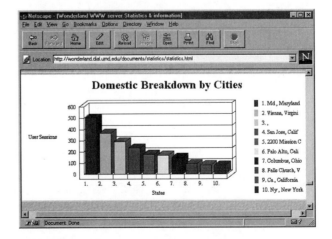

Dealing with File Fragmentation

Virtually all operating systems are plagued with the problem of disk fragmentation. Disk fragmentation occurs when files are added and deleted from a hard drive over a certain period of time. Although it takes a while for a disk to be fragmented, it can seriously affect the performance of applications that frequently access the hard drive. At the time of this writing, only one disk defragmenting program, Diskeeper by Executive Software, is capable of defragmenting NTFS (NT File System) volumes. Before purchasing Diskeeper, you might want to find out if your hard drives are fragmented using a fragmentation-analysis utility that's distributed free of charge.

> **URL**
>
> A disk-fragmentation analysis utility can be downloaded from the Sunbelt Software Distribution Inc. Web site:
>
> `http://www.ntsoftdist.com/ntsoftdist/`

Checking for Disk Fragmentation

The disk-fragmentation analysis utility looks similar to Figure 24.16. By selecting Select Disk from the Analysis menu, a disk volume can be selected to analyze using a dialog box similar to the one shown in Figure 24.17. Note that there are two versions of disk-fragmentation analysis utilities. The first version analyzes only NTFS volumes and the other analyzes only FAT volumes. Depending on the kinds of partitions you have, you might want to download one or both utilities.

FIGURE 24.16.

The disk-fragmentation analysis utility.

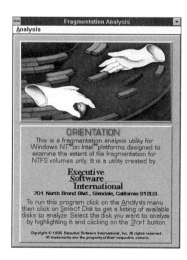

FIGURE 24.17.

Selecting a volume to check for disk fragmentation.

After the disk selected in Figure 24.17 is analyzed, a report similar to the one in Figure 24.18 will be displayed. Select Analysis|Reading for more information about interpreting results as shown in Figure 24.18. Generally, if *Average fragments per file* is greater than 1.3, you will be able to increase the performance of your system by defragmenting the volume that was analyzed.

FIGURE 24.18.

A disk-fragmentation analysis report.

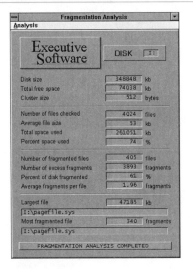

Defragmenting a Fragmented Hard Drive

Diskeeper can be used to defragment a fragmented hard drive. The Diskeeper application is shown in Figure 24.19. A remote NT computer can be defragmented using the Network menu option shown in Figure 24.19. The Defragment menu option can be used to defragment disk partitions by selecting drives as shown in Figure 24.20.

Certain files, such as Windows NT page files, should not be defragmented. Such files can be excluded using the Select Files and Drives to Exclude dialog box shown in Figure 24.21.

FIGURE 24.19.

The Diskeeper disk-defragmenting utility.

FIGURE 24.20.

Selecting a partition to be defragmented by Diskeeper.

FIGURE 24.21.

Various files and drives can be excluded to be defragmented by Diskeeper.

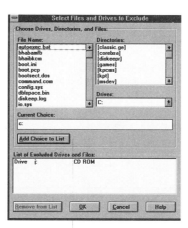

Diskeeper can be configured to defragment drives when the system is idle as well as at a certain preset time. The dialog box shown in Figure 24.22 can be used to configure Diskeeper to defragment a drive when the system is not expected to be heavily used.

FIGURE 24.22.

Diskeeper can be configured to defragment drives at a preset time.

If you are using Windows NT 3.51, you need to uninstall Diskeeper each time a service pack is applied to your system. This is because Diskeeper replaces several core NT system files. After applying a service pack, you need to download a new version of Diskeeper specially designed for the service pack if you are using NT 3.51. If you install Diskeeper and later upgrade to NT 4.0, it is recommended that you uninstall Diskeeper before upgrading to NT 4.0.

This inconvenience has been taken care of in Windows NT 4.0. NT 4.0 has built-in hooks for disk-defragmenting utilities such as Diskeeper.

Windows NT Service Packs

Windows NT service packs are freely made available by Microsoft to fix various bugs in released versions of Windows NT. Your NT system should be updated with new service packs when they are available at Microsoft's FTP site.

Windows NT service packs can be downloaded from the following FTP site:

`ftp://ftp.microsoft.com/bussys/winnt/winnt-public/fixes/`

Note that Windows NT service packs are cumulative. For example, if the latest service pack available is service pack 4, you do not need to apply service packs 1 through 4. Downloading and applying service pack 4 is sufficient.

> **TIP**
>
> Apply new Windows NT service packs if a certain problem you are having is addressed by the service pack or a problem you might potentially have is addressed by it. Although service packs are very safe, they can cause problems in certain rare cases. It is a good idea to monitor Windows NT mail lists and newsgroups for a day or two for any potential problems before applying a new service pack.

When installing service packs, be sure to use the -d option when decompressing the service-pack distribution file. This ensures that any directory structures within the archive are preserved when the service-pack distribution file is decompressed.

Useful Windows NT Utility Applications

A few utilities that can make Windows NT easier to use are listed next. These utilities make it easy to launch and manage Windows NT programs.

RipBar Pro

Although the Start button in Windows NT 4.0 makes it easier to launch various applications, virtually all applications are over three mouse clicks away. Sometimes, this makes it cumbersome to select various programs to launch. RipBar Pro solves this problem by providing a palette of application icons as shown in Figure 24.23.

FIGURE 24.23.

RipBar Pro makes it easy to launch various programs.

By using the dialog box shown in Figure 24.24 and the Tuck Away option, more desktop space can be gained by hiding RipBar Pro just as you can hide the Windows NT Start bar.

FIGURE 24.24.
RipBar Pro can be made to Auto Hide by using the Tuck Away option.

URL

The latest version of RipBar Pro can be downloaded from the following URL:
`http://ourworld.compuserve.com:80/homepages/SoftDesign/RipBAR.htm`

TopDesk

When several Windows applications are open at the same time, they can clutter the desktop and make it rather challenging to locate a program. This problem can be solved by using a virtual desktop utility similar to TopDesk. As shown in Figure 24.25, TopDesk can be used to create virtual desktop workspace screens. By using the mouse, it is possible to switch from one virtual desktop workspace screen to the other.

FIGURE 24.25.
TopDesk can be used to create virtual desktop workspace screens.

TopDesk can be configured to have additional virtual windows and various hot keys by using the dialog box shown in Figure 24.26.

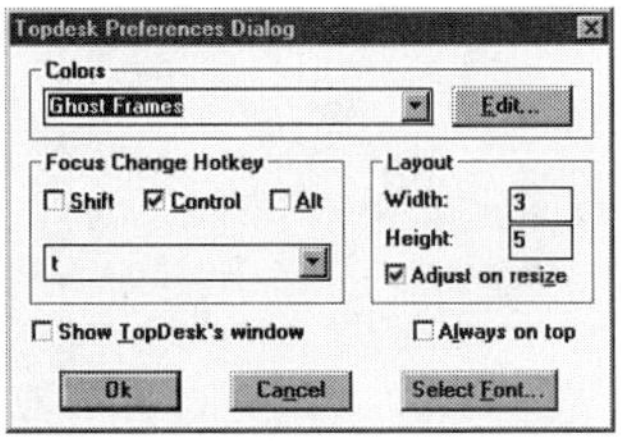

FIGURE 24.26.
TopDesk configuration dialog box.

URL

A copy of TopDesk can be downloaded from the following URL:

`http://www.winsite.com/win3/desktop/`

Windows NT Resource-Kit Utilities

It is highly recommended that you purchase a copy of the Windows NT resource kit if you use Windows NT extensively to perform various tasks. In addition to a number of useful utilities, it also includes additional documentation for Windows NT that is very helpful for administering and maintaining Windows NT systems. A few useful NT resource-kit applications are listed in the next few sections.

Process Viewer

Process Viewer can be used to find out information about applications running on an NT system and *kill* applications that are no longer responding to user input. In addition to this, Process Viewer also can be used to change the priority of a process by using one of the priority buttons shown in Figure 24.27.

FIGURE 24.27.

Process Viewer can be used to administer various applications running on an NT system.

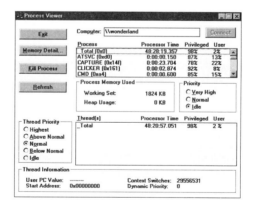

Quick Slice

Although it can't be used to control applications running on a server, Quick Slice is extremely useful in finding out how various applications use the CPU. For example, if the response time of an NT server is unusually slow, it is possible that an errant application is taking up too much CPU time. Such applications can be easily isolated using Quick Slice as shown in Figure 24.28.

FIGURE 24.28.

Quick Slice can be used to find out how the CPU of an NT server is utilized by various applications.

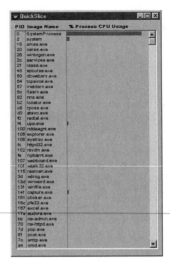

Task Scheduler

The Command Scheduler application of the NT resource kit is a very handy program that can be used to schedule various applications to be run at a certain time.

Summary

Numerous utilities are available for Windows NT to make it easier to administer and manage an NT server. These utilities increase the performance of Windows NT and make it easier to use and manage various Windows programs.

The "Monitoring Web Server Accesses" section demonstrated how to calculate Web-server access statistics using a Web-server log file analyzing application called WebTrends. Afterwards, various aspects of disk fragmentation were discussed and you were shown how to defragment fragmented Windows NT disk partitions. It is important that you stay up-to-date with various Windows NT service packs. Service packs are updates to Windows NT that are released by Microsoft to address various undesirable "features" of Windows NT. Obtaining and installing Windows NT service packs were covered to help keep your NT server up-to-date with the latest Windows NT operating system files. The chapter ended with a discussion of several Windows NT utility applications that can be used to make it easier to use Windows NT.

What's Next?

The next chapter discusses various issues related to setting up and configuring the Windows NT FTP service. The Windows NT FTP service can be used to make various files available to Internet users. You will learn about various aspects of setting up and configuring the Windows NT FTP service as well as security issues associated with setting up an FTP server.

VIII

Enhancing the Capabilities of Your Server

25

Setting Up and Configuring the Windows NT FTP Service

This chapter demonstrates how to set up and configure the Windows NT FTP service. You will be able to make better use of the FTP service by first exploring why you should set up an FTP server. The first section helps you understand the advantages of installing an FTP server on your system. After demonstrating how to install the FTP service, you are shown how it can be configured by using the Control Panel. Although most key features of the FTP service can be controlled via the Control Panel, it is possible to control all aspects of the FTP service by using the registry. Therefore, in order to help you customize the FTP service to better meet your needs, this chapter also illustrates in detail how to modify various features of the Windows NT FTP service by making changes to the registry. Because security is a major concern when setting up any Internet service, an entire section of this chapter is devoted to FTP server security; it covers various security implications of setting up an FTP server and discusses how to avoid possible security breaches on your system due to the FTP service. After reading this chapter, you should be familiar with all aspects of configuring the Windows NT FTP service to distribute information on the Internet in a manner that will not compromise the security of your system.

TECHNICAL NOTE

The Windows NT FTP service complies with requirements for an FTP server defined in the RFCs (Requests for Comments) 959 and 1123.

Why Set Up an FTP Server

Now that you have set up your Web site and have it configured to meet your needs, you might wonder why you should go to all the trouble of setting up an FTP server. Although you can use your Web server to distribute information, you should consider setting up an FTP server if you plan to distribute files such as application programs and documentation that are not meant to be utilized with a Web browser. Setting up a Web server alone might not be sufficient to distribute information because users might not always have access to a Web browser to access your files. On the other hand, due to its text-based nature, almost any *shell account* that has Internet access is capable of accessing an FTP site to upload and download files. For this reason, many users who might not be able to access your Web site will be able to access the same information by using your FTP server. Although text-based Web browsers such as Lynx exist, they are not really meant for downloading and uploading files.

Another reason for setting up an FTP server is the large amount of requests that might need to be fulfilled by your Web server. If your Web server is already handling a large amount of HTTP requests, using an FTP server to distribute files takes away some of the load that must be handled by your Web server. By having a separate service take care of file distribution, you will be able to liberate your Web server for exclusively processing regular HTTP requests.

Also, because the FTP service uses its own log file, it makes matters easier for you to keep track of who accesses what from your system. For example, if you are making certain applications available for download via FTP as opposed to HTTP, you will be able to easily determine who is accessing those files without having to go over a very large Web server access log file. In addition to this, by setting up an FTP server, you also will have better control of various users who upload and download files.

Due to the reasons enumerated in the preceding, and for many other reasons, it is beneficial for you and your users to set up an FTP server on your system. Although there are a few negative aspects associated with setting up an FTP server such as security, there are ways of minimizing such risks. This chapter shows you how to set up an FTP server in a way that will minimize security risks later. However, before such issues are addressed, you first need to install the FTP server on your system. The FTP service is provided with the Windows NT distribution CD-ROM and is very easy to install by following the directions listed in the next section.

Installing the FTP Server

Installing and setting up the Windows NT FTP service is relatively simple. The FTP service is not installed initially by default due to various security risks associated with an FTP server. Soon after installing the FTP service, in the "FTP Server Security" section, you are shown how to secure your FTP server to avoid security breaches. (Be sure to read the section on FTP server security!) Please skip to the next section, which deals with configuring various aspects of the FTP server, if you have already installed the NT FTP service.

SECURITY

The FTP service uses clear text passwords and usernames. For this reason, if someone is "eavesdropping," this person will be able to intercept the password and user ID that's used to access the FTP account. Sensitive information should therefore never be made available to users via FTP unless the information is protected with a robust encryption technology such as PGP (Pretty Good Privacy).

ADMINISTRATION

Due to security issues, you need to be a user who is logged on as the administrator or a user who is a member of the administrator's group before proceeding to install the NT FTP service. You also need the Windows NT distribution CD-ROM because the FTP service is contained on it.

The NT FTP service is installed using the Control Panel application. Invoke the Control Panel application from Program Manager and double-click the Network icon. You see a window that looks similar to the window shown in Figure 25.1. When the Network Settings dialog box appears, click the Add Software button to install the FTP service.

FIGURE 25.1.

The Windows NT FTP service is installed using the Network Settings application.

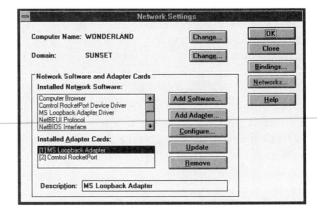

When you click the Add Software button, Windows NT prepares and presents you with a list of network software that you can install on your system. Because the FTP service is a TCP/IP-based service, you should select TCP/IP Protocol and related components from the pull-down menu, as shown in Figure 25.2. Later, you are given a choice of various TCP/IP-based components to install.

FIGURE 25.2.

You can install the Windows NT FTP service by selecting TCP/IP Protocol and related components from the pull-down menu.

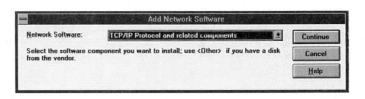

After selecting TCP/IP Protocol and related components, click on Continue to install the FTP service. At this point, you are presented with a list of TCP/IP components that you can install on your system. Various TCP/IP components that already are installed on your system are displayed in red, indicating that you cannot install those services.

If the FTP Server Service is displayed in red with the File Sizes column having a value of 0, it's a good indication that the NT FTP server is already installed on your system. If you are having problems using the FTP service, it also might mean that the FTP server installation on your system has become corrupt. In the latter case, go back to the Network Settings dialog box shown in Figure 25.1, find the FTP server installation among the list of Installed Network Software, and remove the FTP Server Service. After removing the FTP server, reboot your server and start again from the beginning of this section to install the FTP service.

To install the FTP service, click on the checkbox next to FTP Server Service, as shown in Figure 25.3. If Connectivity Utilities are not already installed on your system, you might want to check that box, as well. Doing so also will install client programs for accessing common Internet services such as Finger, FTP, and telnet.

FIGURE 25.3.

Use the Windows NT TCP/IP Installation Options menu to install the NT FTP service by selecting it and pressing the Continue button.

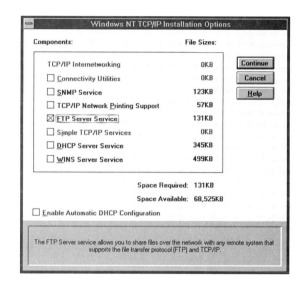

After pressing the Continue button, you are reminded, as shown in Figure 25.4, about the security risk associated with installing the FTP Server Service. At the end of this chapter, you will be shown how to deal with various security issues related to setting up the NT FTP server, so click on the Yes button to proceed with the installation.

FIGURE 25.4.

You will be warned about security risks associated with setting up an FTP server when installing the NT FTP service.

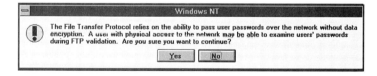

You are now presented with the FTP Service configuration dialog box, similar to the one shown in Figure 25.5. You use this dialog box to configure key aspects of the FTP server, such as home directories of users, maximum number of users allowed at a time, anonymous account settings, and so on.

FIGURE 25.5.

The FTP Service configuration dialog box is used to configure key aspects of the FTP service.

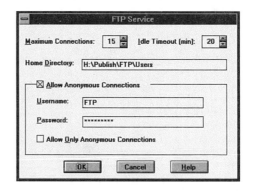

With this dialog box, you can begin to configure your FTP server. Maximum Connections and Idle Timeout are two self-explanatory fields you can change based on your preferences. It is a good idea to specify an idle time-out value that is just a few minutes long to avoid unauthorized access to your FTP server. The Maximum Connections value can be specified depending on the bandwidth of your Internet connection. For example, if your Internet link is just a 28.8 kbps connection, limit the number of connections to about 2. Next, type in the path name of the directory that will contain user directories of users who will be accessing your FTP server. Select an *NTFS (NT File System)* partition for your user directories because the NT FTP service uses NTFS security when determining which FTP users have which rights. If you select a FAT (File Allocation Table) partition, you won't be able to assign user permissions to your FTP users via the File Manager. After typing the path name of the directory containing user directories, check the Allow Anonymous Connections checkbox, as shown in Figure 25.5, to allow anonymous access to your FTP site.

SECURITY

Although you can use the guest account as the account that's used by the anonymous access account, you might want to create a new account that will be used by the anonymous access account. For the purpose of this example, a new user account called FTP will be created to be used by the anonymous access account. More information about creating this account and setting file permissions will be discussed in the "FTP Server Security" section of this chapter. To control who has access to your system, you should disable the guest account unless you need it for some other purpose.

After following the instructions listed earlier in this chapter and pressing the OK button in Figure 25.5, the FTP server is fully installed on your system. When the Network Settings dialog box is invoked from the Control Panel, FTP server will be among the items listed under Installed Network Software, as shown in Figure 25.6. In the future, if you need to configure various options of the FTP server shown in Figure 25.5, you can do so by selecting FTP Server from the Network Settings dialog box and pressing the Configure button. After installing the FTP server, you need to reboot your server. By going into Control Panel and invoking the Services application before doing so, you can make sure that the FTP Server Service is configured to start automatically. By having the FTP service start automatically as soon as your server boots up and establishes its Internet connection, the FTP server will be ready to serve users even if no one is logged on to your server. After rebooting your server, please proceed to the next section to configure various aspects of your FTP server.

FIGURE 25.6.

You can alter various options of the FTP server by selecting FTP Server and pressing the Configure button.

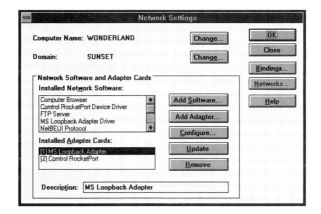

Configuring the FTP Server

In order to configure the FTP server and set user permissions, invoke the Control Panel after rebooting your system. In order to set user permissions and configure the FTP server, you need to log on as the administrator or as a user with administrative permissions. As you can see in Figure 25.7, after rebooting the server a new icon called FTP Server is visible in the Control Panel. Shortly, you will be shown how you can use this application to monitor the status of your FTP server by finding out who is logged on. By using this application, it is also possible to disconnect users and set read/write file permissions for various disk partitions.

By executing the FTP Server application from the Control Panel, you can change various aspects of the FTP server to suit your needs. When you execute the FTP Server icon, you are presented with a dialog box like the one shown in Figure 25.8. As you can see, the FTP Server application displays users who are currently logged on to your FTP server. Because this listing is not automatically updated, you need to manually update it by pressing the Refresh button to get up-to-date information. You also can limit partitions to which users have access via the FTP server by pressing the Security button.

FIGURE 25.7.

You can use the FTP Server application in the Control Panel to monitor the status of your FTP server and disconnect users, as well as set access permissions for various disk partitions.

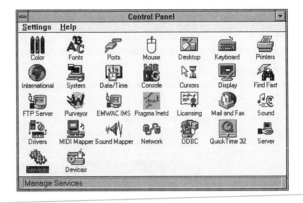

FIGURE 25.8.

You can use the FTP Server application from the Control Panel to determine who is connected to your FTP server as well as to set access permissions for various disk partitions.

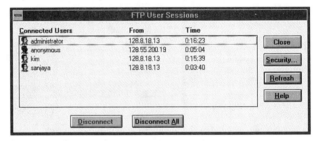

When you press the Security button in Figure 25.8, you can set file permissions for various partitions of your system. A dialog box similar to the one shown in Figure 25.9 appears.

FIGURE 25.9.

The FTP Server Security dialog box is used to specify file access permissions for various disk partitions.

SECURITY

File permissions of users will be overridden by permissions set in the dialog box shown in Figure 25.9. For example, if a user's home directory is in the H: drive and this user has access to all other partitions of the system but only partition H: is assigned read permissions, this user will be restricted to H: and will not be able to access files in any other partition.

The FTP Server Security dialog box is used to specify which disk partitions can be accessed by a user authenticated to access your FTP site. Because rights specified in this dialog box supersede user rights, you can safely lock away users from all partitions that contain sensitive information. By utilizing this dialog box, you should take away read and write permissions from all partitions that contain such sensitive information. Ideally, you should limit FTP access to one NTFS partition to keep things simple.

Defining User Home Directories

When setting up user home directories, an NTFS partition should be used to enforce security on users accessing your FTP site. If a FAT partition is used, you won't be able to limit user access to a certain subdirectory. Although it's possible to use a FAT partition and limit access by restricting access to other disk partitions, this is not a very elegant solution because even an anonymous user will be able to freely roam about the entire directory structure of a FAT partition. The same goes for *HPFS (High Performance File System)* partitions. Because HPFS does not implement file security, it will provide the same level of security FAT provides, which is not much.

> **SECURITY**
>
> Use a different partition than the Windows NT System partition for the FTP server. Although file permissions can be set via NTFS, it's preferable to use a partition that does not contain sensitive information to store user directories that are used by the FTP server. Doing so ensures that even if you make an oversight when setting user permissions, it will not adversely affect the security of your system.

As shown in Figure 25.5, for the purpose of this example, all user directories are stored in the H:\Publish\FTP\Users directory. By creating user directories immediately below this directory, when a user logs on, the user is automatically transferred to his or her directory. The directory structure for user directories specified in Figure 25.5 is listed in Figure 25.10. By setting up a similar directory structure, you can set up the FTP server to automatically take a user who logs on to your FTP site to his or her directory.

For security reasons, you might not want certain directories to be visible to users. You can hide directories you want to keep hidden by invoking the File Manager, selecting the file or directory you want to hide, and then selecting File and Properties (the shortcut for this is Alt+Enter). When the file properties for the file or directory selected earlier are displayed, you can hide the directory by checking the Hidden checkbox.

FTP Server Registry Entries

Although you can modify most major aspects of the FTP server by following the directions listed earlier in the chapter, you can fine-tune various characteristics of your FTP server by making changes to various registry keys. The next few sections demonstrate how you can alter various aspects of your FTP server via the registry.

FIGURE 25.10.

Sample directory structure for home directories of users.

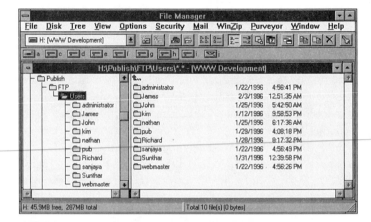

CAUTION

As always, when making changes to the registry, be sure to change only registry keys that are documented. Altering other registry keys can adversely affect the well-being of your system.

Although most registry keys listed in the next section are optional, you must change one registry key so that users can access your FTP site by using a Web browser. If you attempt to access your FTP site by using a version of Netscape prior to version 2.0, you will not get a listing of files. This is because by default, when a listing of files and directories is requested, the NT FTP server displays this data in the MS-DOS directory listing format. However, most Web browsers such as versions of Netscape prior to 2.0 expect the listing to be in the UNIX directory listing format. In order for the directory listing to appear correctly in Web browsers that expect directory lists to be in UNIX format, you need to add a certain registry key.

REGISTRY

After you make changes to the registry, it is necessary to stop and restart the FTP service for the changes to take effect. The FTP service can be stopped and restarted by invoking the Control Panel, executing the services applet, selecting the FTP service, and then stopping and restarting the FTP service.

Registry keys listed in the next few sections are all relative to

```
HKEY_LOCAL_MACHINE\SYSTEM
        \CurrentControlSet
                \Services
                        \Ftpsvc
                                \Parameters
```

Changing Directory Listing Style

In order to change the directory listing style of the NT FTP server to UNIX directory listing style, you have to add the following registry key:

```
Registry key: MsdosDirOutput
Data Type: REG_DWORD, binary
Range: 0 or 1
Value: 1 for MS DOS style directory listing
       0 for UNIX style directory listing
```

When this key is added with a value of 0, the output of the DIR command looks like the output of the UNIX ls -l command. This registry key also changes the slash that's used when the current directory is requested with the PWD command. When the value of MsdosDirOutput is 1 (true), the path contains backward slashes (\). On the other hand, if MsdosDirOutput is 0 (false), the path contains forward slashes (/). An example of what directory listings look like when MsdosDirOutput is 1 and 0 appears in Figures 25.11 and 25.12, respectively.

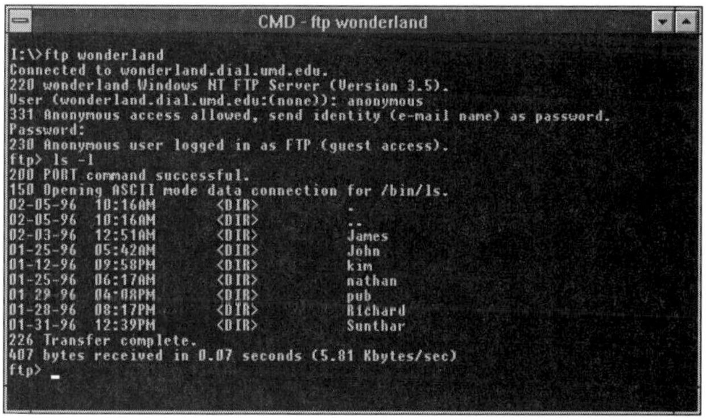

FIGURE 25.11.

Directory listing produced by the ls -l *command when* MsdosDirOutput *is set to* 1 *(default).*

Annotating Directories

When a user accesses a directory on your FTP server, you can inform the user about the contents of the directory by displaying a message. Directories can be annotated by using the following registry key:

```
Registry key: AnnotateDirectories
Data Type: REG_DWORD,binary
Range: 0 or 1
Value: 1 send directory annotations
       0 do not send directory annotations
```

FIGURE 25.12.

Directory listing produced by the ls -l *command when* MsdosDirOutput *is set to* 0.

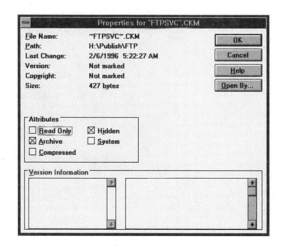

When AnnotateDirectories is set to 1, every time a user changes directories, the FTP server attempts to open a file named ~FTPSVC~.CKM in the new directory. If this file is found, the contents of this file are displayed to the user. This file is usually a *hidden* file. By making this file a hidden file, if a user requests a directory listing, this file will not be visible to the user. A file can be made into a hidden file by selecting it in File Manager, pressing Alt + Enter, and checking the Hidden checkbox, as shown in Figure 25.13.

FIGURE 25.13.

The directory description file (~FTPSVC~.CKM) can be hidden from directory listings by using the File Manager and making it a hidden file.

> **TIP**
>
> The directory annotation feature can be used to inform users where certain files are located and whom they should contact if they run into problems.

Specifying Idle Time-Out Period

You can specify the *idle time-out period* for FTP sessions by setting the following registry key. The user will be logged off automatically if a logon is idle for more than ConnectionTimeout seconds. Make sure the idle time-out period is no longer than a few minutes, unless you have a very good reason for having a longer idle time-out period. If the idle time-out period is too long and a user forgets to log out, someone else can potentially use the active logon to gain unauthorized access to your server.

```
Registry key: ConnectionTimeout
Data Type: REG_DWORD
Range: Value given in seconds
Value: Can be set to the number of seconds the FTP service will allow an FTP
session to be idle
```

> **TIP**
>
> If you do not want your FTP service to disconnect people after a session has been idle, you can set the value of ConnectionTimeout to 0. When ConnectionTimeout is set to 0, idle clients may remain connected indefinitely.

Welcome Message

You also can have a *welcome message* displayed each time a user accesses your FTP server and is validated. In order to define a welcome message, the following registry key needs to be defined with a greeting message:

```
Registry key:    GreetingMessage
Data Type:       REG_MULTI_SZ
Range:           Strings
value            Welcome message
```

> **NOTE**
>
> When a user logs on to your FTP server as an anonymous user and specifies an e-mail address starting with -, the greeting message you just set will not be sent.

Exit Message

You can display an *exit message* when a user logs off the FTP server. This message is contained in the following registry key:

```
Registry key: ExitMessage
Data Type:    REG_SZ
Range:        Text Message
Value:        Can be set to any text message you want to be displayed.
```

Maximum Number of Connections

You can use the registry key MaxConnections to define the maximum number of connections that will be served by the FTP service. By modifying the following registry key, the number of users who can connect to the FTP server at any given time can be controlled. If you are connected to the Internet with a POTS link, limit the number of users to no more than five. If you are using an ISDN line, you may allow up to 25 users to connect to your FTP site at the same time. You may allow a few hundred FTP users to connect to the FTP server at the same time if you are connected to the Internet with a T1 line.

```
Registry key:    MaxConnections
Data Type:       REG_DWORD
Range:           Number
Value            Number of FTP users you allow.
```

> **NOTE**
>
> In order to allow an unlimited number of simultaneous users to access your FTP server, MaxConnections can be set to 0. I don't recommend that you set this value to 0, unless you have a very good reason for doing so.

Maximum Connections Reached Message

The message defined in this registry key is displayed if a user tries to connect to the FTP server when the FTP server is already serving the maximum amount of connections allowed defined in the registry key MaxConnections:

```
Registry key:    MaxClientsMessage
Data Type:       REG_SZ
Range:           Message
Value            Message to be displayed when the FTP server is servicing the
maximum number of FTP users allowed and a new user attempts to log on to the FTP
server.
```

Home Directories

There are two ways to define home directories for FTP users. One way is to go to the Control Panel, execute the network applet, and define the user home directory path (as shown in Figure 25.5). The other way is to modify the following registry key:

```
Registry key:      HomeDirectory
Data Type:         REG_EXPAND_SZ
Range:             Path name
Value              Path to the user's home directory
```

If a user does not have permission to access the directory specified in this registry key, the user is refused access. An event is written to the Windows NT event log if a user tries to log on to the FTP server and the FTP service finds the user's home directory inaccessible.

> **NOTE**
>
> When allowing anonymous FTP, be sure to limit the file access permissions of the user account used by the FTP server to determine anonymous user file access rights. You should make sure that this account has permissions to access only directories you want to be made public.

Logging File Accesses

```
Registry key:  LogFileAccess
Data Type:     REG_DWORD
Range:         0-2
Value:         A value between 0 and 2. The default value 0 does not log accesses.
```

The FTP log file is very valuable. It's the key to determining who accessed what from your FTP server. If LogFileAccess is set to either 1 or 2, it will create a log file to record all file accesses. The log file will be created in the same directory that the FTP service is in. This directory is typically the %SYSTEMROOT%\SYSTEM32 directory. By setting this registry key to 1, a file named FTPSVC.LOG will be created to log all file accesses. If it is set to 2, each day a new log file is created. This log file is named Ftyymmdd.LOG, where yy is the year, mm is the month, and dd is the day.

FTP Server Security

Security is a major concern when an Internet service is set up on any server. Although various tips on security were provided earlier in this chapter, this section summarizes those issues and discusses additional security issues in greater detail. By following the tips and suggestions in this chapter, you will be able to secure your system and use the FTP server in a manner that will not compromise its security.

Limiting FTP Server Access Times

If you are hosting your Web site on Windows NT server, you have more control of when FTP users can log on to the FTP server. However, if you are hosting your Web site using Windows NT Workstation, you do not have control of when users can log on to the FTP server. The

NT FTP server application respects user access times that can be defined in User Manager. For example, as shown in Figure 25.14, a user can be assigned logon hours. In order to invoke the dialog box in Figure 25.14, choose a user in User Manager and select User | Properties from the menu bar. When the User Properties dialog box is displayed, press the Hours button.

FIGURE 25.14.

On Windows NT Server, it's possible to limit the logon hours of users. Logon times set with User Manager are respected by the Windows NT FTP service.

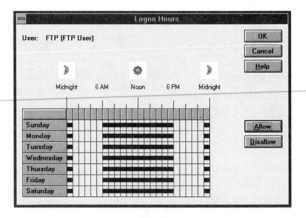

> **NOTE**
>
> The FTP service needs to be stopped and restarted after any user logon hours are changed using the User Manager.

Using FTP to Update Files on a Web Server

If files at your Web site need to be updated by users, it's convenient to set up an FTP account so that users who have to update contents at your Web site will be able to log on to your FTP server and update necessary files. Although this may seem to be a very innocent process, there is a major security issue you should be concerned with when allowing users access to your Web server's directory structure. No FTP account should ever have permission to access your Web server's CGI directory. The reason for this is that any executable file in the CGI directory of your Web server can be executed simply by using a Web browser after the file is uploaded to your Web server's CGI directory. You might think that if you allow only users you trust access to your CGI directory, you need not worry about compromising the security of your Web site. However, allowing users access to the CGI directory can result in very severe security nightmares. Because FTP uses clear text passwords and usernames for user authentication, when users connect to your FTP server, someone can potentially eavesdrop and intercept the password and user ID of a legitimate user. For this reason, you also should ensure that no FTP user has access to your Web server's CGI directory. The FTP server should only allow users to access directories that they need to access.

Summary of FTP Server Security Tips

It's better to limit FTP access to one disk partition. This partition should be an NTFS partition and should not be used to store sensitive information.

No FTP user should have access to your Web server's CGI directory. Allowing an FTP user to upload files to this directory is similar to allowing anyone to upload applications and run them on your server—not a very good thing as far as security is concerned.

You should be aware of risks associated with clear text passwords and user IDs that the FTP server uses. This does not mean that you should now go ahead and uninstall the FTP server. It simply means that users who have FTP access to your system should be able to access only the directories they need to access.

File availability can be limited by specifying access times for your FTP users if you are running Windows NT server. For example, if a user has to periodically upload a new file to your Web server with FTP each day in the morning, you can disable this account from noon until morning.

If the FTP server is used only for file distribution to anonymous users, you should configure the FTP service to accept only anonymous logins. This will prevent regular users trying to log on to the FTP server using their username and password, thus compromising the security of your system.

Administering the FTP Server

After setting up the FTP server, it has to be administered to keep it functioning smoothly. New user accounts have to be created to accommodate needs, and file permissions have to be changed to meet various needs. The following sections discuss a few helpful tips that will aid you in administering your FTP server.

Safely Shutting Down the FTP Service

Unless it is very urgent, you should not shut down the FTP server by stopping the FTP service from the Services application found in the Control Panel. Doing this will immediately disconnect all users from the FTP server. Users who were downloading the last few bytes of a multimegabyte file will not be delighted about getting disconnected. A better way of stopping the FTP server is by using the Pause option in Control Panel's Services application. If you need to bring down the FTP service, you should first check to see if any users are logged on to the FTP server by invoking the FTP Server application from the Control Panel. If users are logged on, the FTP server can be paused and can allow users to complete their file transfers. When the FTP service is paused, all current user sessions will remain active until users log out. However, new FTP connections will not be honored. After all users have logged off the server, it's possible to stop the FTP server without affecting any file transfers.

Analyzing the FTP Server Access Log

You can find out various access statistics for your FTP server by analyzing its log file. For each file opened by a user, a new line is added to the FTP server log file. This log file is invaluable in determining who accessed what from your FTP server. FTP server access log files are usually stored in the `%SYSTEMROOT%\SYSTEM32` directory. In order for the FTP server to log accesses, the registry key `LogFileAccess` must be defined. Please refer to the section "FTP Server Registry Entries" for more information about this key. Each line of the FTP server log file contains information about files that are opened by the user. The information stored in the FTP server access log file is in the following order:

- User's IP Address.
- Username: If this is an anonymous login, the password supplied becomes the username.
- Action: Specifies if a file was opened, created, or appended.
- Complete path name of file that was manipulated by the user.
- Date and time the action took place.

File accesses are logged to the FTP file access log file as follows:

```
*************** FTP SERVER SERVICE STARTING Tue Feb 06 08:16:41 1996
128.8.18.13 sanjaya opened H:\FTP\LaunchCodes.TXT Tue Feb 06 08:19:28 1996
128.8.18.13 sanjaya opened H:\ FTP\TreasureMap.TXT Tue Feb 06 08:19:43 1996
*************** FTP SERVER SERVICE STOPPING Tue Feb 06 08:20:37 1996
```

Summary

This chapter covered various aspects of setting up and configuring the Windows NT FTP service. Although there are certain security risks involved, as long as the FTP server is used properly, these risks can be minimized. You can use the tips and discussions presented in this chapter to make sure your system's security is not compromised due to the FTP server. This chapter also covered different ways of customizing the NT FTP service to meet your needs. In addition to using Control Panel applications to configure the FTP service, you were shown how to modify various aspects of the service by directly making changes to the registry.

What's Next?

The next chapter will demonstrate how to set up the free EMWAC SMTP mail server for sending and receiving Internet e-mail. A number of commercial mail servers also are covered in the following chapter to provide you with an overview of different mail servers available for Windows NT. By evaluating their capabilities, you will be able to select the mail server that best suits your needs. The following chapter also demonstrates how to set up `blat`, a command-line SMTP mail-sending utility.

26

Setting Up a Mail Server

This chapter demonstrates how to set up and configure the Freeware *EMWAC (European Microsoft Windows NT Academic Center)* mail server to send and receive Internet e-mail. After reading this chapter, you will be able to set up a fully functional *SMTP (Simple Mail Transport Protocol)* mail server complete with mail list capabilities. At the end of this chapter, you also will learn about other e-mail servers available for NT. Although you can rely on an external Internet mail server, there are many benefits in setting up your own mail server. If you are relying on an external mail server, the following lists a few advantages of setting up your own SMTP mail server:

- You can communicate with Internet users without depending on an external mail server.
- Your e-mail is delivered promptly. Often, external mail servers handle a large amount of e-mail messages. This can cause e-mail messages to queue and get delayed.
- You have dependable and reliable access to incoming mail and the capability to send outgoing e-mail messages. If something should go wrong with the external mail server, your e-mail may get lost or delayed by as much as a few days!
- You can add new user accounts immediately or delete existing accounts as needed.
- If you must rely on an external mail server, you can use an e-mail server set up on your system as a backup mail server.

Due to this and other reasons, when establishing a presence on the Internet, it's important that you set up your own SMTP mail server. Although there are several commercial e-mail servers available for Windows NT, you can obtain a free e-mail server for Windows NT from the EMWAC Web site. The EMWAC *Internet Mail Service (IMS)* is part of its *Internet tool chest for Windows NT*, which is a collection of Windows NT Internet tools.

URL

The EMWAC Internet tool chest for Windows NT consists of a Freeware HTTP server, Gopher server, WAIS server, WAIS toolkit based on FreeWAIS 0.3, Internet Mail server, and a Finger server. For more information about the Internet tool chest for Windows NT, visit `http://www.emwac.ed.ac.uk/html/toolchst.htm`.

NOTE

Although the EMWAC mail server is provided free of charge, it comes with limited support. If prompt support is of importance to you, one of the commercial mail servers listed at the end of this chapter might better suit your needs. Although you can use the Freeware EMWAC mail server for most of your e-mail needs, there are more advanced mail servers available for Windows NT that provide additional functionality not offered by the EMWAC IMS.

You need the following in order to install the EMWAC mail service:

- Intel, Digital Alpha, or MIPS processor-based computer.
- Windows NT 3.51 Server or Workstation with TCP/IP installed, configured, and functioning properly to access the Internet.
- An NTFS partition.
- Access to a Domain Name Server. This Domain Name Server service might be locally set up on your server or provided as a service by your Internet access provider.
- At least 16 megabytes of RAM. 24 megabytes or more is recommended.

NOTE

Please note that the following directions are for installing version 0.60 of the Freeware EMWAC mail server. If you are installing a later version, the installation procedure may be slightly different from the directions that follow.

Obtaining the Software

Installing the EMWAC mail server is very easy and can be accomplished in just a few minutes. Before beginning to install the mail server, you need to log on to your Windows NT system as the administrator or as a user with administrative privileges. IMS comes in three flavors, depending on the platform you are using:

IMSi386.ZIP	Intel version
IMSAlpha.ZIP	Alpha version
IMSMips.ZIP	MIPS version

Please download the correct version of the EMWAC mail server from the following URL.

URL

You can obtain the EMWAC IMS from

`http://emwac.ed.ac.uk/html/internet_toolchest/ims/install.htm`

After downloading the software, copy the distribution file to a temporary directory. Then, decompress the distribution file to the same temporary directory. The EMWAC mail service distribution file consists of the following files:

SMTPDS.EXE	The SMTP Delivery Agent
SMTPRS.EXE	The SMTP receiver service

POP3S.EXE	The POP3 server service
IMS.CPL	The Control Panel applet used to configure various aspects of the IMS
IMSCMN.DLL	A DLL containing common code used by various IMS services
COPYRITE.TXT	Copyright information about the IMS software
READ.ME	Summary of new features, how to obtain support, and so on

URL

When installing the IMS, if additional information is needed, it can be obtained from

```
http://emwac.ed.ac.uk/html/internet_toolchest/ims/ims.htm
```

NOTE

Please note that you will not be able to start the mail services by executing the .EXE files from the command prompt. The .EXE files are Windows NT services and need to be installed from the command prompt before they can be started as services.

Removing a Prior Version

Before proceeding to install the EMWAC mail service, you have to remove any prior IMS installations from your system. The current version of IMS you might have installed can be determined by logging on to the directory (usually %SYSTEMROOT%\SYSTEM32) containing the mail service files and typing **SMTPDS -version**.

CAUTION

When installing a new version of IMS, it's not sufficient to simply stop the mail services, copy the new files over existing files, and restart the mail services. This can bring about undesired results because different versions may use different registry entries.

In order to remove an older version of IMS, the mail services first need to be stopped. This can be accomplished by invoking the Services applet from the Control Panel and stopping the mail services. The three mail services will typically contain the strings SMTP, EMWAC, and POP3. After stopping the mail services, you can remove them from your system by executing SMTPDS.EXE, SMTPRS.EXE, and POP3S.EXE from the command prompt with the `-remove` argument.

After removing the earlier version of IMS, the new version can be installed. You might need to reboot your system before new IMS files can be copied over the old files.

Installing the EMWAC Mail Server

After obtaining the IMS software and decompressing the distribution file to a temporary directory, you need to copy the essential mail service files to a permanent directory. Because most Windows NT services are located in `%SYSTEMROOT%\SYSTEM32`, you might want to copy IMS files to that directory. Listed next are essential IMS files that you need to copy to either `%SYSTEMROOT%\SYSTEM32` or a permanent directory:

- IMS.CPL (Must be located in `%SYSTEMROOT%\SYSTEM32`)
- SMTPDS.EXE
- SMTPRS.EXE
- POP3S.EXE
- IMSCMN.DLL

After copying IMS.CPL to your `%SYSTEMROOT%\SYSTEM32` directory, when you invoke the Control Panel, you will see the EMWAC mail services icon among other Control Panel icons, as shown in Figure 26.1. Then, by using the `-INSTALL` argument, install all three executable mail service files. This is done by logging on to the permanent directory to which you copied the executable files and typing the following:

```
SMTPRS -INSTALL
SMTPDS -INSTALL
POP3S -INSTALL
```

FIGURE 26.1.

After IMS.CPL is copied to the `%SYSTEMROOT%\`
`SYSTEM32` *directory, the EMWAC mail service icon is visible in the Control Panel.*

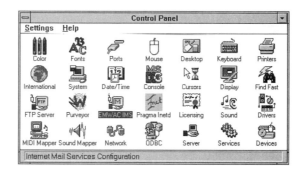

After installing the preceding three programs, they will register themselves with Windows NT's service manager. At this time, if you invoke the Services applet from the Control Panel, you will see the following three mail services installed on your system, as shown in Figure 26.2:

■ EMWAC POP3 Server

■ EMWAC SMTP Delivery Agent

■ EMWAC SMTP Receiver

FIGURE 26.2.

After installing the three mail service applications, they are visible in Control Panel's Services applet.

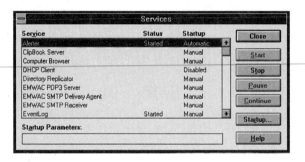

Because the mail server has to be continuously functioning to receive Internet e-mail, it should be set up to start as soon as your server boots. By configuring the EMWAC IMS to start automatically, as soon as your server boots and establishes the Internet link, the mail server will become immediately operational. Because IMS is an NT service, upon establishing the Internet link, even if no one is logged on to your server, the IMS will start accepting e-mail.

You can set up the EMWAC mail services to start automatically by going into Control Panel | Services and selecting all three mail services, one at a time, and changing the startup value to Automatic, as shown in Figure 26.3.

FIGURE 26.3.

By changing the startup value to Automatic in the Control Panel, the EMWAC mail services can be configured to start functioning as soon as NT boots up.

Configuring the EMWAC Mail Server

After installing the IMS, you need to configure it by running the mail server configuration applet from the Control Panel. The EMWAC Internet Mail Services applet is shown in Figure 26.4 and is very easy to use. As shown in Figure 26.4, the configuration applet contains a tabbed data entry form with various input controls. The first tabbed sheet enables you to customize various directories that will be used by the IMS. If you would like to keep all user e-mail in its respective directories, you can specify a virtual path name by appending %USERNAME% to the end of the path name. For example, by specifying a directory such as I:\USERS\MAIL\%USERNAME% as the mailbox directory, all user e-mail will be stored in its own directory in the I:\USERS\MAIL\ directory. If you would rather have all e-mail stored in a directory that's relative to a user's home directory, you also can specify a path such as %HOME%\INETMAIL\INBOX.

FIGURE 26.4.
The EMWAC Internet Mail Services applet.

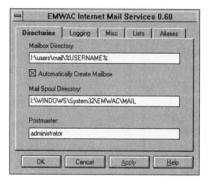

> **NOTE**
>
> Please note that after making any changes in the IMS configuration applet, you need to manually stop and restart all three mail services for the changes to take effect.

After specifying mail directories, you need to designate a user who will be the postmaster for your system. If mail traffic on your system is low, you might want to define the administrator as the postmaster. However, if you expect to process a large number of e-mail messages, you might want to create a new user and designate this user to be the postmaster. After providing a valid NT username as the postmaster and specifying valid directories, the IMS is configured and ready to use. However, before users can log on to read their e-mail, user accounts have to be assigned a certain Windows NT user right. Also, don't forget to stop and restart the mail services for the changes you just made to take effect.

Setting Up User Permissions

Before users can log on to the mail server from various mail clients to read their e-mail, they should be given the Advanced Windows NT user right "Log on as a batch job." In order to assign this right to a single user, or many users, the User Manager program has to be invoked. After selecting a user or group you wish to allow to log on and read e-mail messages, click on Policies and then User Rights. When the User Rights Policy dialog box appears, click on the Show Advanced User Rights checkbox so that the advanced user right "Log on as a batch job" becomes visible in the pull-down list, as shown in Figure 26.5. After clicking on the Show Advanced User Rights checkbox, you can select additional users or groups you wish to provide e-mail services by clicking on the Add button. After selecting additional users and groups, click on OK to assign the advanced user right "Log on as a batch job" to users and groups you selected. Then, users and groups this right was assigned to will be able to send and receive Internet e-mail using the EMWAC IMS.

SECURITY

Rather than selecting individual users one by one and assigning them the "Log on as a batch job" user right, you can create a user group called *EMWAC Mail Users*. This group can be assigned the user right "Log on as a batch job." Then, users you wish to provide e-mail services to can be made members of this group. This will allow you to have more control of who can use your Internet mail server.

FIGURE 26.5.

The advanced user right "Log on as a batch job" has to be assigned from User Manager to users and/or groups to whom you wish to provide e-mail services.

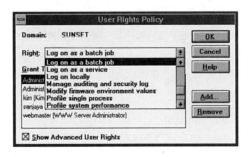

After following these steps, the EMWAC mail server is now configured and ready to accept and deliver Internet e-mail.

URL

You can obtain additional installation instructions for installing the EMWAC mail server from

`http://emwac.ed.ac.uk/html/internet_toolchest/ims/install.htm`

Setting Up E-Mail Aliases

Mail messages received by the IMS can be configured to be redirected to another address. For example, if e-mail to `info@domain.name` has to be redirected to `webmaster@domain.name`, an alias can be created for `info@domain.name`. This is done by executing the IMS applet from the Control Panel and clicking on the Aliases tab; then you can create an alias, as shown in Figure 26.6. In the space provided for the username, type the user for whom you would like to create an e-mail alias. In the case of this example, the username will be `info`. In the space provided for Map to, type the address to where you want the e-mail redirected. For the purpose of this example, the Map to username is `webmaster`.

FIGURE 26.6.

You can create an e-mail alias by specifying the user whose e-mail you want to be redirected and the e-mail address to where you want the e-mail to be redirected.

Then, click on Set to define the alias and click on OK to get rid of the dialog box. In order for the change to take effect, don't forget to stop and restart the mail services. After the mail services are stopped and restarted, all e-mail directed to `info@domain.name` will be redirected to `webmaster@domain.name`.

You also can use wildcards to define e-mail aliases. For example, the alias `T*Y` would match any username that begins with a *T* and ends with a *Y*. Please note that aliases are not case-sensitive. Also, e-mail aliases are processed from top to bottom. Therefore, it's a good idea to move all aliases with wildcards to the bottom of the list to avoid misdirection of e-mail.

Using the EMWAC Mail Server for Mailing Lists

The EMWAC IMS also enables you to define Internet mailing lists. With the aid of mailing lists, it's possible to create discussion groups via e-mail. To create a mailing list, invoke the IMS applet from the Control Panel and click on the Lists tab. At first, the Lists tab doesn't contain any predefined e-mail lists and looks like the dialog box shown in Figure 26.7.

In order to define an e-mail list, press the Add button of the Lists tab. You see a new dialog box similar to the one shown in Figure 26.8.

FIGURE 26.7.

You can use the Lists tab of the IMS configuration applet to define e-mail lists.

FIGURE 26.8.

By clicking on Add from the Lists tab, you can create new mailing lists and insert or delete mail list users.

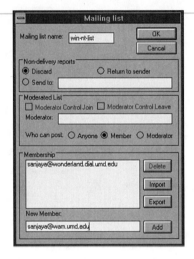

You can create an e-mail list by using the dialog box shown in Figure 26.8. For the purpose of this example, you are shown how to create a mailing list called win-nt-list with two list members. The list will be set up so that only members of the list can post messages to the list, and undeliverable messages will be discarded. Also, the list will be configured so that users can join and leave the list at any time without moderator intervention.

When creating an e-mail list, you first need to give the list a name. This name is typed in the space provided for the Mailing list name. After typing the name of the e-mail list, you need to decide what should be done about non-deliverable mail message reports. The options you have are Discard, Return to sender, and Send to. This information is used by the mailing list when it cannot deliver a message to a certain user. This can be due to an e-mail server being down, incorrect e-mail address, network problems, and so on. If this option is set to Discard, all messages that cannot be delivered will be discarded without generating any reports. The Return to sender option will send a message non-delivery report to the sender. By using the last option, Send to, you can have all undeliverable messages directed to a certain e-mail address. For the purpose of this example, Discard is selected.

You can set up the new e-mail list you're creating as a moderated or unmoderated mail list. If you would like the list to be moderated by someone, you need to type this user's e-mail address in the space provided. The moderator can be set up to control those leaving and joining the mail list. Unless you are maintaining a low-volume, private e-mail list, you should not set up the moderator to control users joining and leaving the list because this can be time-consuming and cause delays. For the purpose of this example, this space is left blank so that users can join and leave the list as they please.

The EMWAC IMS also enables you to control who is allowed to post messages to the mail list. The three options you have available are Anyone, Member, and Moderator. By selecting Member, you can make sure that only members who subscribe to the mail list can post messages. In this example, the mail list is configured to enable only members to post messages.

If you have a text file of users, you can use the Import/Export feature to add or save several users at the same time. When importing a file, each line of the file should contain only a comment or information for one user. Lines that begin with a # are interpreted as comments. The general format of text files that can be imported is

```
# Comment
FirstName LastName <userID@domain.name>
```

It's possible to manually add users to the mail list by typing the e-mail address of users in the space under New Member and clicking on the Add button, as shown in Figure 26.8. (By using the Delete button, you can delete users from the list.) After adding users, the mail list is now all set up and ready to serve users. However, before the mail server starts accepting list e-mail, the IMS service has to be stopped and restarted for the changes to take effect.

Internet users can join an existing mail list by sending a message to the list server with the text SUBSCRIBE as the body of the message. Users should direct list commands to the address of the e-mail list with -request appended to the name of the mail list. For example, the mail list you just created is called win-nt-list. Therefore, commands to this mail list should be directed to win-nt-list-request@domain.name.

The next sections discuss the list commands understood by IMS. These commands should be sent as the body of the message with the string -request appended to the list name.

SUBSCRIBE or JOIN

Users can use SUBSCRIBE or JOIN to subscribe to an existing mail list by including the string SUBSCRIBE or JOIN in the body of the e-mail message. After the IMS receives a subscribe request, it responds by sending a message to the sender indicating if the user was successfully subscribed. However, if Moderator Configured Join is enabled, all subscribe messages will be sent to the moderator of the list.

UNSUBSCRIBE **or** LEAVE

Use the UNSUBSCRIBE or LEAVE command to leave a mail list. If Moderator Control Leave is enabled for a mail list a user wants to unsubscribe from, the unsubscribe message will be forwarded to the moderator of the list. Then, the moderator needs to manually delete the user from the mail list. For the purpose of this example, if a user wants to leave the mailing list that was just created (win-nt-list@domain.name), the request should be sent to win-nt-list-request@domain.name with the body of the message being UNSUBSCRIBE.

HELP

The HELP command sends to the user that requested the information a list of commands that are understood by IMS mail list server.

STOP

The STOP command prevents IMS from processing the remainder of a message searching for list commands. The STOP command is particularly useful when a user whose mail client automatically inserts a signature subscribes to a mail list. By using the STOP command immediately after the list server command, the list server will stop processing the remainder of the message and not attempt to interpret the user's signature as a list command.

EMWAC Mail Server Registry Entries

Although most aspects of the EMWAC mail service can be configured via the Control Panel applet, some settings cannot be modified using the Control Panel program. In order to change these settings, you need to make various changes to certain registry keys. Listed next are a few important registry entries used by the EMWAC IMS.

CAUTION

You need to be careful when making changes to the registry to alter various attributes of the EMWAC mail service. When making changes to the registry, please be sure to make modifications only to specific registry entries.

REGISTRY

The registry keys listed next are common to more than one mail service. These keys can be found at

HKEY_LOCAL_MACHINE\SOFTWARE\EMWAC\IMS

- Registry key name: `MailInBoxDir`

  Data type: `REG_SZ`

  Description: Each EMWAC IMS user must have a mail box. This registry key defines the location of each user's mail box.

  Default: `%HOME%\INETMAIL\INBOX`

- Registry key name: `AutoCreateInboxDir`

  Data type: `REG_DWORD`

  Description: If a user's mail box directory does not already exist, it will be automatically created when needed if `AutoCreateInboxDir` is set to 1.

  Default: 1

- Registry key name: `LocalFailuresToPostmaster`

  Data type: `REG_DWORD`

  Description: By changing `LocalFailuresToPostmaster` to a nonzero value, all delivery failures will be copied to the postmaster account.

  Default: 0

- Registry key name: `MailSpoolDir`

  Data type: `REG_SZ`

  Description: When new mail is accepted for delivery or is being transported within your system, the EMWAC IMS needs a place to store these messages. The location these messages can be stored in is defined in this registry key.

  Default: `%SystemRoot%\EMWAC\MAIL`

- Registry key name: `Postmaster`

  Data type: `REG_SZ`

  Description: The IMS needs to know a user who will act as a postmaster for your system. The postmaster account is defined in this registry key.

  Default: administrator

SMTP Receiver

Listed next are SMTP receiver service specific registry keys.

REGISTRY

SMTP receiver service specific registry keys are located at

`HKEY_LOCAL_MACHINE\SYSTEM\CurrentControlSet\Services\SMTPRS\Parameters`

■ Registry key name: `InlogEnabled`

Data type: `REG_DWORD`

Description: If this value is a nonzero value, SMTP receive service activities will be logged.

Default: 0.

■ Registry key name: `ProhibitMailRelay`

Data type: `REG_DWORD`

Description: The SMTP mail service can deliver messages to users of your local machine as well as the Internet. When this registry value is zero, mail addressed to sites other than the local machine also will be accepted for delivery.

Default: 0

SMTP Delivery Agent

Listed next is an SMTP delivery service related registry key.

REGISTRY

SMTP delivery service related registry keys can be found at

`HKEY_LOCAL_MACHINE\SYSTEM\CurrentControlSet\Services\SMTPDS\Parameters`

■ Registry key name: `OutlogEnabled`

Data type: `REG_DWORD`

Description: SMTP delivery service activities can be logged by assigning a nonzero value to this registry key.

Default: 0

POP3 Server

POP3-specific configuration information is stored under the following registry key.

REGISTRY

POP3 server related registry entries can be found at

`HKEY_LOCAL_MACHINE\SYSTEM\CurrentControlSet\Services\POP3S\Parameters`

■ Registry key name: `MessageExtension`

Data type: `REG_SZ`

Description: When a user's e-mail is received by IMS, it is stored in each user's mail box directory until it is retrieved by the user with the aid of a mail client application. As shown in Figure 26.9, all user e-mail is stored in the user's mail box directory with the default extension .MSG. This extension can be changed by modifying this registry key.

Default: MSG

FIGURE 26.9.

All user e-mail is stored in each user's mail box directory with the extension defined in the registry key `MessageExtension`.

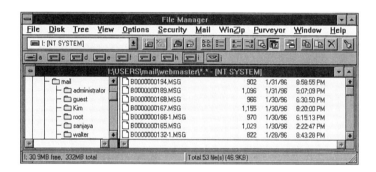

■ Registry key name: `Timeout`

Data type: `REG_DWORD`

Description: The idle time-out period can be defined in seconds by modifying this registry key.

Default: 600

■ Registry key name: `Pop3LogEnabled`

Data type: `REG_DWORD`

Description: If this value is nonzero, POP3 logging is enabled.

Default: 0

Setting Up a Command-Line Mail Sender

In addition to providing users the capability to send and receive Internet e-mail, you can use the e-mail server you just set up for a variety of other purposes. A handy way to keep track of various activities scheduled to run on your server is to have the results of those activities e-mailed to you. This can be done with the aid of a command-line mail sender such as `Blat`. For example, when performing a tape backup, the results of the backup, such as error messages, can be saved to a log and e-mailed to the system administrator.

TOOLS

By installing Blat on your server, you will be able to set up batch scripts that e-mail you results of various tasks such as tape backups. Blat also is used by CGI programs to e-mail user feedback and comments.

Blat is a public domain Windows NT console utility that sends the contents of a file as an e-mail message using SMTP. Blat is useful for creating scripts where mail has to be sent automatically (CGI scripts, results of backups, batch jobs, and so on). You can install Blat in just a few minutes after downloading it from the Web site listed next.

URL

You can obtain Blat from

`http://gepasi.dbs.aber.ac.uk/softw/blat.html`

After downloading Blat, you need to install it on your NT server. Blat is distributed with the source code. The only two files you really need are Blat.exe and gwinsock.dll. These two files should be located in the `%SystemRoot%\SYSTEM32` directory. After decompressing the Blat distribution file, you need to copy Blat.exe and gwinsock.dll to `%SystemRoot%\SYSTEM32`. Then, you can install Blat on your system by typing

Blat -install your_site_address your_userid@your_site_address

Example:

```
your_site_address = wonderland.dial.umd.edu
your_userid@your_site_address = sanjaya@wonderland.dial.umd.edu
```

After typing the command preceding this paragraph, Blat will install itself and let you know that the SMTP server was set properly.

TIP

At this point, if you want to quickly e-mail a file, you can do so by typing

`Blat <filename> -t <recipient>`

Other NT Mail Servers

In addition to the EMWAC mail service, there are a number of other mail servers for Windows NT. Although these mail servers are not free, they come with better support than the

EMWAC server and provide additional functionality. Mail servers listed next are also more robust and secure.

NTMail Mail Server

NTMail is a set of feature-rich mail services for Windows NT. These services provide a computer running Windows NT Server or Workstation with SMTP and POP3 services for sending and receiving Internet e-mail. NTList is an addition to NTMail and provides additional functionality by providing list server capabilities.

> **URL**
>
> You can find the latest version of NTMail and its documentation at Internet Shopper's WWW site. You can obtain NTMail from
>
> `http://www.net-shopper.co.uk/software/ntmail/index.htm`

The following are some features of NTMail:

- Utilizes Windows NT's own user database or user accounts in the registry. When NT's user accounts are used, a new NTMail account will be created for users of your NT server when the user's first e-mail message is received by NTMail.
- Restrictions can be imposed on incoming mail based on message size and domain name.
- Supports "holiday messages" when users are away. Users also can change their holiday message from anywhere on the Internet by filling in a form and submitting it.
- Has a mail server activity log that logs various user activity including incorrect password login attempts.
- Messages can be forwarded or automatically responded to with a predefined message. When automatically responding to a message, fields from the original message can be used to personalize the message being sent.
- Includes a finger server that provides information about users such as the number of unread messages and the user's *plan*. The user's plan is a short text description that will be displayed when someone queries an NTMail user with a finger client.

Post.Office Mail Server

Post.Office is a secure and easy-to-use mail service for Windows NT. In addition to providing SMTP and POP3 services, Post.Office also includes an integrated finger server. One of the highlights of Post.Office is its capability to be administered via a Web browser using forms. If you don't always have ready access to your NT server, you should consider Post.Office because it can be administered remotely using a Web browser.

The following are some features of Post.Office:

■ In order to ensure that your system's security is not compromised, Post.Office functions independently from NT's user database. Therefore, in order to use Post.Office, users do not require an account in your NT system.

■ Only users of certain domains and hosts can be allowed to access the mail server.

■ If tampering or an attempted security breach is suspected, Post.Office sends a warning message to the System Administrator.

■ With the aid of forms, virtually all aspects of the mail server can be administered and configured from anywhere on the Internet.

■ When you go on vacation, Post.Office can be configured to send an automatic message to users who send you e-mail.

URL

You can obtain Post.Office mail server for Windows NT from

`http://www.software.com/prod/po/po.html`

MetaInfo's Sendmail with POP3

MetaInfo's Sendmail for Windows NT is a direct port of the UNIX version 8.7 of Sendmail. This mail server brings the power, flexibility, and efficiency of UNIX into the user-friendly and reliable environment of Windows NT.

Following are some features of MetaInfo's Sendmail:

■ Can be used as a mail server for multiple domains hosted on the same computer.

■ The POP3 server is integrated with NT user manager to provide all users of your system Internet e-mail capabilities. New POP3 accounts are automatically created for valid NT users.

■ Mail to a user can be automatically forwarded by using a .Forward file.

URL

You can obtain MetaInfo's Sendmail with POP3 from MetaInfo's Web site at

`http://www.metainfo.com/MetaInfo/Sendmail/Homepage.htp`

Summary

This chapter demonstrated how to install and configure the Freeware EMWAC mail server. All aspects of setting up the mail server, from where to obtain the software to giving users necessary permissions to read their e-mail, were covered. It also discussed how to use the mail list feature of the EMWAC mail server. By following directions given in this chapter, you can install and configure the EMWAC mail server to run on your system. To provide you with an overview of various commercial mail servers available for NT, several commercial mail servers also were discussed at the end of this chapter. If you require more information about these mail servers, their URLs also were given. In addition to setting up the EMWAC mail server, you also were shown how to install and use Blat, a command-line SMTP mail sending program.

What's Next?

Aside from the EMWAC mail list server, there are several other mail list programs available for Windows NT that offer more functionality. Although you can use the EMWAC list server to host a mail list, it's not very customizable. The next chapter demonstrates how to set up a more feature-rich mail list server for NT. The following chapter also demonstrates how you can effectively use a mail list server to distribute information as well as create discussion groups on the Internet.

27

Setting Up a
Mail-List Server

Since the beginning of the Internet, e-mail has been used by millions of people to communicate with each other. The Internet is no longer the simple network that existed a few years ago. It's becoming more complex as new information distribution technologies such as MBone (Multicast Backbone on the Internet) are implemented for tasks such as distributing multicast video streams on the Internet. However, with the advent of all these technologies, Internet e-mail has survived for over a decade and will continue to be a major medium of information exchange among Internet users.

Mail-list servers use Internet e-mail as the principle means of communication. As shown in Figure 27.1, a mail-list server functions by distributing a message sent to it to all its members.

FIGURE 27.1.

When a message is sent to a mail-list server, it is sent to all users who subscribe to the mail list.

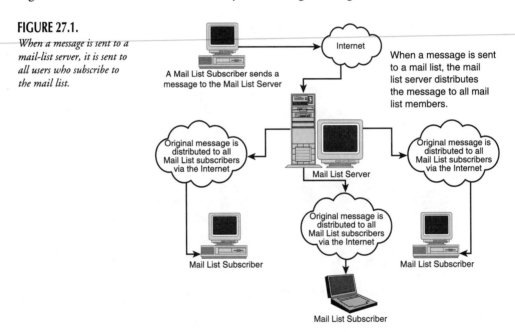

There are many advantages to setting up a mail-list server. As you will learn shortly, it is very easy to set up a mail-list server and use it for a variety of tasks. Let us first examine some reasons for setting up a mail-list server and find out how others are using them.

Why Set Up a Mail-List Server?

Unlike other Internet information-distribution services, the amount of work involved in hosting a mail-list server increases with the number of users who are subscribed to various mail lists. Depending on the number of users being serviced by the list server, a fair amount of network resources and time might be needed to maintain it. Before investing valuable resources to maintain a list server, it is worthwhile to explore why you should set up a mail-list server. Since you are reading this chapter, you must probably already have some very good reasons for setting up a mail-list server. Before discussing issues related to setting up and maintaining a list server, the next few sections discuss why you should set up a list server, and they explain, using examples, how a mail-list server can be used to its maximum potential.

How a Mail-List Server Complements a Web Site

Web sites are very effective for distributing information on the Internet. However, Web sites typically require users to visit that particular Web site for information. If the Web site contains valuable information, users who visit it will probably add it to their list of Internet bookmarks. If a user has been on the Internet for a while, this new bookmark will become one of a few hundred bookmarks. Often, when new and interesting information is added to a Web site, there is no way to inform those who will find the new information useful. This is a major drawback associated with solely relying on a Web site to distribute information. A mail-list server can be used to effectively nullify this drawback, with which virtually all Web sites are plagued.

A list server complements a Web site by providing the content publisher another way of distributing information and inviting users to visit the Web site for more detailed information. For example, you might want to create a newsletter and e-mail it to an interested group of people via a mail list to keep them informed of latest developments related to your organization and summarize new additions that were made to its Web site. If a user is interested in a particular summary, the user can then visit the corporate Web site for more detailed information. Refer to Figure 27.2 for an example of how a newsletter can be used to attract users to a Web site. Figure 27.2 contains part of the Advanced Systems User Group's (ASUG) monthly electronic newsletter. ASUG is a Windows NT user group in the Washington D.C. area, and as you can see, the monthly newsletter is used to invite its members to visit the ASUG Web site for more information. A mail-list server complements a Web site because it can be used to attract visitors.

FIGURE 27.2.

A newsletter distributed via a mail list can be used to invite list members to visit a Web site for more information.

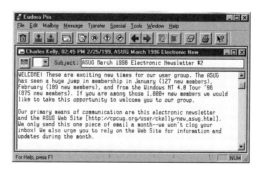

Benefits of Setting Up a Mail-List Server

A mail-list server can be used for a variety of tasks. Many organizations use mail-list servers to keep customers informed of new developments and host public discussion forums on the Internet. For example, at the time of this writing, a Yahoo! search on the search string "`mail list`" found 845 matches. As you can see in Figure 27.3, these matches are for Internet mail lists that discuss various topics.

FIGURE 27.3.

A Yahoo! search alone yields about 850 different topics covered by various Internet mail lists.

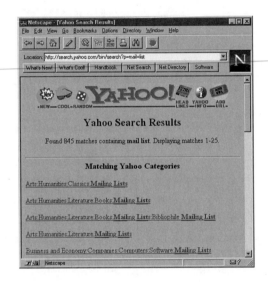

The large number of topics listed in Figure 27.3 proves the usefulness of mail-list servers. Listed next are various benefits of setting up a mail-list server. Some of these benefits will be discussed in greater detail shortly.

- ■ Obtain user feedback
- ■ Discuss a topic in detail
- ■ Keep users informed
- ■ Discuss various hobbies and interests
- ■ Distribute an electronic publication
- ■ Provide technical support
- ■ Product updates
- ■ Question and answer forum
- ■ Public service

Obtain User Feedback

The ability to obtain user feedback is a major advantage in setting up a mail-list server. Although e-mail can be used for the same purpose, it does not give users the chance to discuss various problems they are having. For example, when a user has a problem with a certain product or service, another mail-list member might be able to help this user by providing a possible solution or work-around to solve the problem. This helps cut down support costs and also provides a way to obtain user feedback.

Discuss a Topic in Detail

Mail lists are well suited for discussing a topic in detail. Because one topic is discussed in detail, such lists usually attract various experts in the field being discussed, and they become a rich source of information for many people. An example of such a list is shown in Figure 27.4.

FIGURE 27.4.

The firewall mail list is an example of a mail list set up to discuss a topic in detail.

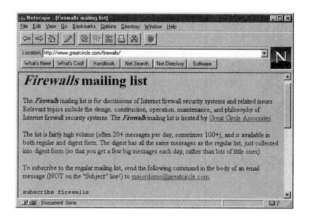

Keep Users Informed

Since the beginning of the Internet, e-mail has been used to keep users informed of new developments. Although it is not necessary to set up a mail list to inform users of new developments, not setting up a mail-list server can turn into a lot of work if you are dealing with a relatively large user database. For example, after requesting to be kept informed of new developments, a user might change his or her mind. In a similar manner, a new user might want to be added to the list so she will be kept informed of new developments. This can create a lot of work; new users have to be manually added to a list, and various users need to be manually deleted from the list. In addition to this, the latest list might not always be available to everyone, and more than one person might need to contact the group of people in the list. Because everything is done manually, when a change is made, it needs to be propagated to everyone else who might need to contact people in the list. This can be unnecessarily time-consuming. On the other hand, a mail list can be set up to automate this process. Users will then be able to join and leave the list by themselves. By using a special password, those who are authorized to *post* to the list will then be able to send messages to the list server. Refer to Figure 27.5 for an example of a mail list set up to keep users informed of new developments.

FIGURE 27.5.

The Internet Shopper NTMail update mail list is an example of a mail list set up to inform customers of new products.

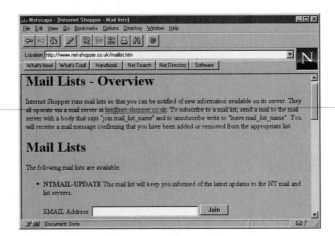

Discuss Various Hobbies and Interests

Mail lists are also effective for creating discussion forums on the Internet for people to discuss various hobbies and interests. Although such forums are not directly beneficial to an organization business-wise, a mail list can be set up to discuss a special interest or hobby as a way of giving something back to the Internet and improving your company's public image. The Yacht mail list shown in Figure 27.6 is an example of a mail list set up to discuss a special interest.

FIGURE 27.6.

The Yacht mail list.

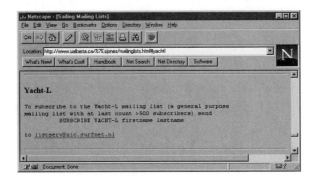

Distribute an Electronic Publication

As shown in Figure 27.7, an electronic publication can be easily distributed to many users using a mail-list server. Again, an advantage of using a mail-list server instead of a mail server alone is the fact that when a mail-list server is used, list members can join and leave the list whenever they want to.

FIGURE 27.7.

The News of the Weird Mailing List is a mail list that has been set up to distribute an electronic publication.

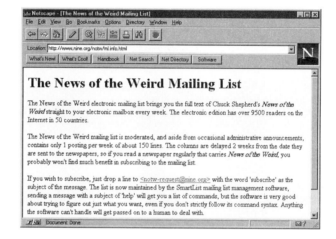

Provide Technical Support

Mail-list servers are well suited for providing technical support to users. Although regular e-mail can be used to do this, it is not very efficient. If one user encounters a problem, it is likely that others will encounter the same problem. When a mail-list server is used, all users who are subscribed to the list server will find out how to deal with many potential problems. This can cut down on the time and resources needed to provide technical support. Furthermore, mail lists also enable users to help each other rather than wait for a technical support person to respond to a message. This does not mean that users should be left to help each other; it can easily lead into a public relations nightmare. It just means that a user having a problem will often find out how to solve the problem in more ways than one.

Public Service

An example of a mail list used to provide a public service is shown in Figure 27.8. The Webserver-NT mail list has been set up by Process Software to discuss various issues related to publishing information on the Internet with Windows NT. Although Process Software does not directly benefit from this mail list, it's a good way to inform Windows NT users about Process Software's Web publishing applications. Setting up a mail list to discuss a product or service you are marketing is often mutually beneficial for you and your users.

FIGURE 27.8.

The Webserver-NT mail list discusses various issues related to developing Web sites on the Internet with Windows NT.

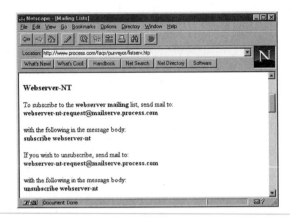

Mail-List Server Requirements and Tips

Listed next are a few tips that will help you host an efficient and user-friendly mail-list server.

Bandwidth Requirements

It is not desirable to host a high-volume mail list on a POTS link to the Internet. This can virtually take away all your limited bandwidth and render your Internet connection worthless. However, if your mail list is going to consist of only a few dozen users, you will be able to make do with a POTS link as long as list members do not send extremely long messages or binary files to your list. On the other hand, if you intend to set up a mail list that is expected to have a few hundred or thousand users, at the very least make sure you have an ISDN line to the Internet.

Hardware Requirements

As far as system resources are concerned, by far the most limiting factor is the bandwidth of your Internet connection. A list server is not very hardware-intensive. A computer running Windows NT with a 486/DX2/66 or better processor will often be sufficient. However, depending on the amount of list members and other applications being run at the same time, additional RAM or processing power may be required. When running a mail-list server along with other network services, a minimum of 24 MB of RAM for NT Workstation and 32 MB of RAM for NT Server is recommended.

Keep Messages Short

You should not use a newsletter distributed via a mail list to list everything that happened in your organization in the last month—from the new lunch menu to a groundbreaking product or service that was just made public. Chances are that your list members already receive dozens of e-mail messages a day. Long messages distract recipients by shifting away their attention from the contents of the message to its length. (Ever read an e-mail message wondering when it will be over?) On the other hand, Web sites are there to provide detailed information. Use your Web site to publish detailed information, keep newsletters short and concise, and include URLs at your Web site for more information.

Things to Watch Out for

There are a few things you should watch out for when hosting a mail list. Unlike other types of information-distribution systems, maintaining a mail list is a rather *sensitive* job. Messages sent to a mail list are distributed to all its list members; a mishap can easily make quite a few people unhappy. Listed next are a few things you should watch out for when putting a mail-list server to use.

Binary Files

You should do everything you can to discourage users from sending binary files to a list server. Although files can be attached to an e-mail message when they are sent, the work involved in dealing with such messages literally multiplies when attachments are involved. For example, if a list has 200 members and a 2 KB file is sent to the list with a 200 KB file attached, over 40 megabytes of data needs to be transmitted by your list server! This is *not* good. If not for the attachment, in order to distribute the message to the list, only 400 KB of data needs to be transmitted. As you can imagine, even if a few people send e-mail messages to a list server with attachments, things can get rather nasty. This situation can cascade into a nightmare if some of these messages get sent back to the mail-list server and get redistributed. Such an incident can easily add several dozen unhappy e-mail messages to your inbox. It is a good idea to make a note of this in the "welcome letter" that is sent to new members as soon as they are subscribed to a mail list. You might want to make the second line of the welcome letter read something similar to: "Please do not send e-mail messages with attachments to this list for any reason." In order to enforce this rule, your list server should let you specify the largest message size it will accept. Messages that are larger than the size specified will then be ignored and not circulated.

Subscribing Users Without Their Knowledge

After setting up a mail-list server, it might be tempting for you to add every person that e-mails you in search of information to a mail list. Although in principle it is a good idea, in reality it can turn into a public relations nightmare. For example, after a few dozen users are subscribed to such a mail list and start exchanging mail messages to and from the list, some are going to wonder how and from where they are getting all these messages. These users might tolerate the e-mail for a while— until a user decides to ask a very simple question on the list. When people intentionally subscribe to a list, they more or less expect this kind of e-mail. However, when users are subscribed to a list without their knowledge and start receiving trivial questions like how to unzip a `.zip` file, they are less tolerant. Therefore, you should avoid subscribing users to a list without their knowledge. If you are still not convinced, I am sure Figure 27.9 will convince you of consequences associated with subscribing users to a list without their permission. What's shown in Figure 27.9 is a number of e-mail messages that resulted from a number of users being automatically subscribed to a list. Just as soon as someone asked a trivial question, several users began sending e-mail to the list asking them to be taken off the list.

FIGURE 27.9.

Subscribing users to a mail list without their permission is not a very good idea and can result in not-so-desirable consequences.

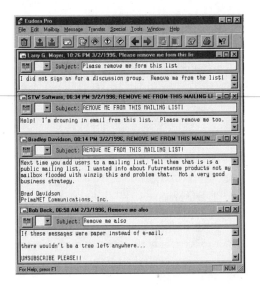

The purpose of Figure 27.9 is not to downgrade the company that automatically subscribed a few users to their mail list. It is merely to show consequences of not asking permission to do so. Incidentally, the company that hosted the mail list in Figure 27.9 makes a wonderful Web-publishing tool that was covered in an earlier chapter.

If you add users to a mail list without their knowledge, make sure it is a very low-volume, *announcement only* mail list that's set up so that its members can't post messages to the list. Such a list can be used to distribute information about new developments, products, and services.

Troublesome Users

Just like the real world, the Internet has its own share of troublesome people who wreak havoc by disrupting the normal flow of things. Because mail lists usually discuss various issues that might challenge ideals and beliefs of some people, it's very easy for someone to start a *flame war*. A flame is generally a bunch of messages that are full of personal insults and very little substance. They often start innocently but can get quite nasty. Flame wars are undesirable. They waste system resources and distract users from more important things that are worth discussing by shifting the focus from the topic being discussed to various personal beliefs and viewpoints. It is important to keep flame wars under control. If a disruptive user is discovered, it is generally desirable to politely e-mail the user and ask the user to stop what he or she is doing. It's not a very good idea to do this publicly. If you still have problems after a number of warnings, you need to take administrative action. In order to do this, you need to have a mail-list server that has special provisions for dealing with such users. The list-server program covered in this chapter has such a provision.

Windows NT Compatible Mail-List Servers

Several mail-list servers are available for Windows NT. URLs of several mail servers that run on Windows NT are listed next. Out of these servers, the remainder of this chapter focuses on installation and configuration issues related to NTList. NTList is a very feature-rich and easy-to-use mail-list server. For your convenience, a copy of NTList is included in the CD-ROM that accompanies the book.

L-Soft International Inc. LISTSERV:

http://www.lsoft.com/

EMWAC Internet Mail Server:

http://emwac.ed.ac.uk/html/internet_toolchest/ims/ims.htm

NTList Mail-List Server:

http://www.net-shopper.co.uk/software/ntmail/ntlist.htm

Installing Mail-List Server Software

NTList is integrated with NTMail, a Simple Mail Transport Protocol (SMTP)/Post Office Protocol (POP) mail server for Windows NT. NTList makes efficient use of system resources by utilizing the capabilities of NTMail to send list-server messages. Although NTMail is included in the CD-ROM, you may want to download the latest version of NTMail from the *Internet Shopper* World Wide Web site.

URL

The latest version of NTMail can be obtained from the *Internet Shopper* Web site:

http://www.net-shopper.co.uk/software/ntmail/index.htm

TECHNICAL NOTE

Requests for Comments (RFCs) are working notes of the Internet research and development community. NTMail is based on several RFCs published by the Internet

Engineering Task Force. These RFCs are RFC 821, RFC 822, RFC 974, RFC 1035, RFC 1123, RFC 1521, and RFC 1725.

More information about these RFCs can be obtained from

`http://www.internic.net/ds/rfc-index.html`

In order to use the functionality of NTList, NTMail has to be installed first.

Installing NTMail

Installing NTMail is very straightforward. First, you need to either download the latest version of NTMail from the URL given earlier or locate the NTMail distribution file in the CD-ROM. Copy the NTMail distribution file to a temporary directory and decompress the `.zip` file. It is recommended that you use a 32-bit file-decompressing utility such as WinZip to ensure any long filenames in the archive are preserved. Also, be sure to use appropriate switches of the file-decompressing utility to make sure that directory path names are preserved. After the NTMail distribution file is decompressed, follow subsequent directions to install NTMail/NTList on your system.

CAUTION

Before installing NTMail, make sure other SMTP and POP3 servers, such as the free EMWAC mail server, are stopped. Failure to do so can complicate the installation process when NTMail attempts to bind with a TCP/IP port on your system.

Execute `setup.exe` to begin the installation process. You will be presented with a dialog box similar to the one shown in Figure 27.10. In this dialog box, you need to provide NTMail with a registration key, the directory you wish NTMail to be installed in, and your domain name. If you intend to use NTMail/NTList, you should register it and obtain a permanent key that does not expire. If not, at the end of each month, you will have to obtain a temporary key from the NTMail distribution site. You will be pleased to know that the developer of NTMail was kind enough to let the readers of this book have an *initial key*. Rather than visit the Internet Shopper Web site to obtain a key, you can type demo to install and use NTMail immediately. Please note that this key will expire at the end of next month, and you will either need to obtain a new key or register your copy of NTMail/NTList after the trial period.

After typing the NTMail key, type the directory you wish NTMail to be installed in and your Internet domain name. Do not select a disk partition that barely has enough room for NTMail. When you start using NTMail for e-mail and NTList to host discussion lists, messages can take up a lot more disk space than NTMail itself. After typing your domain name, press OK to continue installing NTMail; the following Windows NT services will be added and started by the NTMail installation program:

■ POP Server

■ POST Server

■ SMTP Server

FIGURE 27.10.

The NTMail setup dialog box is used by NTMail to gather critical installation information.

In addition to this, as shown in Figure 27.11, three new icons will also be added to Control Panel:

■ **NTMail**—For configuring various features of NTMail

■ **NTMail Users**—For managing NTMail users

■ **NTList**—For configuring various features of NTList

FIGURE 27.11.

The NTMail installation program adds three new icons to Control Panel.

NTMail is now installed and ready for use. The following section demonstrates how to create NTMail user accounts.

Creating User Accounts

After NTMail is set up, it is recommended that you at least create an account for yourself and another account for the Web administrator of your system (usually called a *Webmaster*). In order to add users to NTMail, execute the NT Users application in Control Panel. You will then see a dialog box similar to the one shown in Figure 27.12.

FIGURE 27.12.

New users can be added to NTMail by executing the NT Users application in Control Panel.

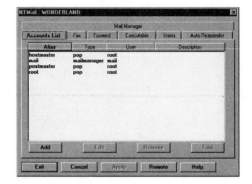

Click the Add button to add a new user. As shown in Figure 27.13, you will then be asked for the type of new user you wish to add. Select User | Holiday Message and press OK to continue.

FIGURE 27.13.

Various types of users can be added to NTMail.

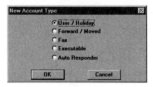

You will then be presented with a dialog box similar to the one shown in Figure 27.14. To create a user account for the Web administrator, type webmaster in the space provided for Username. If the NTMail username just typed in is also a Windows NT username, NTMail gives the option of either using the password in the NT user database or a new NTMail password. For example, if webmaster was also an NT user, webmaster can be added to use the NT user database password, by clicking on Add. The same account can also be added to use a different password by clicking on the password checkbox, typing a password, and clicking Add. Additional aliases for a user can be specified by typing them in the space provided for Aliases.

After webmaster is added as an NTMail user, as shown in Figure 27.15, the user Accounts List will be updated to reflect the new user who was added.

In order to save the changes you made, click Apply. When you exit the NTMail Users application, you will see a dialog box similar to the one shown in Figure 27.16. Answer Yes to this dialog box, and the changes you made will be updated to relevant NTMail services.

FIGURE 27.14.

The Users tab can be used to add new users.

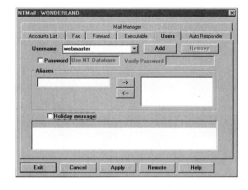

FIGURE 27.15.

The Accounts List tab lists all NTMail users.

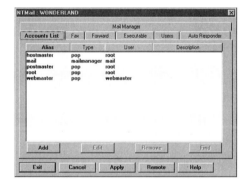

FIGURE 27.16.

NTMail provides an option to update new configuration information to NTMail services when exiting the NTMail Users application.

Using NTMail

At this point, NTMail is fully functional. NTMail users can now receive e-mail provided that the NT machine is properly connected to the Internet. You can test NTMail by sending a message to *NTMailUser@your.Internet.address*. Mail messages sent to NTMail users can be read using a number of mail clients such as Pegasus Mail and Eudora. If you are looking for a feature-rich, free mail client, use either Microsoft Exchange Client that comes with NT 4.0 or Pegasus Mail.

URL

Pegasus Mail can be obtained free of charge from

`http://www.cuslm.ca/pegasus/`

URL

Eudora is a Windows NT-compatible mail client. It comes in two versions. The "light" version is freeware but has limited capabilities. The "pro" version is more feature rich. Eudora can be obtained from

`http://www.qualcomm.com/ProdTech/quest/`

Monitoring Mail-Server Statistics

NTMail statistics can be obtained and monitored using Performance Monitor. In order to monitor NTMail statistics, invoke Performance Monitor and select Edit | Add To Chart. This will bring up an Add to Chart dialog box similar to the dialog box in Figure 27.17. This dialog box can be used to add various NTMail performance counters to Performance Monitor.

FIGURE 27.17.

Various NTMail performance counters can be added to Performance Monitor's chart.

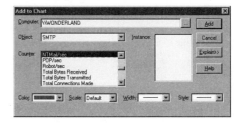

By adding various NTMail counters to the chart, you can monitor various statistics as shown in Figure 27.18.

FIGURE 27.18.

NTMail performance counters can be monitored using Performance Monitor.

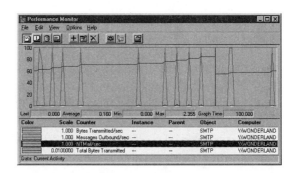

In addition to monitoring counters, by adding NTMail counters to "alerts" it is even possible to configure various programs to run when certain conditions are met. This is a powerful feature. For example, under the POP object, there is a counter by the name of Failed Authorizations/Sec. A high Failed Authorizations/Sec count is a harbinger of a possible system-security breach. Using Performance Monitor, you can set up a program to be executed when such a counter is suspiciously high. It is a good idea to invest in an application that can send text messages to alphanumeric pages. By using such an application along with Performance Monitor, even if you are fast asleep at 3 in the morning, you will know if someone is trying to break into one of your mail servers!

Creating and Managing Mail Lists

Now that NTMail is all set up, you can set up e-mail lists by configuring NTList. NTList is configured using the NTList application in Control Panel. When the NTList application is first invoked, it will look similar to Figure 27.19. By default, no mail lists are present.

FIGURE 27.19.

When the NTList configuration application is first invoked, it does not contain any e-mail lists.

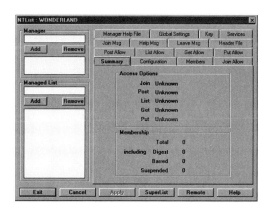

NTMail uses *list managers* to manage various mail lists by helping group various mail-list topics into mail-list categories. For example, a list manager called "NT-Request" can be created to manage Windows NT-related discussion lists. As you can see, breaking down various mail lists into categories and creating a list manager for each category helps mail lists to be managed in a logical manner.

For the purpose of this example, you will be shown how to create an e-mail list to discuss Web-publishing issues related to Windows NT. This mail list will be called WWW-NT. As mentioned earlier, before creating an e-mail list, a list manager has to be created. Because the WWW-NT mail list discusses various issues related to using Windows NT, the list manager can be called NT-Request. In order to create this list, first create a list manager by the name of NT-Request. After highlighting the list manager just created, create a Managed List by the name of WWW-NT. The NTList configuration application will now look similar to Figure 27.20.

A mail list can be set up very easily by following the directions. In order to make the WWW-NT mail list operational, it is required that you update the NTMail service. This can be done by exiting the NTList configuration application and answering Yes to a dialog box similar to the one shown in Figure 27.16.

FIGURE 27.20.

Mail lists are created by creating a managed list under a list manager.

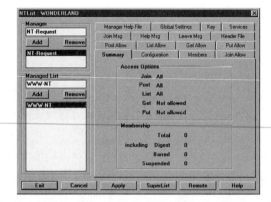

NOTE

NTList services have to be restarted in order for any changes to take effect.

At this time, if a message similar to the one shown in Figure 27.21 is sent to the mail list, the sender will receive a message similar to the one shown in Figure 27.22 confirming the list subscription was a success. In addition to this, another message will be sent to the list subscriber detailing various list-server commands. These commands will be covered shortly.

FIGURE 27.21.

Message sent to list server to subscribe to the WWW-NT mail list.

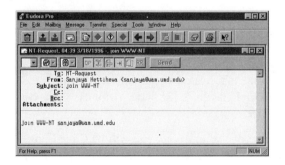

FIGURE 27.22.

Message sent by NTList to confirm the addition of a new user to the WWW-NT mail list.

NOTE

The purpose of this chapter is not to comprehensively cover all aspects of configuring NTList and NTMail. Instead, it is to provide you an overview of various benefits associated with setting up a mail-list server and a brief overview of how NTMail and NTList can be used to set up an Internet mail list. Please refer to NTMail and NTList documentation included in the CD-ROM for additional configuration information.

List-Server Commands

All list-server commands are handled by *list managers*. Users can join and leave a mail list as well as perform a few other tasks by sending commands to the list manager. Unlike users, *list moderators* can send administrative commands to the *list manager* using a password. Listed next are various list server commands supported by NTList.

JOIN **and** SUBSCRIBE

Users can join a mail list by sending either a JOIN or SUBSCRIBE message to the list manager. For example, if the user whose e-mail address is carina@CreativeLink.com wants to join the WWW-NT mail list created earlier, she'd have to send the following message to the list manager (NT-Request).

```
JOIN WWW-NT carina@CreativeLink.com
password <mail list password if set>
```

or

```
SUBSCRIBE WWW-NT carina@CreativeLink.com
password <mail list password if set>
```

DIGEST

Some users prefer to receive one large e-mail message from a mail list at the end of the day as opposed to many small e-mail messages at all times of the day. This option can be set by using the DIGEST command as outlined next.

```
DIGEST <list name> <e-mail address>
password <mail list password if set>
```

In order for this feature to work, the list should have the Log Messages checkbox enabled in the NTList configuration application, as shown in Figure 27.23. If a digest user wants to receive messages in real time once again, that user has to send a JOIN message to the list manager, as outlined earlier.

FIGURE 27.23.

In order for the mail-list digest feature to work, the Log Messages checkbox has to be checked.

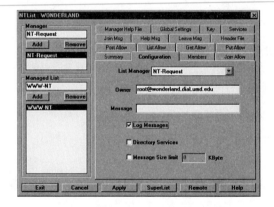

LEAVE and UNSUBSCRIBE

List members can leave the list by sending the following message to the list manager:

```
LEAVE <list name> <user's e-mail address>
password <mail list password if set>
```

or

```
UNSUBSCRIBE <list name> <user's e-mail address>
password <mail list password if set>
```

Help

If an invalid command or list name is sent to the list manager, the list manager's help file will be sent to the user. This message can be edited as shown in Figure 27.24. The same help message is sent to new subscribers.

FIGURE 27.24.

*The Help Msg tab of the
NTList configuration
application can be used to
edit the help message of a
mail list.*

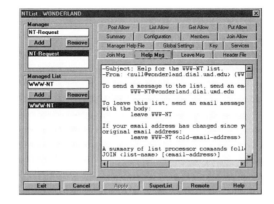

LIST

If it is allowed, the LIST command can be used by users to obtain a list of users who subscribe
to the mail list. This list can be sorted by domain name or alphabetical order. The syntax of the
LIST command is as follows:

```
LIST <list name> <sort method>
```

where <sort method> can be ALPHA or DOMAIN.

PASSWORD

This command is used along with other commands that require a password. In addition to
administrative commands discussed shortly, various list commands can be restricted by assigning a password using various Allow tabs (Post Allow, List Allow, Get Allow) of the NTList
configuration application.

Administrative Commands

Administrative commands can be used to obtain various information about the status of the list
server and also perform administrative tasks. In order for administrative commands to function,
a registry key by the name of ListServerPassword has to be created, as shown in Figure 27.25.

REGISTRY

The registry key ListServerPassword has to be created in order for mail-list server
administrative commands to be interpreted by the list server.

```
    Key Name:          SOFTWARE\InternetShopper\Mail\Parameters

    Value Name:        ListServerPassword
```

```
Type:              REG_SZ

Data:              <Password of List>
```

FIGURE 27.25.

*A registry key
(*ListServerPassword*)
has to be added before
administrative commands
can be sent to a mail-list
manager.*

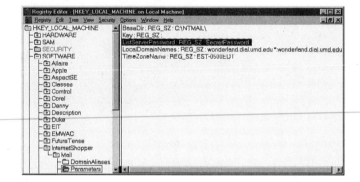

The following administrative commands are supported by NTList:

RESEND

Causes the list manager to send a digest of the list to all members who have requested digest messages.

```
RESEND <listname> [day month year]
PASSWORD <list password>
```

Example:

```
RESEND WWW-NT 18 03 1996
PASSWORD ListServerPassword
```

VERIFY

The VERIFY command is used to obtain a list of invalid user e-mail addresses. NTList compiles this report by contacting the mail server of each list subscriber and validating their e-mail address. The syntax of the VERIFY command is as follows:

```
VERIFY <list name>
PASSWORD <ListServerPassword>
```

Summary

Mail lists are different from other Internet information-distribution applications discussed earlier because they are highly interactive. Managing a mail list may involve some extra effort to keep the list functioning smoothly. However, when used properly, there are many advantages in setting up a mail-list server. By referring users to a Web site for more information via a newsletter, a mail-list server can be used to complement information distributed by a Web site. Windows NT mail-list servers are extremely easy to set up and administer. As shown earlier, the mail-list server included in the CD-ROM can be set up and put to use in a matter of minutes. By using a mail-list server to host discussion forums, you will be able to take advantage of various unique benefits offered by mail lists and make users more productive.

What's Next?

The next chapter discusses how to set up a domain name server under Windows NT. Whenever you connect to an Internet host—for example, www.microsoft.com—a domain name server translates www.microsoft.com into an Internet Protocol address such as 198.105.232.4 before the connection is made,. This process is crucial for locating and connecting to various Internet hosts. The following chapter demonstrates how to set up and configure a domain name server.

28

Setting Up a Domain Name Server

Although Internet Service Providers (ISPs) usually provide Domain Name Service (DNS) to their customers, setting up your own domain name server is beneficial. You can use a local domain name server to cache DNS queries and save bandwidth. In addition, you no longer have to depend on your ISP for DNS. Domain name servers of ISPs sometimes go down, and waiting until someone takes care of the problem can be frustrating. This problem can be solved by setting up your own domain name server.

The purpose of this chapter is to demonstrate how you can set up NT BIND to function as a secondary caching domain name server. The subject of DNS administration, however, cannot be covered in one chapter. DNS administration can become complicated, depending on the structure of your network and your ISP's network. Indeed, entire books have been dedicated to the subject of DNS administration. For additional information about using and configuring the domain name server discussed in this chapter, refer to the book *DNS and BIND* by O'Reilly Associates. Although this book is based on the UNIX version of BIND, material discussed in it also applies to the Windows NT version of BIND. You might also want to refer to the file BOG.WRI included in the NT BIND distribution file for additional information; this file is in Windows Write format. After you read the following sections, you will be able to install NT BIND on your system and configure it to act as a caching secondary domain name server. Refer to BIND documentation and the book *DNS and BIND* for information about configuring BIND as a primary domain name server and using it to assign DNS aliases to various computers on your network.

Obtaining BIND for Windows NT

You can obtain a copy of BIND for NT free of charge. To download it, send an e-mail message to the following:

```
access@drcoffsite.com
```

In a few minutes, you get an e-mail message containing directions for obtaining NT BIND via FTP. This e-mail message contains the username and password that you should use to access the NT BIND FTP site. After you connect to the FTP site, look for the file INDEX in the root directory. Use this file to determine the latest version of BIND for NT. The latest version is distributed with and without the source code. Unless you are interested in the source code, download the binary distribution file that does not contain the source code.

URL

NT BIND download source:
```
http://canon.bhs.com/scripts/appctr.idc?udir=DNS
```

At the time of this writing, the NT BIND distribution file that includes a Setup Wizard does not run on Windows NT 4.0. In the next section, therefore, you learn how to set up NT BIND using a distribution file that does not include the Setup Wizard. Note that both of these versions contain exactly the same program. One uses a GUI setup program; the other does not. Most likely, by the time you read this chapter, the GUI installation program will function with Windows NT 4.0. If it does not, simply download the distribution file that includes a non-GUI installation program. The name of this file should be something similar to ntdns493relbin-nongui.zip.

The following directions and configuration settings apply to both distribution files. If you are using the GUI setup program, directions for installing BIND will be simpler than those that follow. In that case, simply run the Installation Wizard (setup.exe) and answer a few configuration questions.

Installing NT BIND

After you download the NT BIND distribution file, copy it to a temporary directory. Then decompress it using a 32-bit file decompression utility. Be sure to enable the option in the file decompression utility to preserve directory names when decompressing the NT BIND distribution file.

If you download the distribution file containing the GUI installation program, a directory named disk1 is created after the distribution file is decompressed. Log on to this directory, and execute the file setup.exe to install NT BIND. Otherwise, log on to the directory contrib\winnt-dist, created after the distribution file is decompressed, and execute the file install.bat.

The installation program installs NT BIND files by copying them into various directories. Then you see the message The "DomainNameService" service was successfully created on-screen. At this point, if you invoke the Control Panel, you see a DNS Controller icon similar to the one shown in the lower right of Figure 28.1. As you learn shortly, you can execute this icon to stop and start the NT BIND DNS.

FIGURE 28.1.
A new icon is added to the Control Panel by the NT BIND installation program.

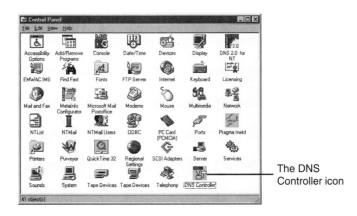

The DNS Controller icon

Before you can use NT BIND, you need to configure it to run as an NT user. You do so by opening the Services application shown in Figure 28.1. To change the user account of the NT BIND service, scroll down the list of services in the Services dialog box, as shown in Figure 28.2, and select the NT BIND service. Then click the Startup button.

FIGURE 28.2.

The NT BIND installation program registers NT BIND as a Windows NT Service.

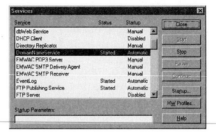

In the Service properties dialog box, which appears after you click the Startup button, you can assign a user account to the NT BIND service, as illustrated in Figure 28.3. In the same dialog box, you can configure the NT BIND service to start automatically after the NT server is booted.

FIGURE 28.3.

The Service properties dialog box of NT BIND.

NT BIND is now installed. However, before you can use it, you must configure it. To configure NT BIND, you edit the file named.boot in the I:\WINDOWS (assuming NT is installed in I:\WINDOWS) directory. You have to edit named.boot depending on your network configuration. Consult the BIND documentation, or contact your ISP for information about editing this file. A thorough overview of BIND configuration settings is beyond the scope of this book because configuration settings in the named.boot file depend on the way your network is set up. The original contents of named.boot are as follow:

```
ORIGINAL NAMED:
directory C:\\var\\named

primary 0.0.127.IN-ADDR.ARPA db.127.0.0
secondary       bethesda.mcs.us.pw.com 155.201.100.10 db.bethesda
secondary       100.201.155.IN-ADDR.ARPA 155.201.100.10 db.155.201.100
secondary       101.201.155.IN-ADDR.ARPA 155.201.100.10 db.155.201.101
cache           . db.cache
```

To configure NT BIND to function as a secondary caching DNS, change the directory (defined by the `directory C:\\var\\named` line) setting to the directory created by NT BIND. Then modify the named.boot file as shown in the following listing. The first `secondary` line configures NT BIND to do secondary DNS servicing for `umd.edu` and to get DNS information from `128.8.76.2` (`ns2.umd.edu`), which is the primary domain name server. This information then is stored in the file named.zoneinfo. The second `secondary` line does the reverse: It configures NT BIND to take an IP address and give the hostname address.

```
directory I:\\var\\named

primary 0.0.127.IN-ADDR.ARPA db.127.0.0
secondary      umd.edu        128.8.76.2       named.zoneinfo
secondary 8.128.in-add.arpa 128.8.76.2 named.inaddr
cache           . db.cache
```

After you configure the NT BIND configuration file, execute the DNS Controller icon in the Control Panel (refer to Figure 28.1). The Domain Name Server dialog box then appears, as shown in Figure 28.4. Click on the Start Server button to start the NT BIND service. Refer to NT BIND documentation for additional information about using this dialog box to configure NT BIND.

FIGURE 28.4.

The Domain Name Server dialog box.

After you start the NT BIND service, follow these directions to verify that NT BIND is installed correctly:

1. Type **nslookup** at the Windows NT command prompt.

   The nslookup prompt then appears on-screen. (The nslookup prompt is just a greater-than sign (>).)

2. At the nslookup prompt, type **server your.server.com**, where your.server.com is the friendly name (Internet address) of your NT machine.

3. At the nslookup prompt, type the name of an Internet server. Then nslookup responds with a message similar to the following:

```
> www.microsoft.com
Server:  wonderland.dial.umd.edu
Address:  128.8.18.13

Name:    www.microsoft.com
Addresses:  198.105.232.5, 198.105.232.6, 198.105.232.4
```

Internet Resources for Additional Help

Consult the following Internet resources for additional information about setting up and using NT BIND. Be sure to subscribe to the NT BIND mailing list if you have any questions about using NT BIND. If you are interested in configuring NT BIND to function as a primary domain name server, you will find information in the NT BIND configuration Web page useful.

NT BIND Mailing List

A mailing list has been set up to discuss various issues related to installing and using NT BIND. Forward suggestions, discussion questions, problems encountered, and suggestions for improvements to the NT BIND mailing list. To join the NT BIND mailing list, send an e-mail message to the following:

```
listserv@drcoffsite.com
```

When you send the e-mail message, be sure to include the following in the body of the message. Be sure to replace *<your name>* with your real name.

```
subscribe bindnt <your name>
```

NT BIND Configuration Web Page

Visit the NT BIND configuration Web page for information about setting up and configuring NT BIND. It includes a step-by-step guide for setting up and configuring NT BIND to function as a primary domain name server. You also can find several sample DNS configuration files at the following Web page.

URL

NT BIND configuration Web page:
```
http://www.telemark.net/~randallg/ntdns.htm
```

Summary

NT BIND is a freeware domain name server that you can set up either as a primary or secondary domain name server. Because its configuration files are compatible with those of the UNIX version of BIND, UNIX BIND documentation also applies to NT BIND. In this chapter, you learned how you can set up NT BIND to function as a secondary domain name server. Refer to NT BIND documentation and Internet resources given at the end of this chapter to learn how you can configure NT BIND to function as a primary domain name server.

What's Next?

The next chapter discusses issues related to setting up a telnet server on your NT server. By reading that chapter, you will learn issues that you need to address when you set up a telnet server. The chapter begins with an introduction to how telnet servers work and how you can benefit from setting up such a server.

Because telnet uses clear-text usernames and passwords, you have to address a number of security issues when setting up a telnet server. In the section titled "Addressing Security Concerns," you learn how to avoid unauthorized access to your NT system via *intercepted* usernames and passwords. You do so by setting up a Perl script to implement *one-time passwords*. To make sure an *intercepted* username and password is not used by an unauthorized person, the moment a user is authorized to log on, the Perl script changes the user's password. The section on security also discusses ways of further securing your server by restricting days and times in which users can connect to your server via telnet. After you read the next chapter, you will be able to set up a telnet server on your NT system without compromising its security.

29

Setting Up a Telnet Server

Unlike previous chapters, this chapter is not about an application that can be used to publish information on the Internet. Instead, it's about an NT service that can be used to make remote-system administration easier. By setting up a telnet service, you will be able to access your server for various system administration tasks from anywhere on the Internet. The chapter begins with a brief discussion about various advantages and drawbacks of setting up a telnet server. Afterwards, you will be presented with a list of telnet servers available for Windows NT. Out of these telnet servers, installation and configuration issues of Pragma Systems InterAccess telnet server will be discussed. Pragma Systems telnet server was chosen because it is robust, supports screens larger than 80 × 24, and all aspects of the server can be administered via an easy-to-use graphical-user interface (GUI). It is also easy to install and configure by designating user-command shells, home directories, and shell-initializing programs. If you need information about other telnet servers listed in this chapter, please visit their respective URLs. All aspects of setting up, configuring, and administering the InterAccess telnet server will be discussed shortly. After completing this chapter, you will be able to compare features of other telnet servers with those of InterAccess and select the telnet server that best suits your needs.

Unlike the command prompt of various flavors of UNIX, Windows NT's command prompt is not very powerful. However, there are a number of ways to extend the capabilities of Windows NT's command prompt. For example, it is possible to define a special shell such as the Hamilton C Shell for Windows NT, to be used by the telnet server. By using such a command shell, you will be able to make use of powerful command-line utilities to make system-administration and -maintenance tasks easier to handle.

Before various telnet servers available for Windows NT are discussed, let's first examine why you should set up a telnet server.

Why Set Up a Telnet Server?

There are many advantages in setting up a telnet server. For example, a telnet server can be used to access your server remotely from virtually anywhere on the Internet. It is possible to use Remote Access Service (RAS) or a third-party, remote-access program to connect to an NT machine, but depending on availability of hardware, software, and other factors, you might not be able to access your server at all times. On the other hand, telnet clients are widely available; all that's usually needed is access to the Internet.

Because the telnet protocol uses *clear text* usernames and passwords to authenticate users, there are various security risks associated with setting up a telnet server. However, in a later section of this chapter you will be shown how to implement a solution to this problem. Although the solution presented is not very elegant, it will make sure that even if someone obtains a username and password by eavesdropping on a telnet session, the password will become useless the moment a user is authenticated. This is accomplished by using a Practical Extraction Report Language (PERL) script to implement One-Time Passwords (OTP) when users telnet into the NT server. More information about this is provided later in this chapter, in the section, "Addressing

Security Concerns." Although Windows NT is an operating system that extensively uses GUIs, a number of tasks can be performed using the NT command prompt. By using various command-shell extenders, NT Resource Kit programs, and other utilities, capabilities of the NT command prompt can be further extended. Listed next are a few tasks that can be accomplished by accessing your NT machine via a telnet server.

- Stop and start services
- Add or delete users
- Change user permissions or login hours
- Copy, move, delete, and edit files
- View the contents of a text file/log file
- Check the status of your server in such areas as free memory, CPU utilization, page-file status, and so on
- Change file permissions
- Shut down/reboot server

As you can see, there are many advantages to setting up a telnet server. Soon after security concerns and various telnet servers available for NT are discussed, you will be shown how to set up a telnet server and customize it to meet your needs.

Security Concerns

At the time of this writing, all telnet servers available for Windows NT use clear-text passwords to authenticate users. Although some UNIX systems use more sophisticated user-authentication systems that validate users using a challenge/response mechanism, this feature is not yet available in telnet servers for Windows NT. It is not very desirable to use clear-text user IDs and passwords, because this can compromise the security of your NT server; a person with malicious intent can log on to your server using an *intercepted* username and password. To avoid such a possibility, the section "Addressing Security Concerns" will demonstrate a technique that can be used to implement OTPs on your telnet server. When OTPs are used, eavesdroppers will not be able to use user IDs and passwords of legitimate users to gain access to your server; one password is good for only one login. However, the implementation of OTPs presented in a later section is not very elaborate. Soon, you will discover what I mean by *not very elaborate*; however, what I am proposing is certainly better than using clear-text user IDs and passwords without any additional security.

Telnet Servers Available for Windows NT

Listed next are URLs of several telnet servers available for Windows NT. Out of these telnet servers, this chapter will discuss installation, configuration and administration issues of Pragma

Systems, InterAccess Telnet server. You may obtain information about other Windows NT telnet servers by visiting their respective URLs:

- Pragma Systems, Inc. InterAccess Telnet Server

  `http://www.ccsi.com:80/pragma/`
- SLnet Telnet Server

  `http://www.seattlelab.com/prodslnet.html`
- Ataman TCP Remote Logon Services—Rlogind, Rexd and Telnetd Services

  `ftp://rmii.com/pub2/ataman/products/`

After learning more about the InterAccess telnet server, you will be able to compare features of it with those of other telnet servers and select the server that best meets your needs.

Overview of the InterAccess Telnet Server

The InterAccess telnet server listens for incoming telnet connections on port 23. When a user connects to the telnet server, he or she is authorized with a username and a password. (See Figure 29.1.)

FIGURE 29.1.

After a telnet server is set up on an NT machine, a user can access it using a telnet client and his or her Windows NT username and password.

When a user is authenticated, he or she is presented with the Windows NT command prompt (`CMD.EXE`). You will be shown how to customize login prompts and change the default command shell in a later section of this chapter.

Installing the InterAccess Telnet Server

You need to be logged on as either the system administrator or a user with administrative rights in order to install the InterAccess telnet server. The server can be installed by executing the `setup.exe` file and specifying the directory you would like the telnet service to be installed in. When installation is complete, a new program group similar to the one shown in Figure 29.2 is created.

FIGURE 29.2.

At the end of the installation process, a new program group is created for the InterAccess telnet server.

After the program group shown in Figure 29.2 is created, execute the INETD icon to start the telnet server. As shown in Figure 29.3, by default, the telnet server is set to start automatically after your system is booted. By going into Control Panel and executing the Services application, the telnet server can be set to start manually, if so desired. The telnet service consumes negligible system resources; the section "Addressing Security Concerns," will deal with security issues associated with running a telnet server. Therefore, it is recommended that you leave this setting as it is.

FIGURE 29.3.

By default, the InterAccess telnet server is configured to start automatically when the system is booted.

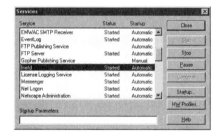

As shown in Figure 29.4, the InterAccess installation process also adds a new icon to the Control Panel. This icon, called Pragma Inetd, can be used to configure various programs to be started by the Inetd service.

FIGURE 29.4.

A new icon is added to Control Panel by the installation program. This icon can be used to configure programs started by the INETD service.

Before users can log on using the telnet server, they need to be assigned the Windows NT user right Log On Locally. This right is assigned by invoking User Manager, choosing users who need telnet access and selecting Policies|User rights from the pull-down menu. You then will see the User Rights Policy dialog box shown in Figure 29.5. The user right Log On Locally can be selected from the pull-down list that lists various user rights. Afterwards, by clicking on the Add button, users or user groups can be given permission to access an NT machine via telnet.

FIGURE 29.5.

The right Log On Locally can be assigned to a user or user group by using User Manager.

It might be easier for you to create a group called Telnet Users and assign the user right Log On Locally to this user group. You then will be able to easily control who has access to your server via telnet by examining members of the Telnet Users group.

Registry Keys

The InterAccess telnet server can be customized by making changes to the registry, as shown in Figure 29.6.

FIGURE 29.6.

The Registry Editor can be used to customize various characteristics of the telnet server.

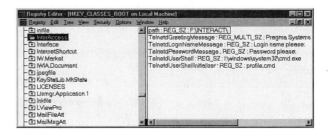

InterAccess Path

The following key contains the directory in which InterAccess is installed. This registry key should not be changed unless the InterAccess directory is moved.

`\\HKEY_CLASSES_ROOT\InterAccess\Path`

Greeting Message

A greeting message can be specified by modifying the following registry key. This greeting will be displayed when a user connects to the telnet server:

`\\HKEY_CLASSES_ROOT\InterAccess\TelnetdGreetingMessage`

The greeting message is a multiline key. Because the value of this key is displayed before a user is authenticated, it can be used to provide an e-mail address or a phone number to contact if assistance is needed.

Login Prompts

As you can see in Figure 29.1, `login name:` is the default user login prompt, and `password` is the default password prompt. These two prompts can be customized by modifying the following two registry keys:

```
\\HKEY_CLASSES_ROOT\InterAccess\TelnetdLoginNameMessage
\\HKEY_CLASSES_ROOT\InterAccess\TelnetdPasswordMessage
```

User Shell

The InterAccess server can be configured to use a shell of your choice. By default, the Windows NT command shell, `CMD.EXE`, is used. If you are more comfortable with a shell such as the Hamilton C-Shell for Windows NT, you can specify that shell to be used as the default user shell by modifying the following registry key:

```
\\HKEY_CLASSES_ROOT\InterAccess\TelnetdUserShell
```

Any character-based program that's compatible with Windows NT can be used as the user shell.

Shell Initialization File

A shell-initialization file can be specified in the registry. Just like the `autoexec.bat` file in DOS, this file is automatically executed each time a user logs on via the telnet server and can be used to set user-environment variables and execute programs.

```
\\HKEY_CLASSES_ROOT\InterAccess\TelnetdUserShellInitializer
```

This key will be used in a later section to implement OTPs on your server.

User Home Directories

The InterAccess server uses home directories specified in the Windows NT account database. The directory `c:\` will be assumed if no home directory is specified for a user.

Home directories can be specified and changed using User Manager. After invoking User Manager, users to which you wish to assign a home directory can be selected. More than one user can be selected by pressing the Ctrl key and clicking on multiple users. After selecting one or more users, select Users|Properties to bring up the User Properties dialog box shown in Figure 29.7.

FIGURE 29.7.

Home directories and login hours, as well as account and group permissions, can be viewed or changed using the User Properties dialog box.

To specify user home directories, click on the Profile button in the dialog box shown in Figure 29.7. You then will be presented with a User Environment Profile dialog box similar to the one shown in Figure 29.8. User Home directories can be defined using this dialog box by typing the full path name of the user's home directory. If more than one user was selected, an implicit path name such as `I:\Users\%USERNAME%` can be specified in this dialog box as shown in Figure 29.8.

FIGURE 29.8.

User home directories can be specified by entering a valid path name in the space provided for the user Home Directory.

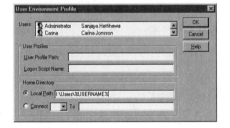

Addressing Security Concerns

When setting up any Internet service, security is a major concern. Because the telnet server presents users with a command prompt after validating a username and a password, precautions must be taken to keep a person with malicious intent from accessing your server using an *intercepted* username and password.

Implementing One-Time Passwords

Because the InterAccess server does not implement One-Time Passwords (OTPs) or a challenge/response mechanism to authenticate users, using clear-text user IDs and passwords can seriously compromise the security of your server.

One solution to this security nightmare is to implement OTPs on your telnet server. In the next section, a mechanism for implementing OTPs on your telnet server is given. In order for this to work, users should be given a list of valid passwords; each password is good enough for only one login. These passwords are saved in a text file and are used by a PERL script to change the user's password as soon as a user is authenticated to log on. You do not have to know how PERL scripts work to implement this PERL script. Full source code of the PERL script is given in the "PERL Script for Implementing One-Time Passwords" section. If PERL is not already installed on your system, refer to Chapter 16, "Introduction to Windows NT CGI Programming," to learn how to obtain and install PERL for Windows NT.

Although it might be cumbersome to create this password file and print a copy of it to users who will be accessing your telnet server, it's far better than compromising the security of your NT server. Many people are only all too familiar with the two commands del *.* and format.

SECURITY

Because passwords of accounts used to access the telnet server may change often, it is recommended that separate *telnet access accounts* be created for users who use the telnet server.

PERL Script for Implementing One-Time Passwords

Listed next is a simple PERL script to implement OTPs on the NT server. In order for this script to work, PERL needs to be installed on your server. If you have not installed PERL on your system already and need assistance installing it, please refer to Chapter 16, "Introduction to Windows NT CGI Programming." For your convenience, the following PERL script is included in the CD-ROM that accompanies the book.

```
# PERL OTP implementation for NT telnet server
# By Sanjaya Hettihewa and John Salmi

# Please change the following to the name of your
# password file as described in Chapter 29
$File    = "passwords";

# Open the password file for reading
open( INPUT, "$File" ) || die( "$File: $!\n" );

# Read contents of the password file into an array
# ( memory )
@Array = <INPUT>;

# Close the password file after reading it
close( INPUT );

# Reverse the order of the lines in the password file
for each ( @Array ) {
        push( @Array2, pop( @Array ));
}

# Free up memory used by Array
undef @Array;
```

```
# Execute command that changes the password
system( pop( @Array2 ));

# Reverse the order again, minus the line just executed
for each ( @Array2 ) {
        push( @Array, pop( @Array2 ));
}

# Rewrite contents of original file, minus the line executed
open( OUTPUT, "> $File" ) ¦¦ die( "$File: $!\n");
print( OUTPUT @Array );
close( OUTPUT );
```

After copying this file to home directories of users who will telnet to your server, change the line $File = "passwords" to the name of your password file (the filename is enclosed within quotation marks). An absolute path name has to be used if this file is not located in the user's home directory. The PERL script then executes the first line of the password file and deletes it from the file. Let us now examine the format of the password file.

Password File Used by PERL Script

The preceding PERL script takes advantage of the fact that user passwords can be changed from the Windows NT command prompt with the following command:

```
NET USER <user_name> <password>
```

where <user_name> is the name of the user you wish to change the password of, and <password> is the new password. The password file is simply a list of NET USER <user_name> <password> commands. The PERL script always executes the first line of this file and deletes it from the file. For example, if the password file is identical to the following listing:

```
net user carina 1
net user carina 12
net user carina 123
net user carina 1234
net user carina 12345
```

each time Carina logs on to the NT server via telnet, the PERL script will change her password by executing the first line of the password file. After this line is executed and a new password is set, that line will be deleted from the password file. For example, the first time Carina logs on, her password will be changed to 1, the second time to 12, and so forth. Because someone eavesdropping on a telnet connection never sees this file being executed by the PERL script, there is no way for an eavesdropper to use the same password used to access the system or find out what the new password is. Because a new password is always used by the PERL script, and a line is deleted from the password file, you should always see to it that there are enough passwords in the password file. It is a good idea to add at least 20 passwords to the password file, print a copy of it, and give it to users who will be connecting to your server.

When selecting passwords, you should make sure passwords that are chosen are not vulnerable to a *dictionary attack*. A dictionary attack uses a computer program to crack a user's password by repeatedly entering common words from a dictionary. When selecting passwords, make sure they are hard to guess by using alphanumeric characters along with other characters, such as those used to punctuate sentences.

Creating the Shell-Initializing File

The shell-initializing file is automatically executed as soon as a user is validated and logged on to your NT server. By adding the PERL script mentioned earlier to the shell-initialization file, the moment a user logs on, the telnet server will execute the PERL script and change the user's password. Because other commands might take a while to complete, the PERL script should be the first command in this file. Listed here is a sample shell-initialization file:

```
@ECHO OFF
ECHO OTP passwords are enabled
ECHO About to change your password
perl PasswordChange.pl
ECHO Your password has been changed
```

In Figure 29.9, you can see how the shell-initialization file gets executed as soon as a user logs on via the telnet server. The name of the shell-initialization file can be specified by modifying the registry, as demonstrated earlier.

FIGURE 29.9.

As soon as a user is validated, the telnet server will execute the shell-initialization file and change the user's password.

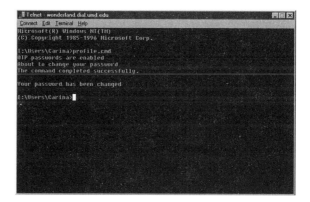

Limiting Access Times

Because InterAccess uses the Windows NT security database to authenticate users, by using User Manager it's possible to allow access to your server via telnet only during certain hours of the day, as described in Figure 29.10. Access can be restricted during certain hours or days by invoking User Manager, choosing Users, and selecting User|Properties. You then will be presented with a dialog box similar to the one shown in Figure 29.10.

FIGURE 29.10.

User Manager can be used to restrict days and hours during which a user can connect to your server via telnet.

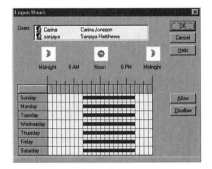

It is a good idea to allow telnet server access only when it is needed. For example, if the telnet server will be used only during regular business hours, access to your server can be restricted during off-business hours.

Administering the Telnet Server

The Telnet Manager icon shown in Figure 29.2 can be used to administer the InterAccess telnet server. Telnet Manager is an easy-to-use, graphical application for managing users connected to any Windows NT machine on the Internet running the InterAccess telnet server. In order to use Telnet Manager, you need to be the system administrator or a user with administrative rights. After invoking the Telnet Manager application, before administering a telnet server, you need to connect to a machine that runs InterAccess. This is done by selecting Manage|New Machine from the menu bar. After selecting New Machine, you will be presented with a dialog box similar to the one shown in Figure 29.11. In this dialog box, type the Internet address of the computer you wish to administer.

FIGURE 29.11.

Before administering a telnet server, you need to connect to it by providing its Internet address.

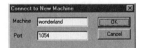

After typing the Internet address, click on the OK button to continue. Next, you will be presented with a User Verification dialog box similar to the one shown in Figure 29.12. Use this dialog box to type in the user name and password of the system administrator or a user account with administrative permissions.

FIGURE 29.12.

A username and a password that has administrative rights are required to manage the telnet server.

After providing a valid username and a password with administrative rights, the Telnet Manager will connect to the server you wish to manage and present you with a list of users logged on to that server. As you can see in Figure 29.13, this list contains usernames of users connected to the telnet server along with the time they logged on. Because this listing does not get updated automatically, View|Refresh needs to be selected to obtain the most up-to-date list of users logged on.

FIGURE 29.13.

After connecting to a computer running InterAccess, User Manager will present you with a list of users logged on to the telnet server.

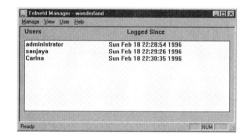

Additional information about a user, such as the process ID of the connection and the machine the user is connecting from, can be obtained by double-clicking on a user listed in Telnet Manager. The information you receive after double-clicking on a user is shown in Figure 29.14.

FIGURE 29.14.

Additional information about a user listed in Telnet Manager.

By choosing a user and selecting User|Logoff, it is also possible to disconnect users from the telnet server.

Uninstalling the Telnet Server

The InterAccess telnet service can be uninstalled by executing the Uninstall InterAccess icon shown in Figure 29.2. To prevent users from losing their work, they should be given a chance to complete it and disconnect from the telnet server before commencing the uninstall process. In the unlikely event you encounter problems with the uninstall program, follow these directions to manually uninstall the telnet service:

1. Make sure all users are logged off the telnet server.
2. Stop the telnet service using the Services application in Control Panel or the `net stop inetd` command.

3. Delete the InterAccess directory and the two files %SYSTEMROOT%/system32/ inetd.cpl and %SYSTEMROOT%/system32/inetdcpa.help.

4. Use the Windows NT Resource Kit utility INSTSRV.EXE to remove the telnet service. The telnet service can be removed by executing the command INSTSRV INETD REMOVE.

Summary

By reading this chapter, you learned about various issues that need to be addressed when setting up a telnet server. The chapter began with an introduction to how telnet servers work and a discussion of how you and your users can benefit from setting up a telnet server. Although only one telnet server was comprehensively covered, at the beginning of the chapter you were provided with a list of Windows NT telnet servers, along with their URLs. Out of these telnet servers, Pragma System's InterAccess telnet server was used to demonstrate how a telnet server can be set up under Windows NT. Virtually all aspects of utilizing and configuring the InterAccess server were covered to demonstrate how it can be customized to suit your needs.

Without compromising your server's security, you can now set up a telnet server on your system and configure it to meet your needs.

What's Next?

In previous chapters, you were shown how to set up a number of information-distribution applications under Windows NT. Although these applications can be used to distribute information, apart from the mail-list server discussed in Chapter 27, "Setting Up a Mail-List Server," none of the applications discussed earlier can be used to host Internet discussion forums. The next chapter demonstrates how to set up a Windows NT NNTP (Network News Transport Protocol) news server to do just this. You are probably already familiar with Internet newsgroups. Internet newsgroups are discussion forums set up on the Internet, where users with similar (or opposing) viewpoints can post messages and discuss various issues. Many newsgroups have been set up, discussing virtually everything imaginable. These newsgroups are hosted using NNTP news servers. There are many benefits to setting up your own news server. After you install and configure it, users will be able to exchange information and discuss various issues. If you are providing a service or selling a product, a news server can be used very effectively to provide customer service as well as technical support.

Although an Internet mail-list server similar to the one discussed in Chapter 27 can be used to create Internet discussion forums using e-mail, there are a number of drawbacks to this. Because there is no automatic archival of messages, it is often hard for users to locate a message that was sent to the list a few weeks ago. On the other hand, a news server can be configured to keep messages active for a certain period of time, allowing users to browse old messages and find out more about a topic previously discussed.

After reading the next chapter, you will discover how easy it is to set up a news server and use it effectively to distribute information and set up discussion forums on the Internet. After putting your news server to use, you will soon ascertain the virtues of setting up an Internet news server. As an added bonus, the next chapter also discusses when you should use an Internet mail-list server or a news server. The following chapter also highlights advantages and drawbacks to using the preceding two servers and discusses how they complement each other.

30

Setting Up an NNTP News Server

Using a Network News Transport Protocol (NNTP) server, you can set up discussion forums on the Internet. Although a Web site is ideal for distributing information on the Internet, it's not always an ideal solution for setting up Internet discussion forums. You can use applications such as WebBoard, described in the next chapter, to set up HTTP-based discussion forums on the Internet. However, such applications have to rely on limited capabilities of various HTML input controls. On the other hand, NNTP servers and clients are designed to handle large volumes of messages. NNTP news reading clients are available for virtually all operating systems and are optimized for reading and posting messages to news servers. For this reason, HTTP-based discussion forums are not suitable for hosting high-volume discussion forums, although they are ideal for setting up low-volume discussion forums.

In this chapter, you learn how you can set up an NNTP server to host public discussion forums on the Internet. Although this chapter does not discuss all aspects of setting up and configuring a news server, after reading it, you will be able to set up a news server at your site and configure it so that users can connect to it to read and post messages. At the end of the chapter, you also learn how you can use an NNTP server to complement information distributed by a Web server.

Applications of an NNTP Server

You can use an NNTP server for a wide variety of tasks. Because it enables users to interact with each other, you can add a new level of interactivity to an Internet server by setting up a news server.

When you introduce a new product, for example, chances are that many of your customers will have similar questions. Although you can treat all these customers individually, you can set up a news server to deal with this situation in a more efficient and cost-effective manner. Users then can connect to the news server and not only post messages when they have questions, but also get answers to them. In addition, users also can discover various innovative ways of solving problems by reading messages posted by others.

In fact, Microsoft just moved its support forums from CompuServe to the Internet after setting up a news server. See Figure 30.1 for an example of how users use the Microsoft news server to obtain technical support.

A news server also can be used to discuss a certain topic and brainstorm new ideas. Not only can you set up a news server on the Internet, but you also can set up one locally on an intranet environment. You might want to consider setting up a newsgroup for each department and various projects. Users then can exchange ideas and opinions with each other and brainstorm innovative solutions with each other.

As you can see, a news server can be used for a wide variety of applications. You should be aware, however, of a few drawbacks associated with using a news server. Some of these drawbacks are listed in the following sections.

FIGURE 30.1.

News servers are ideal for providing technical support to users.

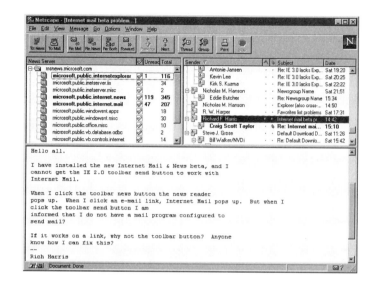

Challenges of Using an NNTP Server

Most commonly used Web browsers such as Internet Explorer and Netscape Navigator have built-in capabilities to participate in news server discussions. After you set up your news server, you can easily add NNTP URLs so that users can connect to your news server and discuss various issues related to the content at your Web site.

Some users might be reluctant to use a news server because the technology seems "new" to them. Try to encourage users to use a news server whenever it can handle a task more efficiently. Once users realize the various benefits offered by news servers, they will start using them more frequently to meet their information needs.

Another drawback of using a news server is its static nature. Although information at a Web site can be made interactive using technologies such as Distributed COM (DCOM), such technologies do not exist for messages posted to a news server. Understand this limitation when you use your news server. Information that is better suited for being published on a Web server should not be published on a news server. Use news servers to publish material that does not require a lot of formatting. Basically, use your news server to post messages that are suitable for discussion by other users.

Installing NetManage's Forum Server

NetManage offers a freeware as well as a commercial NNTP news server for Windows NT. The purpose of the following sections is not to cover both versions of these news servers comprehensively. Such coverage is beyond the scope of this book. However, you do learn how you can use NetManage's NNTP server to set up discussion forums on the Internet.

The freeware version of NetManage's NNTP is similar to the commercial version, but the commercial version has the following added features:

- NNTP Security—Controls access to news server data.
- XOVER—Supports "overview databases" for increased performance.
- GUI Install—Installs the news server easily.

The commercial NNTP server is actually part of NetManage's Intranet Server. Intranet Server is a suite of information distribution and management servers that includes a Domain Name Server (DNS), HyperText Transport Protocol Server (HTTP), Network File System (NFS), Line Printer Daemon (LPD), Directory, and NetTime server.

Visit the NetManage Web site for more information about NetManage's Intranet Server. You also can download NetManage's freeware news server from the same Web site.

URL

NetManage Intranet Server information page:
```
http://www.netmanage.com/netmanage/intra_server/index.html
```

URL

NetManage freeware NNTP server download page:
```
http://www.netmanage.com/netmanage/nns/index.html
```

If you obtain a copy of the NetManage Intranet Server, run the file setup.exe to install the NNTP server and other servers included in the Intranet Server package. If you download the freeware server, be sure to unzip the distribution file using a 32-bit file-decompressing program that preserves long filenames. After you decompress the distribution file, refer to the file usrguide.doc for detailed information about installing the freeware NNTP server. Proceed to the next section after installing the news server to learn how you can use the NNTP server to set up online discussion forums on the Internet.

Configuring the NNTP Server

After you install the news server, it registers itself as a service, as shown in Figure 30.2. I recommend that you allow the news server to start automatically and remain running because it consumes negligible system resources when it is not in use.

FIGURE 30.2.

The NNTP server functions as a Windows NT service.

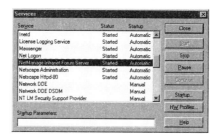

Before you configure the news server, locate the file newsctl.exe. You use this file to issue commands to the news server to do various tasks such as create and delete newsgroups. Also note that after you make any configuration changes using the newsctl.exe program, you need to enter the command **newsctl reload** at the Windows NT command prompt for the changes to take effect. If you want to enable Internet users to connect to your news server to read and post messages, you have to edit the nntp.access file with a text editor such as notepad. In this file, locate the `default access section`, and change it as follows:

```
## Restricted access entry; server is shipped with this by default
## *:: -no- : -no- :!*

## Unrestricted access entry—any client may read and post and servers
## must be explicitly included below
*:Read Post:::*
```

After you make this change, be sure to enter the **newsctl reload** command. Internet users then can connect to your news server to read and post messages.

At this point, you can connect to your news server by using a news reading/posting client, such as Netscape Navigator, as shown in Figure 30.3.

FIGURE 30.3.

Users can use a news reading/posting client to connect to the news server soon after it is set up.

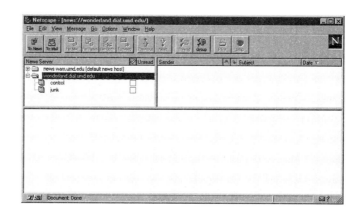

Creating Newsgroups

You can create new newsgroups by using the newsctl.exe file. The syntax for creating new newsgroups is as follows:

```
NEWSCTL NEWGROUP <group name> <Access Control> <Creators name>
```

The `Access Control` parameter can have one of the values shown in Table 30.1.

Table 30.1. `Access Control` parameter values.

Value	Description
Y	New posts are allowed.
n	New posts are not allowed.
m	Moderated newsgroup. All newsgroup posts directed at the newsgroup are mailed to the moderator.

Creating a newsgroup is easy. Simply log on to the directory containing the file newsctl.exe and use the command just shown to create newsgroups. You can create a newsgroup named VBScript, for example, by using the command `newsctl newgroup VBScript y`. Note that the `Creators name` parameter is not required for creating public newsgroups. At this time, if a user connects to the news server with a news client, he or she sees the newsgroup just created, as shown in Figure 30.4.

FIGURE 30.4.

A newsgroup listing after adding a newsgroup to the news server.

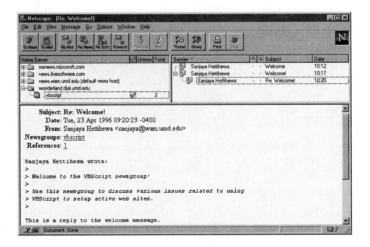

Deleting Newsgroups

Using newsctl.exe, you also can delete newsgroups. The syntax for deleting newsgroups is as follows:

```
NEWSCTL rmgroup <Name of newsgroup>
```

Note that if you accidentally delete an existing newsgroup, you can recover it by immediately re-creating the newsgroup with its same name.

Setting Newsgroup Expiration

By default, the news server expires (deletes) messages seven days after they are posted. Using the expire.ctl file, you can define expiration dates for the entire news server or individual newsgroups. The format of entries of the expire.ctl is as follows:

```
<newsgroup range>:<newsgroup type>:<minimum>:<default>:<maximum>
```

The parameters are as follows:

<newsgroup range>—You can replace this parameter with the name of a newsgroup such as comp.windows.NT or comp.* to match all newsgroups of the comp. hierarchy (such as comp.Windows.NT and comp.microsoft.bob).

<newsgroup type>—You should replace this parameter with either an A or M. Use A to specify unmoderated newsgroups and M to specify moderated newsgroups.

<minimum>—This parameter indicates the minimum time period, in number of days, a message should be kept active. Note that you can replace this value with never to keep messages active for an indefinite period of time.

<default>—This parameter indicates the default time period, in number of days, a message should be kept active. Note that you can replace this value with never to keep messages active for an indefinite period of time.

<maximum>—This parameter indicates the maximum time period, in number of days, a message should be kept active. Note that you can replace this value with never to keep messages active for an indefinite period of time.

Generally, you should not define a newsgroup to always have messages active for an indefinite number of days. If it is not a high-volume newsgroup, however, and is used to post important announcements and discussions related to them, you might want to set that newsgroup to keep its messages forever. For other newsgroups, depending on the amount of drive space you have free, and the number of messages, pick a value between 7 and 30 days. Expiring messages before seven days is not recommended because users find it difficult to get more information about discussions that began a week before.

Using an NNTP Server to Complement a Web Server

As I mentioned previously, you can use an NNTP server to complement a Web site. How can you do this when both servers rely on two separate protocols? The answer is that integrating the two protocols is easy. Always keep in mind that your Web server is for publishing information and your NNTP server is for users to discuss information published at your Web site. Although you can publish information using an NNTP server, doing so is actually a step backward because you forgo all the new technologies that are available to format content published at a Web site.

Most modern Web browsers such as Netscape Navigator and Internet Explorer come with built-in news reading capabilities. Take advantage of these capabilities by using both protocols. A URL can connect to a news server as easily as it can connect to a Web server, provided that the Web browser supports news reading. When you publish information, simply create a link to one of your newsgroups using the URL format `news:\\server.com`. Users then can browse the contents at your Web site and discuss those contents using your news server.

Where to Go from Here

In this chapter, you learned only the basics of setting up and using an NNTP news server. News servers can be used to communicate with each other through the exchange of messages. Also, if you are using the commercial version of the news server discussed in this chapter, you can further configure it by administering various security options on the server.

After you are comfortable with creating and managing a few newsgroups, you should read the documentation included in the news server distribution file. This comprehensive documentation covers all aspects of using the news server. The preceding sections were meant to get you started with using the news server to host public discussion forums on the Internet.

Summary

Setting up an NNTP news server is a great way to add a new level of interactivity to a Web site. Because the most widely used Web browsers—Internet Explorer and Netscape Navigator— both support NNTP news reading, users browsing a Web site can participate in discussions using a news server. You can easily set up a news server and enable users browsing a Web site to access it to participate in online discussions.

What's Next?

The next chapter discusses a number of other applications that you can use to publish information on the Internet. Although these applications are different from applications discussed in most of this book, they add a new level of interactivity to a Web site.

31

Setting Up a Web Conferencing System

By setting up a Web conferencing system, you can enable users browsing a Web site to communicate with each other. Although you can use an Internet news server to set up discussion forums on the Internet, a Web conferencing system is more suitable for hosting relatively low-volume discussion forums. As you learn in this chapter, a Web conferencing system can also be used effectively in an intranet environment.

The purpose of this chapter is to discuss various advantages of setting up a Web conferencing system. You also learn how you can use WebBoard to implement a Web conferencing system at your Web site and set up discussion forums on the Internet. Visit the following Web site for the most up-to-date information about WebBoard.

URL

The WebBoard (Web conferencing system) information Web site:

http://WebBoard.ora.com/

Benefits of Setting Up a Web Conferencing System

With all the Internet information systems discussed previously in this book, you might wonder why you should go to the trouble of setting up a Web conferencing system. Setting up such a system offers many advantages.

A Web conferencing system complements information distributed with a Web site. Although thousands or even millions of users can browse a Web site, they never get to interact with each other. For the most part, a Web site is just a one-way flow of information. A Web site can be used to its maximum potential if you set up a Web conferencing system and allow users browsing it to communicate.

Due to the nature of the Internet community, a Web site typically attracts a diverse audience of users. These users bring with them valuable knowledge and experiences. A Web conferencing system can be used to share this knowledge and experiences with others. It can also be used to find innovative solutions to various problems. You can use a Web conferencing system, for example, to post various problems and find innovative solutions to them. As demonstrated in this chapter, a Web conferencing system can be used to convert a Web site into a two-way medium of information distribution. Naturally, a Web conferencing system is also ideal for providing technical support because it can be used to tap into resources of users browsing a Web site.

You also can use a Web conferencing system in an intranet environment. You can create a Web page, for example, for various projects that are in progress. Rather than send e-mail to one or two individuals about various issues, you can use a Web conferencing system to share these issues with a diverse group. This approach promotes teamwork, collaboration, and makes the work environment more productive.

You might also want to create a series of Web pages for various proposals. Employees can then create Web pages for each proposal and post them on an intranet Web server for others to browse. Such a Web page can have a link to a Web discussion forum. Other employees can then read the proposal, make comments, suggest refinements, and discuss various issues related to implementing the proposal. This is an example of how various strengths of the Web can be exploited in an intranet by setting up a Web conferencing system. Web forums can also be used to brainstorm solutions to various problems. Create a set of Web pages for various problems and link them to a Web discussion forum. As you can see, you can accomplish a great deal by turning the Web, an otherwise one-way medium of information distribution, into a two-way medium of information distribution and assimilation.

Another advantage of using WebBoard is the fact that it uses the formatting capabilities of HTML to present information in a visually appealing manner. Messages posted on a Web discussion forum, for example, can contain inline movies, sound clips, Java applets, and links to other Web pages. In addition, users do not need special software to participate in HTTP-based discussion forums. WebBoard seamlessly integrates with your Web site and provides a single, familiar, and easy-to-use interface.

The following sections demonstrate how you can set up WebBoard to create a discussion forum on the Internet. Note that these sections cover only the procedures necessary to set up a discussion forum with WebBoard. Download a copy of WebBoard and experiment with it to learn how you can use some of its advanced capabilities to create an information-rich Web site.

Installing WebBoard

You can install WebBoard in just a few minutes. At the time of this writing, WebBoard requires a WinCGI-compliant Web server, such as WebSite; however, this situation may have changed by the time you read this chapter. Chances are, in addition to the WinCGI version, at least an ISAPI version of WebBoard will be available at O'Reilly's Web site. You can download the latest version of WebBoard from the following Web site.

URL

The WebBoard (Web conferencing system) software download page:

```
http://software.ora.com/download/
```

After you download WebBoard, copy it to a temporary directory and execute the installation program. The installation program first presents you with a dialog box similar to the one shown in Figure 31.1. In the Choose Destination Location dialog box, you enter the target directory for WebBoard. After you select a directory, click the Next button to continue.

> **CAUTION**
>
> For security reasons, the destination directory of WebBoard should not be a child of your Web server's document root directory.

FIGURE 31.1.
Selecting the destination directory of WebBoard.

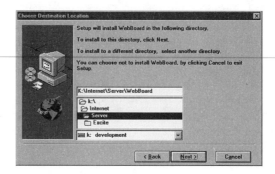

Using the Select CGI-WIN Directory dialog box shown in Figure 31.2, select your Web server's CGI-WIN directory. Note that the version of WebBoard used in this example supports only WinCGI-compliant Web servers. The version available by the time you read this chapter will most likely support ISAPI-compliant Web servers as well. Refer to your Web server documentation and configuration settings for the location of the CGI directory requested by the installation program.

FIGURE 31.2.
The CGI directory selection dialog box.

After you select the CGI-WIN directory, click the Next button to continue. The Select Program Manager Group dialog box shown in Figure 31.3 then appears. Use this dialog box to select the name of WebBoard's Windows NT Start Menu folder and click OK.

FIGURE 31.3.

Start Menu folder selection dialog box.

The installation program then inserts WebBoard icons into the Windows NT Start Menu folder selected in Figure 31.3 and terminates with a Setup Complete dialog box similar to the one shown in Figure 31.4.

FIGURE 31.4.

The Setup Complete dialog box displayed after WebBoard is successfully installed.

After you install WebBoard, the WebBoard Server application is added to the Windows NT "Startup" folder. When a user logs in to the system, the WebBoard Server is automatically started. By the time you read this chapter, WebBoard should be implemented as a Windows NT service, so this information might not apply to you. Visit O'Reilly's Web site for the most up-to-date information regarding this matter. The Windows NT Start Menu folder created by the installation program is shown in Figure 31.5.

FIGURE 31.5.

The Windows NT Start Menu folder created by the WebBoard installation program.

The last dialog box displayed by the installation program may ask you to reboot your server to complete installing WebBoard. If such a dialog box appears, acknowledge it and reboot your server before continuing.

Establishing an Administration Account

After you install WebBoard, you can use a Web browser to administer all aspects of WebBoard. Before you create discussion forums, though, you have to create an administration account. Make sure that both the WebBoard server and the Web server are functioning normally before you create this account.

If you are using the WebSite Web Server from O'Reilly Associates, two directory mappings that are required for the proper execution of WebBoard are automatically set. If you are not running the WebSite Web Server, create the following two directory mappings before proceeding any further:

■ URL alias /wbimages should be mapped to \WebBoard\images.

■ URL alias /Webboard should be mapped to your Web server's WinCGI directory.

WebBoard assigns administrative permissions to the first user who logs in. Therefore, it is essential that you log in and establish an administration account as soon as WebBoard is installed. Use a Web browser to look up the URL http://your.server.com/WebBoard/$Webb.exe after installing WebBoard. WebBoard then asks for a username and a password, as shown in Figure 31.6. Type in a username and a password, and click the OK button. Note that in the dialog box shown in Figure 31.6, you specify the username and password of the WebBoard administrator. Therefore, select a username and password that you are not likely to forget. Of course, you should make them hard to guess as well.

FIGURE 31.6.

Specifying a username and password for a WebBoard administrator account.

WebBoard next displays a Web page similar to the one shown in Figure 31.7. On this Web page, you confirm the creation of a new account with the username and password supplied in the Username and Password dialog box. Select the graphic titled "I am entering as a new user" to log in as the WebBoard administrator.

On the New User Web page shown in Figure 31.8, you supply new user information for WebBoard. After you type in the requested information, click the Login as a New User button located at the bottom of the form.

After you submit the form, WebBoard displays a Web page similar to the one shown in Figure 31.9. Click the MAIN MENU graphic on this Web page to access WebBoard's Main Menu.

FIGURE 31.7.

The new user confirmation Web page.

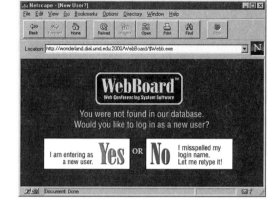

FIGURE 31.8.

The form used to obtain information about new users.

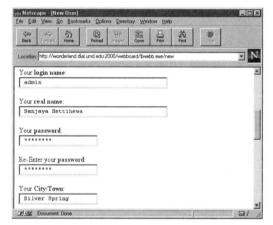

FIGURE 31.9.

WebBoard greets new users with a welcome message.

Setting Up Discussion Forums

Using the WebBoard Main Menu, shown in Figure 31.10, you can access various features of WebBoard. Refer to the WebBoard documentation for information about various options shown on this Web page. Select List Conferences to create a new discussion forum. Note that you need to be logged in as the WebBoard administrator to create new discussion forums.

FIGURE 31.10.

The WebBoard Main Menu.

You can add new forums using the Web page shown in Figure 31.11. From this form, WebBoard obtains various information about the forum being created. You can assign a short name, description, and several other settings to the new discussion forum. Finally, click the Add This Conference button located at the bottom of the form to create the forum.

FIGURE 31.11.

Creating a new WebBoard conference.

The WebBoard forum created in Figure 31.11 is shown in Figure 31.12. On this Web page, you select various WebBoard forums to visit, and if you are the administrator, you can access the Admin Control Panel. The number of messages in each discussion forum is displayed next to the name of the discussion forum.

FIGURE 31.12.

WebBoard conferences.

When you select a new WebBoard forum, you see a Web page similar to the one shown in Figure 31.13. By default, WebBoard forums do not contain any messages. It is a good idea to post a welcome message after creating a discussion forum to welcome users and inform them about the purpose of the discussion forum.

FIGURE 31.13.

A forum created with the form shown in Figure 31.11.

Posting Messages on a WebBoard Discussion Forum

By selecting the Post option in the Web page shown in Figure 31.13, users can post messages. Other users can then respond to messages posted, as shown in Figure 31.14. Replies to original posts are indented to make it easier to locate new discussion topics. After a message is posted, the subject title, the name of the user who posted the message, and the time and date of the message are displayed, as you can see in the figure.

FIGURE 31.14.

Messages posted on a WebBoard discussion forum.

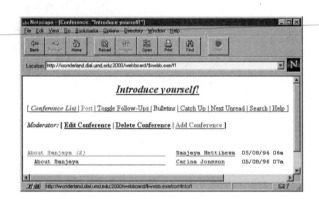

Monitoring WebBoard Accesses

Using the WebBoard Server application, shown in Figure 31.15, you can monitor WebBoard accesses. The WebBoard Server application displays the name of the last user who logged in to WebBoard and the total number of posts and requests served by WebBoard. You can reset these two values by clicking them.

FIGURE 31.15.

The WebBoard Server application.

You can obtain detailed information about WebBoard accesses from the WebBoard Activity Log. As shown in Figure 31.16, the Activity Log logs all WebBoard accesses, including user authentication attempts. You can use the Activity Log to discover possible breaches of security and determine which areas of WebBoard are more popular.

FIGURE 31.16.
The WebBoard Activity log.

Where to Go from Here

WebBoard supports many advanced features that you can use to manage discussion forums hosted with WebBoard. Take some time to experiment with WebBoard, and go over its documentation to learn how to use WebBoard to its maximum potential. Also, create a Web page similar to the one shown in Figure 31.17 and include a link on it to access WebBoard. Do not just create a link to WebBoard, because a user might get confused if he or she just sees a dialog box that asks for a username and a password. Use a Web page, similar to the one shown in the figure, to inform users that they should type in a username and a password before they can participate in discussion forums using WebBoard.

FIGURE 31.17.
Create a Web page with instructions for accessing WebBoard.

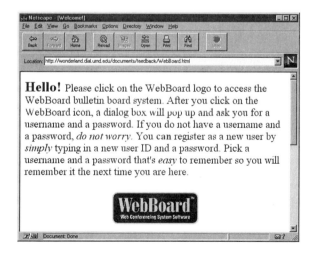

Summary

You can use WebBoard to set up a Web conferencing system and allow users navigating a Web site to interact. Because conference forums set up with WebBoard are accessible via a Web browser, they are easily accessible to users browsing a Web site. A Web site, which is mostly a one-way medium of information distribution, can be turned into a two-way medium of information distribution if you set up a Web conferencing system. You can also use WebBoard to allow users browsing a Web site to communicate with each other, and you can convert a Web site to a rich and diverse source of information.

What's Next?

Congratulations! You've just finished reading the last chapter of this book. Apart from the appendixes and the index, nothing else is left after this chapter. I hope you enjoyed reading this book and that you have learned how you can use Windows NT to publish information effectively on the Internet.

If you have any comments about this book, please let me know. If you would like to see additional information about a certain topic covered in this book in the next edition let me know that, too. I'll try my best to research it and include coverage of it in the next edition. Watch out for the next edition of this book in about an year or so!

In the meantime, visit my Web site for the most up-to-date information about using Windows NT to publish information on the Internet.

URL

NetInnovation.COM Windows NT resources Web site:

`http://WWW.NetInnovation.COM`

IX

Appendixes

Windows NT Resources
on the Internet

The Internet offers many Windows NT resources that are freely available to anyone. Even though you can call Microsoft for questions related to Windows NT, you might first want to find out if anyone else has come across the same problem and learn what was done to solve it, possibly saving you some time and money. Another advantage of posting questions on the Internet is that they are read by a diverse group of people. Therefore, responses you get will be greatly varied and will include a wide range of experiences. You can take advantage of this by sifting through the different responses and selecting the best solution that suits your needs.

Where to Go When You Need Help

With a few exceptions, the Internet is generally a friendly place where people sometimes go a little out of their way to help those who need help. If you are supporting Windows NT, consider joining one or more Windows NT Internet mailing lists. In the next section, you learn about various Windows NT mailing lists and get directions for joining them. In addition to joining various mailing lists, you can also browse Windows NT newsgroups and participate in various discussions; these Internet options enable you to keep up-to-date with new information and learn from the experiences of others.

Windows NT Mailing Lists

Windows NT mailing lists are a rich source of information related to Windows NT. Most people who subscribe to these mailing lists use Windows NT everyday and are quite helpful when someone has a problem. Before you join a mailing list, be aware that some of them generate quite a few e-mail messages each day. If you don't want to receive dozens of e-mail messages daily, it's better not to subscribe to a mailing list. In my opinion, however, the knowledge that you can gain from being in one or more mailing lists is well worth the extra e-mail. By joining a mailing list, you not only get a chance to find solutions to various questions, but you also are able to discuss topics related to Windows NT with other NT users. By sharing your experiences with others, and by learning from the experiences of others, you will be able to find innovative ways of accomplishing your objectives. It's a safe bet that you'll see me occasionally in some of the Windows NT mailing lists provided next.

> **TIP**
>
> If your e-mail application supports "rules," use them to divert e-mail from mailing lists to a folder. This will make sure dozens of messages you get from various mailing lists do not distract you from reading your personal and business e-mail. It's generally a good idea to use a different folder for each mailing list so that when you have some free time, you can open a folder and read all the messages.

To join any of the following Windows NT mailing lists, simply send an e-mail message to the addresses listed. Be sure the body of your message contains the appropriate text listed. Usually, after a few hours, you will start receiving messages directed to the list you sent the subscription request to.

> **TIP**
>
> When you're subscribed to a mailing list, you will receive a "welcome message" that contains information about the mailing list. Be sure to save this message; it also contains information regarding how to unsubscribe from the mailing list in case you change your mind. Some list members are not very friendly when "unsubscribe messages" are sent to the mailing list!

For discussions related to Windows NT-based WWW servers:

Send e-mail to: `webserver-nt-request@DELTA.PROCESS.COM`
Include this in body of message: `subscribe webserver-nt`

Send e-mail to: `http_winnt@Emerald.NET`
Include the string `subscribe` in the subject line; leave the body blank

For general discussions related to Windows NT:

Send e-mail to: `list@bhs.com`
Include this in body of message: `join iwntug`

Send e-mail to: `mailbase@mailbase.ac.uk`
Include this in body of message: `join windows-nt`

Send e-mail to: `listserv@eva.dc.lsoft.com`
Include this in body of message: `subscribe winnt-l`

Windows NT Resources on the World Wide Web

There are many resourceful Windows NT Web sites on the Internet. The following WWW sites are devoted solely to Windows NT. You might want to add some of these sites to your favorite Web browser's bookmark list, visit them every now and then to keep up-to-date with information related to Windows NT, and find solutions to various problems.

Microsoft Windows NT Version 3.51 Hardware Compatibility List

`http://www.microsoft.com/NTServer/HCL/hclintro.htm`

Visit this URL to determine whether a peripheral in question is compatible with Windows NT. If you don't see an item in the hardware compatibility list, it doesn't necessarily mean that it's not compatible with Windows NT. In such a case, you might want to contact the hardware manufacturer for information about Windows NT compatibility.

Microsoft Windows NT from a UNIX Point of View

`http://www.microsoft.com/BackOffice/reading/nt4unix.htm`

This paper provides a technical overview of Windows NT for the information technology professional with a strong background in UNIX. It approaches the subject from the UNIX point of view and relates the concepts of Windows NT to corresponding ones found in UNIX. The paper begins with a technical comparison of the two operating systems and moves on to cover how the two can coexist in a heterogeneous environment. The paper finishes with a brief section describing some of the tools available to aid developers in creating applications for both platforms.

FAQ for Porting from UNIX to Windows NT

`http://www.shore.net/~wihl/unix2nt.html`

If you're interested in learning about NT versions of UNIX and TCP/IP utilities, visit this URL. You might find these utilities quite useful. This site also contains a list of frequently asked questions about how to port UNIX applications to Microsoft's Windows NT. This URL is particularly informative to anyone who intends to port UNIX applications to Windows NT, and it's typically updated with new information about once a month.

Windows NT on the Internet

`http://www.neystadt.org/winnt`

This site contains many resources about using Windows NT to host a Web site and set up other Internet information distribution applications.

European Microsoft Windows NT Academic Center (EMWAC)

`http://www.emwac.ed.ac.uk/`

EMWAC acts as a focus for activities and events that support the use of Windows NT. This is a very informative Web site to find various Internet tools and services for Windows NT. Be sure to browse the Internet Tool Chest for Windows NT at this site for various NT Internet applications such as Finger Server, Gopher Server, HTTP Server, Internet Mail Server , WAIS Server, and WAIS Toolkit.

Digital's Windows NT Home Page

`http://www.windowsnt.digital.com/`

This URL leads you to the Windows NT resources page at Digital; this page contains many Windows NT information resources. If you're hosting your Web server on an Alpha, you'll find this Web site particularly useful.

Beverly Hills Software Windows NT Resource Center

`http://www.bhs.com`

The Beverly Hills Software Windows NT Resource Center is an excellent source for Windows NT resources and information. Beverly Hills Software is an Internet consulting and presence firm that specializes in the design, installation, and implementation of Microsoft Windows NT-based Internet servers.

Microsoft NT Server Web Site

`http://www.microsoft.com/ntserver`

This site contains many Windows NT server resources as well as information about creating Web sites using Windows NT.

Self-Reported Windows NT Links

`http://COBA.SHSU.edu/messages/nt-list.htm`

This site contains hundreds of Windows NT resources that are self-reported. If you set up your own Windows NT resources page, add it to the list found at this Web page.

San Diego Windows NT User Group (SDWNTUG)

`http://www.fbsolutions.com/sdwntug`

The mission of SDWNTUG is to promote the use of Windows NT Server and Workstation and to act as a conduit for the free exchange of information and discussion of NT-related issues.

NT Web Server Security Issues

`http://www.telemark.net/~randallg/ntsecure.htm`

Visit this site to find how you can make your NT Web server on the Internet more secure.

NT Web Server Resource Guide

http://mfginfo.com/htm/website.htm

A comprehensive list of Windows NT software and resources to host a Windows NT-based Web site.

Rick's Windows NT Information Center

http://rick.wzl.rwth-aachen.de/rick

A large number of Windows NT links to NT download sites, user groups and associations, newsgroups, mailing lists, and so forth.

Information on NT

http://infotech.kumc.edu/winnt/

This Web site contains many Windows NT resources, including information about Remote Access Server and Windows NT file archives, as well as other Windows NT resources on the Web.

Sanjaya's Windows NT Resource Center

http://Wonderland.dial.umd.edu/~NT

Contains numerous Windows NT information resources. This resource center is maintained by me and contains information about hosting a Windows NT-based Web site and setting up various Internet information systems on the Internet. You can also find at this Web site information about various NT applications and other Windows NT resources on the Internet.

Windows NT Software on the World Wide Web

There are many Web sites on the Internet that distribute Windows NT software. You'll be able to accomplish certain tasks more efficiently by utilizing the utilities and applications found in the Web sites listed next. You'll also find applications that provide solutions to limitations of NT, such as a lack of a disk quota management.

Internet Shopper

http://www.net-shopper.co.uk/

Internet Shopper is a company dedicated to the promotion of Windows NT on all platforms. At the Internet shopper Web site, you'll find a number of Internet services for Windows NT.

Internet applications found at this Web site include mail server, mail list server, NNTP news server, and Domain Name Service.

California State University Windows NT Shareware Archive

`http://coyote.csusm.edu/cwis/winworld/nt.html`

This site contains a very extensive collection of Windows NT shareware applications as well as device drivers and Windows NT ports of useful UNIX utilities.

NT PERL Distribution Site

`ftp://ntperl.hip.com/ntperl/`

You can obtain the latest version of NT PERL free of charge from this FTP site. PERL is a very powerful programming language commonly used to develop Web CGI programs.

NT DNS

`http://www.telemark.net/~randallg/ntdns.htm`

This link is very useful if you need to set up a Domain Name Service (DNS) server on a Windows NT machine. This link provides you with a free Windows NT port of UNIX Bind.

Pragma Systems Telnet Server

`http://www.ccsi.com:80/pragma/`

Pragma Systems has a telnet server for Windows NT that can be used to connect to a Windows NT Internet server via telnet. You can download an evaluation version of the InterAccess Telnet Server for Windows NT from the preceding Web page.

Sunbelt International

`http://www.ntsoftdist.com/ntsoftdist/`

At the Sunbelt International Web site, you'll find numerous Windows NT disk management utilities, such as a utility to check disk fragmentation.

Carmel Anti-Virus for Windows NT

`http://www.fbsolutions.com/ntav`

Carmel Anti-virus is a Windows NT virus detection and eradication utility.

Windows NT/Web Authoring Newsgroups

Listed next are a few Internet newsgroups that discuss issues relating to Web site development. In order to keep up to date with new technologies and learn innovative ways of distributing information on the Internet, it's a good idea to visit the following newsgroups occasionally:

```
comp.infosystems.www.servers.ms-windows
comp.infosystems.www.servers.misc
comp.infosystems.www.browsers.ms-windows
comp.infosystems.www.authoring.cgi
comp.infosystems.www.authoring.misc
```

A number of newsgroups have been set up on the Internet for discussions related to Windows NT. In order to take part in these discussions, you might want to check out some of the following newsgroups:

```
comp.os.ms-windows.nt.pre-release
comp.os.ms-windows.nt.misc
comp.os.ms-windows.nt.setup.misc
comp.os.ms-windows.nt.setup.hardware
comp.os.ms-windows.nt.admin.networking
comp.os.ms-windows.nt.admin.misc
comp.os.ms-windows.nt.software.backoffice
```

B

Ports Associated with Internet Services

Port numbers of various well-known Internet services are listed in Table B.1. These ports are defined in RFC 1060. Please refer to RFC 1060, by visiting the following URL, for a comprehensive listing and discussion of various ports defined in RFC 1060.

URL

RFC 1060 defines TCP/IP ports of well-known Internet services.

```
http://www.pmg.lcs.mit.edu/cgi-bin/rfc/view?number=1060
```

Table B.1. Well-known Internet services' port numbers.

Port Number	Service Name	Description
5	RJE	Remote Job Entry
7	ECHO	Echo
9	DISCARD	Discard
11	USERS	Active Users
13	DAYTIME	Daytime
17	QUOTE	Quote of the Day
19	CHARGEN	Character Generator
20	FTP-DATA	File Transfer [Default Data]
21	FTP	File Transfer [Control]
23	TELNET	Telnet
25	SMTP	Simple Mail Transfer Protocol
37	TIME	Time
42	NAMESERVER	Host Name Server
43	NICNAME	Who Is
49	LOGIN	Login Host Protocol
53	DOMAIN	Domain Name Server
67	BOOTPS	Bootstrap Protocol Server
68	BOOTPC	Bootstrap Protocol Client
69	TFTP	Trivial File Transfer
79	FINGER	Finger
93	DCP	Device Control Protocol
101	HOSTNAME	NIC Host Name Server
107	RTELNET	Remote Telnet Service

Port Number	Service Name	Description
109	POP2	Post Office Protocol - Version 2
110	POP3	Post Office Protocol - Version 3
113	AUTH	Authentication Service
115	SFTP	Simple File Transfer Protocol
119	NNTP	Network News Transfer Protocol
123	NTP	Network Time Protocol
129	PWDGEN	Password Generator Protocol
130	CISCO-FNA	CISCO FNATIVE
135	LOC-SRV	Location Service
136	PROFILE	PROFILE Naming System
137	NETBIOS-NS	NETBIOS Name Service
138	NETBIOS-DGM	NETBIOS Datagram Service
139	NETBIOS-SSN	NETBIOS Session Service
144	NEWS	NewS
150	SQL-NET	SQL-NET
152	BFTP	Background File Transfer Program
153	SGMP	SGMP
156	SQLSRV	SQL Service
161	SNMP	SNMP
162	SNMPTRAP	SNMPTRAP
192	OSU-NMS	OSU Network Monitoring System
194	IRC	Internet Relay Chat Protocol
197	DLS	Directory Location Service
1198	DLS-Mon	Directory Location Service Monitor

C

In addition to regular alphanumeric characters, special characters can be added to an HTML document using the ISO8859-1 table shown in Table C.1. It is easy to add special characters to an HTML document. For example, if you'd like the copyright symbol (©) to appear somewhere in an HTML document, just insert © or © where you'd like the © symbol to appear. Note that the semicolon *is* necessary. An example of how special characters can be used in a Web page is given next. The Web page shown in Figure C.1 was created using the following HTML code:

```
<HTML>
<HEAD><TITLE>HTML Special character demonstration</TITLE>
</HEAD>
<BODY TEXT="#000000" LINK="#FF0000" VLINK="#808080" ALINK="#FF0080">

<H1>
Web pages can be
&#205;      <!-- Í -->
&ntilde;    <!-- ñ -->
t           <!-- t -->
&euml;      <!-- ë -->
r           <!-- r -->
n           <!-- n -->
&acirc;     <!-- â -->
t           <!-- t -->
&iuml;      <!-- ï -->
&ocirc;     <!-- ô -->
&ntilde;    <!-- ñ -->
&agrave;    <!-- à -->
l           <!-- l -->
&iacute;    <!-- í -->
z           <!-- z -->
&euml;      <!-- ë -->
&ETH;       <!-- Ð -->
<BR>
using special HTML character sequences!
</H1>

</BODY>
</HTML>
```

FIGURE C.1.

Web pages can be ÍñtërnâtïöñàlízëÐ using special HTML character sequences.

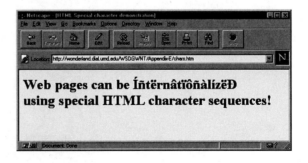

URL

Visit the following URL for more information about adding special characters to a Web page.

`http://www.uni-passau.de/%7Eramsch/iso8859-1.html`

TIP

It is recommended that you use numeric codes from Table C.1. Character codes are not always equally interpreted by some browsers.

Table E.1. The ISO8859-1 table of special characters.

Description	Character	Numeric Code	Character Code
Quotation mark	"	"	"
Ampersand	&	&	&
Less-than sign	<	<	<
Greater-than sign	>	>	>
Non-breaking space			
Inverted exclamation	¡	¡	¡
Cent sign	¢	¢	¢
Pound sterling	£	£	£
General currency sign	¤	¤	¤
Yen sign	¥	¥	¥
Broken vertical bar	¦	¦	¦
Section sign	§	§	§
Dieresis	¨	¨	¨
Copyright	©	©	©
Feminine ordinal	ª	ª	ª
Left angle quote	«	«	«
Not sign	¬	¬	¬
Soft hyphen	-	­	­
Registered trademark	®	®	®

continues

Table E.1. continued

Description	Character	Numeric Code	Character Code
Macron accent	¯	&#175;	&macr;
Degree sign	°	&#176;	&deg;
Plus or minus	±	&#177;	&plusmn;
Superscript two	²	&#178;	&sup2;
Superscript three	³	&#179;	&sup3;
Acute accent	´	&#180;	&acute;
Micro sign	µ	&#181;	&micro;
Paragraph sign	¶	&#182;	&para;
Middle dot	·	&#183;	&middot;
Cedilla	¸	&#184;	&cedil;
Superscript one	¹	&#185;	&sup1;
Masculine ordinal	º	&#186;	&ordm;
Right angle quote	»	&#187;	&raquo;
Fraction one-fourth	¼	&#188;	&frac14;
Fraction one-half	½	&#189;	&frac12;
Fraction three-fourths	¾	&#190;	&frac34;
Inverted question mark	¿	&#191;	&iquest;
Capital A, grave accent	À	&#192;	&Agrave;
Capital A, acute accent	Á	&#193;	&Aacute;
Capital A, circumflex accent	Â	&#194;	&Acirc;
Capital A, tilde	Ã	&#195;	&Atilde;
Capital A, dieresis	Ä	&#196;	&Auml;
Capital A, ring	Å	&#197;	&Aring;
Capital AE ligature	Æ	&#198;	&AElig;
Capital C, cedilla	Ç	&#199;	&Ccedil;
Capital E, grave accent	È	&#200;	&Egrave;
Capital E, acute accent	É	&#201;	&Eacute;
Capital E, circumflex accent	Ê	&#202;	&Ecirc;
Capital E, dieresis	Ë	&#203;	&Euml;
Capital I, grave accent	Ì	&#204;	&Igrave;
Capital I, acute accent	Í	&#205;	&Iacute;
Capital I, circumflex accent	Î	&#206;	&Icirc;

Description	Character	Numeric Code	Character Code
Capital I, dieresis	Ï	&#207;	&Iuml;
Capital Eth, Icelandic	Ð	&#208;	&ETH;
Capital N, tilde	Ñ	&#209;	&Ntilde;
Capital O, grave accent	Ò	&#210;	&Ograve;
Capital O, acute accent	Ó	&#211;	&Oacute;
Capital O, circumflex accent	Ô	&#212;	&Ocirc;
Capital O, tilde	Õ	&#213;	&Otilde;
Capital O, dieresis	Ö	&#214;	&Ouml;
Multiply sign	×	&#215;	&times;
Capital O, slash	Ø	&#216;	&Oslash;
Capital U, grave accent	Ù	&#217;	&Ugrave;
Capital U, acute accent	Ú	&#218;	&Uacute;
Capital U, circumflex accent	Û	&#219;	&Ucirc;
Capital U, dieresis	Ü	&#220;	&Uuml;
Capital Y, acute accent		&#221;	&Yacute;
Capital THORN, Icelandic		&#222;	&THORN;
Small sharp s		&#223;	&szlig;
Small a, grave accent		&#224;	&agrave;
Small a, acute accent		&#225;	&aacute;
Small a, circumflex accent		&#226;	&acirc;
Small a, tilde		&#227;	&atilde;
Small a, dieresis		&#228;	&auml;
Small a, ring		&#229;	&aring;
Small ae diphthong (ligature)		&#230;	&aelig;
Small c, cedilla		&#231;	&ccedil;
Small e, grave accent		&#232;	&egrave;
Small e, acute accent		&#233;	&eacute;
Small e, circumflex accent		&#234;	&ecirc;
Small e, dieresis		&#235;	&euml;
Small i, grave accent		&#236;	&igrave;
Small i, acute accent		&#237;	&iacute;
Small i, circumflex accent		&#238;	&icirc;

continues

Table E.1. continued

Description	Character	Numeric Code	Character Code
Small i, dieresis	ï	&#239;	&iuml;
Small eth, Icelandic	ð	&#240;	&eth;
Small n, tilde	ñ	&#241;	&ntilde;
Small o, grave accent	ò	&#242;	&ograve;
Small o, acute accent	ó	&#243;	&oacute;
Small o, circumflex accent	ô	&#244;	&ocirc;
Small o, tilde	õ	&#245;	&otilde;
Small o, dieresis	ö	&#246;	&ouml;
Division sign	÷	&#247;	&divide;
Small o, slash	ø	&#248;	&oslash;
Small u, grave accent	ù	&#249;	&ugrave;
Small u, acute accent	ú	&#250;	&uacute;
Small u, circumflex accent	û	&#251;	&ucirc;
Small u, dieresis	ü	&#252;	&uuml;
Small y, acute accent	ý	&#253;	&yacute;
Small thorn, Icelandic	þ	&#254;	&thorn;
Small y, dieresis	ÿ	&#255;	&yuml;

D

Internet Country/ Identification Codes

Listed here are various Internet country and identification codes. These codes can be used to analyze an Internet address and determine its origin.

AD	Andorra
AE	United Arab Emirates
AF	Afghanistan
AG	Antigua and Barbuda
AI	Anguilla
AL	Albania
AM	Armenia
AN	Netherlands Antilles
AO	Angola
AQ	Antarctica
AR	Argentina
AS	American Samoa
AT	Austria
AU	Australia
AW	Aruba
AZ	Azerbaijan
BA	Bosnia and Herzegovina
BB	Barbados
BD	Bangladesh
BE	Belgium
BF	Burkina Faso
BG	Bulgaria
BH	Bahrain
BI	Burundi
BJ	Benin
BM	Bermuda
BN	Brunei Darussalam
BO	Bolivia
BR	Brazil
BS	Bahamas
BT	Bhutan
BV	Bouvet Island
BW	Botswana
BY	Belarus
BZ	Belize
CA	Canada
CC	Cocos (Keeling) Islands
CF	Central African Republic
CG	Congo
CH	Switzerland

CI	Cote D'Ivoire (Ivory Coast)
CK	Cook Islands
CL	Chile
CM	Cameroon
CN	China
CO	Colombia
CR	Costa Rica
CS	Czechoslovakia (former)
CU	Cuba
CV	Cape Verde
CX	Christmas Island
CY	Cyprus
CZ	Czech Republic
DE	Germany
DJ	Djibouti
DK	Denmark
DM	Dominica
DO	Dominican Republic
DZ	Algeria
EC	Ecuador
EE	Estonia
EG	Egypt
EH	Western Sahara
ER	Eritrea
ES	Spain
ET	Ethiopia
FI	Finland
FJ	Fiji
FK	Falkland Islands (Malvinas)
FM	Micronesia
FO	Faroe Islands
FR	France
FX	France, Metropolitan
GA	Gabon
GB	Great Britain (UK)
GD	Grenada
GE	Georgia
GF	French Guiana
GH	Ghana
GI	Gibraltar
GL	Greenland
GM	Gambia

GN	Guinea
GP	Guadeloupe
GQ	Equatorial Guinea
GR	Greece
GS	S. Georgia and S. Sandwich Islands
GT	Guatemala
GU	Guam
GW	Guinea-Bissau
GY	Guyana
HK	Hong Kong
HM	Heard and McDonald Islands
HN	Honduras
HR	Croatia (Hrvatska)
HT	Haiti
HU	Hungary
ID	Indonesia
IE	Ireland
IL	Israel
IN	India
IO	British Indian Ocean Territory
IQ	Iraq
IR	Iran
IS	Iceland
IT	Italy
JM	Jamaica
JO	Jordan
JP	Japan
KE	Kenya
KG	Kyrgyzstan
KH	Cambodia
KI	Kiribati
KM	Comoros
KN	Saint Kitts and Nevis
KP	Korea (North)
KR	Korea (South)
KW	Kuwait
KY	Cayman Islands
KZ	Kazakhstan
LA	Laos
LB	Lebanon
LC	Saint Lucia
LI	Liechtenstein
LK	Sri Lanka

LR	Liberia
LS	Lesotho
LT	Lithuania
LU	Luxembourg
LV	Latvia
LY	Libya
MA	Morocco
MC	Monaco
MD	Moldova
MG	Madagascar
MH	Marshall Islands
MK	Macedonia
ML	Mali
MM	Myanmar
MN	Mongolia
MO	Macau
MP	Northern Mariana Islands
MQ	Martinique
MR	Mauritania
MS	Montserrat
MT	Malta
MU	Mauritius
MV	Maldives
MW	Malawi
MX	Mexico
MY	Malaysia
MZ	Mozambique
NA	Namibia
NC	New Caledonia
NE	Niger
NF	Norfolk Island
NG	Nigeria
NI	Nicaragua
NL	Netherlands
NO	Norway
NP	Nepal
NR	Nauru
NT	Neutral Zone
NU	Niue
NZ	New Zealand (Aotearoa)
OM	Oman
PA	Panama
PE	Peru

PF	French Polynesia
PG	Papua New Guinea
PH	Philippines
PK	Pakistan
PL	Poland
PM	St. Pierre and Miquelon
PN	Pitcairn
PR	Puerto Rico
PT	Portugal
PW	Palau
PY	Paraguay
QA	Qatar
RE	Reunion
RO	Romania
RU	Russian Federation
RW	Rwanda
SA	Saudi Arabia
SB	Solomon Islands
SC	Seychelles
SD	Sudan
SE	Sweden
SG	Singapore
SH	St. Helena
SI	Slovenia
SJ	Svalbard and Jan Mayen Islands
SK	Slovak Republic
SL	Sierra Leone
SM	San Marino
SN	Senegal
SO	Somalia
SR	Suriname
ST	Sao Tome and Principe
SU	USSR (former)
SV	El Salvador
SY	Syria
SZ	Swaziland
TC	Turks and Caicos Islands
TD	Chad
TF	French Southern Territories
TG	Togo
TH	Thailand
TJ	Tajikistan
TK	Tokelau

TM	Turkmenistan
TN	Tunisia
TO	Tonga
TP	East Timor
TR	Turkey
TT	Trinidad and Tobago
TV	Tuvalu
TW	Taiwan
TZ	Tanzania
UA	Ukraine
UG	Uganda
UK	United Kingdom
UM	US Minor Outlying Islands
US	United States
UY	Uruguay
UZ	Uzbekistan
VA	Vatican City State
VC	Saint Vincent and the Grenadines
VE	Venezuela
VG	Virgin Islands (British)
VI	Virgin Islands (U.S.)
VN	Vietnam
VU	Vanuatu
WF	Wallis and Futuna Islands
WS	Samoa
YE	Yemen
YT	Mayotte
YU	Yugoslavia
ZA	South Africa
ZM	Zambia
ZR	Zaire
ZW	Zimbabwe
COM	US Commercial
EDU	US Educational
GOV	US Government
INT	International
MIL	US Military
NET	Network
ORG	Non-Profit Organization
ARPA	Old Style Arpanet
NATO	NATO Field

Index

HTML in 10 seconds!*

No kidding.
In the time it takes
for a good slurp of coffee, *HTML Transit* generated this Web page.

Say hello to the template.

HTML Transit takes a new approach to online publishing, using a high-speed production template. It's fast and easy. You can turn a 50-page word processing file into multiple, linked HTML pages—complete with graphics and tables—in less than 10 mouse clicks. From scratch.

Customize your template—formatting, backgrounds, navigation buttons, thumbnails—and save even more time. Now in just 4 clicks, you can crank out an entire library of custom Web pages with no manual authoring.

Take a free test drive.

Stop working so hard. Download an evaluation copy of *HTML Transit* from our Web site:

http://www.infoaccess.com

Your download code is **MCML46**. (It can save you money when you order *HTML Transit*.)

Buy HTML Transit risk free.

HTML Transit is just $495, and is backed by a 30-day satisfaction guarantee. To order, call us toll-free at **800-344-9737**.

InfoAccess

InfoAccess, Inc.
(206) 747-3203
FAX: (206) 641-9367
Email: info@infoaccess.com

▶ **Automatic HTML from native word processor formats**
▶ **Creates HTML tables, tables of contents & indexes**
▶ **Graphics convert to GIF or JPEG, with thumbnails**
▶ **Template control over appearance and behavior**
▶ **For use with Microsoft® Windows®**

HTML Transit is a trademark of InfoAccess, Inc. Microsoft and Windows are registered trademarks of Microsoft Corporation.
*Single-page Microsoft Word document with graphics and tables, running on 75MHz Pentium. Conversion speed depends on document length, complexity and PC configuration.

Designing and Implementing Microsoft Internet Information Server

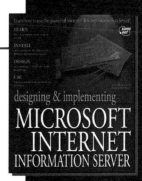

— *Arthur Knowles & Sanjaya Hettihewa*

This book details the specific tasks in setting up and running a Microsoft Internet Information Server. Readers will learn troubleshooting, network design, security, and cross-platform integration procedures.

$39.99 USA, $56.95 CDN, ISBN 1-57521-168-8, 350 pp.

Building an Intranet with Windows NT 4.0

— *Scott Zimmerman & Tim Evans*

This hands-on guide teaches readers how to set up and maintain an efficient Intranet with Windows NT. It comes complete with a selection of the best software for setting up a server, creating content, and for developing Intranet applications.

CD-ROM includes a complete Windows NT Intranet toolkit with a full-featured Web server, Web content development tools, and ready-to-use Intranet applications.

Includes complete specifications for several of the most popular Intranet applications, group scheduling, discussions, database access, and more.

$49.99 USA, $70.95 CDN, ISBN 1-57521-137-8, 600 pp.

Windows NT 4.0 Server Unleashed

— *Jason Garms, et al*

The Windows NT server has been gaining tremendous market share over Novell and the new upgrade—which includes a Windows 95 interface—and is sure to add momentum to its market drive. To that end, *Windows NT 4.0 Server Unleashed* is written to meet that growing market. It provides information on disk and file management, integrated networking, BackOffice integration, and TCP/IP protocols.

$55.00 USA, $77.95 CDN, ISBN 0-672-30933-5, 1,100 pp.

Web Site Administrator's Survival Guide

— *Jerry Ablan & Scott Yanoff, et al*

This is a detailed, step-by-step book that guides the Web administrator—the person responsible for keeping a Web site up and running—through the process of selecting Web server software and hardware, installing and configuring a server, and administering the server on an ongoing basis.

$49.99 USA, $70.95 CDN, ISBN 1-57521-018-5, 784 pp.

The Internet Business Guide, Second Edition

— Rosalind Resnick & Dave Taylor

Updated and revised, this guide will inform and educate the business community on how they can use the Internet to increase profit, reach a broader market, track down business leads, and access critical information.

$25.00 USA, $35.95 CDN, ISBN 1-57521-004-5, 496 pp.

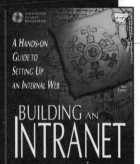

Building an Intranet

— Tim Evans

Building an Intranet will be the first book to focus on using Web technology to provide information for a company internally. The reader will learn how to choose hardware and software, how to set up a secure Web server, and how to make a company's applications Web-aware.

$55.00 USA, $77.95 CDN, 1-57521-071-1, 720 pp.

HTML, JAVA, CGI, VRML, SGML Web Publishing Unleashed

— William Stanek

Includes sections on how to organize and plan your information, design pages, and become familiar with hypertext and hypermedia. Choose from a range of applications and technologies, including Java, SGML, VRML, and the newest HTML and Netscape extensions.

$49.99 USA, $70.95 CDN, 1-57521-051-7, 960 pp.

Teach Yourself Web Publishing with HTML in 14 Days, Premier Edition

— Laura Lemay

This book teaches everything about publishing on the Web. In addition to its exhaustive coverage of HTML, it also gives readers hands-on practice with designing and writing HTML documents.

$39.99 USA, $56.95 CDN, ISBN 1-57521-014-2, 840 pp.

Add to Your Sams Library Today with the Best Books for Programming, Operating Systems, and New Technologies

The easiest way to order is to pick up the phone and call

1-800-428-5331

between 9:00 a.m. and 5:00 p.m. EST.
For faster service please have your credit card available.

ISBN	Quantity	Description of Item	Unit Cost	Total Cost
0-672-30844-4		Designing and Implementing Microsoft Internet Information Server	$39.99	
1-57521-137-8		Building an Intranet with Windows NT 4 (Book/CD-ROM)	$49.99	
1-57521-087-8		CGI Developer's Guide (Book/CD-ROM)	$45.00	
0-672-30933-5		Windows NT 4 Server Unleashed (Book/CD-ROM)	$55.00	
0-672-30735-9		Teach Yourself the Internet, Second Edition	$25.00	
1-57521-041-X		The Internet Unleashed 1996 (Book/CD-ROM)	$49.99	
0-57521-018-5		Web Site Administrator's Survival Guide (Book/CD-ROM)	$49.99	
1-57521-004-5		The Internet Business Guide, Second Edition	$25.00	
1-57521-071-1		Building an Intranet Web (Book/CD-ROM)	$55.00	
1-57521-092-4		Web Page Wizardry: Wiring Your Site for Sound and Action (Book/CD-ROM)	$39.99	
1-57521-014-2		Teach Yourself Web Publishing with HTML in 14 Days (Book/CD-ROM)	$39.99	
1-57521-051-7		Web Publishing Unleashed (Book/CD-ROM)	$49.99	
❏ 3 ½" Disk		Shipping and Handling: See information below.		
❏ 5 ¼" Disk		TOTAL		

Shipping and Handling: $4.00 for the first book, and $1.75 for each additional book. Floppy disk: add $1.75 for shipping and handling. If you need to have it NOW, we can ship product to you in 24 hours for an additional charge of approximately $18.00, and you will receive your item overnight or in two days. Overseas shipping and handling adds $2.00 per book and $8.00 for up to three disks. Prices subject to change. Call for availability and pricing information on latest editions.

201 W. 103rd Street, Indianapolis, Indiana 46290

1-800-428-5331 — Orders   1-800-835-3202 — FAX   1-800-858-7674 — Customer Service

Book ISBN 1-57521-089-4

Installing Your CD-ROM

The companion CD-ROM contains software developed by the authors, as well as an assortment of third-party tools and product demos. The disc is designed to be explored using a CD-ROM Menu program. Using the Menu program, you can view information concerning products and companies, and install programs with a single click of the mouse. To run the Menu program, follow these steps:

Windows NT installation instructions:

1. Insert the CD-ROM disc into your CD-ROM drive.

2. From File Manager or Program Manager, choose Run from the File menu.

3. Type `<drive>\setup` and press Enter, where `<drive>` corresponds to the drive letter of your CD-ROM drive. For example, if your CD-ROM is drive D:, type `D:\setup` and press Enter.

NOTE

For best results, set your monitor to display between 256 and 64,000 colors. A screen resolution of 640×480 pixels is also recommended. If necessary, adjust your monitor settings before using the CD-ROM.